The Right to Information Act, 2005

Introduction by

U.N. Gupta

ATLANTIC

PUBLISHERS & DISTRIBUTORS (P) LTD

Published by

ATLANTIC

PUBLISHERS & DISTRIBUTORS (P) LTD
7/22, Ansari Road, Darya Ganj,
New Delhi-110002
Phones : 2327 3880, 23275880, 23280451
Fax : +91-11-23285873
Web : www.atlanticbooks.com
E-mail : info@atlanticbooks.com

Branch Office
5, Nallathambi Street, Wallajah Road,
Chennai-600 002
Phones : +91-44-64611085, 32413319
E-mail : chennai@atlanticbooks.com

Printed in India at Nice Printing Press, A-33/3A, Site-IV, Industrial Area, Sahibabad, Ghaziabad, U.P.

PREFACE

The Right to Information Act, 2005 fulfils necessity of the present epoch of 'preserving the paramountcy of democratic ideal' over dissipating forces being felt since 1970s. All polities of the world within their distinctive pattern have felt for new or increased participation of people in maintaining democracy; a system plagued by the disease of official secrecy and resulting corruption to a point of its general breakdown. The Indian RTI Act, 2005 and its predecessor Freedom of Information Act, 2002 are the result of a people's movement supported by elected legislature that shows distrust of the official secrecy system and prevailing administrative corruption by 'sitting on files' on the pretext of maintaining official secrecy. The Indian experiment is an advanced step in this direction since RTI Act creates a legal obligation on all authorities—executive, legislative and judicial—to provide sincere and correct information to people in the format in which applicants want it within a time frame or suffer punishment for the lapse. The RTI Act has a statutory status but it over reaches the constitutional positions or categories and privileges when these are operated through administrative functions. The Act does not possess the feature of basic structure of the Constitution and its future lies in the success of its Information Commissions in achieving the aims enshrined in its preamble by their integrity and understanding of the values to be protected—that is the right of people to get information.

Sweden was the first country to make available Right to Information to the people through a law in eighteenth century. The USA enacted a detailed Freedom of Information Act in 1966 and other States followed this. England enacted this law in 2000 as a right granted as a matter of grace of Her Majesty to the people. Now over 150 nations—both democratic or autocratic—

have such a law but none of them creates a punishable offence where information is not properly given or is delayed. The path that the Right to Information Act, 2005 is to tread is new and novel in international perspective. There are as yet no set precedents and the official record of the orders and decisions of the Central or State Information Commissions constituted under the Act. However, in India there are actively motivated purposeful multimedia, newspapers, Internet websites and non-governmental organizations that seek information and give coverage to the reactions of Central and State Information Commissions. Even BBC (British Broadcasting Corporation) has given frequent coverage to the developments under RTI Act of India since it has made government/public authorities answerable under it. Hence, while producing the book on the principles and their actual application in India I found that there was a lot of vacuum but Internet websites and media coverage of Right to Information made the work purposeful. I appreciate the role of Internet websites and media and acknowledge the use of media coverage. Invariably, I have referred to the source or writer of news coverage.

In writing the Introduction to this book, I have alluded to the background developments in India through Supreme Court on right to freedom of information, right to know, right to privacy, judicial analysis of administrative powers and rights of people, among other related ideas. Exposition of this line of background in the book is necessary since the RTI Act, 2005 is now a significantly important part of Indian constitutional law also. In a case seeking information concerning correspondence between President and Prime Minister that took place some years ago on a politically sensitive issue, the Central Information Commission had referred to more than five Supreme Court judgments before issue of order in favour of applicant. It should be remembered that there is always a wide gap among the ideals to be achieved, drafting language used to achieve those ideals, interpretations given to the words used, the wisdom of the administrative workforce and the interests claimed by the persons governed by an Act. This is more so here since information alone without a remedy for the wrong revealed is no good. The RTI Act somewhat falls short on this score and the work done by the

Central or State Public Information Commissions many times lead people to dead end. There is a need for a supplement to this Act on this score.

The Right to Information Act, 2005 has attracted international attention since it makes government a receptive, transparent and accountable collection of identified public authorities. The Act is of immense value to information seeking general public, scholars of constitutional law and thousands of public authorities in India that have to supply information. The RTI Act takes pride in its being a helping hand besides providing information. To cite a few examples: it has helped pensioners to get their dues, exposed employment generation schemes, led to better roads for Gagepalli town, helped Greenpeace movement in its fight for the people against the harm caused by artificial grains and vegetables, fined policemen for laxity, restored people's right to water in Leolari town, helped in unearthing corruption in the procurement of medical supplies in a public sector undertaking, helped municipality in getting its dues from government, exposed absence of safety measures to life and health of people if the Rawatbhata Atomic Power Station (RAPS) was destroyed or damaged by an object from space particularly a meteorite, etc. It has even helped the leader of opposition in Rajya Sabha in retrieving illusive information from ministry of home affairs. When an applicant was aggrieved by judicial process and felt that he was not getting justice, the Central Information Commission even organized a video-conferencing with two officials of Supreme Court to convince the applicant that the information supplied to him was correct and the remedy that he was seeking was in nature of advice and this was not within the competence of CIC.

I am immensely thankful to Dr. K.R. Gupta, Honorary Advisor, Atlantic Publishers and Distributors (P) Ltd., New Delhi, for persistently motivating me to complete the book.

U.N. Gupta

CONTENTS

PART I
INTRODUCTION

INTRODUCTION

U.N. Gupta

THE RIGHT TO INFORMATION IN INDIAN DEMOCRACY

The Right to Information Act, 2005 in its preamble regards the Act as essential and supplemental to democratic ideals under the Indian Constitution. In the year 2007, India celebrated 60 years of parliamentary democracy. For sure India is now a matured democratic republic. There are various institutional requirements and standards for judging the maturity of democracy. The freedom of press and media, right to know, right to dissent, freedom of speech, the continuance of cabinet system of government after periodic elections, regular parliamentary sessions and existence of independent judicial system are measures of success, stability and confidence in the democratic governmental system. Enlightened public opinion, which successfully asserts itself, is essential for democracy and this requires unhindered flow of information and free expression of adverse or conflicting opinions and views on matters of public interest. In India as in other countries, the right of people to access to the inner hidden side of administration as democratic ideal has developed gradually at the end of the last century.

Since 1950 when the present Constitution came into existence the democracy has thrived in India, though there have been periods when Indian political downbeats appear to have led to the fears that Indian democracy was in a sinking boat. The gravest of such moments had come when internal emergency of 1975 had throttled expression of public opinion alongwith political opposition to the government. The curtailment of freedom of speech and expression of people including the right to dissent marked this period of constitutional autocracy. People did observe, listened, noticed quietly and reacted to the contents of an autocratic rule within the framework of the Constitution; and through the same Constitution they did succeed and restored democracy alongwith the right of dissent after the internal emergency was lifted in 1977. Restoration of short eclipsed democracy in 1975 was followed by disapproval of emergency government through the election to the House of People that resulted in absolute majority to the erstwhile parliamentary opposition. This has been remarkable achievement of the people's democracy.[1] The first thing the new government did, was to restore freedom of press and the right to know of the people and to make sure that these and aligned rights which generate enlightened public opinion could never be constitutionally curtailed. These have come to be a basic feature of Indian Constitution.

Further, people and also the patrons of the government of modern States have been immensely interested in clean public administration. Corruption, favoritism and misuse of power have been ages old problems based on the situation that there existed a wall of separation between rulers and subjects. The British period of Indian history was based on this political demarcation. Sweden is known to be the first country, which moved in opposite direction and in 1766 enacted the Freedom of Press Act that allowed scanning of the government documents for public good[2] on the 'Principle of Public Access'. The principle has come to mean that the general public are to be guaranteed an unobstructed view of the activities pursued by the government and local authorities; that all documents handled by the authorities are open to public scrutiny unless a legislation explicitly and specifically makes it otherwise; and that each request for information is to be handled individually. The right of people to

1. Mahatma Gandhi had appropriately cautioned: "The real *Swaraj* (independence) will come not by the acquisition of authority by a few but by the acquisition of capacity by all to resist authority when abused."
2. The process was termed in Swedish language as '*Offenlightsprincipen*', that is, 'The Principle of Public Access'.

be kept informed in a democracy means that even some information normally regarded to be confidential or secret can be passed on to the individuals, press or other media without the risk of criminal charges while the informer is to be immune from a criminal offence of letting out official secrets.

On these lines more than seventy countries around the world[1] have enacted legislation on freedom of information in one form or other. It can be mentioned that: in USA the Freedom of Information Act was enacted in 1966 supplemented with the Electronic Freedom of Information Amendment in 1996; in France this freedom was secured by Act No. 78—753 of 1978; in Australia similar Freedom of Information Act was enacted in 1982; in Canada the federal legislation, namely Access to Information Act and its supplement the Privacy Act were enacted in 1983; in Ireland the Freedom of Information Act was enforced in 1998 while in United Kingdom this Freedom of Information Act was put on Statute Book in 2000. In Europe most of the States have separately enacted information acts but at the same time the European Union (EU) has (i) the Regulation 1049/2001 regarding public access to the documents of the European Parliament, the Council and the Commission, (ii) the Directive 2003/98/EC sets out rules and procedure for 're-use' of public sector information resources for further exploitation. India started in 2002 with Freedom of Information Act on US and British patterns but due to operational difficulties present Right to Information Act, 2005 replaced this. In American slang these laws that set rules for access to information on public documents and records are known as 'sunshine' laws.

As a matter of fact, the freedom of information and acceptance of transparency in administration *require* a minimum of political stability, maturity and self-confidence on the part of both of the people and the persons who run the government. Autocracy, modern military dictatorship included, is the easiest known form of government but it is riddled with administrative tyranny and suppression or ridicule of the liberties of the people. There is more of ruler and subject like relationship between government and people. Welfare of people depends on

1. *Wikipedia*: Freedom of Information Legislation.

administrative benevolence and that is also asserted generally as justification for autocracy set against a democratic rule. After a short autocratic rule of 1975-77, the Indian democracy took another twenty-five years for enacting the Freedom of Information Act,[1] 2002 that was followed by the present Right to Information Act in 2005. In the meantime eight States of India, *viz*, Tamil Nadu, Goa, Rajasthan, Karnataka, Maharashtra, Madhya Pradesh, Assam, Jammu and Kashmir and Delhi had already enacted their respective Right to Information Acts.[2] Bringing out transparency in administration[3] for antidote against undue secrecy of files and concealment of official decision making steps has become 'good politics' both at Central and State levels in India. Transparency has come to mean openness, communication between people and administration, accountability of public authorities for what these do and a step for fight against corruption.

The Seventh Schedule of the Constitution of India regulates the constitutional format for legislation on 'right to information' by Union or State Governments. The 'right to information' as such is not specified as an item of legislative powers in either of the Union, State or Concurrent Lists of the Seventh Schedule. It has been said that legislation on this is a 'residuary matter' under Article 248 of the Constitution of India and so only Parliament can make law on this. However, in all federal States countries including India have enacted freedom of information laws. For India the reason is also that right to information is essential part of the constitutional Fundamental Rights and as such neither of the governments, Union or States, can make any law[4] that violates

1. This Act remained inoperative since it was not notified in Official Central Gazette as required by the legislative process.
2. The present Act is not to apply to the State of Jammu and Kashmir only.
3. The concept compares favorably with the provisions of U.S. Freedom of Information Act (FOIA).
4. The Union Government can make laws on Union List, Concurrent List and on residuary matters, if and when any. Every State can make a law for the welfare of people and on sixty-three items in the State List and forty-seven items in Concurrent List. Both make laws subject to limitations set by the Constitution.

the 'right to information'.[1] Any law dealing with the Right to Information would be a law enacted under Clauses (2) to (6) of Article 19. Since it also touches the Right to Privacy of persons it would have to be a 'procedure established by law' under Article 21 of the Constitution.

On the other hand, the Right to Information Acts seek to help people in obtaining information against the concealment and secrecy by the government bodies of material facts under all Acts made by them. The central purpose to Right to Information Act is to reduce corruption wherever possible and to bring about transparency in government dealings. Ultimately openness to administrative acts and documents leads to democratic 'government by the people for the people'. It is that to obtain information from public authorities by concerned persons for public or personal good is an auxiliary right or obligation. The primacy of Central legislation over existing legislations including State legislations is set by its Section 22 of the RTI Act under which its provisions 'shall have effect notwithstanding anything inconsistent' in any other law. As such it is for the people to choose between the Union and State made laws on the subject in order to obtain information, whichever is more conducive to his interest.[2] Different from some other Constitutions in the Constitution of India there is duality in making laws shared by Union and State Governments but not the matter of their enforcement since both set of laws are enforced by the same administrative authorities and judiciary on territorial basis for jurisdiction. The central RTI Act, 2005 does not mention the situation of the State enacted various RTI Acts. It is for the States to abandon them or for the concerned individuals to choose the

---

1. In USA Freedom of Information is derived from the First Amendment and so primarily Federal Government can make law on it when the law relates to federal public authorities. But the residuary powers under the Constitution are with States and these make Freedom of Information laws for State public authorities and documents. Further the first ten Amendments of US Constitution are applicable to States as well.
2. The State RTI Acts have entirely different set of provisions and rules for tight to information.

advantageous forum. Also the Act does not mention who will bear the expenditure on State Information Commissions. As can be read, the present Act gives positive directions to the State governments to constitute State Information Commissions 'to exercise the powers conferred on and to perform the functions assigned to it under this Act'[1] and to make necessary 'rules to carry out the provisions of this Act'.[2]

What is remarkable in Indian RTI Act, 2005 is the setting up of independent Central and State Information Commissions which are statutory but are given status analogous to judiciary, Public Service Commissions and Indian Election Commission. Transparency and exposure in public are inimical to administrative corruption and this does not happen when administrative officials give information of their own conduct.

Preamble to the RTI Act, 2005

Preamble of an Act is meant to be the key for understanding the purpose and pursuit of the Act in few and well defined words. It indicates the source and background philosophy of the Act and by its enacting clause the Act is made enforceable in the territory. The substantive law follows or 'walks after', the preamble.

It is noticed that the nomenclature of the RTI Act varies in India. Some countries use the term "Access to Information", others use "Freedom of Information" but Indian Act calls it "Right to Information". It can be said that 'access' is one sided and is authority friendly; it is more procedural in content.[3] 'Freedom' is also one sided and functions under the principle "freedom of one is to match with equal freedom of others"; freedom and liberty are political slogans in nature. 'Right' is a legal term different from 'power', 'immunity', 'liberty' or 'privilege'; it is a legal term and jurisprudentially "rights and duties are correlated". There can be no 'right' without a corresponding legal 'duty to submit' to the right. It would be

1. The Act: Chapter IV.
2. The Act: Section 27.
3. The principle is elaborated under footnote 2, *above*.

seen that replacement of Indian Freedom of Information Act 2002 by repeal by Right to Information Act, 2005 is much on these lines though it visualizes democracy as based on access to information. It can also be mentioned as an analysis that the US Freedom of Information Act enacted in 1966 strengthened the democratic and legal rights of people in presidential form of government by introducing the concept of 'openness' and 'transparency' in the conduct of executive or government, the UK the Freedom of Information Act put on Statute Book in 2000 and promulgated in 2005 granted access to people to the records of executive as Her Majesty's 'grace' in the parliamentary form of government. The earlier Indian Freedom of Information Act of 2002 granted access to records of public authorities somewhere in between 'charity' and 'grace' maintaining the holiness of the administration. The Act of 2005 on the other hand as would be observed has made good efforts to make it 'right to information' subject to education, intelligence and paying capacity of common citizen in ways better than as in parliamentary form of Government of England.

Preamble of the Right to Information Act, 2005 accordingly sets the ideals and objectives of the Act; though it is much more wide and comprehensive worded than the rights and obligations enacted under it. It sets to provide a practical regime of right to information for citizens to secure 'access' to information under the control of public authorities in order to promote transparency and accountability in the working of every public authority. The reason for the right of access to information is linked with democracy, the need to have 'an informed citizenry', administrative transparency and accountability of government to the people. The Constitution of India regards the people of India as real sovereign and regards the government and the people as supplementing each other.[1] There is to be no or minimum of secrecy between government and the people. The 'informed'

1. Preamble to the Constitution of India rests the sovereignty with the people of India: "WE, THE PEOPLE OF INDIA, having solemnly resolved to constitute India into a [SOVEREIGN SOCIALIST SECULAR DEMOCRATIC REPUBLIC] and to secure to all its citizens...".

citizens and the electorate are necessary for keeping the executive and elected government chaste. Through the Act people participate in forcing the government to be sincere and not to seek the cover of secrecy. The Preamble of the Act boldly mentions:

> *Whereas* the Constitution of India has established democratic Republic;
>
> *And whereas* democracy requires an informed citizenry and transparency of information which are vital to its functioning and also to contain corruption[1] and to hold Governments and their instrumentalities accountable to the governed;
>
> *And whereas* revelation of information in actual practice is likely to conflict with other public interests including efficient operations of the Governments, optimum use of limited fiscal resources and the preservation of confidentiality of sensitive information;
>
> *And whereas* it is necessary to harmonize these conflicting interests while preserving the paramountcy of the democratic ideal;
>
> Now, therefore, it is expedient to provide for furnishing certain information to citizens who desire to have it.

Understandably it is necessary to look at the parameters of 'democracy'[2] relevant under the Act particularly since it deals with a constitutional right of people. The citizens judge the elected governments by their performance during their tenure, the

1. Prevention of Corruption Act, 1988, separately deals with this aspect of punishment and accountability of widely defined 'public servants' on whom this Act applies. Also the Indian Penal Code deals with various aspects of corruption for criminal prosecution and punishment.
2. Democracy under the Constitution of India is part of its 'basic structure' that cannot be made to vanish. Minerva Mills Ltd. v. Union of India, *AIR* 1980 SC 1789; Any law which violated the principle of free and fair elections that are essential postulates of 'democracy' and so part of 'basic structure' of the Constitution, cannot be taken away: Smt. Indira Gandhi v. Raj Narain, (1976) 2 *SCR* 347.

necessary information is provided by the independent media and inquiries by people. When there is malfunctioning of the government, masses are dissatisfied and individual cases of injustice mount up, the people through ballot, that is democratic process, change or elect another government. Here people so far reacted against misadministration through parliamentary debates. This brings in the Indian Constitution the Preamble[1] of which goes into details of the purposes to be achieved by 'democratic republic'. The openness or transparency of government establishment has to be part of the Constitution for achievement of real 'democratic republic'. It is suffice to mention here that the Act is primarily concerned with economic, political or social 'justice' and 'liberty' of thought and expression and for preventing denial of equality of opportunity, for all of which a lot of information is always necessary. Where an employed person is dissatisfied with a decision involving his service or promotion, or where the license to carry out a profession is cancelled or not given and he needs information to contest the action against his interest it becomes a matter of economic justice. Preamble is no doubt an integral part of the act as matter of interpretation of statutes but it intrinsically is confined to the ideals and objectives of the Act. It is not a source of substantive rights under the Act but it serves to be an aid in interpreting ambiguous terms or fixing the parameters of the meaning of any term used in the Act.[2] But where the operative part of the Act is clear, preamble has no value and the rights and obligations of the people are governed by the operative part of the Act.[3] As such the operative provisions of this Act limit the ideal or concept of 'democracy' where right to information is involved. Equally Section 8 of the

1. Preamble to the Constitution of India mentions as its ideals the securing to all its citizens of:

   "JUSTICE, social, economic and political;

   LIBERTY of thought, expression, belief, faith and worship;

   EQUALITY of status and of opportunity; and to promote among them all;

   FRATERNITY assuring the dignity of the individual and the unity and integrity of the Nation."

2. State of Bombay v. Atma Ram S. Vaidya *AIR* 1951 SC 157.
3. A.K. Gopalan v. State of Madras, *AIR* 1950 SC 27.

Act irrespective of the meaning or scope of democracy restricts 'transparency' in administration by providing wide exceptions.

The operative part of the RTI Act puts into effect the ideals set in its preamble. It is a public law that is related to the structure, powers, rights and the activities of public authorities and goes into details of the administrative ladder for obtaining information, what kind of information cannot be obtained and the government bodies or agencies that remain outside the purview of the Act. However, the regime set by the Act is limited to the obligation of public authorities to provide such 'information to citizens who desire to have it'. The other half, that is, to what extent and how the information received under the Act can remedy the harm suffered by a citizen or do justice to him against oppression or corruption, are matters on which the Act and its preamble are silent though the Central Information Commission has in various individual cases before it, referred to here subsequently in the commentary on the Act, provided necessary or some relief to persons seeking information.

Both from historical and practical perspective the RTI Act is supplementary to freedom of press or media, investigative journalism, personal liberty[1] and people's right to know as part of the development process of their personality and at the same time fortifies democracy by curtailing individual's 'right of privacy' or sovereign's 'right of secrecy'. It exposes corruption or gross negligence[2] and works for transparency in administration.

1. Personal liberty in its true sense means freedom of an individual from such undue restrictions which obstruct the growth and free exercise of his personality. It is the duty of Government to help him by reaching to all necessary information. Hence, the need for RTI Act, 2005.
2. As practical illustration: The University of Allahabad introduced a combined research entrance test (CRET) for all applicants of all its teaching departments in 2007. Most of the candidates found that their subjects of specialization in which they wanted to enroll as research scholars were ignored in the CRET. The harried lot applied for various informations under the RTI Act. Amongst one reply for information, the University acknowledged that it had not prepared any syllabus for holding CRET at all. Meanwhile the Allahabad High Court stayed the announcement of CRET result: 'Many CRET Candidates seek Information under RTI', *The Times of India,* Lucknow ed. 13 November 2007, TNN, 2 (Unreported matter).

On the other hand, 'right of secrecy' whether of individual or government is a wall set in front of right to information. Information sought by media and journalist is *pro bono publico* (for public good) while information sought by individual is for his personal enlightenment or for redressal of his grievances for which he holds a public authority responsible.

The Right to Information: A Fundamental Right

The constitutional concept of the right to information proceeds through 'Right to Freedoms' in Part IV guaranteeing 'Fundamental Rights' to the citizens and persons and has three parts:

(a) Right to acquire information that leads to the formation of views or grievances;

(b) Right to disseminate information, in meetings, through press or media, etc; and

(c) Right to be informed in advance involving obligation on the other persons or authorities to keep people 'informed', *viz*, the display of information or statutory warnings such as: 'Mutual Fund Investments are subject to Market Risks',[1] 'Cigarette Smoking is Injurious to Health',[2] composition of or ingredients of a medicine on the bottle, or maximum retail price of merchandize for sale, or the financial status of companies seeking investment from public, requirement that the name of printer, publisher and place of printing be printed on a book or paper,[3] etc. This is a section of right to information that depends on various other statutory requirements and it is directly not a subject matter of RTI Act, 2005.

(a) Acquiring information—The freedom of information includes both receiving and expression or use of information since the problems of life, success in life and dealing with adversities compel people to seek information. Few people seek information for the sake of information; there is always a purpose

1. Redisuary Non-Banking Companies (Reserve Bank) Directions 1987.
2. Cigarette (Regulation of Production, Supply and Distribution) Act, 1975.
3. Press and Registration of Books Act, 1867, Section 3.

behind the effort. Human problems and their solution cannot be separated from the subject and the RTI Act, 2005 is to be examined in this perspective. Historically, in India the right to know or freedom of information is, apart from various Acts and Statutes, implicit in the section of Fundamental Rights Part of the Constitution entitled 'Right to Freedoms' covering its Articles 19 to 22. The right to acquire information is regarded as part of 'social justice', more so because in busy everyday life individuals have little time to know and so information necessary for them should be at hand through press or otherwise. It developed out of social justice that has reference to interaction within society while political justice is related to art of government with reference to people's participation in it and economic justice touches both equal distribution of wealth by the government and toleration of acquired property rights of members *inter se*.

Acquisition of information depends on:

(i) Freedom of speech and expression which in turn depends on acquisition of basic knowledge by a person or newspaper, this is popularly called 'right to know' as part of social justice and right to the development of personality in society,

(ii) Freedom for trade unions[1] to know the business details and financial condition of company for bargaining bonus, etc.,

(iii) Right to life and to personal liberty,[2]

(iv) Freedom to travel, particularly abroad, for acquiring knowledge,[3]

(v) The right to promote business or occupation through

---

1. All India Bank Employees Association v. National Industrial Tribunal, (1963) 3 *Supreme Court Reports* 269: Effect of Section 34A of Banking Companies Act on trade union activities. Held:

"The right to form unions under Article 19(1)(c) carried with it a guarantee of their effective functioning and unions could not function effectively in respect of industrial disputes if relevant and necessary materials were shut out under the provisions of the Act."

2. Article 21 of the Constitution.

3. Articles 19(1) and 21: Satwant Singh Sawhney v. Assistant Passport Officer, *All India Reporter* 1967 SC 1836.

advertisements, giving information to clients, etc, and

(vi) The right to be informed of the grounds of arrest in criminal prosecution and preventive detention.[1]

The freedom of speech and expression is not possible unless people are freely allowed to acquire knowledge of their liking, develop their minds and freely communicate with other members of society. To achieve this the right to information has developed constitutionally.

The Right to Know: All individuals have a 'right to know', that is, to be in knowledge of the daily happenings and the real truth of all that is of concern to them; it may be emphasized that the real truth is opposite of vagueness, rumors and falsehood and requires verification at individual and technical level. The right to know gives a broader horizon to the right to live successfully, honorably and competitively on our land under Article 21 of the Constitution. Right to life under Article 21 implies knowledge of the means of making livelihood, of professional know-how and of surrounding perils and dangers. In sequence, Article 21 of the Constitution guarantees the right to information as part of 'personal liberty' to every person. It enacts: "No person shall be deprived of his life or personal liberty except according to procedure established by law". The term 'personal liberty' is interpreted to imply all those freedoms that are necessary to develop personality and also to make utmost use of his personality. Knowledge is the base of personality and it is the means by which it can be acquired are part of personal liberty. Education, travel, discussions for exchange of views, professional skills, job satisfaction, earning money are all conducive to growth of personal liberty and these are protected by this article. Negatively, unless there is a law persons enjoy personal liberty unrestrictedly. The 'right to know' is the sum total of the various attributes of personal liberty and it includes the right to receive and to give information. Article 19(1) of the

1. Article 22 of the Constitution.

Constitution has separately guaranteed these attributes.[1] The result is that in so far as an attribute of 'personal liberty' comes under Article 19(1) the restrictions, if any, are placed on them must be in accordance with clauses (2) to (6) of Article 19; otherwise conditions of Article 21 shall apply. This is the constitutional setup in which 'right to information' is a fundamental right.

On economic front, people have the right to know so as to escape fraud and in order to be able to make their career, successfully participate in social life development in the industrial life of democratic India.[2]

The Constitution of India under its Article 22 creates an obligation directly for disclosure or giving of 'information' to a detained person.

From the very outset of the Constitution, arrest and preventive detention under Article 22 has been under scrutiny including his rights to know and to be informed about the 'grounds' on which arrest has been made.

Clause (1) has laid down that: "(1) No person who is arrested shall be detained in custody without being *informed*, as soon as may be, of the grounds for such arrest..."; and

Clause (5) has laid down that: "(5) When any person is detained in pursuance of an order made under any law providing for preventive detention, the authority making the order shall, as soon as may be, *communicate* to such person the grounds on which the order has been made and shall afford him the earliest opportunity of making a representation against the order".

A vast legal assessment of the rights of detained persons, whether on criminal charges or under preventive detention, to know and to be informed and to be communicated of the grounds

---

1. The 'right to hold acquire and dispose of property' vide Article (1) (f) since the Constitution (Forty-fourth Amendment) Act 1978 continues to be protected by the Constitution but under Article 301A. It is now a constitutional right and not a 'Fundamental Right'.
2. Reliance Petrochemicals Ltd. v. Indian Express Newspapers Bombay (P) Ltd., (1988) 4 *SCC* 592.

of detention has taken place through the judgments of the Supreme Court. This has been both with reference to the 'content of information' and the 'delay' involved in making of the communication that is information should be promptly given.

Presently the RTI Act, 2005 is limited to obtaining of information from 'public authorities' by those who 'want to have it' and extends only 'to information accessible under this Act'. Exceptions have been made both with regard to items of information and to the sensitive instrumentalities of government. However, the Act has drawn immense discussions on genus to which this concept belongs in order to set the parameters of inquiry from the government and government controlled or financed authorities. This is an innovation in favour of persons who want to know and get information.

(b) Disseminating information, expressing views and freedom of press—Providing information, religious, political, economic or cultural which people would like to know is part of 'democratic' system envisaged in preamble of RTI Act, 2005 though the source and content of information under the Act are limited. The Supreme Court has asserted,[1] that the freedom of speech and expression guaranteed by Article (19)(1)(a) included the 'Freedom of Press'. For propagating and communicating his ideas to others a citizen has the right to publish them, to disseminate them and to circulate them, either by words of mouth, writing, picture, television or in any manner of his choice. The right of expression extends not merely to the matter that the citizen is entitled to circulate but also to the volume of circulation and also the volume of news and views. Freedom of press motivates a person to seek information under the RTI Act since it enlightens him about the personal interests he should protect by seeking information from 'public authorities'. The interests might be personal, social, cultural, economic or political and 'public authorities' of welfare State deal now with all of them.

---

1. Sakal Papers (P) Ltd. v. Union of India, (1962) 3 *Supreme Court Reports* 842; S. Rangarajan v. P. Jagjivan Ram, (1989) 2 *Supreme Court Cases* 574.

Newspapers, pamphlets, magazines, news-channels of television are various other sources of information and are covered by freedom of press as provider of information to the needy public. The RTI Act requires all public authorities maintaining libraries to include these in the 'information' list that is mandatory to be displayed.

Further,[1] freedom of press is the heart of social and political intercourse. The freedom of expression has four broad social purposes to serve: (i) it helps an individual to attain self-fulfillment, 'by artistic and scholarly endeavors of all sorts', (ii) to assist in discovery of truth, (iii) it strengthens the capacity of individual in participating in decision making, and (iv) it provides a mechanism by which it would be possible to establish a reasonable balance between stability and social change.

On political platform, the freedom of expression allows political discourse that is necessary in any country that aspires for democracy. However, imparting of information by those who provide information of that which people 'ought to know', helps in making or giving plurality of opinions and information on public issues to people. "A successful democracy posits an 'aware' citizenry. Diversity of opinions, views, ideas and ideologies is essential to enable the citizens to arrive at informed judgment on all issues touching them".[2] On democratic front, transparency that the RTI Act functions to achieve in public dealings is essential to the concept of right to information. The Supreme Court declared:[3]

> The people of this country have a *right to know* every public act, everything that is done in a public way, by their public functionaries. They are entitled to know the particulars of every public transaction in all its bearing. The right to know, which is

1. See: Indian Express Newspapers (Bombay) (P) Ltd. v. Union of India, (1985) 1 *Supreme Court Cases* 641; David Feldman, *Civil Liberties and Human Rights.*
2. Secretary, Ministry of Information and Broadcasting v. Cricket Association of Bengal, (1995) 2 *Supreme Court Cases* 300.
3. State of U.P. v. Raj Narain, (1975) 4 *SCC* 428.

> derived from the concept of freedom of speech, though not absolute, is a factor which should make one wary, when secrecy is claimed for transactions which...have no repercussions on public security.

While deliberating on a citizen's right to freedom of information, the Supreme Court observed the people have a 'right to know' through information about the affairs of the elected Government, which seeks to formulate sound policies aimed at their welfare.[1]

The freedom of public discussion, political or religious lectures, educational institutions, press or media are meant to make it possible for interested persons 'to inform other people' what the latter 'ought to now'. In one of its first judgments the Supreme Court[2] dealing with the freedom of press held that:

It "lay at the foundation of all democratic organizations; for without political discussions no public education so essential for proper functioning of the processes of popular government is possible" further that "All members of the society should be able to form their own beliefs and communicate them freely to others. In sum the fundamental principle here is the people's *right to know*." However, the press should not violate the individual's right to privacy as enshrined in Article 21 of the Constitution as part of their right to life and personal liberty.

It is to be noted that collective right to know results in the formation of 'public opinion'. The mobile 'public opinion' has an important role in modern democracy where governments stay in power through ballots. Contrarily in autocracies there is suppression of any development of public opinion against the ruling political party so that there is no cross-examination of government actions and policies. Public opinion requires 'freedom of discussion' for its evolution and this freedom in turn depends on the right of people to be freely informed through media and by piercing of the veil of governmental secrecy. Freedom of discussion is indispensable for mobility and enlightenment of

1. Dinesh Trivedi v. Union of India, (1997) 4 *SCC* 306.
2. Romesh Thappar v. State of Madras, 1950 *Supreme Court Reports* 594.

public opinion. Dissident groups of the day become power wielders of tomorrow in democracy. This freedom of press has been regarded as 'pillar of individual liberty which has been unfailingly guarded by the Courts'.[1] The journalists also have a right to know in order to educate people and supply information of a wide range and the RTI Act is a help to them.

In another case[2] related to freedom of press, the Supreme Court held that it is both a right and a duty:

> Press has a fundamental right to express itself; the community has a *right to be supplied with information*; and the Government has duty to educate the people. (Italics added).

It is further emphasized by Supreme Court that:[3]

> A free and healthy press is indispensable to the functioning of a true democracy. In a democratic set-up, there has to be an active and intelligent participation of the people in all spheres and affairs of their community as well as the State. It is their right to be kept informed about current political, social, economic and cultural life as well as the burning topics and important issues of the day in order to enable them to consider and form broad opinion about the same and the way in which they are being managed, tackled and administered by the Government and its functionaries. To achieve this objective the people need a clear and truthful account of events, so that they may form their own opinion and offer their own comments and viewpoints on such matters and issues and select their further course of action. The primary function, therefore, of the press is to provide comprehensive

1. Express Newspapers P. Ltd. v. Union of India, (1986) 1 *Supreme Court Cases,* 133.
2. Bennett Coleman & Co. v. Union of India, (1972) 2. *Supreme Court Cases* 788.
3. In re: Hari Jai Singh and Another & In re: Vijay Kumar, (1966) 6 *Supreme Court Cases* 466.

> and objective information of all aspects of the country's political, social, economic and cultural life. It has an educative and mobilizing role to play. It plays an important role in molding public opinion it can be an instrument of social change. It may be pointed out here that Mahatma Gandhi in his autobiography has stated that one of the objectives of the newspaper is to understand the proper feelings of the people and give expression to it; another is to arouse among the people certain desirable sentiments; and the third is to fearlessly express popular defects. It, therefore, turns out that the press should have the right to present anything which it thinks fit for publication.

Of course, the freedom of press is subject to the restrictions of Article 19(2) of the Constitution. It has been further clarified by the Supreme Court[1] that:

> But it has to be remembered that this freedom of press is not absolute, unlimited and unfettered at all times and in all circumstances as giving an unrestricted freedom of speech and expression would amount to an uncontrolled license. If it were wholly free even from reasonable restraints it would lead to disorder and anarchy. The freedom is not to be misunderstood as to be a press free to disregard its duty to be responsible. In fact, the element of responsibility must be present in the conscience of the journalists. In an organized society, the rights of the press have to be recognized with its duties and responsibilities towards the society. Public order, decency, morality and such other things must be safeguarded. The protective cover of press freedom must not be thrown open for wrong doings. If a newspaper publishes what is improper, mischievously false or illegal and abuses its liberty it must be punished by court of law.

---

1. In re: Hari Jai Singh and Another & In re: Vijay Kumar, (1966) 6 *Supreme Court Cases* 466.

Historically, this freedom of press no doubt owes its origin to the interpretations of 'freedom of speech and expression' under Article 19(1)(a). But, it is interesting that the RTI Act, 2005 has a much broad outlook and it nowhere links 'right to information' to 'freedom of speech and expression' as is commonly understood. As such it is applicable to situations in a much wider perspective. Information may be needed and be relevant to maintain freedoms mentioned in several of its manifestations under Article 19(1) of the Constitution and more. The right to information under the RTI Act will have its parameters according to the context and the related restrictions under Article 19 clauses (2) to (6) of the Constitution.

(c) *Right to be Informed in Advance:* As already observed it is a section of right to information that depends on various other statutory requirements and it is not a subject matter of RTI Act, 2005. Latter deals with the information that is already with public authorities.

Dissemination of Information

Public authorities—The RTI Act is concerned with dissemination of information held by Government departments and establishments for transparency in administration and for control and limitation of bureaucratic corruption. The information has to be provided by public authorities that are responsible for the departments under them. It is to be noted also that 'public authorities' have wider spread out content than the term 'State' under Part IV of the Constitution against which the freedom of speech and expression is claimed. The term public authorities under the RTI Act has more functionaries than contained in the definition of 'State' under Article 12 of the Constitution of India against whom fundamental rights are available.

Comparatively when the right to information is considered to be an application of Article 19:[1] its scope under the Act is much narrowed down by the limitations set in its Clauses (2) to

1. "(1) All citizens shall have the right—(a) to freedom of speech and expression."

(6) than under the Act. The reason is that under Article 12 the State "includes the Government and Parliament of India and the Legislature of each of the States and all local or other authorities within the territory of India or under the control of the Government of India". The term 'other authorities' have been interpreted in the Constitution alongwith the words 'under control of the Government of India' and include all administrative instrumentalities and statutory and non-statutory bodies which are being financed by the State. The words 'under the control' have been elaborated and extended both to administrative and financial aspects and institutions receiving regular grants-in-aid are subject to the Fundamental Rights. The Universities, statutory public corporations or social institutions, among others, though autonomous but which receive regular government financial aid are covered by Article 12 of the Constitution though these are not engaged directly for the purposes of public administration as generally understood.

But, the 'public authorities' under Section 2(h) of the RTI Act, 2005 has wider application. It includes all authority or body or institutions (1) constituted under Constitution, like, Lok Sabha, Ministries, Prime Ministers Office (PMO), Minority or Backward-class Commissions, Union or State Secretariats, Public Service Commissions, etc.; (2) governmental instrumentalities constituted by any Union or State Act or notification under an Act, e.g. Prasaar Bharti; (3) any autonomous body "owned, *controlled* or substantially financed, like Central Universities; non-Government organization, directly or indirectly by funds provided by the appropriate Government". The Act includes in the ambit of the definition of public authorities the NGOs and privately-run organizations when these are not fully self-financed and have received initial or maintenance grants from the government, such as donation of land by State Government, e.g. research institute.[1]

---

1. CIC/WB/A/2006/00548, Decision on 13 April 2007; In the matter of Greenpeace activist Divya Raghunandan: Meena Menon 'Make data on GM crop tests public: CIC' *The Hindu* e-paper, 19 April 2007, Order was issued on 13 April 2007.

Thus the Act goes into details of a 'public authority' by examining as to how it might be constituted, under whose control it works and who finances it. The all-encompassing words of Section 2(h) foreclose or narrow down any debate for excluding particular bodies from being 'public authority' against whom the right to avail information shall be applicable. As for the companies, a company may be government company or private company depending on shares ownership. The government or Public Sector Undertakings are companies[1] and are subject to RTI Act, 2005. It is interesting that while companies with public share capital are autonomous bodies but many of their functions come under the purview of Company Law Board and those activities include donations to political parties admissible under Section 293A of the Companies Act.[2] As a result, in order to ensure transparency of the funding process of political parties the private companies the Companies Act has made this process subject to the RTI Act, 2005. Regulations of donations to political parties are related to 'political justice' under the Preamble

---

1. There are two types of Public Sector Undertakings (PSU): (i) statutory corporations (for example, the Damodhar Valley Corporation, the Food Corporation of India, the Central or State Warehousing Corporations) and (ii) government-owned or -controlled companies, which are established under the Companies Act, with not less than 51 per cent of paid-up share capital held by the Central Government or by any State government or partly or wholly by both and which include holding companies with more than 50 per cent of the share capital of their subsidiaries.
2. Under this Section, companies (excluding government companies and those less than three years old) can donate funds to any political party or for any political purpose to any person in any financial year, in amounts not exceeding 5 per cent of the average net profit in the three immediately preceding financial years. Such contribution can be made by a resolution authorizing such action passed at a meeting of the company's board of directors. The Companies Act also requires the disclosure of the details of such contributions in the company's profit and loss accounts. Any contravention of these requirements attracts stringent measures, including fines up to three times the amount contributed and three years' imprisonment of the officer responsible for the default. The Section 291A was added in the Company Act by the Election and Other Related Laws (Amendment) Act, 2003.

to the Constitution of India. The Representation of Peoples Act through Indian Election Commission also subjects political parties to RTI Act in so far as the information about any political party, *viz*, funds and donations received, is or can be with the Commission.

Under the RTI Act the 'Public Authorities' are central to the system evolved by Section 4 of the Act, for supply of information related to the units falling under their jurisdiction. They are under section 4(1)(a) in an obligation to maintain all the records of the body, organization or institution duly categorized and indexed in a manner and form suitable for dissemination of information that may be sought, this shall include a statement of the categories of documents held by it or are under its control; under Section 1(b) to publish details about self (body, organization or institution) for public use and information (i) the particulars of the organization, functions and duties; (ii) the categories, powers and duties of the officers and employees alongwith their monthly salaries or remunerations; (iii) the procedure prescribed or followed by the body for its decision-making process including the subdivisions or hierarchy of authority for supervision and accountability for acting according to norms set by it for duly discharge of its functions; (iv) the manual containing rules, regulations, norms, instructions, etc. on which the body functions or on which the officers and employees function; (v) where the public authority functions through board, councils, committees constituted by two or more persons, the powers, functions and other details connected with them including the information whether the meetings and/or reports and minutes of their proceedings are open and accessible to public or not; (vi) the budget allocation of each agency alongwith plans for expenditure and reports of actual expenditure where the body functions through agencies; (vii) where subsidy, concessions, permits or authorizations grants are made the details of such programmes and the details of entitled beneficiaries; (viii) the process, procedures and particulars of facilities for obtaining information by public; and (ix) the names, designation and other particulars of Public Information Officers and Assistant Public Information Officers appointed by it and put in charge of providing information to people requesting information under the Act. These public authorities are storehouse managers of all information about their units and are expected to provide information in the most cost effective that is asked for in the format provided by Sections 6 and 7 of the Act. The prescribed fee for information has to be paid though this is also subject to appeal.

Where policy decisions affecting public are taken,[1] it is required that the body should make appropriate public announcements and Section 4(1)(d) directs that all administrative and quasi-judicial decisions that are taken should be communicated to affected persons alongwith reasons.

Information Officers of Public Authorities: The Act makes it mandatory for the public authorities to appoint specific information officers in all of their units. There are to be Central Public Information Officers for all bodies, organizations or institutions functioning under Central Government; and State Public Information Officers for bodies, organizations or institutions functioning under State Government. For the units of the public authority there are to be Central Assistant Public Information Officers or State Assistant Public Information Officers. The respective 'public authority' under Central or State governments appoint these Officers under Section 5 of the Act.[2] Applications for information or appeals against information supplied or refused are received by them on behalf of concerned public authority also.

The Act permits use of electronic media also for obtaining information from public authority in addition to request in writing made on prescribed format specifying the particulars of information sought and prescribed fees. The channels are separate for obtaining information from Central and State as mentioned

1. Section 4 (1):...(c) publish all relevant facts while formulating important policies or announcing the decisions which affect public; (d) provide reasons for its administrative or quasi-judicial decisions to affected persons.
2. Section 5 of the Act provides the details of the duty of these Central or State Public Information Officers and Assistant Public Information Officers of receiving applications from public seeking information.

earlier. An applicant-making request for information is not required to give any reason for requesting the information or any other personal details except those that may be necessary for contacting him.[1]

The Central Public Information Officer or State Public Information Officers, as the case may be, are to supply the information 'as expeditiously as possible, and in any case within thirty days of the receipt of the request'. Otherwise, the Officer is 'deemed to have refused the request' and the further prescribed proceedings for review or appeal against the refusal shall follow. Sections 8 and 9 provide the specific grounds and reasons for rejection of the request for information, elaborated here subsequently. Where the information requested relates to another person or authority, termed as 'third party', the provisions of Section 11 follow. Here, when the Officer intends to disclose any information which 'relates to or has been supplied by a third party and has been treated as confidential by that third party', the latter gets a *locus standi* in the matter including the right to be heard and making a representation against the disclosure before it is made. Except in case of patents, copyright or any other 'trade and commercial secrets' protected by law the 'disclosure may be allowed if the public interest in disclosure outweighs in importance any possible harm or injury to the interests of such third party'. There are counter rights for third party under Section 11 (2) and (3) and his representations are to be taken into consideration.[2] If any request for information has been rejected by Central Public Information Officer or State Public Information Officers, latter shall under Section 7(8) communicate to the person making the request,—

(i) the reasons for such rejection;

(ii) the period within which an appeal against such rejection may be preferred; and

(iii) the particulars of the appellate authority.

1. Section 6(2) of the Act.
2. The Act: Section 7 (7).

The Act is serious in ensuring dissemination of information. It provides for 'imposition of penalties' on Central or State Public Information Officers for unexplained delays and lapses. Under Section 20 of the RTI Act, the Central and State Public Information Officers are liable to pay Rs. 250 for each day of delay, subject to a maximum of Rs. 25,000 only. The Central or State Information Commission can ask the public authority that has denied information to compensate the applicant for any loss incurred. In the commentary cases inviting penalty are also mentioned. The Central or State Information Commission can also recommend departmental disciplinary action against a Central and State Public Information Officer for intentionally obstructing the furnishing of information, denying or destroying information or providing misleading information.

Exempted Public Authorities

The RTI Act, 2005 exempts by Section 24, Second Schedule the intelligence and security organizations established by Central Government only from its purview. These number nineteen as at present, such as, Intelligence Bureau, Directorate of Revenue Intelligence, etc. and are mentioned in Second Schedule vide Section 24 of the Act. Any information furnished by such organizations to Central Government cannot be disclosed in national interest. The Central Government may, by notification in the Official Gazette, amend the Second Schedule by including therein or excluding any other intelligence or security organizations. Such notification. The notification being delegated legislation shall be laid before each House of Parliament.

This exemption, at the same time, shall not apply to allegations or 'corruption and human rights violations'. When information is sought in respect of allegations of violation of human rights, the information shall only be provided after the approval of the Central Information Commission, and when approval is given such information shall be provided within forty-five days from the date of the receipt of request.

Exemptions from Disclosure

This is an important part of the Act and is most controversial also. While democracy requires transparency in public administration dealings, both internal and in relation to public, the State and government officers need a cover of secrecy upto a point in order to achieve functional efficiency and success. The foreign countries organize espionage in India, which gather and work on pieces of information appearing in media as a source of information. Police cannot catch and convict criminals when these have knowledge of police actions if the criminals have their contacts in police set-up. In commercial competition, one manufacturer say of electronic goods or car would like to know the future planning by fellow manufacturer to be at par or better. For individual citizens personal liberty and development of personality includes right to privacy, and so on. Sections 8, 9 and 10 find a balance between information that should not be divulged, dissemination of which be delayed or be made with conditions. Dissemination under the Act means: "making the information known or communicated to the public through notice boards, newspapers, public announcements, media broadcasts, the internet or any other means, including inspection of offices of any public authority". Under the Act, in a matter of controversy, it is for the public authority to prove that the information is to be kept secret under Section 8.

Section 8 in some matters grants absolute exemption and accordingly no information is to be given on such matters and so it denies the right to obtain information and the Public Information Officers have no discretion but to withhold the information in following matters. Here, the public interest in maintaining the secrecy outweighs the public interest likely to be served by disclosing the information. Then there are other matters of where the exemption is conditional or discretionary and as a change brought about by the Act the disclosure of such information is considered to be in 'larger public interest'. This is decided by Central or State Public Information Officers and is a matter for appeal to the Central or State Information Commission.

1. Absolute exemption—State secrets the "disclosure of which would prejudicially affect the sovereignty and integrity of India, the security, strategic, scientific or economic interests of the State, relation with foreign State or lead to incitement of an offence". Here each of several matters included has a bundle of undefined details or concepts:

(a) 'Sovereignty and integrity' include secrecy in 'Act of State', foreign policies and relations with other States at sovereign level such as making or non-making of treaties with particular States.

The 'Act of State' has reference to sovereign power of dealing with (i) foreign countries by war or peace; (ii) aliens in foreign territory, granting or refusal of visa to foreigners or (iii) the policies followed in international organizations, like United Nations or World Trade Organization, etc.

A citizen can put sovereignty and security of State in jeopardy: 'Sedition' is the crime by an individual directed against the State or the country. Disloyalty to nation can lead to punishment under Section 124A of Indian Penal Code for crime of sedition that enacts: "Whoever by words, either spoken or intended to be read, or by or by visible representation, or otherwise excites or attempts to excite, feelings of disaffection to the Government established by law in India" commits the offence of sedition. Disaffection means[1] "hatred, enmity, dislike, hostility, contempt and every form of ill-will to the Government". This has been qualified to some extent by the interpretation in 1942 given to sedition by the Indian Federal Court:

> The first and fundamental duty of every government is the preservation of order, since order is the condition precedent to all civilization and the advance of human happiness"...Sedition law "is the answer of the State to those who for the purpose of attacking or subverting it, seek to disturb its tranquility, to create public disturbance and to promote disorder, or who '*incite others to do so*'. Words, deeds or writings constitute sedition.[2]

In independent India the Supreme Court of India had before it the question whether Sections 124A and 505 of the Indian Penal Code had become void in view of the freedom of speech

1. Queen Empress v. Bal Gangadhar Tilak, *I.L.R.* 22B. 112 (134).
2. Niharendu v Emperor, *FCR* 1942 38.

and expression vide provisions of Article 19(1)(a) of the Constitution guaranteeing the latter freedom to very citizen. Therefore, for harmonizing the two, for crime of sedition it was necessary that the words incited or had the tendency to incite public disorder alongwith creating disaffection or feeling of enmity against the government. A mere criticism of government though strongly worded would be within the reasonable limits of Article 19(2) is part of freedom of speech and expression.

Freedom of obtaining information by media or individuals through RTI Act is adjustable accordingly. Only sedition related information has to be withheld by Central or State Public Information Officers. However, though not mentioned in the Act, all continuing criminal and civil proceedings in courts are beyond the reach of RTI Act.

(b) 'Strategic' matters high policy oriented matters of foreign relations are related to defence of country and include preference in armaments, defence policies, deployment of forces, etc. Strategic matters concern the survival and finding balance of military power with other States involving armed forces of the country. These matters are vital and are subject to espionage activities by other States. The Indian Official Secrets Act 1923 makes any acquisition or possession of such information a severely punishable crime.

(c) Internal 'security' arrangements include police and dealing with terrorists, divisive politics involving use of force; information of such arrangements and deployments are out of reach of RTI Act under Section 8.

(d) Internal and external economic, commercial and trade policies of government include a wide spectrum. Participation in economic globalization imperatives, internal free or mixed economy preferences, fixing currency exchange rates, and so on. RTI Act cannot be used to know the government's arterial actions and decisions on such matters.

(e) 'Scientific' and technological expertise of national interest developed or held by the government, as in military establishment or government companies or factories; and 'economic interests of the State' include trade, foreign exchange regulation and other such policies the determination of which is sovereign right of India.

(f) The disclosure of such information that might lead to 'incitement of an offence' is a new addition to the idea of State secrecy. The 'offence' naturally must be of grave nature; 'public disorder' is an offence of grave nature while breach or threat to 'law and order' is not so. Normally the government vigilance departments gather vital information, or commissions are appointed after a sensational crime to investigate and report to government. Such information is to be kept secret or confidential when its disclosure would lead to public disorder. It has been evaluated that 'law and order', 'public order', and 'security of State' are distinct but overlapping concepts. "Whereas every breach may amount to disturbance of law and order, every such breach may not amount to disturbance of public order and every public disorder may not prejudicially affect the security of State."[1] 'Incitement of an offence' under the RTI Act is a condition that is part of the function of State to maintain public order and Security of State. Public order is synonymous with public peace, safety and tranquility.[2] When a person incites an offence it should lead to punishable crimes under Indian Penal Code, such as, abetment, conspiracy, waging or abetting a war against Government of India, sedition, spreading communal disharmony, or criminal intimidation, among others. Else, in grave situation preventive action might be taken. Under the National Security Act 1980, Section 3 provides that the Central Government

---

1. Romesh Thapar v State of Madras, *AIR* 1950 SC 594; Shah, G. M. v State of J.K. AIR 1980 SC 594.
2. Ram Manohar Lohia v State of Bihar, *AIR* 1966 SC 740.

or the State Government when (a) satisfied with respect to the person that with a view to preventing him from acting in any manner prejudicial to the defence of India, the relations of India with foreign powers, of the security of India, or (b) when satisfied with respect to the person that with a view to preventing him from acting in any manner prejudicial to the maintenance of public order, may if it is necessary to do so, make an order directing such person be detained. The RTI Act maintains secrecy of related information possessed by public authorities in the national interest.

2. Information to be given under conditions—Under RTI Act the information sought may be:

(a) subject to processes of any court of law during pendency of a civil or criminal case or tribunal, and subject to laws for the Contempt of Courts;

(b) subject 'contempt' of each House of Parliament and State Legislatures, that is, the information disseminated must not cause breach of the 'privileges' of Parliament or the State Legislatures;

(c) excluded when it relates to cabinet papers of Prime Minister or Chief Ministers including records of deliberations of the Council of Ministers, Secretaries and other officers, i.e. Prime Ministers Office (PMO) or Secretaries. However, exception is made for the decisions of Council of Ministers, the reasons thereof, and the material on the basis of which the decisions were taken shall be public matter after the decision has been taken, and the matter is complete, or over: The advice given by Ministers including Prime Minister to President is *per se* not a privileged matter for Section 8 of RTI Act.

It is to be noted on the side of definition that the Union and State Public Service Commissions, Election Commission, Attorney General Offices though these have constitutional status, are not exempted from the obligation of disseminating information under Section 8 of RTI Act.

Judicial Secrecy: The Contempt of Courts Act 1970 regulates the privileges of judiciary in this matter and their violation constitutes contempt of court. However, in addition it provides: (a) the conditions when publication and distribution of a matter will not be contempt; (b) that 'fair and accurate' reports of judicial proceedings are not contempt of court; (c) that 'fair criticism' of judicial act is not contempt of court; and (d) that complaint against presiding officers of 'subordinate courts' to High Court only is not contempt of court.

The powers under contempt of court do not cover administration of non-judicial staff and general administration and these are subject to RTI Act.

Parliamentary Secrecy: Privileges of Parliament and State Legislatures under Articles 105 and 194 of the Constitution are identical and remain undefined by law, as required under Clauses (2) of respective Articles.[1] There is freedom of speech for members and it is the right of 'Speaker' or 'Chairman' of the House to

---

1. Article 105. Powers, privileges, etc. of the House of Parliament and of the members and committees thereof.
   (i) Subject to the provisions of this Constitution and to the rules and standing orders regulating the procedure of Parliament, there shall be freedom of speech in Parliament.
   (ii) No member of Parliament shall be liable to any proceedings in any court in respect of any thing said or any vote given by him in Parliament or any committee thereof, and no person shall be so liable in respect of the publication by or under the authority of either House of Parliament of any report, paper, votes or proceedings.
   (iii) In other respects, the powers, privileges and immunities or each House of Parliament, and of the members and the committees of each House, shall be such as may from time to time defined by Parliament by law and, until so defined. [shall be those of that House and of its members and committees immediately before the coming into force of section 15 of the Constitution (Forty-fourth Amendment) Act, 1978].
   (iv) The provisions of clauses (1), and (3) shall apply in relation to persons who by virtue of this Constitution have the right to speak in, and otherwise to take part in the proceedings of, a House of Parliament or any committee thereof as they apply in relation to members of Parliament.

regulate the proceedings. The Constitution also gives power to each House of Parliament by Article 118 and State Legislatures by Article 208 to frame rules for regulation and for conduct of their business including public relations. Where any person commits breach of its privileges each House has the power to command presence before it of outside offenders before it and to give or impose punishment, which may extend to commitment in prison for the duration of its ongoing session.

Accordingly, any information sought under RTI Act from the public authorities appointed by the Houses will be subject to these constitutional provisions.

Executive Secrecy: The President,[1] Council of Ministers and Secretaries constitute the performing executive under the Constitution of India. Their deliberations when in writing on any subject are subject to secrecy; however, after they take a decision, the matter is treated as public, and thereafter it becomes subject to RTI Act. Further, information which would impede the processes relating to maintenance of public order and 'law and order' and enforcement of various laws, such as, Prevention of Food Adulteration Act 1954 National Security Act 1980, Prevention of Corruption Act 1988, or Narcotic Drugs & Psychotropic Substances Act 1985, etc., investigation, or apprehension or prosecution of offenders, cannot be disclosed. Section 5 of Official Secrets Act 1923 even in its amended form prohibits disclosure or dissemination of matter in normal official documents.

Noting on Files and Handwritten Deliberations or Advice: These have constituted a lively debate in relation to the powers of Central or State Information Commissions to order the public authorities to disclose these 'Noting on Files and Handwritten Deliberations' to applicants for information.

Noting on Files is Part of an Ages Old System: The noting starts from the lowest official ladder in a department till the appropriate officer takes a decision or finally order is issued. Noting by successive officers on files through whom these move is usual feature for taking of Government decisions. When there is delay or a person is aggrieved by a decision he seeks information

1. Governors in case of States are executive heads.

under the RTI Act now. The question is what is a document for dissemination of information asked for by the applicant? Do the noting in files constitute the document or only the decisions? Some of the notings are confidential, some are against and some noting are favourable to a person. This was a matter that was raised and discussed in Parliament at the time of its enactment also. When the new RTI Act replaced Freedom of Information Act 2002 on May 12, 2005, the term "file notings" was not included in the definition of information given in Section 2(f) of RTI Act, 2005. It meant that file notings were or were not part of information remained vague under the Act.

Subsequently, after the RTI Act came into operation the different Government Departments took different stand on the matter. Ideologically for democracy demands for 'transparency' and 'accountability' are quite appealing to the men in offices also, consequently the Government has faced affirmations and rejection of the idea that 'all' official files should be subject to the new RTI Act within its own cadres also. The Central Information Commission in a case[1] *Satyapal* vs. *TCIL* had observed:[2]

> In the system of functioning of public authorities, a file is opened for every subject/matter dealt with by the public authority. While the main file would contain all the materials connected with the subject/matter, generally, each file also has what is known as note sheets, separate from but attached with the main file. Most of the discussions on the subject/matter are recorded in the note sheets and decisions are mostly based on the recording in the note sheets and even the decisions are recorded on the note sheets. These recordings are generally known as "file

1. (CIC) No. ICPB/A-1/CIC/2006.
2. (CIC) No. ICPB/A-1/CIC/2006: In this matter, the Central Public Information Officer (CPIO) of TCIL had declined to supply a copy of a document to the applicant for information on the ground that the same forms part of "file noting" which, according to him is exempted under the RTI Act. The first Appellate Authority also confirmed the decision of the CPIO. The appellant before CIC contended that he has the right to seek information contained in the "file notings".

> notings". Therefore, no file would be complete without note sheets having "file notings". In other words, note sheets containing "file notings" are an integral part of a file. Sometimes, notings are made on the main file also, which obviously would be a part of the file itself. In terms of Section 2(i), a record includes a file and in terms of Section 2(j) right to information extends to accessibility to a record. Thus, a combined reading of Sections 2(f), (i)&(j) would indicate that a citizen has the right of access to a file of which the file notings are an integral part. If the legislature had intended that "file notings" are to be exempted from disclosure, while defining a "record" or "file" it could have specifically provided so. Therefore, we are of the firm view, that, in terms of the existing provisions of the RTI Act, a citizen has the right to seek information contained in "file notings" unless the same relates to matters covered under Section 8 of the Act.

The reaction from the side of Government to this ruling was in the form of a move to amend the RTI Act for giving effect to the Government standpoint. The proposed Right to Information (Amendment) Bill 2006 had generated a lot of adverse criticism in Parliament, media and public. However, due to dissentions and lack of support in Parliament the Government has dropped the move to adopt the Right to Information (Amendment) Bill 2006 in the August 2006 session of Parliament which would have kept out of information to public the 'file noting in some areas'.[1]

The case for the view of Government seems to be fortified by a stay granted by Delhi High Court in another pending case dealing with correspondence of advice given by Prime Minister to President against decision of CIC.[2]

---

1. 'Govt drops move to amend Right to Information Act': PTI news from New Delhi, *Times of India* 19 Aug 2006, 1637 hrs IST.
2. Appeal No. CIC/MA/A/2006/00121 'Court Stays Order seeking Copies of Narayanan, Vajpayee Letters': Staff Reporter, *The Hindu, e-paper*, 23 Aug 2006: In the matter of application for information by C. Ramesh of Vellore, discussed in detail earlier.

Whether the Government will pursue the Proposed Amendment in future is uncertain and till then the ruling of CIC shall prevail.

3. Information concerning a Third Person—(a) Any information with a public authority is to be refused when received from a third person in official way that relates to patent laws, copyrights or his trade secrets and when its disclosure will harm his competitive position. But when the public authority is 'satisfied that the larger public interest warrants the disclosure of such information' and the conditions of Section 11 in favour of third person have been met, the disclosure of such information under RTI Act may be made.

(b) Any information with a public authority received from a third person marked as confidential by the latter or where 'fiduciary relationship' such as between doctor and patient, advocate and litigant, husband and wife, insurance company and insured, taxman and tax-payer, etc. exist under law, the information cannot be disseminated. However, when the public authority is 'satisfied that the larger public interest warrants the disclosure of such information' and the conditions of Section 11 in favour of third person have been met, the disclosure of such information under RTI Act may also be made.

4. Dissemination of information received from a 'foreign government' in confidence by the public authority cannot be done.

5. Any information of personal nature that has no relationship to any public activity or interest cannot be disclosed unless the Central or State Public Information Officer or the appellate authority in the 'larger public interest' justifies its disclosure.

6. A public authority may under paragraph (2) of Section 8 of RTI Act allow access to information covered by Section 5 of the Official Secrets Act after he specifically decides that 'public interest in disclosure outweighs the harm to the protected interest' notwithstanding the Official Secrets Act.

The Information Commissions

The RTI Act, 2005 has made unique beginning of creating independent and autonomous Information Commissions that operate separately for Central Government establishment and State Government establishments, in keeping with the federal structure of the Constitution:

1. The Central Information Commission[1] has its headquarter in New Delhi is composed of Chief Election Commissioner and upto ten Central Information Commissioners, all appointed by the President for tenure of five years or the age of 65 whichever is earlier. These are to be "persons of eminence in public life with wide knowledge and experience in law, science and technology, social service, management, journalism, mass media or administration and governance". They have the status and salary at par with Chief Election Commissioner and Election Commissioners functioning under the Constitution. They can be removed only by order of the President on the ground of proved misbehavior or incapacity after the Supreme Court, on a reference made to it by the President, has, on inquiry, reported that the Chief Information Commissioner or any Information Commissioner, as the case may be, ought to on such ground be removed. Also the President can remove by order from office the Chief Information Commissioner or any Information Commissioner if the Chief Information Commissioner or a Information Commissioner, as the case may be, only when—

(a) He is adjudged an insolvent; or

(b) He has been convicted of an offence which, in the opinion of the President, involves moral turpitude; or

(c) He engages during his term of office in any paid employment outside.

2. State Information Commissions—Likewise, every State has to constitute its own (name of the State) State Information Commission[2] naming the city of its head quarter. It is composed

1. Chapter III, Sections 12 to 14 of the Act.
2. Chapter IV Sections 15 to 17.

of State Chief Information Commissioner and the State Information Commissioners. The Governor of the State shall appoint these. The salaries and allowances payable to and other terms and conditions of service (a) of the State Chief Information Commissioner shall be the same as that of an Election Commissioner; and (b) of the State Information Commissioner shall be the same as that of the Chief Secretary to the State Government. The Governor can remove them from their office by his order on the ground of proved misbehavior or incapacity after the approval of the Supreme Court, on a reference made to it by the Governor after an inquiry. The Governor can also by order remove from office the State Chief Information Commissioner or any State Information Commissioner if the Chief Information Commissioner or a Information Commissioner, as the case may be, on the same grounds as apply for members of Central Information Commission. All these have tenure of five years or the age of 65 whichever is earlier. For qualification, these are "persons of eminence in public life with wide knowledge and experience in law, science and technology, social service, management, journalism, mass media or administration and governance".

The State Information Commissions are to function autonomously without being subjected to directions by any other authority under this Act, that is, there is no subordination of State Information Commissions to Central Information Commission. The general superintendence, direction and management of the affairs of the State Information Commission vests in the State Chief Information Commissioner who is assisted by the State Information Commissioners and these exercise all such powers and do all such acts and things which may be exercised or done by the State Information Commission. The State Government shall provide the State Chief Information Commissioner and the State Information Commissioners with such officers and employees as may be necessary for the efficient performance of their functions under this Act, and the salaries and allowances payable to and the terms and conditions of service of the officers and other employees appointed for the purpose of this Act shall be such as may be prescribed duties of his office; or

(d) He is, in the opinion of the President, unfit to continue in office by reason of infirmity of mind or body; or

(e) He has acquired such financial or other interest as is likely to affect prejudicially his functions as the Chief Information Commissioner or a Information Commissioner.

The Central Information Commission functions autonomously without being subjected to directions by any other authority under this Act. The general superintendence, direction and management of the affairs of the Central Information Commission vests in the Chief Information Commissioner who is assisted by the Information Commissioners and these exercise all such powers and do all such acts and things which may be exercised or done by the Central Information Commission.

The Central Government provides the Chief Information Commissioner and the Information Commissioners such officers and employees as may be necessary for the efficient performance of their functions under this Act, and the salaries and allowances payable to and the terms and conditions of service of the officers and other employees appointed for the purpose of this Act shall be such as may be prescribed.

3. **Powers and functions of Information Commissions**—The Constitution of India has by its Part XI divided legislative and administrative powers and functions between the Union and the States. Accordingly, the Central Information Commission is to deal with those public authorities which function under laws made by Union while the State Information Commissions deal with functions taking place under the laws enacted by the respective States. This is irrespective of the administrative authorities, which are enforcing both Union and State enacted laws within their territorial Jurisdiction. The district magistrates while enforcing Union (central) laws in the district would be subject to Central Information Commission and while enforcing State enacted laws would be subject to the jurisdiction of State Information Commission. There is obvious overlapping of jurisdictions and the RTI Act makes it a duty of Information Commissions, Central or State, to transmit the applications for

information received from public to the appropriate other forum without making the public suffer.

Each Commission requires each Government department or organization to appoint one Public Information Officer.

In general the powers and functions of the two Commissions are similar and are three: (1) To help citizen—seeking information in reaching the appropriate public authority; this might involve inquiry whether an authority is public authority or is otherwise.

(2) When the Public Information Officer of the public authority has dealt with the request for information, it may suffer from various considerations, *viz.*, that the information is denied, cannot be given or can be partly given for reasons stated, that the information given is inaccurate or evasive, that a third party is involved whose permission is to be cleared, or that the person making the request does not agree with the amount of fee to be charged, etc., which keep the request for information pending.

(3) In all circumstances, the person seeking information can 'appeal' to the Central Information Commission or State Information Commission against the decision of Public Information Officers of public authorities.

(4) When the Public Information Officer is inaccurate, tardy or inefficient and does not maintain the time schedule set by the Act in dissemination of information sought, the Information Commissions can punish him with fines.

The precise details are discussed in the notes and comments on provisions of Chapters III, IV and V of the Act subsequently.

Under the Freedom of Information Act 2002 there was no provision for the two autonomous Information Commissions and for this omission it had come into severe criticism. The Public Information Officers were the last authority and there was no provision for appeals beyond their authority; the time schedules were recommendatory and not mandatory, much as in England under the Freedom of Information Act 2000. The result as feared was that the Public Information Officers being part of administrative machinery could delay or suppress correct information. In England for the purposes of U.K. Freedom of Information Act 2000 (1) the Data Protection Commissioner of

Data Protection Act 1998 is additionally the Information Commissioner; (2) the Data Protection Tribunal is additionally the Information Tribunal. There is no independent *ombudsman* type body to enforce freedom of information. Somehow British activists on freedom of information find Indian experiment with autonomous body independent of government directions and pressures, as interesting for other States if not for England. The British Government's Department of International Development (DFDI) and London-based consultancy Adam Smith International (ISL) are cooperating with Indian Government in a detailed evaluation of the working of RTI Act during the two years after it came into force.

Miscellaneous Settings in the Act

The Chapter VI of the RTI Act provides for smooth working of the Act and for removing difficulties and doubts in its operation.

1. The Act protects for things done in good faith under the Act or the rules made thereunder. However, this does not exclude the exercise of powers not granted by the Act and to criminal offences for which criminal proceedings are instituted. Departmental actions against officers and staff under the Act are also not excluded. There is to be no criminal or civil liability of officers under the Act or any rule made under it for anything that is done in good faith.[1]

2. The information given under RTI Act is governed by the limitations set by the Act itself and it overrides secrecy under Official Secrets Act 1023 and any other such law,[2] like the Evidence Act, for the time being in force or in any instrument having effect by virtue of any law other than this Act. This fulfils a long felt demand as against claim of secrecy for any official document under this Act, and is discussed in detail in commentary on Section 8(2) of the RTI Act, 2005.

3. Since the Central and State Information Commissions have independent standing the question arises about the

1. RTI Act, 2005: Section 21.
2. RTI Act, 2005: Section 2 RTI Act, 2005: Section 22.

jurisdiction that the High Courts exercise over legal actions and interpretations under the Acts by Union or State Legislatures. As the Act provides no authority, implying executive mainly, can substitute its judgment for any order passed under this RTI Act otherwise than by an appeal made under the provisions of the Act.

However, this does not push out the jurisdiction of the High Court under Article 226 of the Constitution by way of writ of certiorari and the appellate jurisdiction of the Supreme Court of India under the Constitution. As the matters are evolving there are cases against interpretations given by Information Commissioners and Information Officers to various provisions of the Act. A person or public authority can also proceed to the High Court claiming relief under the doctrine of ultra vires; this aspect is appropriately discussed in the Commentary.

4. Under Article 24 the Second Schedule lists nineteen intelligence and security organizations established by Central Government are to be out of the purview of the Act accept for information sought that pertains to allegation of corruption and violation of human rights. These intelligence-gathering organizations of the Government for the security of the country are specifically exempted from the operation of RTI Act by Schedule two of the Act.

5. The RTI Act, 2005 has provided autonomy and independence to the Central Information Commission and State Information Commission comparable to the judiciary. But at the same time the Central Information Commission and State Information Commission have been rooted in democratic parliamentary system. The Commissions are to make annual reports on the implementation of the Act to the Central or State Governments as the case may be.[1]

The Act has evolved a system for 'laying off annual report of the work done under the Act to be made to the Parliament or the State Legislature. The Members of Parliament or State Legislature have the right to make suggestions for improvement in working of the Commissions and of criticizing them for

1. RTI Act, 2005: Section 25.

sluggishness. This provision also provides a window for amending the Act where it falters in the achievement of democratic ideals.

6. The Commissions and the public authorities are to maintain regular contact with the people informing the latter about the procedures, reports, notices about the fee payable, its location and address, etc.[1]

7. The rule making power including removal of difficulties under the Act is with the Central Government, State Government and the Competent Authorities and the procedures set by the Act is to be followed.[2]

1. RTI Act, 2005: Section 26.
2. RTI Act, 2005: Section 27, 28, 29 & 30.

PART II

THE RIGHT TO INFORMATION ACT, 2005

(No. 22 of 2005)

THE RIGHT TO INFORMATION ACT, 2005 (NO. 22 OF 2005)

An Act to provide for setting out the practical regime of right to information for citizens to secure access to information under the control of public authorities, in order to promote transparency and accountability in the working of every public authority, the constitution of a Central Information Commission and State Information Commissions and for matters connected therewith or incidental thereto.

Whereas the Constitution of India has established democratic Republic;

And whereas democracy requires an informed citizenry and transparency of information which are vital to its functioning and also to contain corruption and to hold Governments and their instrumentalities accountable to the governed;

And whereas revelation of information in actual practice is likely to conflict with other public interests including efficient operations of the Governments, optimum use of limited fiscal resources and the preservation of confidentiality of sensitive information;

And whereas it is necessary to harmonise these conflicting interests while preserving the paramountcy of the democratic ideal;

Now, therefore, it is expedient to provide for furnishing certain information to citizens who desire to have it.

Be it enacted by Parliament in the Fifty-sixth Year of the Republic of India as follows:

CHAPTER I

PRELIMINARY

1. Short title, extent and commencement.—1. This Act may be called the Right to Information Act, 2005.

2. It extends to the whole of India except the State of Jammu and Kashmir.

3. The provisions of sub-section (1) of section 4, sub-sections (1) and (2) of section 5, sections 12, 13, 15, 16, 24 , 27 and 28 shall come into force at once, and the remaining provisions of this Act shall come into force on the one hundred and twentieth day[1] of its enactment.

2. Definitions.—In this Act, unless the context otherwise requires—

(a) "appropriate Government" means in relation to a public authority which is established, constituted, owned, controlled or substantially financed by funds provided directly or indirectly—

(i) by the Central Government or the Union Territory administration, the Central Government;

(ii) by the State Government, the State Government;

(b) "Central Information Commission" means the Central Information Commission constituted under sub-section (1) of section 12;

(c) "Central Public Information Officer" means the Central Public Information Officer designated under sub-section (1) and includes a Central Assistant Public Information Officer designated as such under sub-section (2) of section 5;

(d) "Chief Information Commissioner" and "Information Commissioner" mean the Chief Information Commissioner and Information Commissioner appointed under sub-section (3) of section 12;

---

1. 12th October, 2005.

(e) "competent authority" means—

(i) the Speaker in the case of the House of the People or the Legislative Assembly of a State or a Union territory having such Assembly and the Chairman in the case of the Council of States or Legislative Council of a State;

(ii) the Chief Justice of India in the case of the Supreme Court;

(iii) the Chief Justice of the High Court in the case of a High Court;

(iv) the President or the Governor, as the case may be, in the case of other authorities established or constituted by or under the Constitution;

(v) the administrator appointed under Article 239 of the Constitution;

(f) "information" means any material in any form, including records, documents, memos, e-mails, opinions, advices, press releases, circulars, orders, logbooks, contracts, reports, papers, samples, models, data material held in any electronic form and information relating to any private body which can be accessed by a public authority under any other law for the time being in force;

(g) "prescribed" means prescribed by rules made under this Act by the appropriate Government or the competent authority, as the case may be;

(h) "public authority" means any authority or body or institution of self-government established or constituted—

(a) by or under the Constitution;

(b) by any other law made by Parliament;

(c) by any other law made by State Legislature;

(d) by notification issued or order made by the appropriate Government, and includes any—

(i) body owned, controlled or substantially financed;

(ii) non-Government organisation substantially financed, directly or indirectly by funds provided by the appropriate Government;

(i) "record" includes—

(a) any document, manuscript and file;

(b) any microfilm, microfiche and facsimile copy of a document;

(c) any reproduction of image or images embodied in such microfilm (whether enlarged or not); and

(d) any other material produced by a computer or any other device;

(j) "right to information" means the right to information accessible under this Act which is held by or under the control of any public authority and includes the right to—

(i) inspection of work, documents, records;

(ii) taking notes, extracts or certified copies of documents or records;

(iii) taking certified samples of material;

(iv) obtaining information in the form of diskettes, floppies, tapes, video cassettes or in any other electronic mode or through printouts where such information is stored in a computer or in any other device;

(k) "State Information Commission" means the State Information Commission constituted under sub-section (1) of section 15;

(l) "State Chief Information Commissioner" and "State Information Commissioner" mean the State Chief Information Commissioner and the State Information Commissioner appointed under sub-section (3) of section 15;

(m) "State Public Information Officer" means the State Public Information Officer designated under sub-section (1) and includes a State Assistant Public Information Officer designated as such under sub-section (2) of section 5;

(n) "third party" means a person other than the citizen making a request for information and includes a public authority.

CHAPTER II

RIGHT TO INFORMATION AND OBLIGATIONS OF PUBLIC AUTHORITIES

3. Right to information.—Subject to the provisions of this Act, all citizens shall have the right to information.

4. Obligations of public authorities.—(1) Every public authority shall—

(a) maintain all its records duly catalogued and indexed in a manner and the form which facilitates the right to information under this Act and ensure that all records that are appropriate to be computerised are, within a reasonable time and subject to availability of resources, computerised and connected through a network all over the country on different systems so that access to such records is facilitated;

(b) publish within one hundred and twenty days from the enactment of this Act—

(i) the particulars of its organisation, functions and duties;

(ii) the powers and duties of its officers and employees;

(iii) the procedure followed in the decision-making process, including channels of supervision and accountability;

(iv) the norms set by it for the discharge of its functions;

(v) the rules, regulations, instructions, manuals and records, held by it or under its control or used by its employees for discharging its functions;

(vi) a statement of the categories of documents that are held by it or under its control;

(vii) the particulars of any arrangement that exists for consultation with, or representation by, the members of the public in relation to the formulation of its policy or implementation thereof;

(viii) a statement of the boards, councils, committees and other bodies consisting of two or more persons constituted as its part or for the purpose of its advice, and as to whether meetings of those boards, councils, committees and other bodies are open to the public, or the minutes of such meetings are accessible for public;

(ix) a directory of its officers and employees;

(x) the monthly remuneration received by each of its officers and employees, including the system of compensation as provided in its regulations;

(xi) the budget allocated to each of its agency, indicating the particulars of all plans, proposed expenditures and reports on disbursements made;

(xii) the manner of execution of subsidy programmes, including the amounts allocated and the details of beneficiaries of such programmes;

(xiii) particulars of recipients of concessions, permits or authorisations granted by it;

(xiv) details in respect of the information, available to or held by it, reduced in an electronic form;

(xv) the particulars of facilities available to citizens for obtaining information, including the working hours of a library or reading room, if maintained for public use;

(xvi) the names, designations and other particulars of the Public Information Officers;

(xvii) such other information as may be prescribed and thereafter update these publications every year;

(c) publish all relevant facts while formulating important policies or announcing the decisions which affect public;

(d) provide reasons for its administrative or quasi-judicial decisions to affected persons.

(2) It shall be a constant endeavour of every public authority to take steps in accordance with the requirements of clause (b) of sub-section (1) to provide as much information *suo motu* to the public at regular intervals through various means of communications, including internet, so that the public have minimum resort to the use of this Act to obtain information.

(3) For the purposes of sub-section (1), every information shall be disseminated widely and in such form and manner which is easily accessible to the public.

(4) All materials shall be disseminated taking into consideration the cost effectiveness, local language and the most effective method of communication in that local area and the information should be easily accessible, to the extent possible in electronic format with the Central Public Information Officer or State Public Information Officer, as the case may be, available free or at such cost of the medium or the print cost price as may be prescribed.

Explanation—For the purposes of sub-sections (3) and (4), "disseminated" means making known or communicated the information to the public through notice boards, newspapers, public announcements, media broadcasts, the internet or any other means, including inspection of offices of any public authority.

5. **Designation of public information officers.**—(1) Every public authority shall, within one hundred days of the enactment of this Act, designate as many officers as the Central Public Information Officers or State Public Information Officers, as the case may be, in all administrative units or offices under it as

may be necessary to provide information to persons requesting for the information under this Act.

(2) Without prejudice to the provisions of sub-section (1), every public authority shall designate an officer, within one hundred days of the enactment of this Act, at each sub-divisional level or other sub-district level as a Central Assistant Public Information Officer or a State Assistant Public Information Officer, as the case may be, to receive the applications for information or appeals under this Act for forwarding the same forthwith to the Central Public Information Officer or the State Public Information Officer or senior officer specified under sub-section (1) of section 19 or the Central Information Commission or the State Information Commission, as the case may be:

Provided that where an application for information or appeal is given to a Central Assistant Public Information Officer or a State Assistant Public Information Officer, as the case may be, a period of five days shall be added in computing the period for response specified under sub-section (1) of section 7.

(3) Every Central Public Information Officer or State Public Information Officer, as the case may be, shall deal with requests from persons seeking information and render reasonable assistance to the persons seeking such information.

(4) The Central Public Information Officer or State Public Information Officer, as the case may be, may seek the assistance of any other officer as he or she considers it necessary for the proper discharge of his or her duties.

(5) Any officer, whose assistance has been sought under sub-section (4), shall render all assistance to the Central Public Information Officer or State Public Information Officer, as the case may be, seeking his or her assistance and for the purposes of any contravention of the provisions of this Act, such other officer shall be treated as a Central Public Information Officer or State Public Information Officer, as the case may be.

6. Request for obtaining information.—(1) A person, who desires to obtain any information under this Act, shall make a request in writing or through electronic means in English or Hindi or in the official language of the area in which the application is being made, accompanying such fee as may be prescribed, to—

(a) the Central Public Information Officer or State Public Information Officer, as the case may be, of the concerned public authority;

(b) the Central Assistant Public Information Officer or State Assistant Public Information Officer, as the case may be, specifying the particulars of the information sought by him or her:

Provided that where such request cannot be made in writing, the Central Public Information Officer or State Public Information Officer, as the case may be, shall render all reasonable assistance to the person making the request orally to reduce the same in writing.

(2) An applicant making request for information shall not be required to give any reason for requesting the information or any other personal details except those that may be necessary for contacting him.

(3) Where an application is made to a public authority requesting for an information—

(i) which is held by another public authority; or

(ii) the subject matter of which is more closely connected with the functions of another public authority,

the public authority, to which such application is made, shall transfer the application or such part of it as may be appropriate to that other public authority and inform the applicant immediately about such transfer:

Provided that the transfer of an application pursuant to this sub-section shall be made as soon as practicable but in no case later than five days from the date of receipt of the application.

7. **Disposal of request.**—(1) Subject to the proviso to sub-section (2) of section 5 or the proviso to sub-section (3) of section 6, the Central Public Information Officer or State Public Information Officer, as the case may be, on receipt of a request under section 6 shall, as expeditiously as possible, and in any

case within thirty days of the receipt of the request, either provide the information on payment of such fee as may be prescribed or reject the request for any of the reasons specified in sections 8 and 9:

Provided that where the information sought for concerns the life or liberty of a person, the same shall be provided within forty-eight hours of the receipt of the request.

(2) If the Central Public Information Officer or State Public Information Officer, as the case may be, fails to give decision on the request for information within the period specified under sub-section (1), the Central Public Information Officer or State Public Information Officer, as the case may be, shall be deemed to have refused the request.

(3) Where a decision is taken to provide the information on payment of any further fee representing the cost of providing the information, the Central Public Information Officer or State Public Information Officer, as the case may be, shall send an intimation to the person making the request, giving—

(a) the details of further fees representing the cost of providing the information as determined by him, together with the calculations made to arrive at the amount in accordance with fee prescribed under sub-section (1), requesting him to deposit that fees, and the period intervening between the despatch of the said intimation and payment of fees shall be excluded for the purpose of calculating the period of thirty days referred to in that sub-section;

(b) information concerning his or her right with respect to review the decision as to the amount of fees charged or the form of access provided, including the particulars of the appellate authority, time limit, process and any other forms.

(4) Where access to the record or a part thereof is required to be provided under this Act and the person to whom access is to be provided is sensorily disabled, the Central Public Information Officer or State Public Information Officer, as the case may be, shall provide assistance to enable access to the information,

including providing such assistance as may be appropriate for the inspection.

(5) Where access to information is to be provided in the printed or in any electronic format, the applicant shall, subject to the provisions of sub-section (6), pay such fee as may be prescribed:

Provided that the fee prescribed under sub-section (1) of section 6 and sub-sections (1) and (5) of section 7 shall be reasonable and no such fee shall be charged from the persons who are below poverty line as may be determined by the appropriate Government.

(6) Notwithstanding anything contained in sub-section (5), the person making request for the information shall be provided the information free of charge where a public authority fails to comply with the time limits specified in sub-section (1).

(7) Before taking any decision under sub-section (1), the Central Public Information Officer or State Public Information Officer, as the case may be, shall take into consideration the representation made by a third party under section 11.

(8) Where a request has been rejected under sub-section (1), the Central Public Information Officer or State Public Information Officer, as the case may be, shall communicate to the person making the request—

(i) the reasons for such rejection;

(ii) the period within which an appeal against such rejection may be preferred; and

(iii) the particulars of the appellate authority.

(9) An information shall ordinarily be provided in the form in which it is sought unless it would disproportionately divert the resources of the public authority or would be detrimental to the safety or preservation of the record in question.

8. Exemption from disclosure of information.— (1) Notwithstanding anything contained in this Act, there shall be no obligation to give any citizen—

(a) information, disclosure of which would prejudicially affect the sovereignty and integrity of India, the security, strategic, scientific or economic interests of the State, relation with foreign State or lead to incitement of an offence;

(b) information which has been expressly forbidden to be published by any court of law or tribunal or the disclosure of which may constitute contempt of court;

(c) information, the disclosure of which would cause a breach of privilege of Parliament or the State Legislature;

(d) information including commercial confidence, trade secrets or intellectual property, the disclosure of which would harm the competitive position of a third party, unless the competent authority is satisfied that larger public interest warrants the disclosure of such information;

(e) information available to a person in his fiduciary relationship, unless the competent authority is satisfied that the larger public interest warrants the disclosure of such information;

(f) information received in confidence from foreign Government;

(g) information, the disclosure of which would endanger the life or physical safety of any person or identify the source of information or assistance given in confidence for law enforcement or security purposes;

(h) information which would impede the process of investigation or apprehension or prosecution of offenders;

(i) cabinet papers including records of deliberations of the Council of Ministers, Secretaries and other officers:

Provided that the decisions of Council of Ministers, the reasons thereof, and the material on the basis of which the decisions were taken shall be made public after the decision has been taken, and the matter is complete, or over:

Provided further that those matters which come under the exemptions specified in this section shall not be disclosed;

(j) information which relates to personal information the disclosure of which has no relationship to any public activity or interest, or which would cause unwarranted invasion of the privacy of the individual unless the Central Public Information Officer or the State Public Information Officer or the appellate authority, as the case may be, is satisfied that the larger public interest justifies the disclosure of such information:

Provided that the information which cannot be denied to the Parliament or a State Legislature shall not be denied to any person.

(2) Notwithstanding anything in the Official Secrets Act, 1923 (19 of 1923) nor any of the exemptions permissible in accordance with sub-section (1), a public authority may allow access to information, if public interest in disclosure outweighs the harm to the protected interests.

(3) Subject to the provisions of clauses (a), (c) and (i) of sub-section (1), any information relating to any occurrence, event or matter which has taken place, occurred or happened twenty years before the date on which any request is made under section 6 shall be provided to any person making a request under that section:

Provided that where any question arises as to the date from which the said period of twenty years has to be computed, the decision of the Central Government shall be final, subject to the usual appeals provided for in this Act.

9. Grounds for rejection to access in certain cases.—Without prejudice to the provisions of section 8, a Central Public Information Officer or a State Public Information Officer, as the case may be, may reject a request for information where such a request for providing access would involve an infringement of copyright subsisting in a person other than the State.

COMMENTS

If a request for information involves an infringement of copyright subsisting in a person other than a State, it may be rejected.

10. Severability.—(1) Where a request for access to information is rejected on the ground that it is in relation to information which is exempt from disclosure, then, notwithstanding anything contained in this Act, access may be provided to that part of the record which does not contain any information which is exempt from disclosure under this Act and which can reasonably be severed from any part that contains exempt information.

(2) Where access is granted to a part of the record under sub-section (1), the Central Public Information Officer or State Public Information Officer, as the case may be, shall give a notice to the applicant, informing—

(a) that only part of the record requested, after severance of the record containing information which is exempt from disclosure, is being provided;

(b) the reasons for the decision, including any findings on any material question of fact, referring to the material on which those findings were based;

(c) the name and designation of the person giving the decision;

(d) the details of the fees calculated by him or her and the amount of fee which the applicant is required to deposit; and

(e) his or her rights with respect to review of the decision regarding non-disclosure of part of the information, the amount of fee charged or the form of access provided, including the particulars of the senior officer specified under sub-section (1) of section 19 or the Central Information Commission or the State Information Commission, as the case may be, time limit, process and any other form of access.

COMMENTS

Where a request for access to information is rejected on the ground that it is in relation to information which is exempted from disclosure, then access may be provided to that part of the record which does not contain any information which is exempted information.

11. Third party information.—(1) Where a Central Public Information Officer or a State Public Information Officer, as the case may be, intends to disclose any information or record, or part thereof on a request made under this Act, which relates to or has been supplied by a third party and has been treated as confidential by that third party, the Central Public Information Officer or State Public Information Officer, as the case may be, shall, within five days from the receipt of the request, give a written notice to such third party of the request and of the fact that the Central Public Information Officer or State Public Information Officer, as the case may be, intends to disclose the information or record, or part thereof, and invite the third party to make a submission in writing or orally, regarding whether the information should be disclosed, and such submission of the third party shall be kept in view while taking a decision about disclosure of information:

Provided that except in the case of trade or commercial secrets protected by law, disclosure may be allowed if the public interest in disclosure outweighs in importance any possible harm or injury to the interests of such third party.

(2) Where a notice is served by the Central Public Information Officer or State Public Information Officer, as the case may be, under sub-section (1) to a third party in respect of any information or record or part thereof, the third party shall, within ten days from the date of receipt of such notice, be given the opportunity to make representation against the proposed disclosure.

(3) Notwithstanding anything contained in section 7, the Central Public Information Officer or State Public Information Officer, as the case may be, shall, within forty days after receipt of the request under section 6, if the third party has been given

an opportunity to make representation under sub-section (2), make a decision as to whether or not to disclose the information or record or part thereof and give in writing the notice of his decision to the third party.

(4) A notice given under sub-section (3) shall include a statement that the third party to whom the notice is given is entitled to prefer an appeal under section 19 against the decision.

COMMENTS

Third Party

According to section 2(n) of the Right to Information Act, 2005 "Third Party" means a person other than the citizen making a request for information and includes public authority.

Right to Impart and Receive Information

The right to impart and receive information is a species of the right of freedom of speech and expression guaranteed by Article 19(1)(a) of the Constitution. A Citizen has a fundamental right to use the best means of imperative and receiving information and as such to have an access to telecasting for the purpose.[1]

All the Agents of Public must be Responsible—

In a government of responsibility where all the agents of public must be responsible for their conduct, there can be but few secrets. The people of this country have a right to know every public act, everything that is done in a public way by their public functionaries. They are entitled to know the particulars of every public transaction in all its bearings. The right to know, which is derived from the concept of freedom of speech, though not absolute, is a factor which should make one wary, when secrecy is claimed for transactions which can, at any rate have repercussion on public security.[2]

---

1. Secretary, ministry of Information and Broadcasting, Govt. of India V. Cricket Association of Bengal, AIR 1995 SC 1236.
2. State of Uttar Pradesh v. Raj Narain, AIR 1978 SC 865: (1975) 4 SCC 428.

Where a Central Public Information Officer or State Public Information Officer, as the case may be, shall within five days give written notice to such third party of the request and of the fact that he intends to disclose the information or record, or part thereof, and invite the third party to make a submission in writing or orally, regarding whether the information should be disclosed and such submission of the third party shall be kept in view while taking a decision about disclosure of information.

CHAPTER III

THE CENTRAL INFORMATION COMMISSION

12. Constitution of Central Information Commission.—(1) The Central Government shall, by notification in the Official Gazette, constitute a body to be known as the Central Information Commission to exercise the powers conferred on, and to perform the functions assigned to, it under this Act.

(2) The Central Information Commission shall consist of—

(a) the Chief Information Commissioner; and

(b) such number of Central Information Commissioners, not exceeding ten, as may be deemed necessary.

(3) The Chief Information Commissioner and Information Commissioners shall be appointed by the President on the recommendation of a committee consisting of—

(i) the Prime Minister, who shall be the Chairperson of the committee;

(ii) the Leader of Opposition in the Lok Sabha; and

(iii) a Union Cabinet Minister to be nominated by the Prime Minister.

Explanation—For the purposes of removal of doubts, it is hereby declared that where the Leader of Opposition in the House of the People has not been recognised as such, the Leader of the single largest group in opposition of the Government in the House of the People shall be deemed to be the Leader of Opposition.

(4) The general superintendence, direction and management of the affairs of the Central Information Commission shall vest in the Chief Information Commissioner who shall be assisted by

the Information Commissioners and may exercise all such powers and do all such acts and things which may be exercised or done by the Central Information Commission autonomously without being subjected to directions by any other authority under this Act.

(5) The Chief Information Commissioner and Information Commissioners shall be persons of eminence in public life with wide knowledge and experience in law, science and technology, social service, management, journalism, mass media or administration and governance.

(6) The Chief Information Commissioner or an Information Commissioner shall not be a Member of Parliament or Member of the Legislature of any State or Union territory, as the case may be, or hold any other office of profit or connected with any political party or carrying on any business or pursuing any profession.

(7) The headquarters of the Central Information Commission shall be at Delhi and the Central Information Commission may, with the previous approval of the Central Government, establish offices at other places in India.

13. Term of office and conditions of service.—(1) The Chief Information Commissioner shall hold office for a term of five years from the date on which he enters upon his office and shall not be eligible for reappointment:

Provided that no Chief Information Commissioner shall hold office as such after he has attained the age of sixty-five years.

(2) Every Information Commissioner shall hold office for a term of five years from the date on which he enters upon his office or till he attains the age of sixty-five years, whichever is earlier, and shall not be eligible for reappointment as such Information Commissioner:

Provided that every Information Commissioner shall, on vacating his office under this sub-section be eligible for appointment as the Chief Information Commissioner in the manner specified in sub-section (3) of section 12:

Provided further that where the Information Commissioner is appointed as the Chief Information Commissioner, his term of office shall not be more than five years in aggregate as the Information Commissioner and the Chief Information Commissioner.

(3) The Chief Information Commissioner or an Information Commissioner shall before he enters upon his office make and subscribe before the President or some other person appointed by him in that behalf, an oath or affirmation according to the form set out for the purpose in the First Schedule.

(4) The Chief Information Commissioner or an Information Commissioner may, at any time, by writing under his hand addressed to the President, resign from his office:

Provided that the Chief Information Commissioner or an Information Commissioner may be removed in the manner specified under section 14.

(5) The salaries and allowances payable to and other terms and conditions of service of—

(a) the Chief Information Commissioner shall be the same as that of the Chief Election Commissioner;

(b) an Information Commissioner shall be the same as that of an Election Commissioner:

Provided that if the Chief Information Commissioner or an Information Commissioner, at the time of his appointment is, in receipt of a pension, other than a disability or wound pension, in respect of any previous service under the Government of India or under the Government of a State, his salary in respect of the service as the Chief Information Commissioner or an Information Commissioner shall be reduced by the amount of that pension including any portion of pension which was commuted and pension equivalent of other forms of retirement benefits excluding pension equivalent of retirement gratuity:

Provided further that if the Chief Information Commissioner or an Information Commissioner if, at the time of his appointment is, in receipt of retirement benefits in respect of any previous service rendered in a Corporation established by or under any Central Act or State Act or a Government company owned or controlled by the Central Government or the State Government, his salary in respect of the service as the Chief

Information Commissioner or an Information Commissioner shall be reduced by the amount of pension equivalent to the retirement benefits:

Provided also that the salaries, allowances and other conditions of service of the Chief Information Commissioner and the Information Commissioners shall not be varied to their disadvantage after their appointment.

(6) The Central Government shall provide the Chief Information Commissioner and the Information Commissioners with such officers and employees as may be necessary for the efficient performance of their functions under this Act, and the salaries and allowances payable to and the terms and conditions of service of the officers and other employees appointed for the purpose of this Act shall be such as may be prescribed.

14. Removal of Chief Information Commissioner or Information Commissioner.—(1) Subject to the provisions of sub-section (3), the Chief Information Commissioner or any Information Commissioner shall be removed from his office only by order of the President on the ground of proved misbehaviour or incapacity after the Supreme Court, on a reference made to it by the President, has, on inquiry, reported that the Chief Information Commissioner or any Information Commissioner, as the case may be, ought to on such ground be removed.

(2) The President may suspend from office, and if deem necessary prohibit also from attending the office during inquiry, the Chief Information Commissioner or Information Commissioner in respect of whom a reference has been made to the Supreme Court under sub-section (1) until the President has passed orders on receipt of the report of the Supreme Court on such reference.

(3) Notwithstanding anything contained in sub-section (1), the President may by order remove the Chief Information Commissioner or any Information Commissioner from office if the Chief Information Commissioner or a Information Commissioner, as the case may be,—

(a) is adjudged an insolvent; or

(b) has been convicted of an offence which, in the opinion of the President, involves moral turpitude; or

(c) engages during his term of office in any paid employment outside the duties of his office; or

(d) is, in the opinion of the President, unfit to continue in office by reason of infirmity of mind or body; or

(e) has acquired such financial or other interest as is likely to affect prejudicially his functions as the Chief Information Commissioner or a Information Commissioner.

(4) If the Chief Information Commissioner or a Information Commissioner in any way, concerned or interested in any contract or agreement made by or on behalf of the Government of India or participates in any way in the profit thereof or in any benefit or emolument arising therefrom otherwise than as a member and in common with the other members of an incorporated company, he shall, for the purposes of sub-section (1), be deemed to be guilty of misbehaviour.

CHAPTER IV

THE STATE INFORMATION COMMISSION

15. Constitution of State Information Commission.— (1) Every State Government shall, by notification in the Official Gazette, constitute a body to be known as the... (name of the State) Information Commission to exercise the powers conferred on, and to perform the functions assigned to it under this Act.

(2) The State Information Commission shall consist of—

(a) the State Chief Information Commissioner, and

(b) such number of State Information Commissioners, not exceeding ten, as may be deemed necessary.

(3) The State Chief Information Commissioner and the State Information Commissioners shall be appointed by the Governor on the recommendation of a committee consisting of—

(i) the Chief Minister, who shall be the Chairperson of the committee;

(ii) the Leader of Opposition in the Legislative Assembly; and

(iii) a Cabinet Minister to be nominated by the Chief Minister.

Explanation—For the purposes of removal of doubts, it is hereby declared that where the Leader of Opposition in the Legislative Assembly has not been recognised as such, the Leader of the single largest group in opposition of the Government in the Legislative Assembly shall be deemed to be the Leader of Opposition.

(4) The general superintendence, direction and management of the affairs of the State Information Commission shall vest in the State Chief Information Commissioner who shall be assisted by the State Information Commissioners and may exercise all such powers and do all such acts and things which may be exercised or done by the State Information Commission autonomously without being subjected to directions by any other authority under this Act.

(5) The State Chief Information Commissioner and the State Information Commissioners shall be persons of eminence in public life with wide knowledge and experience in law, science and technology, social service, management, journalism, mass media or administration and governance.

(6) The State Chief Information Commissioner or a State Information Commissioner shall not be a Member of Parliament or Member of the Legislature of any State or Union territory, as the case may be, or hold any other office of profit or connected with any political party or carrying on any business or pursuing any profession.

(7) The headquarters of the State Information Commission shall be at such place in the State as the State Government may, by notification in the Official Gazette, specify and the State Information Commission may, with the previous approval of the State Government, establish offices at other places in the State.

COMMENTS

Every State Government has to constitute a State Information Commission to exercise the powers conferred on, and to Perform the functions assigned to, it under the Act. The State Information Commission shall consist of (i) the State Chief Information Commissioner; and (ii) State Information Commissioners, not exceeding ten. The State Chief Information Commissioner and the State Information Commissioners shall be appointed by the Governor on the recommendation of a committee consisting of (a) the Chief Minister, who shall be the chairperson of the committee; (b) the Leader of Opposition in the Legislative Assembly; and (c) a Cabinet Minister to be nominated by the Chief Minister.

16. Term of office and conditions of service.—(1) The State Chief Information Commissioner shall hold office for a term of five years from the date on which he enters upon his office and shall not be eligible for reappointment:

Provided that no State Chief Information Commissioner shall hold office as such after he has attained the age of sixty-five years.

(2) Every State Information Commissioner shall hold office for a term of five years from the date on which he enters upon his office or till he attains the age of sixty-five years, whichever is earlier, and shall not be eligible for reappointment as such State Information Commissioner:

Provided that every State Information Commissioner shall, on vacating his office under this sub-section, be eligible for appointment as the State Chief Information Commissioner in the manner specified in sub-section (3) of section 15:

Provided further that where the State Information Commissioner is appointed as the State Chief Information Commissioner, his term of office shall not be more than five years in aggregate as the State Information Commissioner and the State Chief Information Commissioner.

(3) The State Chief Information Commissioner or a State Information Commissioner, shall before he enters upon his office make and subscribe before the Governor or some other person

appointed by him in that behalf, an oath or affirmation according to the form set out for the purpose in the First Schedule.

(4) The State Chief Information Commissioner or a State Information Commissioner may, at any time, by writing under his hand addressed to the Governor, resign from his office:

Provided that the State Chief Information Commissioner or a State Information Commissioner may be removed in the manner specified under section 17.

(5) The salaries and allowances payable to and other terms and conditions of service of—

(a) the State Chief Information Commissioner shall be the same as that of an Election Commissioner;

(b) the State Information Commissioner shall be the same as that of the Chief Secretary to the State Government:

Provided that if the State Chief Information Commissioner or a State Information Commissioner, at the time of his appointment is, in receipt of a pension, other than a disability or wound pension, in respect of any previous service under the Government of India or under the Government of a State, his salary in respect of the service as the State Chief Information Commissioner or a State Information Commissioner shall be reduced by the amount of that pension including any portion of pension which was commuted and pension equivalent of other forms of retirement benefits excluding pension equivalent of retirement gratuity:

Provided further that where the State Chief Information Commissioner or a State Information Commissioner if, at the time of his appointment is, in receipt of retirement benefits in respect of any previous service rendered in a Corporation established by or under any Central Act or State Act or a Government company owned or controlled by the Central Government or the State Government, his salary in respect of the service as the State Chief Information Commissioner or the State Information Commissioner shall be reduced by the amount of pension equivalent to the retirement benefits:

Provided also that the salaries, allowances and other conditions of service of the State Chief Information Commissioner and the State Information Commissioners shall not be varied to their disadvantage after their appointment.

(6) The State Government shall provide the State Chief Information Commissioner and the State Information Commissioners with such officers and employees as may be necessary for the efficient performance of their functions under this Act, and the salaries and allowances payable to and the terms and conditions of service of the officers and other employees appointed for the purpose of this Act shall be such as may be prescribed.

17. Removal of State Chief Information Commissioner or State Information Commissioner.—(1) Subject to the provisions of sub-section (3), the State Chief Information Commissioner or a State Information Commissioner shall be removed from his office only by order of the Governor on the ground of proved misbehaviour or incapacity after the Supreme Court, on a reference made to it by the Governor, has on inquiry, reported that the State Chief Information Commissioner or a State Information Commissioner, as the case may be, ought to on such ground be removed.

(2) The Governor may suspend the State Chief Information Commissioner or a State Information Commissioner from office, and if deem necessary prohibit also from attending the office during inquiry, in respect of whom a reference has been made to the Supreme Court under sub-section (1) until the Governor has passed orders on receipt of the report of the Supreme Court on such reference.

(3) Notwithstanding anything contained in sub-section (1), the Governor may by order remove the State Chief Information Commissioner or a State Information Commissioner from office if a State Chief Information Commissioner or a State Information Commissioner, as the case may be,—

(a) is adjudged an insolvent; or

(b) has been convicted of an offence which, in the opinion of the Governor, involves moral turpitude; or

(c) engages during his term of office in any paid employment outside the duties of his office; or

(d) is, in the opinion of the Governor, unfit to continue in office by reason of infirmity of mind or body; or

(e) has acquired such financial or other interest as is likely to affect prejudicially his functions as the State Chief Information Commissioner or a State Information Commissioner.

(4) If the State Chief Information Commissioner or a State Information Commissioner in any way, concerned or interested in any contract or agreement made by or on behalf of the Government of the State or participates in any way in the profit thereof or in any benefit or emoluments arising therefrom otherwise than as a member and in common with the other members of an incorporated company, he shall, for the purposes of sub-section (1), be deemed to be guilty of misbehaviour.

CHAPTER V

POWERS AND FUNCTIONS OF THE INFORMATION COMMISSIONS, APPEAL AND PENALTIES

18. Powers and functions of commission.—(1) Subject to the provisions of this Act, it shall be the duty of the Central Information Commission or State Information Commission, as the case may be, to receive and inquire into a complaint from any person—

(a) who has been unable to submit a request to a Central Public Information Officer or State Public Information Officer, as the case may be, either by reason that no such officer has been appointed under this Act, or because the Central Assistant Public Information Officer or State Assistant Public Information Officer, as the case may be, has refused to accept his or her application for information or appeal under this Act for forwarding the same to the Central Public Information Officer or State Public Information Officer or Senior Officer specified in sub-section (1) of section 19 or the Central Information Commission or the State Information Commission, as the case may be;

(b) who has been refused access to any information requested under this Act;

(c) who has not been given a response to a request for information or access to information within the time limit specified under this Act;

(d) who has been required to pay an amount of fee which he or she considers unreasonable;

(e) who believes that he or she has been given incomplete, misleading or false information under this Act; and

(f) in respect of any other matter relating to requesting or obtaining access to records under this Act.

(2) Where the Central Information Commission or State Information Commission, as the case may be, is satisfied that there are reasonable grounds to inquire into the matter, it may initiate an inquiry in respect thereof.

(3) The Central Information Commission or State Information Commission, as the case may be, shall, while inquiring into any matter under this section, have the same powers as are vested in a civil court while trying a suit under the Code of Civil Procedure, 1908, in respect of the following matters, namely—

(a) summoning and enforcing the attendance of persons and compel them to give oral or written evidence on oath and to produce the documents or things;

(b) requiring the discovery and inspection of documents;

(c) receiving evidence on affidavit;

(d) requisitioning any public record or copies thereof from any court or office;

(e) issuing summons for examination of witnesses or documents; and

(f) any other matter which may be prescribed.

(4) Notwithstanding anything inconsistent contained in any other Act of Parliament or State Legislature, as the case may be, the Central Information Commission or the State Information Commission, as the case may be, may, during the inquiry of any complaint under this Act, examine any record to which this Act applies which is under the control of the public authority, and no such record may be withheld from it on any grounds.

19 Appeal.—(1) Any person who, does not receive a decision within the time specified in sub-section (1) or clause (a) of sub-section (3) of section 7, or is aggrieved by a decision of the Central Public Information Officer or State Public Information Officer, as the case may be, may within thirty days from the expiry of such period or from the receipt of such a decision prefer an appeal to such officer who is senior in rank to the Central Public Information Officer or State Public Information Officer as the case may be, in each public authority:

Provided that such officer may admit the appeal after the expiry of the period of thirty days if he or she is satisfied that the appellant was prevented by sufficient cause from filing the appeal in time.

(2) Where an appeal is preferred against an order made by a Central Public Information Officer or a State Public Information Officer, as the case may be, under section 11 to disclose third party information, the appeal by the concerned third party shall be made within thirty days from the date of the order.

(3) A second appeal against the decision under sub-section (1) shall lie within ninety days from the date on which the decision should have been made or was actually received, with the Central Information Commission or the State Information Commission:

Provided that the Central Information Commission or the State Information Commission, as the case may be, may admit the appeal after the expiry of the period of ninety days if it is satisfied that the appellant was prevented by sufficient cause from filing the appeal in time.

(4) If the decision of the Central Public Information Officer or State Public Information Officer, as the case may be, against which an appeal is preferred relates to information of a third party, the Central Information Commission or State Information

Commission, as the case may be, shall give a reasonable opportunity of being heard to that third party.

(5) In any appeal proceedings, the onus to prove that a denial of a request was justified shall be on the Central Public Information Officer or State Public Information Officer, as the case may be, who denied the request.

(6) An appeal under sub-section (1) or sub-section (2) shall be disposed of within thirty days of the receipt of the appeal or within such extended period not exceeding a total of forty-five days from the date of filing thereof, as the case may be, for reasons to be recorded in writing.

(7) The decision of the Central Information Commission or State Information Commission, as the case may be, shall be binding.

(8) In its decision, the Central Information Commission or State Information Commission, as the case may be, has the power to—

(a) require the public authority to take any such steps as may be necessary to secure compliance with the provisions of this Act, including—

(i) by providing access to information, if so requested, in a particular form;

(ii) by appointing a Central Public Information Officer or State Public Information Officer, as the case may be;

(iii) by publishing certain information or categories of information;

(iv) by making necessary changes to its practices in relation to the maintenance, management and destruction of records;

(v) by enhancing the provision of training on the right to information for its officials;

(vi) by providing it with an annual report in compliance with clause (b) of sub-section (1) of section 4;

(b) require the public authority to compensate the complainant for any loss or other detriment suffered;

(c) impose any of the penalties provided under this Act;

(d) reject the application.

(9) The Central Information Commission or State Information Commission, as the case may be, shall give notice of its decision, including any right of appeal, to the complainant and the public authority.

(10) The Central Information Commission or State Information Commission, as the case may be, shall decide the appeal in accordance with such procedure as may be prescribed.

COMMENTS

First Appeal: 30-day Period of Limitation

Any citizen who does not receive a decision within the time specified or in aggrieved person of decision of Central Government Public Information Officer can appeal within 30 days from expiry of such period or receipt of such a decision, to such officer or State Public Information Officer in each public authority.

Second Appeal

A second appeal against the decision of Central Public Information Officer or State Public Information Officer can be filed within 90 days from the date on which the decision should have been made or was actually received, with the Central Information Commission or the State Information Commission.

Extension of Period

In first Appeal:

If the senior Central Public Information Officer or the Senior State Public Information Officer is satisfied that there was sufficient cause for not filing the appeal in time, he can admit the appeal after the expiry of the period of 30 days.

In Second Appeal

The Central Information Commission or State Information Commission, if is satisfied that there was sufficient cause for not filing the appeal within 90 days, he can admit the appeal after expiry of period of 90 days.

20. Penalties.—(1) Where the Central Information Commission or the State Information Commission, as the case may be, at the time of deciding any complaint or appeal is of the opinion that the Central Public Information Officer or the State Public Information Officer, as the case may be, has, without any reasonable cause, refused to receive an application for information or has not furnished information within the time specified under sub-section (1) of section 7 or malafidely denied the request for information or knowingly given incorrect, incomplete or misleading information or destroyed information which was the subject of the request or obstructed in any manner in furnishing the information, it shall impose a penalty of two hundred and fifty rupees each day till application is received or information is furnished, so however, the total amount of such penalty shall not exceed twenty-five thousand rupees:

Provided that the Central Public Information Officer or the State Public Information Officer, as the case may be, shall be given a reasonable opportunity of being heard before any penalty is imposed on him:

Provided further that the burden of proving that he acted reasonably and diligently shall be on the Central Public Information Officer or the State Public Information Officer, as the case may be.

(2) Where the Central Information Commission or the State Information Commission, as the case may be, at the time of deciding any complaint or appeal is of the opinion that the Central Public Information Officer or the State Public Information Officer, as the case may be, has, without any reasonable cause and persistently, failed to receive an application for information or has not furnished information within the time specified under sub-section (1) of section 7 or malafidely denied the request for information or knowingly given incorrect, incomplete or misleading information or destroyed information which was the subject of the request or obstructed in any manner in furnishing the information, it shall recommend for disciplinary action against the Central Public Information Officer or the State Public Information Officer, as the case may be, under the service rules applicable to him.

COMMENTS

Imposition of Penalty

Where the Central Public Information Officer or the State Public Information officer, without any reasonable cause refuses to receive an application for information or does not furnish infromation within time specified or malafidely denies the request for Information or gives incorrect, incomplete, misleading, or destroyed Information knowingly, then the Central Information Commission or State Information Commission can imopose a penalty of Rs. 250 each day till application is received or information is furnished but the total amount of such penalty shall not exceed Rs. 25,000 subject to opportunity of being heard to be given to that Information Officer otherwise the order of penalty shalll be set aside.

No Appeal against the Order of Penalty

The Central Information Officer and the State Information Officer cannot appeal against the order of the Central Information Commission or State Infromation Commission.

CHAPTER VI

MISCELLANEOUS

21. Protection of action taken in good faith.—No suit, prosecution or other legal proceeding shall lie against any person for anything which is in good faith done or intended to be done under this Act or any rule made thereunder.

22. Act to have overriding effect.—The provisions of this Act shall have effect notwithstanding anything inconsistent therewith contained in the Official Secrets Act, 1923, and any other law for the time being in force or in any instrument having effect by virtue of any law other than this Act.

23. Bar of jurisdiction of courts.—No court shall entertain any suit, application or other proceeding in respect of any order made under this Act and no such order shall be called in question otherwise than by way of an appeal under this Act.

24. Act not to apply to certain organisations.—(1) Nothing contained in this Act shall apply to the intelligence and security organisations specified in the Second Schedule, being organisations established by the Central Government or any information furnished by such organisations to that Government:

Provided that the information pertaining to the allegations of corruption and human rights violations shall not be excluded under this sub-section:

Provided further that in the case of information sought for is in respect of allegations of violation of human rights, the information shall only be provided after the approval of the Central Information Commission, and notwithstanding anything contained in section 7, such information shall be provided within forty-five days from the date of the receipt of request.

(2) The Central Government may, by notification in the Official Gazette, amend the Schedule by including therein any other intelligence or security organisation established by that Government or omitting therefrom any organisation already specified therein and on the publication of such notification, such organisation shall be deemed to be included in or, as the case may be, omitted from the Schedule.

(3) Every notification issued under sub-section (2) shall be laid before each House of Parliament.

(4) Nothing contained in this Act shall apply to such intelligence and security organisation being organisations established by the State Government, as that Government may, from time to time, by notification in the Official Gazette, specify:

Provided that the information pertaining to the allegations of corruption and human rights violations shall not be excluded under this sub-section:

Provided further that in the case of information sought for is in respect of allegations of violation of human rights, the information shall only be provided after the approval of the State Information Commission and, notwithstanding anything contained in section 7, such information shall be provided within forty-five days from the date of the receipt of request.

(5) Every notification issued under sub-section (4) shall be laid before the State Legislature.

25. Monitoring and reporting.—(1) The Central Information Commission or State Information Commission, as the case may be, shall, as soon as practicable after the end of each year, prepare a report on the implementation of the provisions of this Act during that year and forward a copy thereof to the appropriate Government.

(2) Each Ministry or Department shall, in relation to the public authorities within their jurisdiction, collect and provide such information to the Central Information Commission or State Information Commission, as the case may be, as is required to prepare the report under this section and comply with the requirements concerning the furnishing of that information and keeping of records for the purposes of this section.

(3) Each report shall state in respect of the year to which the report relates—

(a) the number of requests made to each public authority;

(b) the number of decisions where applicants were not entitled to access to the documents pursuant to the requests, the provisions of this Act under which these decisions were made and the number of times such provisions were invoked;

(c) the number of appeals referred to the Central Information Commission or State Information Commission, as the case may be, for review, the nature of the appeals and the outcome of the appeals;

(d) particulars of any disciplinary action taken against any officer in respect of the administration of this Act;

(e) the amount of charges collected by each public authority under this Act;

(f) any facts which indicate an effort by the public authorities to administer and implement the spirit and intention of this Act;

(g) recommendations for reform, including recommendations in respect of the particular public authorities, for the development, improvement, modernisation, reform or amendment to this Act or other legislation or common law or any other matter relevant for operationalising the right to access information.

(4) The Central Government or the State Government, as the case may be, may, as soon as practicable after the end of each year, cause a copy of the report of the Central Information Commission or the State Information Commission, as the case may be, referred to in sub-section (1) to be laid before each House of Parliament or, as the case may be, before each House of the State Legislature, where there are two Houses, and where there is one House of the State Legislature before that House.

(5) If it appears to the Central Information Commission or State Information Commission, as the case may be, that the practice of a public authority in relation to the exercise of its functions under this Act does not conform with the provisions or spirit of this Act, it may give to the authority a recommendation specifying the steps which ought in its opinion to be taken for promoting such conformity.

26. Appropriate government to prepare programmes.—(1) The appropriate Government may, to the extent of availability of financial and other resources,—

(a) develop and organise educational programmes to advance the understanding of the public, in particular of disadvantaged communities as to how to exercise the rights contemplated under this Act;

(b) encourage public authorities to participate in the development and organisation of programmes referred to in clause (a) and to undertake such programmes themselves;

(c) promote timely and effective dissemination of accurate information by public authorities about their activities; and

(d) train Central Public Information Officers or State Public Information Officers, as the case may be, of public authorities and produce relevant training materials for use by the public authorities themselves.

(2) The appropriate Government shall, within eighteen months from the commencement of this Act, compile in its official language a guide containing such information, in an easily comprehensible form and manner, as may reasonably be required by a person who wishes to exercise any right specified in this Act.

(3) The appropriate Government shall, if necessary, update and publish the guidelines referred to in sub-section (2) at regular intervals which shall, in particular and without prejudice to the generality of sub-section (2), include—

(a) the objects of this Act;

(b) the postal and street address, the phone and fax number and, if available, electronic mail address of the Central Public Information Officer or State Public Information Officer, as the case may be, of every public authority appointed under sub-section (1) of section 5;

(c) the manner and the form in which request for access to an information shall be made to a Central Public Information Officer or State Public Information Officer, as the case may be;

(d) the assistance available from and the duties of the Central Public Information Officer or State Public Information Officer, as the case may be, of a public authority under this Act;

(e) the assistance available from the Central Information Commission or State Information Commission, as the case may be;

(f) all remedies in law available regarding an act or failure to act in respect of a right or duty conferred or imposed by this Act including the manner of filing an appeal to the Commission;

(g) the provisions providing for the voluntary disclosure of categories of records in accordance with section 4;

(h) the notices regarding fees to be paid in relation to requests for access to an information; and

(i) any additional regulations or circulars made or issued in relation to obtaining access to an information in accordance with this Act.

(4) The appropriate Government must, if necessary, update and publish the guidelines at regular intervals.

27. Powers to make rules by appropriate government.— (1) The appropriate Government may, by notification in the Official Gazette, make rules to carry out the provisions of this Act.

(2) In particular, and without prejudice to the generality of the foregoing power, such rules may provide for all or any of the following matters, namely—

(a) the cost of the medium or print cost price of the materials to be disseminated under sub-section (4) of section 4;

(b) the fee payable under sub-section (1) of section 6;

(c) the fee payable under sub-sections (1) and (5) of section 7;

(d) the salaries and allowances payable to and the terms and conditions of service of the officers and other employees under sub-section (6) of section 13 and sub-section (6) of section 16;

(e) the procedure to be adopted by the Central Information Commission or State Information Commission, as the case may be, in deciding the appeals under sub-section (10) of section 19; and

(f) any other matter which is required to be, or may be, prescribed.

28. Power to make rules by competent authority.—(1) The competent authority may, by notification in the Official Gazette, make rules to carry out the provisions of this Act.

(2) In particular, and without prejudice to the generality of the foregoing power, such rules may provide for all or any of the following matters, namely:—

(i) the cost of the medium or print cost price of the materials to be disseminated under sub-section (4) of section 4;

(ii) the fee payable under sub-section (1) of section 6;

(iii) the fee payable under sub-section (1) of section 7; and

(iv) any other matter which is required to be, or may be, prescribed.

29. Laying of rules.—(1) Every rule made by the Central Government under this Act shall be laid, as soon as may be after it is made, before each House of Parliament, while it is in session, for a total period of thirty days which may be comprised in one session or in two or more successive sessions, and if, before the expiry of the session immediately following the session or the successive sessions aforesaid, both Houses agree in making any modification in the rule or both Houses agree that the rule should not be made, the rule shall thereafter have effect only in such modified form or be of no effect, as the case may be; so, however, that any such modification or annulment shall be without prejudice to the validity of anything previously done under that rule.

(2) Every rule made under this Act by a State Government shall be laid, as soon as may be after it is notified, before the State Legislature.

30. Power to remove difficulties.—(1) If any difficulty arises in giving effect to the provisions of this Act, the Central Government may, by order published in the Official Gazette, make such provisions not inconsistent with the provisions of this Act as appear to it to be necessary or expedient for removal of the difficulty:

Provided that no such order shall be made after the expiry of a period of two years from the date of the commencement of this Act.

(2) Every order made under this section shall, as soon as may be after it is made, be laid before each House of Parliament.

31. Repeal.— The Freedom of Information Act, 2002 is hereby repealed.

THE FIRST SCHEDULE

[*See* sections 13(3) and 16(3)]

FORM OF OATH OR AFFIRMATION TO BE MADE BY THE CHIEF INFORMATION COMMISSIONER/THE INFORMATION COMMISSIONER/THE STATE CHIEF INFORMATION COMMISSIONER/THE STATE INFORMATION COMMISSIONER

"I, ..., having been appointed Chief Information Commissioner/Information Commissioner/State Chief Information Commissioner/State Information Commissioner swear in the name of God / solemnly affirm that I will bear true faith and allegiance to the Constitution of India as by law established, that I will uphold the sovereignty and integrity of India, that I will duly and faithfully and to the best of my ability, knowledge and judgment perform the duties of my office without fear or favour, affection or ill-will and that I will uphold the Constitution and the laws.".

THE SECOND SCHEDULE

[*See* section 24]

INTELLIGENCE AND SECURITY ORGANISATION ESTABLISHED BY THE CENTRAL GOVERNMENT

1. Intelligence Bureau.
2. Research and Analysis Wing of the Cabinet Secretariat.
3. Directorate of Revenue Intelligence.
4. Central Economic Intelligence Bureau.
5. Directorate of Enforcement.
6. Narcotics Control Bureau.

7. Aviation Research Centre.
8. Special Frontier Force.
9. Border Security Force.
10. Central Reserve Police Force.
11. Indo-Tibetan Border Police.
12. Central Industrial Security Force.
13. National Security Guards.
14. Assam Rifles.
15. Sashtra Seema Bal.[1]
16. Special Branch (CID), Andaman and Nicobar.
17. The Crime Branch-C.I.D.-CB, Dadra and Nagar Haveli.
18. Special Branch, Lakshadweep Police.
19. Special Protection Group.
20. Defence Research and Development Organization.
21. Border Road Development Board.
22. Financial Intelligence Unit, India.[2]

---

1. Subs by G.S.R. 347, dated 28th September, 2005, for S. No. 15. S. No. 15 before substitution stood as under:
   "15. Special Service Bureau."
2. Ins. By G.S.R. 347, dated 28th September, 2005.

THE RIGHT TO INFORMATION (REGULATION OF FEE AND COST) RULES, 2005*

In exercise of the powers conferred by clauses (b) and (c) of sub-section (2) of section 27 of the Right to Information Act, 2005 (22 of 2005), the Central Government hereby makes the following rules, namely:

1. Short title and commencement.—(1) These rules may be called the Right to Information (Regulation of Fee and Cost) Amendment Rules, 2006.

(2) They shall come into force on the date of their publication in the Official Gazette.

2. Definitions.—In the rules, unless the context otherwise requires,—

(a) "Act" means the Right to Information Act, 2005;

(b) "section" means section of the Act;

(c) all other words and expressions used herein but not defined and defined in the Act shall have the meanings assigned to them in the Act.

3. A request for obtaining information under sub-section (1) of section 6 shall be accompanied by an application fee of rupees ten by way of cash against proper receipt or by demand draft or bankers cheque [or Indian Postal Order] payable to the Accounts Officer of the public authority.

---

* *Vide* G.S.R. 336(E), published in the Gazette of India, Pt. II, Sec. 3(i), dated 1st October, 2005.

4. For providing the information under sub-section (1) of section 7, the fee shall be charged by way of cash against proper receipt or by demand draft or bankers cheque or Indian Postal Order payable to the Accounts Officer of the public authority at the following rates—

(a) rupees two for each page (in A-4 or A-3 size paper) created or copied;

(b) actual charge or cost price of a copy in larger size paper;

(c) actual cost of price for samples or models; and

[(d) for inspection of records, no fee for the first hour; and a fee of rupees five for each fifteen minutes (or fraction thereof) thereafter.][1]

5. For providing the information under sub-section (5) of section 7, the fee shall be charged by way of cash against proper receipt or by demand draft or bankers cheque [or Indian Postal Order][2] payable to the Accounts Officer of the public authority at the following rates—

(a) for information provided in diskette or floppy rupees fifty per diskette or floppy; and

(b) for information provided in printed form at the price fixed for such publication or rupees two per page of photocopy for extracts from the publication.

---

1. Subs. by G.S.R. 649(E), dated 27th October, 2005, for clause (d) (w.e.f. 28-10-2005). Clause (d), before substitution, stood as under:
"(d) for inspection of records, no fee for the first hour; and a fee of rupees five for each fifteen minutes (or fraction thereof) thereafter.".
2. Ins. by G.S.R. 294(E), dated 17th May, 2006 (w.e.f. 18-5-2006)

THE CENTRAL INFORMATION COMMISSION (APPEAL PROCEDURE) RULES, 2005[1]

In exercise of the powers conferred by clauses (e) and (f) of sub-section (2) of section 27 of the Right to Information Act, 2005 (22 of 2005), the Central Government hereby makes the following rules, namely:

1. Short title and commencement.—(1) These rules may be called the Central Information Commission (Appeal Procedure) Rules, 2005.

(2) They shall come into force on the date[2] of their publication in the Official Gazette.

2. Definitions.—In these rules, unless the context otherwise requires,—

(a) "Act" means the Right to Information Act, 2005;

(b) "Section" means section of the Act.

(c) "Commission" means the Central Information Commission;

(d) Words and expressions used herein and not defined but defined in the Act, shall have the meanings respectively assigned to them in that Act.

3. Contents of appeal.—An appeal to the Commission shall contain the following information, namely:

(i) name and address of the appellant;

---

1. *Vide* G.S.R. 650(E), Government of India, Ministry of Personnel, Public Grievances and Pensions, dated 28th October, 2005 (w.e.f. 28-10-2005).
2. Came into force on 28-10-2005.

(ii) name and address of the Central Public Information Officer against the decision of whom the appeal is preferred;

(iii) particulars of the order including number, if any, against which the appeal is preferred;

(iv) brief facts leading to the appeal;

(v) if the appeal is preferred against deemed refusal, the particulars of the application, including number and date and name and address of the Central Public Information Officer to whom the application was made;

(vi) prayer or relief sought;

(vii) grounds for the prayer or relief;

(viii) verification by the appellant; and

(ix) any other information which the Commission may deem necessary for deciding the appeal.

4. Documents to accompany appeal.—Every appeal made to the Commission shall be accompanied by the following documents, namely:

(i) self-attested copies of the Orders or documents against which the appeal is being preferred;

(ii) copies of documents relied upon by the appellant and referred to in the appeal; and

(iii) an index of the documents referred to in the appeal.

5. Procedure in deciding appeal.—In deciding the appeal the Commission may:

(i) hear oral or written evidence on oath or on affidavit from concerned or interested person;

(ii) peruse or inspect documents, public records or copies thereof;

(iii) inquire through authorised officer further details or facts;

(iv) hear Central Public Information Officer, Central Assistant Public Information Officer or such Senior Officer who decide the first appeal, or such person against whom the complaint is made, as the case may be;

(v) hear third party; and

(vi) receive evidence on affidavits from Central Public Information Officer, Central Assistant Public Information Officer, such Senior Officer who decides the first appeal, such person against whom the complaint lies or the third party.

6. Service of notice by Commission.—Notice to be issued by the Commission may be served in any of the following modes, namely:

(i) service by the party itself;

(ii) by hand delivery (dasti) through Process Server;

(iii) by registered post with acknowledgment due; or

(iv) through Head of Office or Department.

7. Personal presence of the appellant or complainant.—(1) The appellant or the complainant, as the case may be, shall in every case be informed of the date of hearing at least seven clear days before that date.

(2) The appellant or the complainant, as the case may be, may at his discretion at the time of hearing of the appeal or complaint by the Commission be present in person or through his duly authorised representative or may opt not to be present.

(3) Where the Commission is satisfied that the circumstances exist due to which the appellant or the complainant, as the case may be, is being prevented from attending the hearing of the Commission, then, the Commission may afford the appellant or the complainant, as the case may be, another opportunity of being heard before a final decision is taken or take any other appropriate action as it may deem fit.

(4) The appellant or the complainant, as the case may be, may seek the assistance of any person in the process of the appeal while presenting his points and the person representing him may not be a legal practitioner.

8. Order of the Commission.—Order of the Commission shall be pronounced in open proceedings and be in writing duly authenticated by the Registrar or any other officer authorised by the Commission for this purpose.

THE LOK SABHA SECRETARIAT RIGHT TO INFORMATION (REGULATION OF FEE AND COST) RULES, 2005*

In exercise of the powers conferred by section 28 of the Right to Information Act, 2005 (Central Act 22 of 2005), the Speaker, Lok Sabha, hereby makes the following rules, namely:

1. Short title and commencement:—(1) These rules may be called the Lok Sabha Secretariat Right to Information (Regulation of Fee and Cost) Rules, 2005.

(2) They shall come into force on the date of their publication in the Official Gazette.

2. Definitions.— In these rules, unless the context otherwise requires.—

(a) "Act" means the Right to Information Act, 2005;

(b) "Section" means section of the Act; and

(c) All other words and expressions used herein but not defined, shall have the meanings respectively assigned to them in that Act.

3. A request for obtaining information under sub-section (1) of section 6 shall be accompanied by an application fee of rupees ten by way of cash against proper receipt or by money order or demand draft or banker's cheque payable to the Drawing and Disbursing Officer, Lok Sabha.

---

* *Vide* G.S.R. 747 (E), dated 27th December, 2005, published in the Gazette of India, Extra., Pt. II, Sec. 3(i), No. 535, dated 27th December, 2005.

4. For providing the information under sub-section (1) of section 7, the fee shall be charged by way of cash against proper receipt or by money order or demand draft or banker's cheque payable to the Drawing and Disbursing Officer, Lok Sabha at the following rates:

(a) rupees two for each page (in A-4 or A-3 size paper) created or copied;

(b) actual charge or cost price of a copy in larger size paper;

(c) actual cost or price for samples or models; and

(d) for inspection of records, no fee for the first hour; and a fee of rupees five for each subsequent hour (or fraction thereof).

5. For providing the information under sub-section (5) of section 7, the fee shall be charged by way of cash against proper receipt or by money order or demand draft or banker's cheque payable to the Drawing and Disbursing Officer, Lok Sabha at the following rates:

(a) for information provided in diskette or floppy rupees fifty per diskette or floppy; and

(b) for information provided in printed form at the price fixed for such publication or rupees two per page of photocopy for extracts from the publication.

PART III

OTHER RELATED LAWS

THE OFFICIAL SECRETS ACT, 1923

[19 OF 1923, DT. 2-4-1923]

An Act to consolidate and amend the law relating to official secrets.

Whereas it is expedient that the law relating to official secrets should be consolidated and amended; it is hereby enacted as follows:

1. Short title, extent and application.—(1) This Act may be called the Official Secrets Act, 1923.

(2) It extends to the whole of India and applies also to servants of the Government and to citizens of India outside India.

2. Definitions.—In this Act, unless there is anything repugnant in the subject or context,

(1) any reference to a place belonging to Government includes a place occupied by any department of the Government, whether the place is or is not actually vested in Government;

(2) expressions referring to communicating or receiving include any communicating or receiving, whether in whole or in part, and whether the sketch, plan, model, article, note, document, or information itself, or the substance, effect or description thereof only be communicated or received; expressions referring to obtaining or retaining any sketch, plan, model, article, note or document, include the copying or causing to be copied of the whole or any part of any sketch, plan, model, article, note or document; and expressions referring to the communication of any sketch, plan, model, article, note or document include the transfer or transmission of any sketch, plan, model, article, note or document;

(3) "document" includes part of a document;

(4) "model" includes design, pattern and specimen;

(5) "munitions of war" includes the whole or any part of any ship, submarine, aircraft, tank or similar engine, arms and ammunition, torpedo, or mine intended or adopted for use in war, and any other article, material or device, whether actual or proposed, intended for such use;

(6) "Office under Government" includes any office or employment in or under an department of the Government[1] [...];

(7) "photograph" includes an undeveloped film or plate;

(8) "prohibited place" means—

(a) any work of defence, arsenal, naval, military or air force establishment or station, mine, minefield, camp, ship or aircraft belonging to, or occupied by or on behalf of Government, any military telegraph or telephone so belonging or occupied, any wireless or signal station or office so belonging or occupied and any factory, dockyard or other place so belonging or occupied and used for the purpose of building, repairing, making or storing any munitions of war, or any sketches, plants, models or documents relating thereto, or for the purpose of getting any metals, oil or minerals of use in time of war;

(b) any place not belonging to Government where any munitions of war or any sketches, models, plans or documents relating thereto, are being made, repaired, gotten or stored under contract with, or with any person on behalf of, Government, or otherwise on behalf of Government;

(c) any place belonging to or used for the purpose of Government which is for the time being declared by the Central Government, by notification in the Official Gazette, to be a prohibited place for the

1. The words "or of the Government of the United Kingdom or of any British possession" omitted by Act 24 of 1967, sec. 3 (w.e.f. 15-8-1967).

purposes of this Act on the ground that information with respect thereto, or damage thereto, would be useful to an enemy, and to which a copy of the notification in respect thereof has been affixed in English and in the vernacular of the locality;

(d) any railway, road way or channel, or other means of communication by land or water (including any works or structures being part thereof or connected therewith) or any place used for gas, water or electricity works or other works for purposes of a public character, or any place where any munitions of war or any sketches, models, plans or documents relating thereto, are being made, repaired, or stored otherwise than on behalf of Government, which is for the time being declared by the Central Government, by notification in Official Gazette, to be a prohibited place for the purposes of this Act on the ground that information with respect thereto, or the destruction or obstruction thereof, or interference therewith, would be useful to an enemy, and to which a copy of the notification in respect thereof has been affixed in English and in the vernacular of the locality;

(9) "sketch" includes any photograph or other mode of representing any place of thing; and

(10) "Superintendent of Police" includes any police officer of a like or superior rank, and any person upon whom the powers of a Superintendent of Police are for the purposes of this Act conferred by the Central Government.

3. Penalties for spying.—(1) If any person for any purpose prejudicial to the safety or interests of the State:

(a) approaches, inspects, passes over or is in the vicinity of, or enters, any prohibited place; or

(b) makes any sketch, plan, model, or note which is calculated to be or might be or is intended to be, directly or indirectly, useful to an enemy; or

(c) obtains, collects, records or publishes or communicates to other person any secret official code or pass word, or any sketch, plan, model, article or note or other document or information which is calculated to be or might be or is intended to be, directly or indirectly, useful to an enemy [or which relates to a matter the disclosure of which is likely to affect the sovereignty and integrity of India, the security of the State or friendly relations with foreign States],

He shall be punishable with imprisonment for a term which may extend, where the offence is committed in relation to any work of defence, arsenal, naval, military or air force establishment or station, mine, minefield, factory, dockyard, camp, ship or aircraft or otherwise in relation to the naval, military or air force affairs of Government or in relation to any secret official code, to fourteen years and in other cases to three years.

(2) On a prosecution for an offence punishable under this section [1][...] it shall not be necessary to show that the accused person was guilty of any particular act tending to show a purpose prejudicial to the safety or interests of the State, and, notwithstanding that no such act is proved against him, he may be convicted if, from the circumstances of the case or his conduct or his known character as proved, it appears that his purpose was a purpose prejudicial to the safety or interests of the State; and if any sketch, plan, model, article, note, document or information relating to or used in any prohibited place, or relating to anything in such a place, or any secret official code or password is made, obtained, collected, recorded, published or communicated by any person other than a person acting under lawful authority, and from the circumstances of the case or his conduct or his known character as proved it appears that his purpose was a purpose prejudicial to the safety or interests of the State, such sketch, plan, model, article, note, document,

1. The words "with imprisonment for a term which may extend to fourteen Years" Omitted by Act 24 of 1967, sec. 6 (w.e.f. 15-8-1967).

[1][information, code or password shall be presumed to have been made], obtained, collected, recorded, published or communicated for a purpose prejudicial to the safety or interests of the State.

2. Subs. by the Act 24 of 1967, sec. 4, for "or information shall be presumed to have been made" (w.e.f. 15-8-1967).

THE PUBLIC RECORDS ACT, 1993

No. 69 of 1993 (21 DECEMBER 1993)

An Act to regulate the management, administration and preservation of public records of the Central Government, Union Territory Administrations, public sector undertakings, statutory bodies and corporations, commissions and committees constituted by the Central Government or a Union Territory Administration and matters connected therewith or incidental thereto.

Be it enacted by Parliament in the Forty-fourth Year of the Republic of India as follows:

1. Short title and commencement.—(1) This Act may be called the Public Records Act, 1993.

(2) It shall come into force, on such date as the Central Government may, by notification in the Official Gazette, appoint.

2. Definitions—In this Act, unless the context otherwise requires— (a) "Board" means the Archival Advisory Board constituted under sub-section (1) of section 13; (b) "Director General" means the Director General of Archives appointed by the Central Government and includes any officer authorized by that Government to perform the duties of the Director General; (c)"Head of the Archives" means a person holding the charge of the Archives of the Union Territory Administration; (d) "prescribed" means prescribed by rules made under this Act; (e) "public records" includes: (i) any document, manuscript and file; (ii) any microfilm, microfiche and facsimile copy of a document; (iii) any reproduction of image or images embodied in such microfilm (whether enlarged or not); and (iv) any other material produced by a computer or by any other device, of any records creating agency; (f) "records creating agency" includes:

(i) in relation to the Central Government, any ministry, department or office of that Government; (ii) in relation to any statutory body or corporation wholly or substantially controlled or financed by the Central Government or commission or any committee constituted by that Government, the offices of the said body, corporation, commission or committee; (iii) in relation to a Union Territory Administration, any department or office of that Administration; (iv) in relation to any statutory body or corporation wholly or, substantially controlled or financed by Union Territory Administration or commission or any committee constituted by that Government, the offices of the said body, corporation, commission or committee; (g) "records officer" means the officer nominated by the records creating agency under sub-section (1) of section 5.

3. Power of the Central Government to co-ordinate, regulate and supervise operations connected with administration, managements *etc.* of public records.—(1) The Central Government shall have the power to coordinate, regulate and supervise the operations connected with the administration, management, preservation, selection, disposal and retirement of public records under this Act.

(2) The Central Government in relation to the public records of the records, creating agencies specified in sub-clauses (i) and (ii) of clause (f) of section 2 and the Union territory Administration in relation to the public records of the records creating agencies specified in sub-clauses (iii) and (iv) of the said clause, may, by order, authorize the Director General on the head of the Archives, as the case may be, subject to such conditions as may be specified in the order, to carry out all or any of the following function, namely: (a) supervision, management and control of the Archives; (b) acceptance for deposit of public records of permanent, nature after such period as may be prescribed; (c) custody, use and withdrawal of public records; (d) arrangement, preservation and exhibition of public records; (e) preparation of inventories, indices, catalogues and other reference media of public records; (f) analyzing, developing, promoting and coordinating the standards, procedures and the techniques for improvement of the records management system;

(g) ensuring the maintenance, arrangement and security of public records in the Archives and in the offices of the records creating agency; (h) promoting utilization of available space and maintenance of equipments for preserving public records; (i) tendering advice to records creating agencies on the compilation, classification and disposal of records and application of standards, procedures and techniques of records management; (j) survey and inspection of public records; (k) organizing training programmes in various disciplines of Archives administration and records management; (l) accepting records from any private source; (m) regulating access to public records; (n) receiving records from delunet bodies and making arrangement for securing public records in the event of national emergency; (o) receiving reports on records management and disposal practices from the records officer; (p) providing authenticated copies of, or extracts from, public records; (q) destroying or disposal of public records; (r) obtaining on lease or purchasing or accepting as gift any document of historical or national importance.

4. Prohibition against taking of public records out of India.—No person shall take or cause to be taken out of India any public records without the prior approval of the Central Government:

Provided that no such prior approval shall be required if any public records are taken or sent out of India for any official purpose.

5. Records Officer.—(1) Every records creating agency shall nominate one of its officers as records officer to discharge the functions under this Act.

(2) Every records creating agency may set up such number of record rooms in such places as it deems fit and shall place each record room under the charge of a records officer.

6. Responsibilities of records officer.—(1) The records officer shall be responsible for: (a) proper arrangement, maintenance and preservation of public records under his charge; (b) periodical review of all public records and weeding out public records of euphomeral value; (c) appraisal of public records which are more than twenty-five years old in consultation with the National Archives of India or, as the case may be, the Archives of the Union territory with a view to retaining public records of permanent value; (d) destruction of public records in such manner and subject to such conditions as may be prescribed under sub-section (1) of section 8; (e) compilation of a schedule of retention for public records in consultation with the National Archives of India or, as the case may be, the Archives of the Union Territory; (f) periodical review for downgrading of classified public records in such manner as may be prescribed; (g) adoption of such standards, procedures and techniques as may be recommended from time to time by the National Archives of India for improvement of record management system and maintenance of security of public records; (h) compilation of annual indices of public records; (i) compilation of organizational history and annual supplement thereto; (j) assisting the National Archives of India or, as the case may be, the Archives of the Union territory for public records management; (k) submission of annual report to the Director General or, as the case may be head of the Archives in such manner as may be prescribed; (l) transferring of records of any defunct body to the National Archives of India or the Archives of the Union Territory, as the case may be, for preservation.

(2) The records officer shall act under the direction of the Director General or, as the case may be, head of the Archives while discharging the responsibilities specified in sub-section (1).

7. Records officer to take appropriate action in the event of unauthorised removal, destruction, etc. of public records in his custody.—(1) The records officer shall, in the event of any unauthorized removal, destruction, defacement or alteration of any public records under his charge, forthwith take appropriate action for the recovery or restoration of such public records.

(2) The records officer shall submit a report in writing to the Director General or as the case may be the head of the Archives without any delay on any information about any unauthorized removal, destruction, defacement or alteration of any public records under his charge and about the action initiated by him and shall take action as he may deem necessary subject to the

directions, if any given by the Director General or, as the case may be, head of the Archives.

(3) The records officer may seek assistance from any government officer or any other person for the purpose of recovery or restoration of public records and such officer or person shall render all assistance to the records officer.

8. Destruction or disposl of public records.—(1) Save as otherwise provided in any law for the time being in force, no public record shall be destroyed or otherwise disposed of excepts in such manner and subject to such conditions as may be prescribed.

(2) No record created before the year 1892 shall be destroyed except where in the opinion of the Director General or, as the case may be, the head of the Archives, it is so defaced or is in such condition that it cannot be put to any archival use.

9. Penalty for contraventions.—Whoever contravenes any of the provisions of section 4 or section 8 shall be punishable with imprisonment for a term which may extend to five years or with fine which may extend to ten thousand rupees or with both.

10. Public records bearing security classification.—No public records bearing security classification shall be transferred to the National Archives of India or the Archives of the Union Territory.

11. Receipt of records from private sources.—(1) The National Archives of India or the Archives of the Union Territory may accept any record of historical or national importance from any private source by way of gift, purchase or otherwise.

(2) The National Archives of India or, as the case may be, the Archives of any Union Territory may, in such manner and subject to such conditions as may be prescribed, make any record referred to in sub-section (1) available to any *bona fide* research scholar.

12. Access to public records.—(1) All unclassified public records as are more than thirty years old and are transferred to the National Archives of India or the Archives of the Union Territory may be, subject to such exceptions and restrictions as may be prescribed made available to any *bona fide* research scholar.

Explanation: For the purposes of this sub-section, the period of thirty years shall be reckoned from the year of the opening of the public record.

(2) Any records creating agency may grant to any person access to any public record in its custody in such manner and subject to such conditions as may be prescribed.

13. Archival Advertisory Board.—(1) The Central Government may, by notification in the Official Gazette, constitute an Archival Advisory Board for the purposes of this Act.

(2) The Board shall consist of the following members, namely:
(a) Secretary to the Government of India in the Ministry of Central Government dealing with Culture—Chairman, ex-officio;

(b) One officer not below the rank of Joint Secretary to the Government of India, each from the Cabinet Secretariat, Ministry of Home Affairs, Ministry of Defence, Ministry of External Affairs, Ministry of Finance and Ministry of Personnel, Public Grievances and Pension—Members, ex-officio;

(c) Two representatives not below the rank of Joint Secretary in the Union Territory Administrations to be nominated by the Central Government—Members;

(d) Three persons to be nominated by the Central Government for a period not exceeding three years, one being an Archivist and two being Professors in the Post-graduate Department of History in any recognized University—Members.

Director General of Archives

The members nominated under clause (d) of sub-section (2) shall be paid such allowances as may be prescribed.

14. Function of the Board.—The Board shall perform the following functions, namely: advise the Central Government and Union Territory Administrations on matters concerning the administration, management, conservation and use of public records; lay down guidelines for training of Archivists; give directions for acquisition of records from private custody; deal with such other matters as may be prescribed.

15. Power of the Director General to lay down norms and standards for cources in archival science.—The Director General shall have the power to lay down norms and standards for courses curricula, assessment and examinations relating to the training in archival science and other ancillary subjects.

16. Protection of action taken in good faith.—No suit, prosecution or other legal proceedings shall lie against any person in respect of anything which is in good faith done or intended to be done in pursuance of this Act or the rules made thereunder.

17. Power to make rules.—(1) The Central Government may, by notification in the Official Gazette, makes rules to carry out the provisions of this Act.

(2) In particular and without prejudice to the generality of the foregoing power, such rules may provide for all or any of the following matters, namely: the period after which public records of permanent nature may be accepted under clause (b) of sub-section (2) of section 3; the manner in which and the conditions subject to which public records can be destroyed under clause (d) of sub-section (1) of section 6; the manner in which periodical review of classified public records for downgrading shall be undertaken under clause (F) of sub-section (1) of section 6; the manner in which the records officer will report to the Director General or the head of the Archives under clause (k) of sub-section (l) of section 6; the manner in which and the conditions subject to which public records may be destroyed or disposed of under sub-section (l) of section 8; the manner in which and the conditions subject to which records of historical or national importance may be made available to research scholar under sub-section (2) of section 11; exceptions and restrictions subject to which public records may be made available to a research scholar under sub-section (1) of section 12; the manner in which and the conditions subject to which any records creating agency may grant to any person access to public records in its custody sub-section (2) of section 12; the allowances payable to members of the Board under sub-section (3) of section 13; the matters with

respect to which the Board may perform its functions under clause (d) of section 14; any other matter which is required to be, or may be, prescribed.

18. Laying of rules before parliament.—Every rule madc under this Act shall be laid, as soon as may be after it is made, before each House of Parliament, while it is in session, for a total period of thirty days which may be comprised in one session or in two or more successive sessions, and if, before the expiry of the session immediately following the session or the successive sessions aforesaid, both Houses agree in making any modification in the rule or both Houses agree that the rule should not be made, the rule shall thereafter have effect only in such modified form or be of no effect, as the case may be; so, however, that any such modification or annulment shall be without prejudice to the validity of anything previously done under that rule.

THE PUBLIC RECORDS RULES, 1997*

In exercise of the powers conferred by sub-section (1) of section 17 of the Public Records Act, 1993 (69 of 1993), the Central Government hereby makes the following rules, namely:

Short title and commencement.— These rules may be called the Public Records Rules, 1997. They shall come into force on the date of their publication in the Official Gazette.

Definitions.— In these rules, unless the context otherwise requires, "Act" means the Public Records Act, 1993 (69 of 1993); "appraisal" means the evaluation of public records in association with the National Archives of India or Archives of the Union Territory as the case may be; "classified records" means the files relating to the public records classified as top-secret, confidential and restricted in accordance with the procedure laid down in the Manual of Departmental Security Instruction circulated by the Ministry of Home affairs from time to time; "custody" means the possession of public records; "defunct body" means a corporate or non-corporate body which has been wound up with no successor to carry on its functions; "Declassification" means downgrade the security classification after their evaluation; "file" means a collection of papers relating to the public records on a specific subject-matter consisting of correspondence, notes and appendix thereto and assigned with a file number; "form" means the form appended to these rules; "private records" means records lying in the possession of a private individual or with any non-governmental organization; "recording" means the process of closing a file after action on all issue considered thereon has been

---

* *Vide* G.S.R. 43, dated 9th January, 1997, published in the Gazette of India, Extra., Pt. II, Sec. (i), dated 18th January, 1997.

completed; "records of permanent nature" means the public records being maintained after recording for a period specified, under sub-rule (1) of rule 5 by the records creating agency in accordance with the procedure laid in its Manual of Office Procedure or Instructions on the subject; "retention Schedule of records" means a schedule which provides the period of retention; "review" means periodical evaluation of recorded files on the expiry of the period of retention for determining their further retention or destruction as the case may be; "section" means the section of the Act; "standing guard file" means a compilation of papers on a particular subject-matter consisting of copies of policy decision, orders, instructions or any another matter incidental thereto arranged in a chronological order; Words and expression used herein and not defined but defined in the Act, shall have the meanings respectively assigned to them in the Act.

Nomination of records officer.—The records creating agency shall by an officers order issued in pursuance of the provision of sub-section (1) of section 5 of the Act nominate one of its officers, not below the rank or grade of a Section Officer, as the Records Officer. A copy of such office order shall forwarded to the Director General or Head of the Archives, as the case may be.

Maintenance of standing guard file.—The Records Officer shall be responsible for maintaining and keeping a standing guard file and proper record of the directions issued by the Director General or Head of the Archives, as the case may be in pursuance of the provisions of sub-section (2) of section 6 and shall produce the same for inspection as and when required by the Director General or Head of the Archives, as the case may be.

Acceptance of public records of permanent nature.—The Director General or Head of the Archives, as the case may be shall accept for deposit and preservation public records of permanent nature which have been retained after recording by the records creating agency in its records room for the last twenty-five years or more.

Records Officer shall intimate to the Director General or Head of the Archives, as the case may be each year before 31st day of January, in form-1 the particulars of all public records of permanent nature which are due for appraisal during the year.

On receipt of an intimation under sub-rule (2), the Director General or Head of the Archives, as the case may be, through his officers shall assist the Records Officer in conducting the appraisal of public records. When the appraisal is over, the Records Officer shall prepare, in triplicate, a transfer list in Form-2 of all public records and deposit the same for preservation with the Director General or Head of the Archives as the case may be who shall after his satisfaction, return one copy of the transfer list to the Records Officer as a receipt of the public records.

If the Records Officer after appraisal deems it necessary to retain any record or file of permanent nature beyond the period of twenty-five years, he may do so for reasons to be recorded in writing and under intimation to the Director General or Head of the Archives as the case may be.

Withdrawal of public records.—If public records deposited and preserved with the Director General or Head of the Archives as the case may be, are required by the records creating agency for any official purpose, then the Records Officer shall send a duly signed and stamped requisition slip in Form-3 to the Director General or Head of the Archives as the case may be.

The public records requisitioned under sub-rule (1) may be returned as soon as the purpose is achieved but shall not be retained beyond the period of six months by the Records Officer or the records creating agency.

Downgrading of classified records.—The records creating agency shall by an office order authorize an officer not below the rank of the Under Secretary to the Government of India to evaluate and downgrade the classified records being maintained by it. A copy of such office order shall be forwarded to the Director General or Head of the Archives, as the case may be.

The officer so authorized under sub-rule (1) shall evaluate the classified records every fifth year for the purpose of down-grading.

After down-grading if the officer declares any record as of permanent nature the same shall be deposited and preserved with the Director General or Head of the Archives , as the case may be, after its appraisal.

The records deposited under this rule can be requisitioned for any official purpose and returned to the Director General or Head of the Archives as the case may be, in the manner provided under rule 6.

Every year in the last week of June and December a half-yearly statement in Form-4 shall be furnished by the officer authorized under sub-rule (1) to the Director General or Head of the Archives, as the case may be on the action taken for evaluation and downgrading the classified records.

Submission of annual report.—The Records Officers nominated under rule 3 shall furnish to the Director General or Head of the Archives as the case may be an Annual Report in Form-5 every year in the month of March of the following year.

The Director General or Head of the Archives as the case may be shall thereafter, submit a report to the Government in the Ministry of Human Resources Development every year on the action taken by the Records Officer in pursuance to the provision of clauses (a) to (1) of sub-section 1 of section 6 of the Act.

Destruction of public records.—No public records shall be destroyed without being recorded and reviewed. In the month of January every year each records creating agency shall record after consulting the records retention Schedule all these files on which action has been completed. This work shall be accomplished in consultation with the Records Officer.

No public records which is more than twenty five-years old shall be destroyed by any records creating agency unless it is appraised.

A list of all such public records which are proposed to be destroyed shall be prepared by the record creating agency in Form-6 and retained permanently for future reference.

The Records Officer shall furnish a half-yearly report in Form-on recording, indexing, reviewing and weeding of records to the Director General or Head of the Archives, as the case may be.

Records shall be destroyed either by burning or shredding in the presence of Records Officer.

Access to private records.—Records acquired from private sources by way of gift or purchase or otherwise shall be made available for *bona fide* research subject to the conditions laid down by the donor.

Research scholars shall submit an application in Form-8 to the Director General or Head of the Archives as the case may be for permission to consult records. The Director General or Head of the Archives as the case may be, may refuse such permission in public interest and for reasons to be recorded on the said application.

Wherever microfilm rolls may be available the original records shall not be supplied for consultation to research scholars. No copy of any records shall be made by any one without the prior permission of the Director General or Head of the Archives, as the case may be.

Access to public records.—The public records accepted for deposit and preservation under sub-rule (1) of rule 5 shall be made available for *bona fide* consultation and research purpose subject to the provision of sub-section (1) of section 12 and the following conditions namely.

A person who intends to consult the public records shall apply to the Director General or Head of the Archives, as the case may be in Form-8. The Director General or Head of the Archives, as the case may be, may refuse such permission in public interest and for reasons to be recorded on the said application.

Foreign nationals intending to consult the public records may be permitted only on the production of letters of introduction from their sponsoring institution and diplomatic Mission.

Record maps and cartographic records relating to the Ministry of External Affairs and Ministry of Defence, in respect of Arunachal Pradesh (including Eastern Section of the Sino-Indian border) Sikkim, Bhutan, Nepal, Tibet, China and Myanmar and areas comprising Pakistan and Bangladesh may be made available for consultation keeping in view the security and the defence of India or of any part of the Territory thereof. Records relating to the Ministry of External Affairs. Home Affairs and Human Resources Development in respect of Jammu and Kashmir (including Gilgit and Chitral) may also be made available for consultation keeping in view the security and defence of India or of any part of the Territory thereof. Provided that the Director General or Head of the Archives as the case may be refuse such consultation.

Wherever microfilm rolls may be made available the original records shall not be supplied for consultation to research scholar.

Reprographic and transcription facilities may be made available on submission of an application in Form-9 and for such services the applicant shall have to make the payment of such services (the applicant shall have to make the payment of such services charges) as may be fixed by the Director General or Head of the Archives as the case may be from time to time.

A person consulting public records for the purpose of research and publishes the work which is based upon the material taken from the said records may acknowledge the same.

A person intending to consult the public records shall not.— Write and put any marks or indications on public records.

Fold, tear, cut, crease, or otherwise damage or mutilate public records; Remove any public records without obtaining the permission from the Director General or Head of the Archives, as the case may be; Be allowed to take any eatable or drinking products or smoking while consulting public records; Place anything or object on any public records with a view to make out any copy of the said records; Disturb or interrupt any other person while consulting the public records; and Behave in a manner which in the opinion of the Director General or Head of the Archives as the case may be is detrimental to the maintenance and preservation of public records.

Allowances to the members of the Archival Advisory Board: The members of the Archival Advisory Board nominated by the Central Government under clause (d) of sub-section 2 of section 13 shall draw travelling allowance and daily allowance for attending the meetings of the Archival Advisory Board at the rates admissible to Group 'A' officers of the Central Government.

Form 1

[*See* sub-rule (2) of rule 5]

PARTICULARS OF RECORDS OF PERMANENT NATURE DUE FOR APPRAISAL DURING THE YEAR ....

Total number of files of 'A' & 'B' categories lying in the records rooms of the records creating agencies	Total numbers of files of 'A' & 'B' categories transferred to records rooms by the Sections during the period under report	Total No. of files referred to under column 1 and 2	Total No. of files due for appraisal	Remarks if any
1	2	3	4	5

Form 2

[*See* sub-rule (3) of rule 5]

TRANSFER LIST

Name of the records creating agency i.e.
Ministry/ Department/Office/Public Undertakings etc. : ....

Name and particulars of the records officer : ....

Name of the Branch/Section: ....

Year: ....

S. No.	File No.	Subject matter of the file	Remarks, if any

....
Signature and seal of the records officer

Form 3

[*See* sub-rule (1) of rule 6]

REQUISITION SLIP

Name of the records creating agency
(i.e. Ministry/Department/Office) : ....

Name and particulars of the records officer : ....

Particulars of records or File No. requisitioned : ....

Purpose for which required : ....

Undertaking by the records officer—I .... hereby declare that the records/file requisitioned shall be returned to the Director General/the head of the Archives before the expiry of six months as required under sub-rule (2) of rule 6.

....

Signature and seal of the records officer

Form 4

[*See* sub-rule (5) of rule 7]

HALF YEARLY STATEMENT ON PERIODICAL REVIEW OF CLASSIFIED RECORDS

Total No. of classified records lying at present in the organisation	No. of classified records due for reviewing	No. of files reviewed and downgraded during the period under report	Remarks

Form 5

[*See* sub-rule (1) of rule 8]

FORM FOR THE SUBMISSION OF ANNUAL REPORT TO DIRECTOR GENERAL OF ARCHIVES/ HEAD OF THE ARCHIVES

1. A. Setting up organised Departmental Records Room—Whether your organisation has set up an organised Records Room, and if so; is the space sufficient?

B. Nomination of Records Officers.—Whether your organisation has nominated an officer as Departmental Records Officer, and if not, give reasons?

C. Training of Records Officer and Staff:

(i) Whether Departmental Records Officer has received training in Records Management?

(ii) Whether the junior staff working in the Departmental Records Room are trained in various aspects of Records Management?

(iii) If not, are you willing to avail training facilities existing at National Archives of India.

D. I. Sharing of space for housing semi-current records at National Archives/Archives of the Union Territory:

(i) Whether your organisation is willing to share space at National Archives, New Delhi and its Records Centres at Jaipur, Pondicherry and Bhubaneswar and Regional Office at Bhopal?

(ii) If yes, please state bulk of records proposed to be transferred.

II (i) Whether your organisation is willing to share space at the Archives of the Union Territory?

2. Periodical recording, reviewing and weeding out of semi-current records:

   (i) Whether your organisation has taken steps for recording, reviewing and weeding out of ephemeral records?

   (ii) Indicate the total number of records recorded, reviewed and weeded out during the period under report.

3. Appraisal of Non-Current records:

   (i) Whether your organisation has initiated action to get non-current records appraised in consultation with National Archives?

   (ii) State the total bulk of records awaiting appraisal.

4. Compilation/Revision of Retention Schedule of Records:

   (i) Whether your organisation has compiled Record Retention Schedule of substantive functions in consultation with National Archives and if not what action do you propose to take?

   (ii) Has your organisation taken steps to revise the above schedule after five years?

5. Periodical review of classified records:

   (i) Whether your organisation has declassified the classified records during the period under report?

   (ii) If not, state reasons?

6. Compilation of Annual Indices to Records:
   (i) Whether your organisation has compiled annual indices?
   (ii) State inclusive years with the name of the series?
7. Compilation of organisational history:

   Has your organisation compiled organisational history, reflecting various functions along with the date of their creation and if so furnish a copy to National Archives.
8. Records of Defunct Bodies:
   (i) Whether your organisation has got records of defunct bodies, give details?
   (ii) If yes, what action have you initiated for their transfer to National Archives?

Form 6

[*See* sub-rule (3) of rule 9]

PARTICULARS OF RECORDS DESTROYED DURING THE YEAR ....

File Nos.	Subject matter of the files	Remarks

Form 7

[*See* sub-rule (4) of rule 9]

QUARTERLY REPORT ON RECORDING, INDEXING, REVIEWING AND WEEDING OF RECORDS DURING THE HALF YEAR ENDING ....

Sl. No.	Total Number of files recorded	Total number of files indexed	Total No. of files reviewed	Total No. of files weeded out, if any	Remarks
1	2	3	4	5	6

Form 8

[*See* rule (2) of rule 10 and clause (i) of sub-rule (1) of rule 11]

APPLICATION FORM FOR PERMISSION TO CONSULT RECORDS

To,

The Director General of Archives,
Government of India,
New Delhi-110001

Sir,

I hereby apply for enrolment as a research scholar for consulting records in the Research Room of the National Archives of India. I agree to comply with the rules and conditions in force and promise to deposit a copy of each of my work based on the materials consulted at the National Archives of India immediately after the publication.

1. Name, including Surname: Sh./ Smt./ Km./ Dr. ....
2. Father's/ Husband's Name: ....
3. Date of Birth: ....
4. Qualifications: ....
5. Nationality: ....
6. Profession: ....
7. Subject of Research: ....
8. University/Institutions* registered with: ....
9. Period for which admission is sought: ....
10. Signature and date: ....
11. Address (i) Local: ....
    (ii) Permanent: ....

---

* Scholars are requested to attach a letter of recommendation from their University/Institution/Department. However, the foreign scholars are requested to bring a letter of accredition from the diplomatic representatives of their country in India as well.

Particulars of records to be consulted:

Sl. No.	Department	Period	Remarks
1.			
2.			
3.			
4.			

Form 9

[*See* clause (v) of sub-rule (1) of rule 11]

APPLICATION FOR REPROGRAPHIC/ TRANSCRIPTION FACILITIES

To, Dated:......................

The Director General of Archives,

National Archives of India,

New Delhi.

Sir,

Kindly supply me Microfilm (NFG/POS) Photo Copies/ Xerox Transcripts of the material(s) indicated in the enclosed list for my research/publication/university. The material is from the Ministry(s) Department(s) of .... It consits of .... items and covers the period from .... to ....

1. I declare that the above material is for my research/ publication/university.
2. I undertake to pay the charges as per schedule of rates prevailing at the time of completion of work. I understand and accept that the estimated cost, when supplied is only tentative and the rates are also liable to revision without notice.
3. The photocopies/transcripts supplied will not be sold/ transferred to any other person without prior permission of the Director General of Archives.
4. The material, if published, will be suitably acknowledged and provisions of copyright, where applicable, will be complied with.

5. I hereby deposit a sum of Rs .... as advance.

Permanent Address
(in block letters)

Yours faithfully

Signature:

Name (in block letters)

Local Address

FOR OFFICE USE

Advance received vide receipt No. .... dated .... for Rs .... services charges have come to Rs .... Balance receipt vide Receipt No. .... dated .... Rs ....

Cleared for photocopying transcription subject to following:

(1) ....

Signature of Archivist

Date:

THE FREEDOM OF INFORMATION ACT, 2002*

An Act to provide for freedom to every citizen to secure access to information under the control of public authorities, consistent with public interest, in order to promote openness, transparency and accountability in administration and in relation to matters connected therewith or incidental thereto.

Be it enacted by Parliament in the Fifty-third Year of the Republic of India as follows:

CHAPTER I

PRELIMINARY

1. Short title, extent and commencement.—(1) This Act may be called the Freedom of Information Act, 2002.

(2) It extends to the whole of India except the State of Jammu and Kashmir.

(3) It shall come into force on such date as the Central Government may, by notification in the Official Gazette, appoint.

2. Definition.—In this Act, unless the context otherwise requires–

(a) "appropriate government" means in relation to a public authority established, constituted, owned, substantially financed by funds provided directly or indirectly or controlled—

(i) by the Central Government, the Central Government;

* Repealed by the Right to Information Act, 2005 (22 of 2005) (w.e.f. 12-10-2005).

(ii) by the State Government, the State Government;

(iii) by the Union territory, the Central Government.

(b) "competent authority" means—

(i) the Speaker in the case of the House of the People or the Legislative Assembly and the Chairman in the case of the Council of States or the Legislative Council;

(ii) the Chief Justice of India in the case of the Supreme Court;

(iii) the Chief Justice of the High Court in the case of a High Court;

(iv) the President or the Governor, as the case may be, in the case of other authorities created by or under the Constitution;

(v) the administrator appointed under Article 239 of the Constitution.

(c) "freedom of information" means the right to obtain information from any public authority by means of—

(i) inspection, taking of extracts and notes;

(ii) certified copies of any records of such public authority;

(iii) diskettes, floppies or in any other electronic mode or through printouts where such information is stored in a computer or in any other device.

(d) "information" means any material in any form relating to the administration, operations or decisions of a public authority;

(e) "prescribed" means prescribed by rules made under this Act by the appropriate Government or the competent authority, as the case may be;

(f) "public authority" means any authority or body established or constituted—

(i) by or under the Constitution;

(ii) by any law made by the appropriate Government, and includes any other body owned, controlled or substantially financed by funds provided directly or indirectly by the appropriate Government;

(g) "Public Information Officer" means the Public Information Officer appointed under sub-section (1) of Section 5;

(h) "record" includes—

(i) any document, manuscript and file;

(ii) any microfilm, microfiche and facsimile copy of a document;

(iii) any reproduction of image or images embodied in such microfilm (whether enlarged or not); and

(iv) any other material produced by a computer or by any other device.

(i) "third party" means a person other than the person making a request for information and includes a public authority.

CHAPTER II

FREEDOM OF INFORMATION AND OBLIGATIONS OF PUBLIC AUTHORITIES

3. Freedom of information.—Subject to the provisions of this Act, all citizen shall have freedom of information.

4. Obligations on public authorities.—Every public authority shall—

(a) maintain all its records, in such manner and form as is consistent with its operational requirements duly catalogued and indexed;

(b) publish at such intervals as may be prescribed by the appropriate Government or competent authority:—

(i) the particulars of its organisation, functions and duties;

(ii) the powers and duties of its officers and employees and the procedure followed by them in the decision making process;

(iii) the norms set by the public authority for the discharge of its functions;

(iv) rules, regulations, instructions, manuals and other categories of records under its control used by its employees for discharging its functions;

(v) the details of facilities available to citizens for obtaining information; and

(vi) the name, designation and other particulars of the Public Information Officer;

(c) publish all relevant facts concerning important decisions and policies that affect the public while announcing such decisions and policies;

(d) give reasons for its decisions, whether administrative or quasi-judicial to those affected by such decisions;

(e) before initiating any project, publish or communicate to the public generally or to the persons affected or likely to be affected by the project in particular, the facts available to it or to which it has reasonable access which in its opinion should be known to them in the best interests of natural justice and promotion of democratic principles.

5. Appointment of Public Information Officers.—(1) Every public authority shall for the purposes of this Act, appoint one or more officers as Public Information Officers.

(2) Every Public Information Officer shall deal with requests for information and shall render reasonable assistance to any person seeking such information.

(3) The Public Information Officer may seek the assistance of any other officer as he considers necessary for the proper discharge of his duties.

(4) Any officer whose assistance has been sought under sub-section (3), shall render all assistance to the Public Information Officer seeking his assistance.

6. Request for obtaining information.—A person desirous of obtaining information shall make a request in writing or through electronic means, to the concerned Public Information Officer specifying the particulars of the information sought by him:

Provided that where such request cannot be made in writing, the Public Information Officer shall render all reasonable assistance to the person making the request orally to reduce it in writing.

7. Disposal of requests.—(1) On receipt of a request under Section 6, the Public Information Officer shall, as expeditiously as possible, and in any case within thirty days of the receipt of the request, either provide the information requested on payment of such fee as may be prescribed or reject the request for any of the reasons specified in Sections 8 and 9:

Provided that where the information sought for concerns the life and liberty of a person, the same should be provided within forty-eight hours of the receipt of the request:

Provided further that where it is decided to provide the information on payment of any further fee representing the cost of providing the information, he shall send an intimation to the person making the request, giving the details of the fees determined by him, requesting him to deposit the fees and the period intervening between the despatch of the said intimation and payment of fees shall be excluded for the purpose of calculating the period of thirty days referred to above.

(2) Before taking any decision under sub-section (1), the Public Information Officer, shall take into consideration the representation made by a third party under Section 11.

(3) Where a request is rejected under sub-section (2), the Public Information Officer shall communicate to the person making request,

(i) the reason for such rejection;

(ii) the period within which an appeal against such rcjections may be preferred;

(iii) the particulars of the appellate authority.

(4) Information shall ordinarily be provided in the form in which it is sought unless it would disproportionately divert the resources of the public authority or would be detrimental to the safety or preservation of the record in question.

8. Exemption from disclosure of information.—(1) Notwithstanding anything hereinbefore contained, the following information not being information relating to any matter referred to in sub-section (2), shall be exempted from disclosure, namely:—

(a) information, the disclosure of which would prejudicially affect the sovereignty and integrity of India, security of the State, strategic scientific or economic interest of India or conduct of international relations;

(b) information, the disclosure of which would prejudicially affect public safety and order, detection and investigation of an offence or which may lead to an incitement to commit an offence or prejudicially affect fair trial or adjudication of a pending case;

(c) information, the disclosure of which would prejudicially affect the conduct of Centre-State relations, including information exchanged in confidence between the Central and State Governments or any of their authorities or agencies;

(d) cabinet papers including records of deliberations of the Council of Ministers, Secretaries and other officers;

(e) minutes or records of advice including legal advice, opinions or recommendations made by any officer of a public authority during the decision making process prior to the executive decision or policy formulation;

(f) trade or commercial secrets protected by law of information, the disclosure of which would prejudicially affect the legitimate economic and commercial interests or the competitive position of a public authority; or would cause unfair gain or loss to any person; and

(g) information, the disclosure of which may result in the breach of privileges of Parliament or the Legislature of a State, or contravention of a lawful order of a court.

(2) Subject to the provisions of clause (a) of sub-section (1), any information relating to any occurrence, event or matter which has taken place occurred or happened twenty-five years before the date on which any request is made under Section 6 shall be provided to any person making a request under that section:

Provided that where any question arises as to the date from which the said period of twenty-five years has to be computed, the decision of the Central Government shall be final.

9. Grounds for refusal to access in certain cases.—Without prejudice to the provisions of Section 8, a Public Information Officer may reject a request for information also where such request—

(a) is too general in nature or is of such a nature that, having regard to the volume of information required to be retrieved or processed would involve unreasonable diversion of the resources of a public authority or would adversely interfere with the functioning of such authority:

Provided that where such request is rejected on the ground that the request is too general, it would be the duty of the Public Information Officer to render help as far as possible to the person making request to reframe his request in such a manner as may facilitate compliance with it;

(b) relates to information that is required by law, rules, regulations or orders to be published at particular time and such information is likely to be so published within thirty days of the receipt of such request;

(c) relates to information that is contained in published material available to public; or

(d) relates to information which would cause unwarranted invasion of the privacy of any person.

10. Severability.—(1) If a request for access to information is rejected on the ground that it is in relation to information which is exempted from disclosure, then notwithstanding anything contained in this Act, access may be given to that part of the record which does not obtain any information that is exempted from disclosure under this Act and which can reasonably be severed from any part that contains exempted information.

(2) Where access is granted to a part of the record in accordance with sub-section (1), the person making the request shall be informed—

(a) that only part of the record requested, after severance of the record containing information which is exempted from disclosure, is being furnished; and

(b) of the provisions of the Act under which the severed part exempted from disclosure.

11. Third party information.—(1) Where a public authority intends to disclose any information or record, or part thereof, on a request made under this Act which relates to, or has been supplied by a third party and has been treated as confidential by that third party, the Public Information Officer shall, within twenty-five days from the receipt of a request, give written notice to such third party of the request and of the fact that the public authority intends to disclose the information or record, or part thereof:

Provided that except in the case of trade or commercial secrets protected by law, disclosure may be allowed if the public interest in disclosure outweighs in importance any possible harm or injury to the interests of such third party.

(2) Where a notice is given by the Public Information Officer under sub-section (1) to a third party in respect of any information or record or part thereof, the third party shall, within twenty days from the date of issuance of notice, be given the

opportunity to make representation against the proposed disclosure.

(3) Notwithstanding anything contained in Section 7, the Public Information Officer shall, within sixty days after receipt of the request under Section 6, if the third party has been given an opportunity to make representation under sub-section (2), make a decision as to whether or not to disclose the information or record or part thereof and give in writing the notice of his decision to the third party.

(4) A notice given under sub-section (3) shall include a statement that the third party to whom the notice is given is entitled to prefer an appeal against the decision under Section 12.

12. Appeals.—(1) Any person aggrieved by a decision of the Public Information Officer may, within thirty days of receipt of such decision, prefer an appeal to such authority as may be prescribed:

Provided that such authority may entertain the appeal after the expiry of the said period of thirty days if it is satisfied that the appellant was prevented by sufficient cause from filing the appeal in time.

(2) A second appeal against the decision under sub-section (1) shall lie within thirty days of such decision, to the Central Government or the State Government or the competent authority, as the case may be:

Provided that the Central Government or the State Government or the competent authority, as the case may be, may entertain the appeal after the expiry of the said period of thirty days if it is satisfied that the appellant was prevented by sufficient cause from filing the appeal in time.

(3) The appeals referred to in sub-sections (1) and (2) shall be disposed of within thirty days of the receipt of such appeals or within such extended period, as the case may be, for reasons to be recorded in writing.

(4) If the decision of the Public Information Officer against which the appeal is preferred under sub-section (1) or sub-section (2) also relates to information of third party, the appellate

authority shall give a reasonable opportunity of being heard to that third party.

CHAPTER III

MISCELLANEOUS

13. Protection of action taken in good faith.—No suit, prosecution or other legal proceeding shall lie against any person for anything which is in good faith done or intended to be done under this Act or any rule made thereunder.

14. Act to have overriding effect.—The provisions of this Act shall have effect notwithstanding anything inconsistent therewith contained in the Official Secrets Act, 1923, and any other law for the time being in force or in any instrument having effect by virtue of any law other than this Act.

15. Bar of jurisdiction of courts.—No court shall entertain any suit, application or other proceeding in respect of any order made under this Act and no such order shall be called in question otherwise than by way of an appeal under this Act.

16. Act not to apply to certain organisations.—(1) Nothing contained in this Act shall apply to the intelligence and security organisations, specified in the Schedule, being organisations established by the Central Government or any information furnished by such organisations to that Government.

(2) The Central Government may, by notification in the Official Gazette, amend the Schedule by including therein any other intelligence or security organisation established by that Government or omitting therefrom any organisation already specified therein and on the publication of such notification, such organisation shall be deemed to be included in or, as the case may be, omitted from the Schedule.

(3) Every notification issued under sub-section (2), shall be laid before each House of Parliament.

(4) Nothing contained in this Act shall apply to such intelligence and security organizations which may be specified, by a notification in the Official Gazette, by a State Government from time to time.

(5) Every notification issued under sub-section (4), shall be laid before the State Legislature.

17. Power to make rules by Central Government.—(1) The Central Government may, by notification in the Official Gazette, make rules to carry out the provisions of this Act.

(2) In particular, and without prejudice to the generality of the foregoing power, such rules may provide for all or any of the following matters, namely—

(a) intervals at which matters referred to in sub-clauses (i) to (vi) of clause (b) of Section 4 shall be published;

(b) the fee payable under sub-section (1) of Section 7;

(c) the authority before whom an appeal may be preferred under sub-section (1) of Section 12;

(d) any other matter which is required to be or may be prescribed.

18. Power to make rules by State Government.—(1) The State Government may, by notification in the Official Gazette, make rules to carry out the provisions of this Act.

(2) In particular, and without prejudice to the generality of the foregoing power, such rules may provide for all or any of the following matters, namely:

(a) the fee payable under sub-section (1) of Section 7;

(b) the authority before whom an appeal may be preferred under sub-section (1) of Section 12;

(c) any other matter which is required to be, or may be, prescribed:

Provided that initially the rules shall be made by the Central Government by notification in the Official Gazette.

19. Rule making power by competent authority.—(1) The competent authority may, by notification in the Official Gazette, make rules to carry out the provisions of this Act.

(2) In particular, and without prejudice to the generality of the foregoing power, such rules may provide for all or any of the following matters, namely:

(a) the fee payable under sub-section (1) of Section 7;

(b) the authority before whom an appeal may be preferred under sub-section (1) of Section 12;

(c) any other matter which is required to be, or may be, prescribed.

20. Laying of rules.—(1) Every rule made by the Central Government under this Act shall be laid, as soon as may be after it is made, before each House of Parliament, while it is in session, for a total period of thirty days which may be comprised in one session or in two or more successive sessions, and if, before the expiry of the session immediately following the session or the successive sessions aforesaid, both Houses agree in making any modification in the rule or both Houses agree that the rule should not be made, the rule shall thereafter have effect only in such modified form or be of no effect, as the case may be, so, however, that any such modification or annulment shall be without prejudice to the validity of anything previously done under that rule.

(2) Every rule made under this Act by a State Government shall be laid, as soon as may be after it is notified, before the State Legislature.

21. Power to remove difficulties.—(1) If any difficulty arises in giving effect to the provisions of this Act, the Central Government may, by order published in the Official Gazette, make such provisions not inconsistent with the provisions of this Act as appear to it to be necessary or expedient for removal of the difficulty:

Provided that no such order shall be made after the expiry of a period of two years from the date of the commencement of this Act.

(2) Every order made under this section shall, as soon as may be after it is made, be laid before the Houses of Parliament.

THE SCHEDULE

(*See* section 16)

INTELLIGENCE AND SECURITY ORGANISATIONS ESTABLISHED BY THE CENTRAL GOVERNMENT

1. Intelligence Bureau.
2. Research and Analysis Wing of the Cabinet Secretariat.
3. Directorate of Revenue Intelligence.
4. Central Economic Intelligence Bureau.
5. Directorate of Enforcement.
6. Narcotics Control Bureau.
7. Aviation Research Centre.
8. Special Frontier Force.
9. Border Security Force.
10. Central Reserve Police Force.
11. Indo-Tibetan Border Police.
12. Central Industrial Security Force.
13. National Security Guards.
14. Assam Rifles.
15. Special Service Bureau.
16. Special Branch (CID), Andaman and Nicobar.
17. The Crime Branch—C.I.D.—CB., Dadra and Nagar Haveli.
18. Directorate of Vigilance including Anti Corruption Branch, National Capital Territory of Delhi.
19. Special Branch, Lakshadweep Police.

PART IV

ALLIED ACTS AND RULES

(Relevant Provisions)

THE ALL INDIA SERVICES (CONDUCT) RULES, 1968

(Relevant Provisions)

2. Definitions.—In these rules, unless the context otherwise requires

(a) "Government" means:

(i) in the case of a member of the Service serving in connection with the affairs of the Union, the Central Government; or

(ii) in the case of a member of the Service serving under a Foreign Government or outside India (whether on duty or on leave), the Central Government; or

(iii) in the case of a member of the Service serving in connection with the affairs of a State, the Government of that State;

Explanation—A member of the Service whose services are placed at the disposal of a company, corporation or other organisation or a local authority by the Central Government or the Government or the Government of a State shall for the purpose of these rules, be deemed to be a member of the Service serving in connection with the affairs of the Union or in connection with the affairs of that State, as the case may be, notwithstanding that his salary is drawn from the sources other than the Consolidated Fund of India or the Consolidated Fund of that State;

*　　　*　　　*　　　*

(c) "member of the Service" means a member of an All India Service as defined in section 2 of the All India Services Act, 1951 (61 of 1951)—

(d) "private undertaking" includes a company, firm or association or body of individuals.

9. Unauthorised communication of information.—No member of the Service shall except in accordance with any general or special order of the Government or in the performance in good faith of duties assigned to him, communicate directly or indirectly any official document or part thereof or information to any Government servant or any other person to whom he is not authorised to communicate such document or information.

Explanation: Quotation by a member of the Service (in his representations to the Head of Office or Head of Department or President) of, or from, any letter circular or office memorandum or from the notes on any file to which he is not authorised to have access, or which he is not authorised to keep in his personal custody or for personal purposes, shall amount to authorised communication of information within the meaning of this rule.

THE ATOMIC ENERGY ACT, 1962
(Relevant Provisions)

3. General powers of the Central Government.—Subject to the provisions of this Act, Central Government shall have power—

(a) to produce, develop, use and dispose of atomic energy either by itself or through any authority or corporation established by it or a Government company and carry out research into any matters connected therewith;

(b) to manufacture or otherwise produce any prescribed or radioactive substance and any articles which in its opinion are, or are likely to be, required for, or in connection with, the production, development or use of atomic energy or such research as aforesaid and to dispose of such described or radioactive substance or any articles manufactured or otherwise produced.

(i) to buy or otherwise acquire, store and transport any prescribed or radioactive substance and any articles which in its opinion are, or are likely to be, required for, or in connection with, the production, development or use of atomic energy; and (ii) to dispose of such prescribed or radioactive substance or any articles bought or otherwise acquired by it either by itself or through any authority or corporation established by it, or by a Government company;

(c) to declare as "restricted information" any information not so far published or otherwise made public relating to—

(i) the location, quality and quantity of prescribed substances and transactions for their acquisition, whether by purchase or otherwise, or disposal, whether by sale or otherwise;

(ii) the processing of prescribed substances and the extraction or production of fissile materials from them;

(iii) the theory, design, construction and operation of plants for the treatment and production of any of the prescribed substances and for the separation of isotopes;

(iv) the theory, design, construction and operation of nuclear reactors; and

(v) research and technological work on materials and processes involved in or derived from items (i) to (iv);

(d) to declare as "prohibited area" any area or premises where work including research, design or development is carried on in respect of the production, treatment, use, application or disposal of atomic energy or of any prescribed substance;

(e) to provide for control over radioactive substances or radiation generating plant in order to—

(i) prevent radiation hazards;

(ii) secure public safety and safety of persons handling radioactive substances or radiation generating plant; and

(iii) ensure safe disposal of radioactive wastes;

(f) to provide for the production and supply of electricity from atomic energy and for taking measures conducive to such production and supply and for all matters incidental thereto either by itself or through any authority or corporation established by it or a Government company;

(g) to do all such things (including the erection of buildings and execution of works and the working of minerals) as the Central Government considers necessary or expedient for the exercise of the foregoing powers.

18. Restriction on disclosure of information.—(1) The Central Government may by order restrict the disclosure of information, whether contained in a document, drawing, photograph, plan, model or in any other form whatsoever, which relates to, represents or illustrates—

(a) an existing or proposed plant used or proposed to be used for the purpose of producing, developing or using atomic energy, or

(b) the purpose or method of operation of any such existing or proposed plant, or

(c) any process operated or proposed to be operated in any such existing or proposed plant.

(2) No person shall—

(a) disclose, or obtain or attempt to obtain any information restricted under sub-section (1), or

(b) disclose, without the authority of the Central Government, any information obtained in the discharge of any functions under this Act or in the performance of his official duties.

(3) Nothing in this section shall apply—

(i) to the disclosure of information with respect to any plant of a type in use for purposes other than the production, development or use of atomic energy, unless the information discloses that plant of that type is used or proposed to be used for the production, development or use of atomic energy or research into any matters connected therewith; or

(ii) where any information has been made available to the general public otherwise than in contravention of this section, to any subsequent disclosure of that information.

THE BUREAU OF INDIAN STANDARDS ACT, 1986
(Relevant Provisions)

30. Certain matters to be kept confidential.—any information obtained by an inspecting officer or the bureau from any statement made or information supplied or any evidence given or from inspection made under the provisions of this act shall be treated as confidential:

Provided that nothing in this section shall apply to the disclosure of any information for the purpose of prosecution under this act.

THE CENTRAL CIVIL SERVICES (CONDUCT) RULES, 1964

(8.2.1) Sub: Communication to the Press by Officials

Reference (i) this office letter of even number dated 4.11.67 communicating *inter alia* the directive issued by the Governing Body of the CSIR at its meeting held on 5.7.1967 to the effect that steps should be taken to put a stop to unauthorised publications in the press in the interest of the efficient working of the CSIR, and (ii) this office endorsement No. 33(11)/67-G(A) dated 2.9.67 circulating Home Ministry's Office Memorandum No. 2519/67. Estt(A) dated 4.7.67 regarding safeguards against leakage of classified official information through the press.

1. The question of communication to the press by officials of the CSIR again came up for discussion at the meeting of the Governing Body held on 24 July 1970.

2. There was considerable discussion. The President, CSIR, summed up that as far as scientific matters were concerned, scientists should have freedom to publish their work and express their views. They should also be encouraged to publish their research findings. Scientists should also have freedom to express their views on scientific policies but when it came to ventilating their personal or individual grievances or expressing their views on organisational matters, it would not be proper for them to go to the press.

3. The Governing Body agreed that the Directors and others should desist from going to the press to ventilate their individual grievances or to express views on organisational matters but that they should have freedom to publicise scientific work and also

express their views on scientific policies and directed that suitable instructions may be formulated and issued in this connection.

4. In. view of the above directive of the Governing Body, the attention of all concerned is, once again, drawn to the relevant provisions in this regard as contained in the Manual of the Office Procedure and the Central Civil Services (Conduct) Rules, 1964, which are reproduced in the enclosed annexure for ready reference and which would apply to CSIR employees subject to the following modifications—

(a) Scientists shall have freedom to publicise scientific work

(b) Scientists shall have the freedom to express their views on scientific policies.

(CSIR Letter No: 1/31/65-VIG., dated 28 November 1970)

Relevant extracts from the provisions in the Central Civil Services (Conduct) Rules, 1964 and the Manual of Ofrice Procedure, as made applicable to the employees of the CSIR.

C.C.S. (Conduct) Rules, 1964: "(8) Connection with Press or Radio: No Government servant shall, except with the previous sanction of the Government or the prescribed authority, or in the *bona fide* discharge of his duties, participate in a radio broadcast or contribute any article or write any letter either in his own name or anonymously, pseudonymously or in the name of any other person to any newspaper or periodical:

Provided that no such sanction shall be required if such broadcast or such contribution is of a purely literary, artistic or scientific character."

11. Unauthorised communication of information: "No Government servant shall, except in accordance with any general or special order of the Government or in the performance in good faith of the duties assigned to him, communicate, directly or indirectly, any official document or any part thereof or information to any Government servant or any other person to whom he is not authorised to communicate such document or information."

"**9. Criticism of Government:** No Government servant shall, in any radio broadcast or in any document published in his own name or anonymously, pseudonymously or in the name of any other person or in any communication to the press or in any public utterance, make any statement of fact or opinion.

(i) which has the effect of an adverse criticism of any current or recent policy or action of the Central Government or a State Government: Provided that in the case of any Government servant included in any category of Government servants specified in the second proviso to sub-rule (3) of Rule 1, nothing contained in this clause shall apply to bonafide expression of views by him as an office bearer of a trade union of such Government servants for purpose of safeguarding the conditions of service of such Government servants or for securing an improvement thereof; or

(ii) which is capable of embarrassing the relations between the Central Government and the Government of any state; or

(iii) Which is capable of embarrassing the relations between the Central Government and the Government of any foreign state.

Provided that nothing in this rule shall apply to any statements made or views expressed by a Government servant in his official capacity or in the due performance of the duties assigned to him."

Manual of Office Procedure

154. Communication of information to the press: "Information to the Press should normally be communicated through the Press information Bureau by an officer authorised to do so."

155. Functions of Information Officer: Information Officers of the Press Information Bureau are attached to every Ministry of the Government of India. It is the duty of an Information Officer, on the one hand, to arrange to give due publicity to the activities of the Ministry to which he is attached and on the other, to keep the Ministry informed of the popular reactions thereto. In order to discharge his duties properly, the Information Officer will maintain a close liaison with the Ministry to which he is attached and the latter will give him the necessary facilities."

161. Communication of information to the press: "Only Ministers, Secretaries or other officers specially authorised by the Minister, may give information or be accessible to the representative of the Press. Any other officer, if approached by a representative of the Press, should refer him to the Principal Information officer of Government of India."

Re-Issue of Press Release, etc.

The policy on issue of press release as also publicity of work done, such as development of processes, etc. in our Laboratories, was reviewed by DGSIR recently. It was felt that while our achievements need to be publicised, and ill-informed criticism of the CSIR should be rebutted, there is need for some caution in this regard. Instances have come to light where premature and undue publicity has been given to the processes developed in the Laboratories which in the long run prove counterproductive.

Press releases, particularly on major issues, should be issued only with DGSIR's approval. Similarly, the Newsletters brought out by the Laboratories and the CSIR News should not also publish premature information about the achievements made in different Laboratories.

(CSIR Circular No. 1(28)/80-E III, dated 24 Nov. 1981).

(8.2.2) Release of Information to the Press

Instructions have been issued by CSIR from time to time regarding the procedure for making available information to the press by the CSIR Laboratories and scientists. According to these instructions while the information on policy matters could be made available to the press only by DGSIR, the information on scientific matters could not be given by a scientist or any other employee below the Director. Instances have however come to notice where individual scientists have given information to the press in violation of these guidelines which has caused embarrassment to the organisation as a whole.

I shall be grateful if these instructions are brought to the notice of all scientists and other employees of your Laboratory for strict compliance. Any violation of these instructions should be seriously viewed and disciplinary action taken.

CSIR Letter No. D.O.No. 1198/86-Vig. dated 19 July 1986.

THE CODE OF CRIMINAL PROCEDURE, 1973

(Relevant Provisions)

50. Person arrested to be informed of grounds of arrest and of right to bail.—(1) Every police officer or other person arresting any person without warrant shall forthwith communicate to him full particulars of the offence for which he is arrested or other grounds for such arrest.

(2) Where a police officer arrests without warrant any person other than a person accused of a non-bailable offence, he shall inform the person arrested that he is entitled to be released on bail and that he may arrange for sureties on his behalf.

50A. Obligation of person making arrest to inform about the arrest, etc. to a nominated person.—(1) Every police officer or other person making any arrest under this Code shall forthwith give the information regarding such arrest and place where the arrested person is being held to any of his friends, relatives or such other persons as may be disclosed or nominated by the arrested person for the purpose of giving such information.

(2) The police officer shall inform the arrested person of his rights under sub-section (1) as soon as he is brought to the police station.

(3) An entry of the fact as to who has been informed of the arrest of such person shall be made in a book to be kept in the police station in such form as may be prescribed in this behalf by the State Government.

(4) It shall be the duty of the Magistrate before whom such arrested person is produced, to satisfy himself that the

requirements of sub-section (2) and sub-section (3) have been complied with in respect of such arrested person.

207. Supply to the accused of copy of police report and other documents.—In any case where the proceeding has been instituted on a police report, the Magistrate shall without delay furnish to the accused, free of cost, a copy of each of the following:

(i) The police report;

(ii) The first information report recorded under section 154:

(iii) The statements recorded under sub-section (3) of section 161 of all persons whom the prosecution proposes to examine as its witnesses, excluding therefrom any part in regard to which a request for such exclusion has been made by the police officer under sub-section (6) of section 173;

(iv) The confessions and statements, if any, recorded under section 164;

(v) Any other document or relevant extract thereof forwarded to the Magistrate with the police report under sub-section (5) of section 173:

Provided that the Magistrate may, after perusing any such part of a statement as is referred to in clause (iii) and considering the reasons given by the police officer for the request, direct that a copy of that part of the statement or of such portion thereof as the Magistrate thinks proper, shall be furnished to the accused:

Provided further that if the Magistrate is satisfied that any document referred to in Clause (v) is voluminous, he shall, instead of furnishing the accused with a copy thereof, direct that he will only be allowed to inspect it either personally or through pleader in court.

208. Supply of copies of statements and documents to accused in other cases triable by Court of Session.—Where, in a case instituted otherwise than on a police report, it appears to the Magistrate issuing process under section 204 that the offence is triable exclusively by the Court of Session, the Magistrate shall without delay furnish to the accused, free of cost, a copy of each of the following:

(i) The statements recorded under section 200 or section 202, or all persons examined by the Magistrate;

(ii) The statements and confessions, if any, recorded under section 161 or section 164;

(iii) Any documents produced before the Magistrate on which the prosecution proposes to rely:

Provided that if the Magistrate is satisfied that any such document is voluminous, he shall, instead of furnishing the accused with a copy thereof, direct that he will only be allowed to inspect it either personally or through pleader in court.

THE COMPANIES ACT, 1956

(Relevant Provisions)

39. Copies of memorandum and articles, etc. to be given to members.—(1) A company shall, on being so required by a member, send to him within seven days of the requirement and subject to the payment of a fee of one rupee, a copy of each of the following documents as in force for the time being:

(a) The memorandum;

(b) The articles, if any;

(c) every other agreement and every resolution referred to in section 192, if and in so far as they have not been embodied in the memorandum or articles.

(2) If a company makes default in complying with the requirements of this section, the company, and every officer of the company who is in default, shall be punishable, for each offence, with fine which may extend to five hundred rupees.

1. Clause (c) omitted by Act 53 of 2000, sec. 10 (w.e.f. 13-12-2000).

2. Subs. by Act 53 of 2000, sec. 10, for "fifty rupees" (w.e.f. 13-12-2000).

40. Alteration of memorandum or articles, etc. to be noted in every copy.—(1) Where an alteration is made in the memorandum or articles of a company, 1[. . .], or any resolution referred to in section 192, every copy of the memorandum, articles, agreement or resolution issued after the date of the alteration shall be in accordance with the alteration.

(2) If, at any time, the company issues any copies of the memorandum, articles resolution or agreement, which are not in accordance with the alteration or alterations made therein before

that time, the company, and every officer of the company who is in default, shall be punishable with fine which may extend to one hundred rupees for each copy so issued.

1. Certain words omitted by Act 53 of 2000, sec. 11 (13-12-2000).
2. Subs. by Act 53 of 2000, sec. 11, for "ten rupees" (w.e.f. 13-12-2000).

53. Service of documents on members by company.—(1) A document may be served by a company on any member thereof either personally, or by sending it by post to him to his registered address, or if he has no registered address in India, to the address, if any, within India supplied by him to the company for the giving of notices to him.

(2) Where a document is sent by post,

(a) service thereof shall be deemed to be effected by properly addressing, prepaying and posting a letter containing the document, provided that where a member has intimated to the company in advance that documents should be sent to him under a certificate of posting or by registered post with or without acknowledgement due and has deposited with the company a sum sufficient to defray the expenses of doing so, service of the document shall not be deemed to be effected unless it is sent in the manner intimated by the member; and

(b) 1[...] such service shall be deemed to have been effected:

(i) in the case of a notice of a meeting, at the expiration of forty-eight hours after the letter containing the same is posted, and

(ii) in any other case at the time at which the letter would be delivered in the ordinary course of post.

(3) A document advertised in a newspaper circulating in the neighbourhood of the registered office of the company shall be deemed to be duly served on the day on which the advertisement appears, on every member of the company who has no registered

address in India and has not supplied to the company an address within India for the giving of notices to him.

(4) A document may be served by the company on the joint-holders of a share by serving it on the joint-holder named first in the register in respect of the share.

(5) A document may be served by the company on the persons entitled to a share in consequence of the death or insolvency of a member by sending it through the post in a prepaid letter addressed to them by name, or by the title of representatives of the deceased, or assignees of the insolvent, or by any like description, at the address, if any, in India supplied for the purpose by the persons claiming to be so entitled, or until such an address has been so supplied, by serving the document in any manner in which it might have been served if the death or insolvency had not occurred.

1. The words "unless the contrary is proved", omitted by Act 65 of 1960, sec. 16 (w.e.f. 28-12-1960).

54. Authentication of documents and proceedings.— Save as otherwise expressly provided in this Act, a document or proceeding requiring authentication by a company may be signed by a director, 1[...] the manager, the secretary or other authorised officer of the company, and need not be under its common seal.

1. The words "the managing agent, secretaries and treasurers" omitted by Act 53 of 2000, sec. 15 (w.e.f. 13-12-2000).

60B. Information memorandum.—(1) A public company making an issue of securities may circulate information memorandum to the public prior to filing of a prospectus.

(2) A company inviting subscription by an information memorandum shall be bound to file a prospectus prior to the opening of the subscription lists and the offer as a red-herring prospectus, at least three days before the opening of the offer.

(3) The information memorandum and red-herring prospectus shall carry same obligations as are applicable in the case of a prospectus.

(4) Any variation between the information memorandum and the red-herring prospectus shall be highlighted as variations by the issuing company.

Explanation: For the purposes of sub-sections (2), (3) and (4), "red-herring prospectus" means a prospectus which does not have complete particulars on the price of the securities offered and the quantum of securities offered.

(5) Every variation as made and highlighted in accordance with sub-section (4) above shall be individually intimated to the persons invited to subscribe to the issue of securities.

(6) In the event of the issuing company or the underwriters to the issue have invited or received advance subscription by way of cash or post-dated cheques or stock-invest, the company or such underwriters or bankers to the issue shall not encash such subscription money or post-dated cheques or stock-invest before the date of opening of the issue, without having individually intimated the prospective subscribers of the variation and without having offered an opportunity to such prospective subscribers to withdraw their application and cancel their post-dated cheques or stock-invest or return of subscription paid.

(7) The applicant or proposed subscriber shall exercise his right to withdraw from the application on any intimation of variation within seven days from the date of such intimation and shall indicate such withdrawal in writing to the company and the underwriters.

(8) Any application for subscription which is acted upon by the company or underwriters or bankers to the issue without having given enough information of any variations, or the particulars of withdrawing the offer or opportunity for cancelling the post-dated cheques or stock-invest or stop payments for such payments shall be void and the applicants shall be entitled to receive a refund or return of its post-dated cheques or stock-invest or subscription moneys or cancellation of its application, as if the said application had never been made and the applicants are entitled to receive back their original application and interest at the rate of fifteen per cent from the date of encashment till payment of realisation.

(9) Upon the closing of the offer of securities, a final prospectus stating therein the total capital raised, whether by way of debt or share capital and the closing price of the securities

and any other details as were not complete in the red-herring prospectus shall be filed in a case of a listed public company with the Securities and Exchange Board and Registrar, and in any other case with the Registrar only.

61. Terms of contract mentioned in prospectus or statement in lieu of prospectus, not to be varied.—A company shall not, at any time, vary the terms of a contract referred to in the prospectus or statement in lieu of prospectus, except subject to the approval of, or except on authority given by, the company in general meeting.

63. Criminal liability for mis-statements in prospectus.—(1) Where a prospectus issued after the commencement of this Act includes any untrue statement, every person who authorised the issue of the prospectus shall be punishable with imprisonment for a term which may extend to two years, or with fine which may extend to fifty thousand rupees, or with both, unless he proves either that the statement was immaterial or that he had reasonable ground to believe, and did up to the time of the issue of the prospectus believe, that the statement was true.

(2) A person shall not be deemed for the purposes of this section to have authorised the issue of a prospectus by reason only of his having given —

(a) the consent required by section 58 to the inclusion therein of a statement purporting to be made by him as an expert, or

(b) the consent required by 2[...] sub-section (3) of section 60.

1. Subs. by Act 53 of 2000, sec. 23, for five thousand rupees (w.e.f. 13-12-2000).
2. The words "clause (b) of" omitted by Act 65 of 1960, sec 19 (w.e.f. 28-12-1960).

64. Document containing offer of shares or ebentures for sale to be deemed prospectus.—(1) Where a company allots or agrees to allot any shares in or debentures of the company with a view to all or any of those shares or debentures being offered for sale to the public, any document by which the offer for sale to the public is made shall, for all purposes, be deemed to be a prospectus issued by the company; and all enactment and rules of law as to the contents of prospectuses and as to liability in respect of statements in and omissions from prospectuses, or otherwise relating to prospectuses, shall apply with the modifications specified in sub-section (3), (4) and (5), and have effect accordingly, as if the shares or debentures had been offered to the public for subscription and as if person accepting the offer in respect of any shares or debentures were subscribers for those shares or debentures, but without prejudice to the liability, if any, of the persons by whom the offer is made in respect of mis-statements contained in the document or otherwise in respect thereof.

(2) For the purposes of this Act, it shall, unless the contrary is proved, be evidence that an allotment of, or an agreement to allot, shares or debentures was made with a view to the shares or debentures being offered for sale to the public if it is shown:

(a) that an offer of the shares or debentures or of any of them for sale to the public was made within six months after the allotment or agreement to allot; or

(b) that at the date when the offer was made, the whole consideration to be received by the company in respect of the shares or debentures had not been received by it.

(3) Section 56 as applied by this section shall have effect as if it required a prospectus to state in addition to the matters required by that section to be stated in a prospectus:

(a) the net amount of the consideration received or to be received by the company in respect of the shares or debentures to which the offer relates; and

(b) the place and time at which the contract under which the said shares or debentures have been or are to be allotted may be inspected.

(4) Section 60 as applied by this section shall have effect as if the persons making the offer were persons named in a prospectus as directors of a company.

(5) Where a person making an offer to which this section relates is a company or a firm, it shall be sufficient if the document referred to in sub-section (1) is signed on behalf of the company or firm by two directors of the company or by not less than one-half of the partners in the firm, as the case may be; and any such director or partner may sign by his agent authorised in writing.

118. Right to obtain copies of and inspect trust deed.— (1) A copy of any trust deed for securing any issue of debentures shall be forwarded to the holder of any such debentures or any member of the company, at his request and within seven days of the making thereof, on payment:

(a) In the case of a printed trust deed, of 1[such sum as may be prescribed]; and

(b) In the case of a trust deed which has not been printed, of 2[such sum as may be prescribed], for every one hundred words or fractional part thereof required to be copied.

(2) If a copy is refused, or is not forwarded within the time specified in sub-section (1), the company, and every officer of the company who is in default, shall be punishable, for each offence, with fine which may extend to 3[five hundred rupees] and with a further fine which may extend to 4[two hundred rupees] for every day during which the offence continues.

(3) The 5[Central Government] may also, by order, direct that the copy required shall forthwith be sent to the person requiring it.

(4) The trust deed referred to in sub-section (1) shall also be open to inspection by any member or debenture holder of the company in the same manner, to the same extent, and on repayment of the same fees, as if it were the register of members of the company.

1. Subs. by Act 31 of 1988. sec. 67, for "the sum of one rupee" (w.e.f. 15-7-1988).
2. Subs. by Act 31 of 1988. sec. 67, for "six annas" (w.e.f. 15-7-1988).
3. Substituted by Act 53 of 2000, sec. 49, for "fifty rupees" (w.e.f. 13-12-2000).

4. Substituted by Act 53 of 2000, sec. 49, for "twenty rupees" (w.e.f. 13-12-2000).
5. Substituted by Act 31 of 1988, sec. 67, for "Court" (w.e.f. 31-5-1991) and again subs. by Act 11 of 2003, sec. 19 for "Company Law Board".

136. Copy of instrument creating charge to be kept by company at registered office.—Every company shall cause a copy of every instrument creating any charge requiring registration under this Part to be kept at the registered office of the company:

Provided that, in the case of a series of uniform debentures, a copy of one debenture of the series shall be sufficient.

144. Right to inspect copies of instruments creating charges and company's register of charges.—(1) The copies of instruments creating charges kept in pursuance of section 136, and the register of charges kept in pursuance of section 143, shall be open during business hours (but subject to such reasonable restrictions as the company in general meeting may impose, so that not less than two hours in each day are allowed for inspection) to the inspection of any creditor or member of the company without fee, at the registered office of the company.

(2) The register of charges kept in pursuance of section 143 shall also be open, during business hours but subject to the reasonable restrictions aforesaid, to the inspection of any other person on payment of a fee of 1[such sum as may be prescribed] for each inspection, at the registered office of the company.

(3) If the inspection of the said copies or register is refused, the company, and every officer of the company who is in default, shall be punishable with fine which may extend to 2[five hundred rupees] and with a further fine which may extend to 3[two hundred rupees] for every day during which the refusal continues.

(4) The 4[Central Government] may also by order compel an immediate inspection of the said copies or register.

1. Subs. by Act 31 of 1988, sec. 67, for "one rupee" (w.e.f. 15-7-1988).
2. Subs. by Act 53 of 2000, sec. 55, for "fifty rupees" (w.e.f. 13-12-2000).

3. Subs. by Act 53 of 2000, sec. 55, for "twenty rupees" (w.e.f. 13-12-2000).
4. Substituted by Act 31 of 1988, sec. 67, for "Court" (w.e.f. 31-5-1991) and again subs. by Act 11 of 2003, sec. 21, for "Company Law Board".

197. Publication of reports of proceedings of general meetings.—(1) No document purporting to be a report of the proceedings of any general meeting of a company shall be circulated or advertised at the expense of the company, unless it includes the matters required by section 193 to be contained in the minutes of the proceedings of such meeting.

(2) If any report is circulated or advertised in contravention of sub-section (1), the company, and every officer of the company who is in default, shall be punishable, in respect of each offence, with fine which may extend to 1[five thousand rupees].

1. Subs. by Act 53 of 2000, sec. 83, for "five hundred rupees" (w.e.f. 13-12-2000).

222. Construction of references to documents annexed to accounts.—References in this Act to documents annexed or required to be annexed to a company's accounts or any of them shall not include the Board's report, the auditors' report or any document attached or required to be attached to those accounts:

Provided that any information which is required by this Act to be given in the accounts, and is allowed by it to be given in a statement annexed to the accounts, may be given in the Board's report instead of in the accounts; and if any such information is so given, the report shall be annexed to the accounts and this Act shall apply in relation thereto accordingly, except that the auditors shall report thereon only in so far as it gives the said information.

223. Certain companies to publish statement in the Form in Table F in Schedule I.—(1) Every company which is a limited banking company, an insurance company or a deposit, provident or benefit society, shall, before it commences business and also on the first Monday in February and the first Monday in August in every year during which it carries on business, make a statement in the Form in Table F in Schedule I, or in a Form as near thereto as circumstances admit.

(2) A copy of the statement, together with a copy of the last audited balance sheet laid before the members of the company, shall be displayed and until the display of the next following statement, shall be kept displayed, in a conspicuous place in the registered office of the company, and in every branch office or place where the business of the company is carried on.

(3) Every member and every creditor of the company shall be entitled, on payment of a sum of eight annas, to be furnished with a copy of the statement, within seven days of such payment.

(4) If default is made in complying with any of the requirements of this section, the company, and every officer of the company who is in default, shall be punishable with fine which may extend to 1[five hundred rupees] for every day during which the default continues.

(5) This section shall not apply to a life assurance company or provident insurance society to which the provisions of the Insurance Act, 1938 (4 of 1938), as to the annual statements to be made by such company or society, apply with or without modifications, if the company or society complies with those provisions.

1. Subs. by Act 53 of 2000, sec. 106, for "fifty rupees" (w.e.f. 13-12-2000).

305. Duty of directors etc. to make disclosure.—(1) Every director, managing director, 2[...] manager or secretary of any company, who is appointed to or relinquishes, the office of director, managing director, 2[...] manager or secretary of any other body corporate, shall, within twenty days of his appointment to, or as the case may be, relinquishment of, such office, disclose to the company aforesaid the particulars relating to the office in the other body corporate which are required to be specified under sub-section (1) of section 303; and if he fails to do so, he shall be punishable with fine which may extend to 3[five thousand rupees].

(2) The provisions of sub-section (1) shall also apply to a person deemed to be a director of the company by virtue of the Explanation to sub-section (1) of section 303 when such person is appointed to, or relinquishes, any of the offices in the other body corporate refer1red to in sub-section (1).

1. Subs. by Act 65 of 1960, sec. 11, for section 305 (w.e.f. 28-12-1960).
2. The words "managing agent, secretaries and treasurers" omitted by Act 53 of 2000, sec. 150 (w.e.f. 13-12-2000).
3. Subs. by Act 53 of 2000, sec. 150, for "five hundred rupees" (w.e.f. 13-12-2000).

306. Register to be kept by Registrar and inspection thereof.—(1) The Registrar shall keep a separate register or registers in which there shall be entered the particulars received by him under sub-section (2) of section 303 in respect of companies, so however, that all entries in respect of each such company shall be together.

(2) The register or registers aforesaid shall be open to inspection by any member of the public at any time during office hours, on payment of the prescribed fee.

307. Register of directors' shareholdings, etc.—(1) Every company shall keep a register showing, as respects each director of the company, the number, description and amount of any shares in, or debentures of, the company or any other body corporate, being the company's subsidiary or holding company, or a subsidiary of the company's holding company, which are held by him or in trust for him, or of which he has any right to become the holder whether on payment or not.

(2) Where any shares or debentures have to be recorded in the said register or to be omitted therefrom, in relation to any director, by reason of a transaction entered into after the commencement of this Act and while he is a director, the register shall also show the date of, and the price or other consideration for, the transaction:

Provided that where there is an interval between the agreement for any such transaction and the completion thereof, the date so shown shall be that of the agreement.

(3) The nature and extent of any interest or right in or over any shares or debentures recorded in relation to a director in the said register shall, if he so requires be indicated in the register.

(4) The company shall not, by virtue of anything done for the purposes of this section, be affected with notice, of, or be put upon inquiry as to, the rights of any person in relation to any shares or debentures.

(5) The said register shall, subject to the provisions of this section, be kept at the registered office of the company, and shall be open to inspection during business hours (subject to such reasonable restrictions as the company may, by its articles or in general meeting, impose, so that not less than two hours in each day are allowed for inspection) as follows:

(a) during the period beginning fourteen days before the date of the company's annual general meeting and ending three days after the date of its conclusion, it shall be open to the inspection of any member or holder or debentures of the company; and

(b) during that or any other period, it shall be open to the inspection of any person acting on behalf of the Central Government or of the Registrar.

In computing the fourteen days and the three days mentioned in this sub-section any day which is a Saturday, a Sunday or a public holiday shall be disregarded.

(6) Without prejudice to the rights conferred by sub-section (5), the Central Government or the Registrar may, at any time require a copy of the said register, or any part thereof.

(7) The said register shall also be produced at the commencement of every annual general meeting of the company and shall remain open and accessible during the continuance of the meeting to any person having the right to attend the meeting.

If default is made in complying with this sub-section the company, and every officer of the company who is in default, shall be punishable with fine which may extend to 1[five thousand rupees].

(8) If default is made in complying with sub-section (1) or (2), or if any inspection required under this section is refused, or if any copy required thereunder is not sent within a reasonable time, the company, and every officer of the company who is in default, shall be punishable with fine which may extend to 2[fifty

thousand rupees] and also with a further fine which may extend to 3[two hundred rupees] for every day during which the default continues.

(9) In the case of any such refusal, thc 4[Ccntral Government or Tribunal, as the case may be], may also, by order, compel an immediate inspection of the register.

(10) For the purposes of this section—

(a) any person in accordance with whose directions or instructions the Board of directors of a company is accustomed to act, shall be deemed to be a director of the company; and

(b) a director of a company shall be deemed to hold, or to have an interest or a right in or over, any shares or debentures, if a body corporate other than the company holds them or has that interest or right in or over them, and either—

(i) that body corporate or its Board of directors is accustomed to act in accordance with his directions or instructions; or

(ii) he is entitled to exercise or control the exercise of one-third or more of the total voting power exercisable at any general meeting of that body corporate.

5[***]

1. Subs. by Act 53 of 2000, sec. 151, for "five hundred rupees" (w.e.f. 13-12-2000).
2. Subs. by Act 53 of 2000, sec. 151, for "five thousand rupees" (w.e.f. 13-12-2000).
3. Subs. by Act 53 of 2000, sec. 151, for "twenty rupees" (w.e.f. 13-12-2000).
4. Subs. by Act 31 of 1988, sec. 67, for "Court" (w.e.f. 31-5-1991) and again subs, by Act 11 of 2003, sec. 35, for "Company Law Board".
5. Sub-section (11) ins. by Act 65 of 1960, sec. 112 (w.e.f. 28-12-1960) and omitted by Act 53 of 2000, sec. 151 (w.e.f. 13-12-2000).

308. Duty of directors and persons deemed to be directors to make disclosure of shareholdings.—(1) Every director of a company, and every person deemed to be a director of the company by virtue of sub-section (10) of section 307, shall give notice to the company of such matters relating to himself as may be necessary for the purpose of enabling the company to comply with the provisions of that section.

(2) Any such notice shall be given in writing, and if it is not given at a meeting of the Board, the person giving the notice shall take all reasonable steps to secure that it is brought up and read at the meeting of the Board next after it is given.

(3) Any person who fails to comply with sub-section (1) or (2) shall be punishable with imprisonment for a term which may extend to two years, or with fine which may extend to 1[fifty thousand rupees], or with both.

1. Subs. by Act 53 of 2000, sec. 152, for "five thousand rupees" (w.e.f. 13-12-2000)

393. Information as to compromises or arrangements with creditors and members.—(1) Where a meeting of creditors or any class of creditors, or of members or any class of members, is called under section 391—

(a) with every notice calling the meeting which is sent to a creditor or member, there shall also be sent a statement setting forth the terms of the compromise or arrangement and explaining its effect; and in particular, stating any material interests of the directors, managing director 1[***] or manager of the company, whether in their capacity as such or as members or creditors of the company or otherwise, and the effect on those interests of the compromise or arrangement if, and in so far as, it is different from the effect on the like interests of other persons; and

(b) in every notice calling the meeting which is given by advertisement, there shall be included either such a statement as aforesaid or a notification of the place at which and the manner in which creditors or members entitled to attend the meeting may obtain copies of such a statement as aforesaid.

(2) Where the compromise or arrangement affects the rights of debenture-holders of the company, the said statement shall give the like information and explanation as respects the trustees of any deed for securing the issue of the debentures as it is required to give as respects the company's directors.

(3) Where a notice given by advertisement includes a notification that copies of a statement setting forth the terms of the compromise or arrangement proposed and explaining its effect can be obtained by creditors or members entitled to attend the meeting, every creditor or member so entitled shall, on making an application in the manner indicated by the notice, be furnished by the company, free of charge, with a copy of the statement.

(4) Where default is made in complying with any of the requirements of this section, the company, and every officer of the company who is in default, shall be punishable with fine which may extend to 2[fifty thousand rupees]; and for the purpose of this sub-section any liquidator of the company and any trustee of a deed for securing the issue of debentures of the company shall be deemed to be an officer of the company:

Provided that a person shall not be punishable under this sub-section if he shows that the default was due to the refusal of any other person, being a director, managing director, 1[***] manager or trustee for debenture holders, to supply the necessary particulars as to his material interests.

(5) Every director, managing director, 1[***] or manager of the company, and every trustee for debenture holders of the company, shall give notice to the company of such matters relating to himself as may be necessary for the purposes of this section; and if he fails to do so, he shall be punishable with fine which may extend to 3[five thousand rupees].

1. The words "managing agent, secretaries and treasurers,"omitted by Act 53 of 2000, sec. 175 (w.e.f. 13-12-2000).
2. Subs. by Act 53 of 2000, sec. 175, for "five thousand rupees" (w.e.f. 13-12-2000).

3. Subs. by Act 53 of 2000, sec. 175, for "five hundred rupees" (w.e.f. 13-12-2000).

424J. Power of Tribunal to call for periodic information.— On receipt of reference under section 424A, the Tribunal may call for any periodic information from the company as to the steps taken by the company to make its net worth exceed the accumulated losses or to make repayment of its debts referred to in that section, as the case may be, and the company shall furnish such information.

461. Books to be kept by liquidator.—(1) The liquidator shall keep, in the manner prescribed, proper books in which he shall cause entries or minutes to be made of proceedings at meetings and of such other matters as may be prescribed.

(2) Any creditor or contributory may, subject to the control of the 1[Tribunal], inspect any such books, personally or by his agent.

1. Subs. by Act 11 of 2003, sec. 70, for "Cour

485. Publication of resolution to wind-up voluntarily.—(1) When a company has passed a resolution for voluntary winding up, it shall, within fourteen days of the passing of the resolution, give notice of the resolution by advertisement in the Official Gazette, and also in some newspaper circulating in the district where the registered office of the company is situated.

(2) If default is made in complying with sub-section (1), the company, and every officer of the company who is in default, shall be punishable with fine which may extend to 1[five hundred rupees] for every day during which the default continues.

For the purposes of this sub-section, a liquidator of the company shall be deemed to be an officer of the company.

1. Subs. by Act 53 of 2000, sec. 192, for "fifty rupees" (w.e.f. 13-12-2000).

488. Declaration of solvency in case of proposal to wind-up voluntarily.—(1) Where it is proposed to wind up a company voluntarily, its directors, or in case the company has more than two directors, the majority of the directors, may, at a meeting of the Board, make a declaration verified by an affidavit, to the effect that they have made a full inquiry into the affairs of the company, and that, having done so, they have formed the opinion that the company has no debts, or that it will be able to pay its debts in full within such period not exceeding three years from the commencement of the winding up as may be specified in the declaration.

(2) A declaration made as aforesaid shall have no effect for the purposes of this Act, unless—

(a) it is made within the five weeks immediately preceding the date of the passing of the resolution for winding up the company and is delivered to the Registrar for registration before that date; and

1(b) it is accompanied by a copy of the report of the auditors of the company (prepared, as far as circumstances admit, in accordance with the provisions of this Act) on the profit and loss account of the company for the period commencing from the date up to which the last such account was prepared and ending with the latest practicable date immediately before the making of the declaration and the balance sheet of the company made out as on the last-mentioned date and also embodies a statement of the company's assets and liabilities as at that date.

(3) Any director of a company making a declaration under this section without having reasonable grounds for the opinion that the company will be able to pay its debts in full within the period specified in the declaration, shall be punishable with imprisonment for a term which may extend to six months, or with fine which may extend to 2[fifty thousand rupees], or with both.

(4) If the company is wound up in pursuance of a resolution passed within the period of five weeks after the making of the declaration, but its debts are not paid or provided for in full within the period specified in the declaration, it shall be presumed, until the contrary is shown, that the director did not have reasonable grounds for his opinion.

(5) A winding up in the case of which a declaration has been made and delivered in accordance with this section is in this Act referred to as "a member's voluntary winding up"; and a winding up in the case of which a declaration has not been so made and delivered is in this Act referred to as a "a creditors' voluntary winding up".

1. Subs. by Act 65 of 1960, sec. 178, for clause (b) (w.e.f. 28-12-1960).
2. Subs. by Act 53 of 2000, sec. 193, for "five thousand rupees" (w.e.f. 13-12-2000).

489. Provisions applicable to a member's voluntary winding up.—The provisions contained in sections 490 to 498, both inclusive, shall subject to the provisions of section 498, apply in relation to a member's voluntary winding up.

548. Books and papers of company to be evidence.—Where a company is being wound up, all books and papers of the company and of the liquidators shall, as between the contributories of the company, be prima facie evidence of the truth of all matters purporting to be therein recorded.

550. Disposal of books and papers of company.—(1) When the affairs of a company have been completely wound up and it is about to be dissolved, its books and papers and those of the liquidator may be disposed of as follows, that is to say:

(a) in the case of a winding up by the Tribunal, in such manner as the Tribunal directs;

(b) in the case of a member's voluntary winding up, in such manner as the company by special resolution directs; and

(c) in the case of a creditor's voluntary winding up, in such manner as the committee of inspection or, if there is no such committee, as the creditors of the company may direct.

(2) After the expiry of five years from the dissolution of the company, no responsibility shall rest on the company, the liquidator, or any person to whom the custody of the books and papers has been

committed, by reason of any book or paper not being forthcoming to any person claiming to be interested therein.

(3) The Central Government may, by rules,

(a) prevent for such period (not exceeding five years from the dissolution of the company) as the Central Government thinks proper, the destruction of the books and papers of a company which has been wound up and of its liquidator; and

(b) enable any creditor or contributory of the company to make representations to the Central Government in respect of the matters specified in clause (a) and to 2[appeal to the Tribunal] from any direction which may be given by the Central Government in the matter.

(4) If any person acts in contravention of any such rules or of any direction of the Central Government thereunder, he shall be punishable with imprisonment for a term which may extend to six months, or with fine which may extend to 3[fifty thousand rupees], or with both.

1. Subs. by Act 11 of 2003, sec. 106, for clause (a).
2. Subs. by Act 11 of 2003, sec. 106, for "appeal to the Court".
3. Subs. by Act 53 of 2000, sec. 209, for "five thousand rupees" (w.e.f. 13-12-2000).

551. Information as to pending liquidations.—(1) If the winding up of a company is not concluded within one year after its commencement, the liquidator shall, unless he is exempted from doing so either wholly or in part by the Central Government, within two months of the expiry of such year and thereafter until the winding up is concluded, at intervals of not more than one year or at such shorter intervals, if any, as may be prescribed, file a statement in the prescribed form and containing the prescribed particulars duly audited, by a person qualified to act as auditor of the company, with respect to the proceedings in, and position of, the liquidation,

(a) in the case of a winding up by or subject to the supervision of the Court, in Court; and

(b) in the case of a voluntary winding up, with the Registrar:

Provided that no such audit as is referred to in this sub-section shall be necessary where the provisions of section 462 apply.

(2) When the statement is filed in Court under clause (a) of sub-section (1), a copy shall simultaneously be filed with the Registrar and shall be kept by him along with the other records of the company.

(2A) Where a statement referred to in sub-section (2) relates to Government company in liquidation, the liquidator shall forward a copy thereof,

(a) to the Central Government, if that Government is a member of the Government company; or

(b) to any State Government, if that Government is member of the Government company; or

(c) to the Central Government and any State Government, if both the Governments are members of the Government company.

(3) Any person stating himself in writing to be a creditor or contributory of the company shall be entitled, by himself or by his agent, at all reasonable times, on payment of the prescribed fee, to inspect the statement, and to receive a copy thereof or an extract therefrom.

(4) Any person untruthfully stating himself to be a creditor or contributor for the above purpose shall be deemed to be guilty of an offence under section 182 of the Indian Penal Code (45 of 1860), and shall, on the application of the liquidator, be punishable accordingly.

(5) If a liquidator fails to comply with any of the requirements of this section, he shall be punishable with fine which may extend to five hundred rupees for every day during which the failure continues:

Provided that if the liquidator makes wilful default in causing the statement referred to in sub-section (1) to be audited by person qualified to act as auditor of the company, the liquidator shall be punishable with imprisonment for a term which may extend to six months, or with fine which may extend to one thousand rupees, or with both.

610. Inspection, production and evidence of documents kept by Registrar.—(1) 2[Save as otherwise provided elsewhere in this Act, any person may]—

(a) inspect any documents kept by the Registrar 3[in accordance with the rules made under the Destruction of Records Act, 1917] being documents filed or registered by him in pursuance of this Act, or making a record of any fact required or authorised to be recorded or registered in pursuance of this Act, on payment for each inspection of 4[such fees as may be prescribed];

(b) require a certificate of the incorporation of any company, or a copy or extract of any other document or any part of any other document to be certified by the Registrar, 5[on payment in advance of 6[such fees as may be prescribed]:

Provided that the rights conferred by this sub-section shall be exercisable—

(i) in relation to documents delivered to the Registrar with a prospectus in pursuance of sub-clause (i) of clause (b) of sub-section (1) of section 60, only during the fourteen days beginning with the date of publication of the prospectus; and at other times, only with the permission of the Central Government; and

(ii) in relation to documents so delivered in pursuance of clause (b) of sub-section (1) of section 605, only during the fourteen days beginning with the date of the prospectus; and at other times, only with the permission of the Central Government.[1]

1. Inserted by the Companies (Amendment) Act, 1996, w.e.f. 1 March 1997.

(2) No process for compelling the production of any document kept by the Registrar shall issue from any Court 7[or the 9(Tribunal)] except with the leave of that Court 7[or the 9(Tribunal)] and any such process, if issued, shall bear thereon a statement that it is issued with the leave of the Court 7[or the 9(Tribunal)].

(3) A copy of, or extract from, any document kept and registered at any of the officers for the registration of companies under this Act, certified to be a true copy under the hand of the Registrar (whose official position it shall not be necessary to prove), shall, in all legal proceedings, be admissible in evidence as of equal validity with the original document. 8[***]

1. Omitted by Act No. 17 of 1969, w.e.f. 3 April 1970.
2. Substituted by Act No. 65 of 1960, for the words "Any person may".
3. Inserted by Act No. 65 of 1960.
4. Substituted by the Companies (Amendment) Act, 1988, w.e.f. 15 July 1988 for the words "a fee of one rupee".
5. Substituted by Act No. 65 of 1960.
6. Substituted by Act No. 65 of 1960.
7. Inserted by the Companies (Amendment) Act, 1988, w.e.f. 31 May 1991.
8. Sub-section (4) omitted by Act No. 65 of 1960.
9. Substituted for "Company Law Board", the words by the Companies (Second Amendment) Act, 2002, w.e.f. 13 January 2003.

610A. Admissibility of microfilms, facsimile copies of documents, computer printouts and documents on computer media as documents and as evidence.—(1) Notwithstanding anything contained in any other law for the time being in force-—

(a) a microfilm of a document or the reproduction of the image or images embodied in such microfilm (whether enlarged or not); or

(b) a facsimile copy of a document; or

(c) a statement contained in a document and included in a printed material produced by a computer (hereinafter referred to as a "computer printout"), if the conditions mentioned in sub-section (2) are satisfied, shall be deemed to be also a document for the purposes of this Act and the rules made thereunder and shall be admissible in any proceedings thereunder, without further proof or production of the original, as evidence of any contents of the original or of any fact stated therein of which direct evidence should be admissible.

(2) The conditions referred to in sub-section (1) in respect of a computer printout shall be the following, namely:

(a) the information contained in the statement reproduces or is derived from returns and document filed by the company on paper or on computer network, floppy, diskette, magnetic cartridge tape, CD-rom or any other computer readable media;

(b) while receiving returns or documents on computer media, necessary checks by scanning the documents filed on computer media will be carried out and media will be duly authenticated by the Registrar; and

(c) the Registrar shall also take due care to preserve the computer media by duplicating, transferring, mastering or storage without loss of data.]

Part XIII

GENERAL

615. Power of central government to direct companies to furnish information or statistics.—(1) The Central Government may, by order, require companies generally, or any class of companies, or any company, to furnish such information or statistics with regard to their or its constitution or working, and within such time, as may be specified in the order.

(2)(a) Every order under sub-section (1) addressed to companies generally or to any class of companies, shall be published in the Official Gazette and in such other manner, if any, as the Central Government may think fit.

(b) The date of publication of the order in the Official Gazette shall be deemed to be the date on which the demand for information or statistics is made on such companies or class of companies, as the case may be.

(3) Every order under sub-section (1) addressed to an individual company shall be served on it in the manner laid down in section 51.

(4) For the purpose of satisfying itself that any information or statistic furnished by a company in pursuance of any order under sub-section (1) is correct and complete, the Central Government may require such company,

(a) to produce such records or documents in its possession or under its control for inspection, before such officer and at such time as may be specified by the Central Government; or

(b) to furnish such further information as may be specified by the Central Government and within such time as may be fixed by it.

(5) The Central Government may also, by order, direct an inquiry to be made by any person or persons named in the order,

(a) for the purpose of obtaining any information or statistics which a company has failed to furnish as required of it by an order under sub-section (1); or

(b) for the purpose of satisfying itself that any information or statistics furnished by a company in pursuance of an order made under sub-section (1) is correct and complete; and in so far as such information or statistics may be found to be incorrect or incomplete, for the purpose of obtaining such information or statistics as may be necessary to make the information to statistics furnished correct and complete; and a person or persons so appointed shall, for the purposes of such inquiry, have such powers as may be prescribed.

(6) If any company fails to comply with an order made under sub-section (1) or (4), or knowingly furnishes any information or statistics which is incorrect or incomplete in any material respect, the company, and every officer thereof who is in default, shall be punishable with imprisonment which may extend to three months, or with fine which may extend to ten thousand rupees, or with both.

(7) An order requiring any information or statistics to be furnished by a company may also be addressed to any person who is, or has at any time been, an officer or employee of the company, and all the provisions of this section, so far as may be, shall apply in relation to such person as they apply in relation to the company:

Provided that no such person shall be punishable under sub-section (6), unless the Court is satisfied that he was in a position to comply with the order and made wilful default in doing so.

(8) Where a body corporate incorporated outside India and having established an office within India, carries on business in India, all references to a company in this section shall be deemed to include references to the body corporate in relation, and only in relation, to such business.

1. The words "one thousand rupees" substituted by the Companies (Amendment) Act, 2000, w.e.f. 14 December 2000.

627. Production and inspection of books where offence suspected.—(1) If, on an application made to a Judge of a High Court in Chambers 3[or Tribunal, as the case may be] by the Public Prosecutor of the State or by the Central Government, 3[or by a company prosecutor appointed under section 624A] it is shown that there is reasonable cause to believe that any person has, while he was an officer of a company, committed an offence in connection with the management of the company's affairs, and that evidence of the commission of the offence is to be found in any books or papers of or under the control of the company, an order may be made—

(i) authorising any person named therein to inspect the said books or papers or any of them for the purpose of investigating, and obtaining evidence of the commission of, the offence; or

(ii) requiring the 1[***] manager of the company or such other officer thereof as may be named in the order, to produce the said books or papers or any of them to a person, and at a place and time, named in the order.

(2) Sub-section (1) shall apply also in relation to any books or papers of a person carrying on the business of banking so far as they relate to the company's affairs, as it applies to any books or papers of or under the control of the company, except that no such order as is referred to in clause (ii) thereof shall be made by virtue of this sub-section.

(3) No appeal shall lie from the decision of a Judge of the High Court 3[or Tribunal, as the case may be] under this section.

1. Omitted by the Companies (Amendment) Act, 2000, w.e.f. 14 December 2000.
2. Inserted by Act No. 65 of 1960.
3. Inserted by the Companies (Second Amendment) Act, 2002, w.e.f. 13 January 2003.

628. Penalty for false statements.—If in any return, report, certificate, balance sheet, prospectus, statement or other document required by or for the purposes of any of the provisions of this Act, any person makes a statement—

(a) which is false in any material particular, knowing it to be false; or

(b) which omits any material fact knowing it to be material; he shall, save as otherwise expressly provided in this Act, be punishable with imprisonment for a term which may extend to two years, and shall also be liable to fine.

THE COMPETITION ACT, 2002

(Relevant Provisions)

57. Restriction on disclosure of information.—No information relating to any enterprise, being an information which has been obtained by or on behalf of the Commission for the purposes of this Act, shall, without the previous permission in writing of the enterprise, be disclosed otherwise than in compliance with or for the purposes of this Act or any other law for the time being in force.

THE CONSTITUTION OF INDIA
(Relevant Provisions)

PREAMBLE

WE, THE PEOPLE OF INDIA, having solemnly resolved to constitute india into a SOVEREIGN SOCIALIST SECULAR DEMOCRATIC REPUBLIC and to secure to all its citizens.

Right to Equality

14. Equality before law.—The State shall not deny to any person equality before the law or the equal protection of the laws within the territory of India.

Right to Freedom

19. Protection of certain rights regarding freedom of speech, etc.—(1) All citizens shall have the right—

(a) To freedom of speech and expression;

(b) To assemble peaceably and without arms;

(c) To form associations or unions;

(d) To move freely throughout the territory of India;

(e) To reside and settle in any part of the territory of India; 1[and]

(f) 2* * * *

(g) To practise any profession, or to carry on any occupation, trade or business.

(2). 3[Nothing in sub-clause (a) of clause (1) shall affect the operation of any existing law, or prevent the State from making any law, in so far as such law imposes reasonable restrictions on the exercise of the right conferred by the said sub-clause in the interests of 4[the sovereignty and integrity of India,] the security of the State, friendly relations with foreign States, public order, decency or morality, or in relation to contempt of court, defamation or incitement to an offence.]

(3) Nothing in sub-clause (b) of the said clause shall affect the operation of any existing law in so far as it imposes, or prevent the State from making any law imposing, in the interests of 4[the sovereignty and integrity of India or] public order, reasonable restrictions on the exercise of the right conferred by the said sub-clause.

(4) Nothing in sub-clause (c) of the said clause shall affect the operation of any existing law in so far as it imposes, or prevent the State from making any law imposing, in the interests of 4[the sovereignty and integrity of India or] public order or morality, reasonable restrictions on the exercise of the right conferred by the said sub-clause.

(5) Nothing in 5[sub-clauses (d) and (e)] of the said clause shall affect the operation of any existing law in so far as it imposes, or prevent the State from making any law imposing, reasonable restrictions on the exercise of any of the rights conferred by the said sub-clauses either in the interests of the general public or for the protection of the interests of any Scheduled Tribe.

(6) Nothing in sub-clause (g) of the said clause shall affect the operation of any existing law in so far as it imposes, or prevent the State from making any law imposing, in the interests of the general public, reasonable restrictions on the exercise of the right conferred by the said sub-clause, and, in particular, 6[nothing in the said sub-clause shall affect the operation of any existing law in so far as it relates to, or prevent the State from making any law relating to,

(i) The professional or technical qualifications necessary for practising any profession or carrying on any occupation, trade or business, or

(ii) The carrying on by the State, or by a corporation owned or controlled by the State, of any trade, business, industry or service, whether to the exclusion, complete or partial, of citizens or otherwise].

1. Ins. by the Constitution (Forty-fourth Amendment) Act, 1978, s. 2 (w.e.f. 20-6-1979).
2. Sub-clause (f) omitted by s. 2, Constitution (Forty-fourth Amendment) Act, 1978 (w.e.f. 20-6-1979).
3. Subs. by the Constitution (First Amendment) Act, 1951, s. 3, for cl. (2) (with retrospective effect
4. Ins. by the Constitution (Sixteenth Amendment) Act, 1963, s. 2.
5. Subs. by the Constitution (Forty-fourth Amendment) Act, 1978, s. 2, for "sub-clauses (d), (e) and (f)" (w.e.f. 20-6-1979).
6. Subs. by the Constitution (First Amendment) Act, 1951, s. 3, for certain words.

21. Protection of life and personal liberty.—No person shall be deprived of his life or personal liberty except according to procedure established by law.

22. Protection against arrest and detention in certain cases.—(1) No person who is arrested shall be detained in custody without being informed, as soon as may be, of the grounds for such arrest nor shall he be denied the right to consult, and to be defended by, a legal practitioner of his choice.

(2) Every person who is arrested and detained in custody shall be produced before the nearest magistrate within a period of twenty-four hours of such arrest excluding the time necessary for the journey from the place of arrest to the court of the magistrate and no such person shall be detained in custody beyond the said period without the authority of a magistrate.

(3) Nothing in clauses (1) and (2) shall apply

(a) To any person who for the time being is an enemy alien; or

(b) To any person who is arrested or detained under any law providing for preventive detention.

(4) No law providing for preventive detention shall authorise the detention of a person for a longer period than three months unless—

(a) An Advisory Board consisting of persons who are, or have been, or are qualified to be appointed as, Judges of a High Court has reported before the expiration of the said period of three months that there is in its opinion sufficient cause for such detention:

Provided that nothing in this sub-clause shall authorise the detention of any person beyond the maximum period prescribed by any law made by Parliament under sub-clause (b) of clause (7); or

(b) Such person is detained in accordance with the provisions of any law made by Parliament under sub-clauses (a) and (b) of clause (7).

(5) When any person is detained in pursuance of an order made under any law providing for preventive detention, the authority making the order shall, as soon as may be, communicate to such person the grounds on which the order has been made and shall afford him the earliest opportunity of making a representation against the order.

(6) Nothing in clause (5) shall require the authority making any such order as is referred to in that clause to disclose facts which such authority considers to be against the public interest to disclose.

(7) Parliament may by law prescribe—

(a) The circumstances under which, and the class or classes of cases in which, a person may be detained for a period longer than three months under any law providing for preventive detention without obtaining the opinion of an Advisory Board in accordance with the provisions of sub-clause (a) of clause (4);

(b) The maximum period for which any person may in any class or classes of cases be detained under any law providing for preventive detention; and

(c) The procedure to be followed by an Advisory Board in an inquiry under sub-clause (a) of clause (4).

1. On the enforcement of s. 3 of the Constitution (Forty-fourth Amendment) Act, 1978, art. 22 shall stand amended as directed in s. 3 of that Act. For the text of s. 3 of that Act, see Appendix III.

Right to Constitutional Remedies

32. Remedies for enforcement of rights conferred by this Part.—(1) The right to move the Supreme Court by appropriate proceedings for the enforcement of the rights conferred by this Part is guaranteed.

(2) The Supreme Court shall have power to issue directions or orders or writs, including writs in the nature of *habeas corpus*, *mandamus*, prohibition, *quo warranto* and *certiorari*, whichever may be appropriate, for the enforcement of any of the rights conferred by the part.

(3) Without prejudice to the powers conferred on the Supreme Court by clauses (1) and (2), Parliament may by law empower any other court to exercise within the local limits of its jurisdiction all or any of the powers exercisable by the Supreme Court under clause (2).

(4) The right guaranteed by this article shall not be suspended except as otherwise provided for by this Constitution.

54. Election of President.—The President shall be elected by the members of an electoral college consisting of—

(a) The elected members of both Houses of Parliament; and

(b) The elected members of the Legislative Assemblies of the States.

1[*Explanation*. In this article and in Article 55, State includes the National Capital Territory of Delhi and the Union territory of Pondicherry.]

1. Ins. by the Constitution (Seventieth Amendment) Act, 1992, s. 2 (w.e.f. 1-6-1995).

78. Duties of Prime Minister as respects the furnishing of information to the President, etc.—It shall be the duty of the Prime Minister—

(a) To communicate to the President all decisions of the Council of Ministers relating to the administration of the affairs of the Union and proposals for legislation;

(b) To furnish such information relating to the administration of the affairs of the Union and proposals for legislation as the President may call for; and

(c) If the President so requires, to submit for the consideration of the Council of Ministers any matter on which a decision has been taken by a Minister but which has not been considered by the Council.

226. Power of High Courts to issue certain writs.—(1) Notwithstanding anything in Article 32, every High Court shall have powers, throughout the territories in relation to which it exercises jurisdiction, to issue to any person or authority, including in appropriate cases, any Government, within those territories directions, orders or writs, including writs in the nature of *habeas corpus, mandamus,* prohibition, *quo warranto* and *certiorari,* or any of them, for the enforcement of any of the rights conferred by Part III and for any other purpose.

(2) The power conferred by clause (1) to issue directions, orders or writs to any Government, authority or person may also be exercised by any High Court exercising jurisdiction in relation to the territories within which the cause of action, wholly or in part, arises for the exercise of such power, notwithstanding that the seat of such Government or authority or the residence of such person is not within those territories.

(3) Where any party against whom an interim order, whether by way of injunction or stay or in any other manner, is made on, or in any proceedings relating to, a petition under clause (1), without—

(a) furnishing to such party copies of such petition and all documents in support of the plea for such interim order; and

(b) giving such party an opportunity of being heard, makes an application to the High Court for the vacation of such order and furnishes a copy of such application to the party in whose favour such order has been made or the counsel of such party, the High Court shall dispose of the application within a period of two weeks from the date on which it is received or from the date on which the copy of such application is so furnished, whichever is later, or where the High Court is closed on the last day of that period, before the expiry of the next day afterwards on which the High Court is open; and if the application is not so disposed of, the interim order shall, on the expiry of that period, or, as the case may be, the expiry of the said next day, stand vacated.

(4) The power conferred on a High Court by this Article shall not be in derogation of the power conferred on the Supreme Court by clause (2) of Article 32.

THE DELIMITATION ACT, 2002

(Relevant Provisions)

An Act to provide for the readjustment of the allocation of seats in the House of the People to the States, the total number of seats in the Legislative Assembly of each State, the division of each State and each Union territory having a Legislative Assembly into territorial constituencies for elections to the House of the People and Legislative Assemblies of the States and Union territories and for matters connected therewith.

Be it enacted by Parliament in the Fifty-third Year of the Republic of India as follows:--

2. Definitions.—In this Act, unless the context otherwise requires,

(a) "article" means an article of the Constitution;

(b) "associate member" means a member nominated under Section 5;

(c) "Commission" means the Delimitation Commission constituted under Section 3;

(d) "Election Commission" means the Election Commission referred to in Article 324;

(e) "member" means a member of the Commission and includes the Chairperson; and

(f) "State" includes a Union territory having a Legislative Assembly but does not include the State of Jammu and Kashmir.

3. Constitution of Delimitation Commission.—As soon as may be after the commencement of this Act, the Central Government shall constitute a Commission to be called the Delimitation Commission which shall consist of three members as follows:

(a) one member, who shall be a person who is or has been a Judge of the Supreme Court, to be appointed by the Central Government who shall be the Chairperson of the Commission;

(b) the Chief Election Commissioner or an Election Commissioner nominated by the Chief Election Commissioner, ex officio:

Provided that after the nomination of an Election Commissioner as a member under this clause, no further nomination under this clause shall be made except to fill the casual vacancy of such member under Section 6; and

(c) the State Election Commissioner of concerned State, ex officio.

Explanation. For the purposes of clause (c), the State Election Commissioner of concerned State, in respect of the duties of the Commission relating to that State, means the State Election Commissioner appointed by the Governor of that State under clause (1) of Article 243K.

4. Duties of the Commission.—(1) The readjustment made, on the basis of the census figures as ascertained at the census held in the year 1971, by the Delimitation Commission constituted under Section 3 of the Delimitation Act, 1972 (76 of 1972), of the allocation of seats in the House of the People to the several States and the total number of seats in the Legislative Assembly of each State shall be deemed to be the readjustment made by the Commission for the purposes of this Act.

(2) Subject to the provisions of sub-section (1) and any other law for the time being in force, the Commission shall readjust the division of each State into territorial constituencies for the purpose of elections to the House of the People and to the State Legislative Assembly on the basis of the census figures as ascertained at the census held in the year 1991:

Provided that where on such readjustment only one seat is allocated in the House of the People to a State, the whole of that State shall form one territorial constituency for the purpose of elections to the House of the People from that State.

5. Associate members.—(1) The Commission shall associate with itself for the purpose of assisting it in its duties in respect of each State, ten persons five of whom shall be members of the House of the People representing that State and five shall be members of the Legislative Assembly of that State:

Provided that where the number of members of the House of the People representing any State is five or less, then, all such members shall be the associate members for that State and in the latter case the total number of associate members shall be less than ten by such number as by which the total number of members of the House of the People representing that State is less than five.

(2) The persons to be so associated with each State shall be nominated, in the case of the members of the House of the People, by the Speaker of that House, and in the case of members of a Legislative Assembly, by the Speaker of that Assembly, having due regard to the composition of the House or, as the case may be, of the Assembly.

(3) The first nominations to be made under sub-section (2)—

(a) shall be made by the Speakers of the several Legislative Assemblies within one month, and by the Speaker of the House of the People within two months, of the commencement of this Act; and

(b) shall be communicated to the Chief Election Commissioner, and where the nominations are made by the Speaker of a Legislative Assembly, also to the Speaker of the House of the People.

(4) None of the associate members shall have a right to vote or to sign any decision of the Commission.

(5) The Commission shall have power to call upon—

(a) the Registrar General and Census Commissioner, India or his nominee; or

(b) the Surveyor General of India or his nominee; or

(c) any other officer of the Central Government or State Government; or

(d) any expert in geographical information system; or

(e) any other person, whose expertise and knowledge are considered necessary by the Commission to provide to it in addition to the assistance provided by the persons referred to in sub-section the officers and persons so called upon shall be duty bound to assist the Commission.

(6) The Secretary to the Election Commission shall be the ex-officio Secretary of the Election Commission and shall discharge his functions with the assistance of the employees of the Commission under the supervision of the Chairperson of the Commission.

6. Casual vacancies.—If the office of the Chairperson or of a member or of an associate falls vacant owing to his death or resignation, it shall be filled as soon as may be practicable by the Central Government or the Speaker concerned under and in accordance with the provisions of Section 3 or, as the case may be, of Section 5.

7. Procedure and powers of the Commission.—(1) The Commission shall determine procedure and shall, in the performance of its functions, have all the powers of a civil court under the Code of Civil Procedure, 1908 (5 of 1908), while trying a suit, in respect of the following matters, namely—

(a) summoning and enforcing the attendance of witnesses;

(b) requiring the production of any document; and

(c) requisitioning any public record from any court or office.

(2) The Commission shall have power to require any person to furnish any information on such points or matters as in the opinion of the Commission may be useful for, or relevant to, any matter under the consideration of the Commission.

(3) The Commission may authorise any of its members to exercise any of the powers conferred on it by clauses (a) to (c) of sub-section (1) and sub-section (2), and any order made or act done in exercise of any of those powers by the member authorised

by the Commission in that behalf shall be deemed to be the order or act, as the case may be, of the Commission.

(4) If there is a difference of opinion among the members, the opinion of the majority shall prevail, and acts and orders of the Commission shall be expressed in terms of the views of the majority.

(5) Commission as well as any group of associate members shall have power to act notwithstanding the temporary absence of a member or associate member or the existence of a vacancy in the Commission or in that or any other group of associate members; and no act or proceeding of the Commission or of any group of associate members shall be invalid or called in question on the ground merely of such temporary absence or of the existence of such vacancy.

(6) The Commission shall be deemed to be a civil court for the purposes of Sections 345 and 346 of the Code of Criminal Procedure, 1973 (2 of 1974).

Explanation. For the purposes of enforcing the attendance of witnesses, the local limits of the jurisdiction of the Commission shall be the limits of the territory of India.

8. Readjustment of number of seats.—The Commission shall, having regard to the provisions of Articles 81, 170, 330 and 332, and also, in relation to the Union territories, except National Capital Territory of Delhi, Sections 3 and 39 of the Government of Union Territories Act, 1963 (20 of 1963) and in relation to the National Capital territory of Delhi sub-clause (b) of clause (2) of Article 239-AA, by order, determine,

(a) on the basis of the census figures as ascertained at the census held in the year 1971 and subject to the provisions of Section 4, the number of seats in the House of the People to be allocated to each State and determine on the basis of the census figures as ascertained at the census held in the year 1991 the number of seats, if any, to be reserved for the Scheduled Castes and for the Scheduled Tribes of the State; and

(b) on the basis of the census figures as ascertained at the census held in the year 1971 and subject to the provisions of Section 4, the total number of seats to be assigned to the Legislative Assembly of each State and determine on the basis of the census figures as ascertained at the census held in the year 1991 the number of seats, if any, to be reserved for the Scheduled Castes and for the Scheduled Tribes of the State:

Provided that the total number of seats assigned to the Legislative Assembly of any State under clause (b) shall be an integral multiple of the number of seats in the House of the People allocated to that State under clause (a).

9. Delimitation of constituencies.—(1) The Commission shall, in the manner herein provided, then, distribute the seats in the House of the People allocated to each State and the seats assigned to the Legislative Assembly of each State as readjusted on the basis of 1971 census to single-member territorial constituencies and delimit them on the basis of the census figures as ascertained, at the census held in the year 1991, having regard to the provisions of the Constitution, the provisions of the Act specified in Section 8 and the following provisions, namely:

(a) all constituencies shall, as far as practicable, be geographically compact areas, and in delimiting them regard shall be had to physical features, existing boundaries of administrative units, facilities of communication and public convenience;

(b) every assembly constituency shall be so delimited as to fall wholly within one parliamentary constituency;

(c) constituencies in which seats are reserved for the Scheduled Castes shall be distributed in different parts of the State and located, as far as practicable, in those areas where the proportion of their population to the total is comparatively large; and

(d) constituencies in which seats are reserved for the Scheduled Tribes shall, as far as practicable, be located in areas where the proportion of their population to the total is the largest.

(2) The Commission shall—

(a) publish its proposals for the delimitation of constituencies, together with the dissenting proposals, if any, of any associate member who desires publication thereof, in the Gazette of India and in the Official Gazettes of all the States concerned and also in such other manner as it thinks fit;

(b) specify a date on or after which the proposals shall be further considered by it;

(c) consider all objections and suggestions which may have been received by it before the date so specified, and for the purpose of such consideration, hold one or more public sittings at such place or places in each State as it thinks fit; and

(d) thereafter by one or more orders determine—

(i) the delimitation of parliamentary constituencies; and

(ii) the delimitation of assembly constituencies, of each State.

10. Publication of orders and their date of operation.— (1) The Commission shall cause each of its orders made under Section 8 or Section 9 to be published in the Gazette of India and in the Official Gazettes of the States concerned and simultaneously cause such orders to be published at least in two vernacular newspapers and publicize on radio, television and other possible media available to the public and after such publication in the Official Gazettes of the States concerned, every District Election Officer shall cause to be affixed, the Gazette version of such orders relating to the area under his jurisdiction, on a conspicuous part of his office for public notice.

(2) Upon publication in the Gazette of India, every such order shall have the force of law and shall not be called in question in any court.

(3) As soon as may be after such publication, every such order shall be laid before the House of the People and the Legislative Assemblies of the States concerned.

(4) Subject to the provisions of sub-section (5), the readjustment of representation of the several territorial constituencies in the House of the People or in the Legislative Assembly of a State and the delimitation of those constituencies provided for in any such order shall apply in relation to every election to the House or to the Assembly, as the case may be, held after the publication in the Gazette of India of that order and shall so apply in supersession of the provisions relating to such representation and delimitation contained in any other law for the time being in force or any order or notification issued under such law insofar as such representation and delimitation are inconsistent with the provisions of this Act.

(5) Nothing in this section shall affect the representation in the House of the People or in the Legislative Assembly of a State until the dissolution of the House or of the Assembly, as the case may be, existing on the date of publication in the Gazette of India of the final order or orders of the Commission relating to the delimitation of parliamentary constituencies or, as the case may be, of the assembly constituencies of that State and any by-election to fill any vacancy in such House or in any such Assembly shall be held on the basis of the provisions of the laws and orders superseded by sub-section (4) as if the said provisions had not been superseded.

(6) The Commission shall endeavour to complete and publish each of its orders referred to in sub-section (1) in the manner provided in that sub-section, within two years of the constitution of the Commission under Section 3.

11. Power to maintain delimitation orders up to date.— (1) The Election Commission may, from time to time, by notification in the Gazette of India and in the Official Gazette of the State concerned,

(a) correct any printing mistake in any of the orders made by the Commission under Section 9 or any error arising therein from an inadvertent slip or omission; and

(b) where the boundaries or name of any district or any territorial division mentioned in any of the said orders are or is altered, make such amendments as appear to it to be necessary or expedient for bringing the orders up to date, so, however, that the boundaries or areas or extent of any constituency shall not be changed by any such notification.

(2) Every notification under this section shall be laid, as soon as may be after it is issued, before the House of the People and the Legislative Assembly of the State concerned.

12. Repeal. The Delimitation Act, 1972 (76 of 1972) is hereby repealed.

THE DESIGNS ACT, 2000
(Relevant Provisions)

2. Definitions.—(1) In this Act, unless the context otherwise requires,

1[(a) "Appropriate laboratory" means a laboratory or organisation—

(i) Recognized by the Central Government;

(ii) Recognized by a State Government, subject to such guidelines as may be prescribed by the Central Government in this behalf; or

(iii) Any such laboratory or organisation established by or under any law for the time being in force, which is maintained, financed or aided by the Central Government or a State Government for carrying out analysis or test of any goods with a view to determining whether such goods suffer from any defect;

2[(aa) "Branch office" means—

(i) Any establishment described as a branch by the opposite party; or

(ii) Any establishment carrying on either the same or substantially the same activity as that carried on by the head office of the establishment;

(b) "Complainant" means—

(i) A consumer; or

(ii) Any voluntary consumer association registered under the companies Act, 1956 (1 of 1956), or under any other law for the time being in force; or

(iii) The Central Government or any State Government, who or which makes a complaint;

2[(iv) One or more consumers where there are numerous consumers having the same interest;]

3[(v) in case of death of a consumer, his legal heir or representative.] who or which makes a complaint;

(c) "Complaint" means any allegation in writing made by a complainant that—

4[(i) An unfair trade practice or a restrictive trade practice has been adopted by 5[any trader or service provider;]

(ii) 6[The goods bought by him or agreed to be bought by him] suffer from one or more defects;

(iii) 7[Service hired or availed of or agreed to be hired or availed of by him] suffer from deficiency in any respect;

8[(iv) a trader or the service provider, as the case may be, has charged for the goods or for the service mentioned in the complaint, a price in excess of the price in excess of the price—

(a) fixed by or under any law for the time being in force;

(b) displayed on the goods or any package containing such goods;

(c) displayed on the price list exhibited by him by or under any law for the time being in force;

(d) agreed between the parties;

9[(v) goods which will be hazardous to life and safety when used are being offered for sale to the public—

(a) in contravention of any standards relating to safety of such goods as required to be complied with, by or under any law for the time being in force;

(b) if the trader could have known with due diligence that the goods so offered are unsafe to the public;

10[(vi) service which are hazardous or likely to be hazardous to life and safety of the public when used, are being offered by the service provider which such person could have known with due diligence to be injurious to life and safety.]

(d) "Consumer" means any person who,

(i) Buys any goods for a consideration which has been paid or promised or partly paid and partly promised, or under any system of deferred payment and includes any user of such goods other than the person who buys such goods for consideration paid or promised or partly paid or partly promised or under any system of deferred payment when such use is made with the approval of such person but does not include a person who obtains such goods for resale or for any commercial purpose; or

(ii) 11[Hires or avails of] any services for a consideration which has been paid or promised or partly paid and partly promised, or under any system of deferred payment and includes any beneficiary of such services other than the person who 8[hires or avails of] the services for consideration paid or promised, or partly paid and partly promised, or under any system of deferred payment, when such services are availed of with the approval of the first mentioned person 11[but does not include a person who avails of such services for any commercial purpose;]

12[*Explanation.* For the purposes of this sub-clause "commercial purpose" does not include use by a consumer of goods bought and used by him and services availed by him exclusively for the purposes of earning his livelihood, by means of self-employment;]

(e) "Consumer dispute" means a dispute where the person against whom a complaint has been made, denies or disputes the allegations contained in the complaint;

(f) "Defect" means any fault, imperfection or shortcoming in the quality, quantity, potency, purity or standard which is required to be maintained by or under any law for the time being in force or 13[under any contract express or implied or] as is claimed by the trader in any manner whatsoever in relation to any goods;

(g) "Deficiency" means any fault, imperfection, shortcoming or inadequacy in the quality, nature and manner of performance which is required to be maintained by or under any law for the time being in force or has been undertaken to be performed by a person in pursuance of a contract or otherwise in relation to any service;

(h) "District Forum" means a Consumer Disputes Redressal Forum established under clause (a) of sec. 9;

(i) "Goods" means goods as defined in the sale of Goods Act, 1930 (3 of 1930);

14[(j) "Manufacturer" means a person who—

(i) Makes or manufactures any goods or parts thereof; or

(ii) Does not make or manufacture any goods but assembles parts thereof, made or manufactured by others; or

(iii) Puts or causes to be put his own mark on any goods made or manufactured by any other manufacturer.]

Explanation. Where a manufacturer despatches any goods or part thereof to any branch office maintained by him, such branch office shall not be deemed to be the manufacturer even though the parts so despatched to it are assembled at such branch office and are sold or distributed from such branch office:

13[(jj) "Member" includes the President and a member of the National Commission or a State Commission or a District Forum, as the case may be;]

(k) "National Commission" means the National Consumer Disputes Redressal Commission established under claux (c) of sec. 9:

l. "National" means a notification published in the official Gazette;

(m) "Person" includes—

(i) A firm whether registered or not;

(ii) A Hindu undivided family;

(iii) A co-operative society;

(iv) Every other association of persons whether registered under the societies Registration Act, 1860 (21 of 1860), or not;

(n) "Prescribed" means prescribed by the rules made by the State Government, or as the case may be, the Central Government under this Act;

2[(nn) "regulation" means the regulations made by the National Commission under this Act;

15[(nnn) "restrictive trade practice" means a trade practice which tends to being about manipulation of price or its conditions of delivery or to affect flow of supplies in the market relating to goods or service in such a manner as to impose on the consumers unjustified costs or restrictions and shall include—

(a) delay beyond the period agreed to be a trader in supply of such goods or in providing the services which has led or is likely to lead to rise in the price;

(b) any trade practice which requires a consumer to buy, hire or avail of any goods or, as the case may be, services as condition precedent to buying, hiring or availing of other goods or services.]

(o) "Services" means service of any description which is made available to potential 16[users and includes, but not limited to, the provision of] facilities in connection with banking. Financing insurance, transport, processing, supply of electrical or other energy, board or lodging or both, 17[housing construction] entertainment, amusement or the purveying of news or other information, but does not include the rendering of any service free of charge or under a contract of personal service;

18[(oo) "spurious goods and services" mean such goods and services which are claimed to be genuine but they are actually not so.]

(p) "State Commission" means a Consumer Disputes Redressal Commission established in a State under clause (b) of sec. 9;

(q) "Trader" in relation to any goods means " a person who sells or distributes any goods for sale and includes the manufacturer thereof, and where such goods are sold or distributed in package form, includes the packer thereof";

19[(r) "Unfair trade practice" means a trade practice which, for the purpose of promoting the sale, use or supply of any goods or for the provision of any service, adopts any unfair method or unfair or deceptive practice including any of the following practices, namely:

1. The practice of making any statement, whether orally or in writing or by visible representation which,
   - (i) Falsely represents that the goods are of a particular standard, quality, quantity; grade-composition, style or model;
   - (ii) Falsely represents that the service of a particular standard, quality or grade;
   - (iii) Falsely represents any re-built, second-hand, renovated, reconditioned or old goods as new goods;
   - (iv) Represents that the goods or service have sponsorship, approval, performance, characteristics, accessories, uses or benefits which such goods or service do not have;
   - (v) Represents that the seller or the supplier has a sponsorship or approval or affiliation which such seller or supplier does not have;
   - (vi) Makes a false or misleading representation concerning the need for, or the usefulness of, any goods or service;
   - (vii) Gives to the public any warranty or guarantee of the performance, efficacy or length of life of a product or of any goods that is not based on an adequate or proper test thereof:

Provided that where a defence is raised to the effect that such warranty or guarantee is based on adequate or proper test, the burden of proof of such defence shall lie on the person raising such defence;

(viii) Makes to the public a representation in a form that purports to be—

(i) A warranty or guarantee of a product or of any goods or service; or

(ii) A promise to replace, maintain or repair an article or any part thereof or to repeat or continue a service until it has achieved a specified result, if such purported warranty or guarantee or promise is materially misleading or if there is no reasonable prospect that such warranty, guarantee or promise will be carried out;

(ix) Materially misleads the public concerning the price at which a product or like products or goods or service, have been or are, ordinarily sold or provided, and, for this purpose, a representation as to price shall be deemed to refer to the price at which the product or goods or service has or have been sold by sellers or provided by suppliers generally in the relevant market unless it is clearly specified to be the price at which the product has been sold or services have been provided by the person by whom or on whose behalf the representation is made;

(x) Gives false or misleading facts disparaging the goods, services or trade of another person;

Explanation. For the purposes of CI. (1), a statement that is:

(a) Expressed on an article offered or displayed for sale, or on its wrapper or container; or

(b) Expressed on anything attached to, inserted in, or accompanying an article offered or displayed for sale or on anything on which the article is mounted for display or sale; or

(c) Contained in or on anything is sold, sent, delivered, transmitted or in any other manner whatsoever made available to a member of the public,

shall be deemed to be a statement made to the public by, and only by, the person who had caused the statement to be so expressed, made or contained;

(2) Permits the publication of any advertisement whether in any newspaper or otherwise, for the sale or supply at a bargain price, of goods or the services that are not intended to be offered for sale or supply at the bargain price, or for a period that is, and in quantities that are, reasonable, having regard to the nature of the market in which the business is carried on, the nature and size of business, and the nature of the advertisement.

Explanation. For the purposes of CI. (2), "bargaining price" means

(a) A price that is stated in any advertisement to be a bargain price, by reference to an ordinary price or otherwise, or

(b) A price that a person who reads, hears or sees the advertisement, would reasonably understand to be a bargain price having regard to the prices at which the product advertised or like products are ordinarily sold.

(3) Permits—

(a) The offering of gifts, prizes or other items with the intention of not providing them as offered or creating impression that something is being given or offered free of charge when it is fully or partly covered by the amount charged in the transaction as a whole;

(b) The conduct of any contest, lottery, game of chance or skill, for the purpose of promoting, directly or indirectly, the sale, use or supply of any product or any business interest.

20[(3A) Withholding from the participants of any scheme offering gifts, prizes or other items free of charge, on its closure the information about final results of the scheme.

Explanation. For the purposes of this sub-clause, the participants of a scheme shall be deemed to have been informed of the final results of the scheme where such results are within a reasonable time published, prominently in the same newspapers in which the scheme was originally advertised.]

(4) Permits the sale or supply of goods intended to be used, or are of kind likely to be used, by consumers, knowing or having reason to believe that the goods do not comply with the standards prescribed by competent authority relating to performance, composition, contents. Design, constructions, finishing or packaging as are necessary to prevent or reduce the risk of injury to the person using the goods.

(5) Permits the hoarding or destruction of goods, or refuses to sell the goods or to make them available for sale or to provide any service, if such hoarding or destruction or refusal raises or tends to raise or is intended to raise, the cost of those or other similar goods or services.

20[(6) Manufacture of spurious goods or offering such goods for sale or adopting deceptive practices in the provision of services.]

(2) Any reference in this Act to any other Act or provision thereof which is not in force in any area to which this Act applies shall be construed to have reference to the corresponding Act or provision thereof in force in such areas.

1. Substituted by Act 50 of 1993, sec. 2 for clause (a) (w.e.f. 18-6-1993).
2. Inserted by Act 50 of 1993, sec. 2 (w.e.f. 18-6-1993).
3. Ins. by Act 62 of 2002, sec. 2 (w.e.f. 15-3-2003).
4. Inserted by Act 50 of 1993, sec. 2 for sub-clause (i) (w.e.f. 18-6-1993).
5. Subs. by Act 62 of 2002, sec. 2, for "any trader" (w.e.f. 15-3-2003).
6. Subs. by Act 50 of 1993, sec. 2, for "the goods mentioned in the complaint" (w.e.f. 18-6-1993).

7. Subs. by Act 50 of 1993, sec. 2, for "the services mentioned in the complaint" (w.e.f. 18-6-1993).
8. Subs. by Act 62 of 2002, sec. 2, for sub-clause "(iv) a trader has charged for the goods mentioned in the complaint a price in excess of the price fixed by or under any time being in force or displayed on the goods or any package containing such goods;" (w.e.f. 15-3-2003).
9. Ins. by Act 50 of 1993, sec. 2 (w.r.e.f. 18-6-1993) and subs. by Act 62 of 2002, sec. for sub-clause "(v) goods which will be hazardous to life and safety when used, are being offered for sale to the public in contravention of the provisions of any law for the time being in force requiring traders to display information in regard to the contents, manner and effect of use of such goods," (w.e.f. 15-3-2003).
10. Sub-clause (vi) along with sub-clause (iv) and (v) subs. For the earlier clauses (iv) and (v) by Act 62 of 2002, sec. 2 (w.e.f. 15-3-2003). 11. subs. by Act 50 of 1993, sec. 2, for "hires" (w.r.e.f. 18-6-1993).
12. Added by Act 62 of 2002, sec. 2, (w.e.f. 15-3-1993).
13. Subs. by Act 62 of 2002, sec. 2, for "Explanation.—for the purposes of sub-clause (i), 'commercial purpose' does not include use by a consumer of goods bought and used by him exclusively for the purpose of earning his livelihood, by means of self-employment:" (w.e.f. 15-3-2003).
14. Subs. by Act 62 of 2002, sec. 2, for clause '(j) "manufacturer" means a person who—
    - (i) makes or manufactures any goods or parts therof; or
    - (ii) does not make or manufacture any goods but assembles parts thereof made or manufactured by

others and claims the end product to be goods manufactured by himself; or

(iii) puts or causes to be put his own mark on any goods made or manufactured by any other manufacturer and claims such goods to be goods manufactured by himself.

Explanation. Where a manufacturer dispatches any goods or part thereof to any branch office maintained by him, such branch office shall not be deemed to be the manufacturer even though the parts so dispatched to it are assembled at such branch office and are sold or distributed from such branch office; (w.e.f. 15-3-2003).

15. Ins. by Act 50 of 1993, sec. 2 (w.r.e.f. 18-6-1993) and subs. by Act 62 of 2002, sec. 2, for clause "(nn) "restrictive trade practice" means any trade practice which requires a consumer to buy, hire or avail of any goods or, as the case may be, services as a condition precedent for buying, hiring or availing of other goods or services;" (w.e.f. 15-3-2003).
16. Clause (nnn) along with clause (nn) subs. For the earlier clause (nn) by Act 62 of 2002, sec. 2 (w.e.f. 15-3-2003).
17. Subs. by Act 62 of 2002, sec. 2, for "users and includes the provision of" (w.e.f. 15-3-2003).
18. Ins. by Act 62 of 2002, sec. 2 (w.e.f. 15-3-2003).
19. Subs. by Act 50 of 1993, sec. 2, for clause (r) (w.r.e.f. 18-6-1993).
20. Ins. by Act 62 of 2002, sec. 2 (w.e.f. 15-3-2003).

THE INDIAN EVIDENCE ACT, 1872
(Relevant Provisions)

123. Evidence as to affairs of State.—No one shall be permitted to give any evidence derived from unpublished official records relating to any affairs of State, except with the permission of the officer at the head of the department concerned, who shall give or withhold such permission as he thinks fit.

124. Official communications.—No public officer shall be compelled to disclose communications made to him in official confidence, when he considers that the public interests would suffer by the disclosure.

125. Information as to commission of offences.—No Magistrate or Police Officer shall be compelled to say whence he got any information as to the commission of any offence, and no Revenue Officer shall be compelled to say whence he got any information as to the commission of any offence against the public revenue.

Explanation. "Revenue-Officer" in this section means any officer employed in or about the business of any branch of the public revenue.

126. Professional communications.—No barrister, attorney, pleader or vakil, shall at any time be permitted, unless with his client's express consent to disclose any communication made to him in the course and for the purpose of his employment as such barrister, pleader, attorney or vakil, by or on behalf of his client, or to state the contents or condition of any document with which he has become acquainted in the course and for the purpose of his professional employment or to disclose any advice given by him to his client in the course and for the purpose of such employment.

Provided that nothing in this section shall protect from disclosure.

1. Any communication made in furtherance of any illegal purpose,
2. Any fact observed by any barrister, pleader, attorney or vakil, in the course of his employment as such showing that any crime or fraud has been committed since the commencement of his employment.

It is immaterial whether the attention of such barrister, pleader, attorney or vakil was or was not directed to such fact by or on behalf of his client.

Explanation. The obligation stated in this section continues after the employment has ceased.

Illustrations:

(a) A, a client, says to B, an attorney, "I have committed forgery and I wish you to defend me."

As the defence of a man known to be guilty is not a criminal purpose, this communication is protected from disclosure.

(b) A, a client, says to B, an attorney, "I wish to obtain possession of property by the use of forged deed on which I request you to sue."

The communication being made in furtherance of criminal purpose, is not protected from disclosure.

(c) A, being charged with embezzlement retains B, an attorney to defend him. In the course of the proceedings B observes that an entry has been made in A's account book, charging A with the sum said to have been embezzled, which entry was not in the book at the commencement of his employment.

This being a fact observed by B in the course of his employment showing that a fraud has been committed since the commencement of the proceedings, it is not protected from disclosure.

THE GEOGRAPHICAL INDICATIONS OF GOODS (REGISTRATION AND PROTECTION) ACT, 1999

(Relevant Provisions)

2. Definitions and interpretation.—(1) In this Act, unless the context otherwise requires,

* * * * * * *

(e) "geographical indication", in relation to goods, means an indication which identifies such goods as agricultural goods natural goods or manufactured goods as originating, or manufactured in the territory of country, or a region or locality in that territory, where a given quality, reputation or other characteristic of such goods is essentially attributable to its geographical origin and in case where such goods are manufactured goods one of the activities of either the production or of processing or preparation of the goods concerned takes place in such territory, region or locality, as the case may be.

Explanation. For the purposes of this clause, any name which is not the name of country, region or locality of that country shall also be considered as the geographical indication if it relates to a specific geographical area and is used upon or in relation to particular goods originating from that country, region or locality, as the case may be;

78. Documents open to public inspection.—(1) The following documents, subject to such conditions as may be prescribed, be open to public inspection at the Geographical Indications Registry, namely:

(a) the register and any document upon which any entry in the register is based;

(b) every notice of opposition to the registration of a geographical indication, application for rectification before the Registrar, counter-statement thereto, and any affidavit or document filed by the parties in any proceedings before the Registrar;

(c) the indexes mentioned in section 77; and

(d) such other documents as the Central Government may, by notification in the Official Gazette, specify:

Provided that where such register is maintained wholly or partly on computer, the inspection of such register under this section shall be made by inspecting the computer print out of the relevant entry in the register so maintained on computer.

(2) Any person may, on an application to the Registrar and on payment of such fee as may be prescribed, obtain a certified copy of any entry in the register or any document referred to in sub-section (1).

THE INDIAN PENAL CODE (45 OF 1860)

(Relevant Provisions)

2. Punishment of offences committed within India.—Every person shall be liable to punishment under this Code and not otherwise for every act of omission contrary to the provisions thereof, of which he shall be guilty within 1[India] 2[***].

1. The original words "the said territories" have successively been amended by the A.O. 1937, the A.O. 1948, the A.O. 1950 and Act 3 of 1951, sec. 3 and Sch. to read as above.
2. The words and figures "on or after the said first day of May 1861" rep. by Act 12 of] 1891, sec. 2 and Sch. I.

11. Person.—The word "person" includes any Company or Association or body of persons, whether incorporated or not.

Section 29A. Electronic record 129A. Electronic record.

The words "electronic record" shall have the meaning assigned to them in clause (t) of sub-section (1) of section 2 of the Information Technology Act, 2000.

1. Ins. by Act 21 of 2000. sec. 91 and Sch. I (w.e.f. 17-10-2000).

29A. Electronic record.—The words "electronic record" shall have the meaning assigned to them in clause (t) of sub-section (1) of section 2 of the Information Technology Act, 2000."

1. Ins. by Act 21 of 2000, sec. 91 and Sch. I (w.e.f. 17-10-2000).

167. Public servant farming an incorrect document with intent to cause injury.—Whoever, being a public servant, and being, as 1[such public servant, charged with the preparation or translation of any document or electronic record, frames, prepares or translates that document or electronic record] in a manner which he knows or believes to be incorrect, intending thereby to cause or knowing it to be likely that he may thereby cause injury to any person, shall be punished with imprisonment of either description for a term which may extend to three years, or with fine, or with both.

1. Subs. by Act 21 of 2000, sec. 91 and Sch. I, for certain words (w.e.f. 17-10-2000).

CHAPTER XVIII

OF OFFENCES RELATING TO DOCUMENTS AND TO [1][...] PROPERTY MARKS

463. Forgery.—[2][Whoever makes any false documents or false electronic record part of a document or electronic record with, intent to cause damage or injury], to the public or to any person, or to support any claim or title, or to cause any person to part with property, or to enter into any express or implied contract, or with intent to commit fraud or that fraud may be committed, commits forgery.

464. Making a false document.—1[A person is said to make a false document or false electronic record:

First—Who dishonestly or fraudulently:

(a) Makes, signs, seals or executes a document or part of a document;

(b) Makes or transmits any electronic record or part of any electronic record;

(c) Affixes any digital signature on any electronic record;

(d) Makes any mark denoting the execution of a document or the authenticity of the digital signature.

---

1. The words "TRADE OR" omitted by Act 43 of 1958, sec. 135 and sch. (w.e.f. 25-11-1959).

2. Subs. by Act 21 of 2000, sec. 91 and Sch. I, for certain words (w.e.f. 17-10-2000).

With the intention of causing it to be believed that such document or part of document, electronic record or digital signature was made, signed, sealed, executed, transmitted or affixed by or by the authority of a person by whom or by whose authority he knows that it was not made, signed, sealed, executed or affixed; or

Secondly—Who, without lawful authority, dishonestly or fraudulently, by cancellation or otherwise, alters a document or an electronic record in any material part thereof, after it has been made, executed or affixed with digital signature either by himself or by any other person, whether such person be living or dead at the time of such alteration; or

Thirdly—Who dishonestly or fraudulently causes any person to sign, seal, execute or alter a document or an electronic record or to affix his digital signature on any electronic record knowing that such person by reason of unsoundness of mind or intoxication cannot, or that by reason of deception practised upon him, he does not know the contents of the document or electronic record or the nature of the alterations.]

Illustrations

(a) A has a letter of credit upon B for rupees 10,000 written by Z. A, in order to defraud B, adds a cipher to the 10,000, and makes the sum 1,00,000 intending that it may be belived by B that Z so wrote the letter. A has committed forgery.

(b) A, without Z's authority affixes Z's seal to document purporting to be a conveyance of an estate from Z to A, with the intention of selling the estate to B, and thereby of obtaining from B the purchase-money. A has committed forgery.

(c) A picks up a cheque on a banker signed by B, payable to bearer, but without any sum having been inserted in the cheque. A fraudulently fills up the cheque by inserting the sum of ten thousand rupees. A commits forgery.

(d) A leaves with B, his agent, a cheque on a banker, signed by A, without inserting the sum payable and authorizes B to fill up the cheque by inserting a sum not exceeding ten thousand rupees for the purpose of making certain payments. B fraudulently fills up the cheque by inserting the sum or twenty thousand rupees. B commits forgery.

(e) A draws a bill of exchange on himself in the name of B without B's authority, intending to discount it as a genuine bill with a banker and intending to take up the bill on its maturity. Here, as A draws the bill with intent to deceive the banker by leading him to suppose that he had the security of B, and thereby to discount the bill, A is guilty of forgery.

(f) Z's will contains the these words "I direct that all my remaining property be equally divided between A, B and C." A dishonestly scratches out B's name, intending that it may be believed that the whole was left to himself and C. A has committed forgery.

(g) A endorses a Government promissory note and makes it payable to Z or his order by writing on the bill the words "Pay to Z or his order" and signing the endorsement. B dishonestly erases the words "Pay to Z or his order", and thereby converts the special endorsement into a blank endorsement. B commits forgery.

(h) A sells and conveys an estate to Z. A afterwards, in order to defraud Z of his estate, executes a conveyance of the same estate to B, dated six months earlier than the date of the conveyance to Z, intending it to be believed that he had conveyed the estate to B before he conveyed it to Z. A has committed forgery.

(i) Z dictates his will to A. A intentionally writes down a different legatee for the legatee named by Z, and by representing to Z that he has prepared the will according to his instructions, induces Z to sign the will. A has committed forgery.

(j) A writes a letter and signs it with B's name without B's authority, certifying that A is a man of good character and in distressed circumstances from unforeseen misfortune, intending by means of such letter to obtain alms from Z and other persons. Here, as A made a false document in order to induce Z to part with property. A has committed forgery.

(k) A without B's authority writes a letter and signs it in B's name certifying to A's character, intending thereby to obtain employment under Z. A has committed forgery in as much as he intended to deceive Z by the forged certificate, and thereby to induce Z to enter into an express or implied contract for service.

Explanation 1: A man's signature of his own name may amount to forgery.

Illustrations

(a) A signs his own name to a bill of exchange, intending that it may be believed that the bill was drawn by another person of the same name. A has committed forgery.

(b) A writes the word "accepted" on a piece of paper and signs it with Z's name, in order that B may afterwards write on the paper a bill of exchange drawn by B upon Z, and negotiate the bill as though it had been accepted by Z. A is guilty of forgery; and if B, knowing the fact, draws the bill upon the paper pursuant to A's intention, B is also guilty of forgery.

(c) A picks up a bill of exchange payable to the order of a different person of the same name. A endorses the bill in his own name, intending to cause it to be believed that it was endorsed by the person whose order it was payable, here A has committed forgery.

(d) A purchases an estate sold under execution of a decree against B. B, after the seizure of the estate, in collusion with Z, executes a lease of the estate of Z at a nominal rent and for a long period and dates the lease six months prior to the seizure, with intent to defraud A, and to cause it to be believed that the lease was granted before the seizure. B, though he executes the lease in his own name, commits forgery by antedating it.

(e) A, a trader, in anticipation of insolvency, lodges effects with B for A's benefit, and with intent to defraud his creditors; and in order to give a colour to the transaction, writes a promissory note binding himself to pay to B a sum for value received, and antedates the note, intending that it may be believed to have been made before A was on the point of insolvency. A has committed forgery under the first head of the definition.

Explanation 2. The making of a false document in the name of a fictitious person, intending it to be believed that the document was made by a real person, or in the name of deceased person, intending it to be believed that the document was made by the person in his lifetime, may amount to forgery.

Illustration

A draws a bill of exchange upon a fictitious person, and fraudulently accepts the bill in the name of such fictitious person with intent to negotiate it. A commits forgery.

2[*Explanation* 3: For the purposes of this section, the expression "affixing digital signature" shall have the meaning assigned to it in clause (d) of sub-section (1) of section 2 of the Information Technology Act, 2000.]

1. Subs. by Act 21 of 2000, sec. 91 and Sch. I, for certain words (w.e.f. 17-10-2000).
2. Ins. by Act 21 of 2000, sec. 91 and Sch. I, (w.e.f. 17-10-2000).

465. Punishment for forgery.—Whoever commits forgery shall be punished with imprisonment of either description for a term which may extend to two years, or with fine, or with both.

466. Forgery of record of court or of public register, etc.—1[Whoever forges a document or an electronic record], purporting to be a record or proceeding of or in a Court of Justice, or a register of birth, baptism, marriage or burial, or a register kept by a public servant as such, or a certificate or document purporting to be made by a public servant in his official capacity, or an authority to institute or defend a suit, or to take any proceedings therein, or to confess judgment, or a power of attorney, shall be punished with imprisonment of either description for a term which may extend to seven years, and shall also be liable to fine.

1[*Explanation*: For the purposes of this section, "register" includes any list, data or record of any entries maintained in the electronic form as defined in clause (r) of sub-section (1) of section 2 of the Information Technology Act, 2000.]

1. Subs. by Act 21 of 2000, sec. 91 and Sch. I, for "Whoever forges a document" (w.e.f. 17-10-2000).

467. Forgery of valuable security, will, etc.—Whoever forges a document which purports to be a valuable security or a will, or an authority to adopt a son, or which purports to give authority to any person to make or transfer any valuable security, or to receive the principal, interest or dividends thereon, or to receive or deliver any money, moveable property, or valuable security, or any document purporting to be an acquaintance or receipt acknowledging the payment of money, or an acquaintance or receipt for the delivery of any moveable property or valuable security, shall be punished with 1[imprisonment for life], or with imprisonment of either description for a term which may extend to ten years, and shall also be liable to fine.

1. Subs. by Act 26 of 1955, s. 117 and Sch. I, for "transportation for life" (w.e.f. 1-1-1956).

468. Forgery for purpose of cheating.—Whoever commits forgery, intending that the 1[document or Electronic Record forged] shall be used for the purpose of cheating, shall be punished with imprisonment of either description for a term which may extend to seven years, and shall also be liable to fine.

1. Subs. by Act 21 of 2000, sec. 91 and Sch. I, for "document forged" (w.e.f. 17-10-2000).

469. Forgery for purpose of harming reputation.—Whoever commits forgery, 1[intending that the document or Electronic Record forged] shall harm the reputation of any party, or knowing that it is likely to be used for that purpose, shall be punished with imprisonment of either description for a term which may extend to three years, and shall also be liable to fine.

1. Subs. by Act 21 of 2000, sec. 91 and Sch. I, for "intending that the documents forged" (w.e.f. 17-10-2000).

470. Forged document or electronic record.—A false document or Electronic Record made wholly or in part by forgery is designated "a forged document or electronic record".

471. Using as genuine a forged document or electronic record.—Whoever fraudulently or dishonestly uses as genuine any 1[document or electronic record] which he knows or has reason to believe to be a forged 1[document or electronic record], shall be punished in the same manner as if he had forged such 2[document or electronic record].

1. Subs. by Act 21 of 2000, sec. 91 and Sch. I, for "document" (w.e.f. 17-10-2000).
2. Subs. by Act 21 of 2000, sec. 91 and Sch. I, for "document forged" (w.e.f. 17-10-12000).

472. Making or possessing counterfeit seal, etc., with intent to commit forgery punishable under section 467.—Whoever makes or counterfeits any seal, plate or other instrument for making an impression, intending that the same shall be used for the purpose of committing any forgery which would be punishable under section 467 of this Code, or, with such intent, has in his possession any such seal, plate or other instrument, knowing the same to be counterfeit, shall be punished with 1[imprisonment for life], or with imprisonment of either description for a term which may extend to seven years, and shall also be liable to fine.

1. Subs. by Act 26 of 1955, sec. 117 and sch. I, for "transportation for life" (w.e.f. 1-1-1956).

473. Making or possessing counterfeit seal, etc. with intent to commit forgery punishable otherwise.—Whoever makes or counterfeit any seal, plate or other instrument for making an impression, intending that the same shall be used for the purpose of committing any forgery which would be punishable under any section of this chapter other than section 467, or, with such intent, has in his possession any such seal, plate or other instrument, knowing the same to be counterfeit, shall be punished with imprisonment of either description for a term which may extend to seven years, and shall also be liable to fine.

474. Having possession of document described in section 466 or 467, knowing it to be forged and intending to use it as genuine.—1[Whoever has in his possession any document or electronic record, knowing the same to be forged, and intending that the same shall fraudulently or dishonestly be used as genuine, shall, if the document or electronic record, is one of the description mentioned in section 466 of this code], be punished with imprisonment of either description for a term which may extend to seven years, and shall also be liable to fine; and if the document is one of the description mentioned in section 467, shall be punished with 2[imprisonment for life], or with imprisonment of either description, for a term which may extend to seven years, and shall also be liable to fine.

1. Subs. by Act 21 of 2000, sec. 91 and Sch. I, for certain words (w.e.f. 17-10-2000).
2. Subs. by Act 26 of 1955, sec. 117 and Sch. I, for "transportation for life" (w.e.f. 1-1-1956).

475. Counterfeiting device or mark used for authenticating documents described in section 467, or possessing counterfeit marked material.—Whoever counterfeits upon, or in the substance or, any material, any device or mark used for the purpose of authenticating any document described in section 467 of this code, intending that such device or mark shall be used for the purpose of giving the appearance of authenticity to any document then forged or thereafter to be forged on such material, or who, with such intent, has in his possession any material upon or in the substance of which any such device or mark has been counterfeited, shall be punished with 1[imprisonment for life], or with imprisonment of either description for a term which may extend to seven years, and shall also be liable to fine.

1. Subs. by Act 26 of 1955, sec. 117 and Sch. I, for "transportation for life" (w.e.f. 1-1-1956).

476. Counterfeiting device or mark used for authenticating 1[documents or electronic record], other than those described in section 467, or possessing counterfeit marked material.— Whoever counterfeits upon, or in the substance of, any material, any device or mark used for the purpose of authenticating any 1[document or electronic record], other than the documents described in Section 467 of this code, intending that such device or mark shall be used for the purpose of giving the appearance of authenticity to any document or electronic record then forged or thereafter to be forged on such material, or who with such intent, has in his possession any material upon or in the substance of which any such device or mark has been counterfeited, shall be punished with imprisonment of either description for a term which may extend to seven years, and shall also be liable to fine.

1. Subs. by Act 21 of 2000, sec. 91 and Sch. I, for "any document" (w.e.f. 17-10-2000).

477. Fraudulent cancellation, destruction, etc. of will, authority to adopt, or valuable security.—Whoever fraudulently or dishonestly, or with intent to cause damage or injury to the public or to any person, cancels, destroys or defaces, or attempts to cancel, destroy or deface, or secretes or attempts to secrete any document which is or purports to be a will, or an authority to adopt a son, or any valuable security, or commits mischief in respect of such document, shall be punished with 1[imprisonment for life], or with imprisonment of either description for a term which may extend to seven years, and shall also be liable to fine.

1. Subs. by Act 26 of 1955, sec. 117 and Sch. I, for "transportation for life" (w.e.f. 1-1-1956).

477A. Falsification of accounts.—1[477A. Falsification of accounts.]

Whoever, being a clerk, officer or servant, or employed or acting in the capacity of a clerk, officer or servant, willfully, and with intent to defraud, destroys, alters, mutilates or falsifies any

2[book, electronic record, paper, writing], valuable security or account which belongs to or is in the possession of his employer, or has been received by him for or on behalf of his employer, or willfully, and with intent to defraud, makes or abets the making of any false entry in, or omits or alters or abets the omission or alteration of any material particular of any material particular form or in, any such 2[book, electronic record, paper, writing], valuable security or account, shall be punished with imprisonment of either description for a term which may extend to seven years, or with fine, or with both.

Explanation: It shall be sufficient in any charge under this section to allege a general intent to defraud without naming any particular person intended to be defrauded or specifying any particular sum of money intended to be the subject of the fraud, or any particular day on which the offence was committed.

1. Added by Act 3 of 1895, sec. 4.
2. Ins. by Information Technology Act, 2000, Sch. 1, (w.e.f. 17-10-2000).

THE INFORMATION TECHNOLOGY ACT, 2000
(Relevant Provisions)

2. Definitions.—(1) In this Act, unless the context otherwise requires,

(a) "access", with its grammatical variation and cognate expressions, means gaining entry into, instructing or communicating with the logical, arithmetical or memory function resources of a computer, computer system or computer network;

(b) "addressee" means a person who is intended by the originator to receive the electronic record but does not include any intermediary;

(c) "adjudicating officer" means an adjudicating officer appointed under sub-section (1) of section 46; "affixing digital signature", with its grammatical variations and cognate expressions means adoption of any methodology or procedure by a person for the purpose of authenticating an electronic record by means of digital signature; "appropriate Government" means as respects any matter—enumerated in List II of the Seventh Schedule to the Constitution; relating to any State law enacted under List III of the Seventh Schedule to the Constitution, the State Government and in any other case, the Central Government; "asymmetric crypto system" means a system of a secure key pair consisting of a private key for creating a digital signature and a public key to verify the digital signature; "Certifying Authority" means a person who has been granted a licence to issue a Digital Signature Certificate under section 24; "certification practice statement" issued by a Certifying Authority to specify the practices that the Certifying Authority employs in issuing Digital Signature Certificates; "computer" means electronic, magnetic, optical or other high-speed date processing device or system which performs logical, arithmetic and memory functions by manipulations of electronic, magnetic or optical impulses, and includes all input, output, processing, storage, computer software or communication facilities which are connected or relates to the computer in a computer system or computer network; "computer network" means the inter-connection of one or more computers through—

* * * *

(i) the use of satellite, microwave, terrestrial line or other communication media; and

(ii) terminals or a complex consisting of two or more interconnected computers whether or not the interconnection is continuously maintained; "computer resources" means computer, computer system, computer network, data, computer database or software; "computer system" means a device or collection of devices, including input and output support devices and excluding calculators which are not programmable and capable being used in conjunction with external files which contain computer programmes, electronic instructions, input data and output data that performs logic, arithmetic, data storage and retrieval, communication control and other functions; "Controller" means the Controller of Certifying Authorities appointed under sub-section (1) of section 17; "Cyber Appellate Tribunal" means the cyber Regulations Appellate Tribunal established under sub-section (1) of section 48; "data" means a representation of information, knowledge, facts, concepts or instruction which are being prepared or have been prepared in a formalised manner, and is intended to be processed, is being processed or has been processed in a computer system or computer network, and may be in any form (including computer printouts magnetic or optical storage media, punched cards, punched tapes) or stored internally in the memory of the computer. "digital signature" means authentication of any electronic record by a subscriber by means of an electronic method or procedure in accordance with the provisions of section 3; "Digital Signature Certificate "means a Digital Signature Certificate issued under sub-section (4) of section 35; "electronic form", with reference to information means, any information generated, sent, received or stored in media, magnetic, optical, computer memory, micro film, computer generated micro fiche or similar device; "Electronic Gazette" means Official Gazette published in the electronic form; "electronic record" means data, record or data generated, image or sound stored, received or sent in an electronic form or microfilm or computer generated micro fiche; "function", in relation to a computer, includes logic, control, arithmetical process, deletion, storage and retrieval and retrieval and communication or telecommunication from or within a computer; "information" includes data, text, images, sound, voice, codes, computer programmes, software and databases or microfilm or computer generated micro fiche; "intermediary" with respect to any particular electronic message, means any person who on behalf of another person receives, stores or transmits that message or provides any service with respect to that message; "key pair", in an asymmetric crypto system, means a private key and its mathematically related public key, which are so related that the public key can verify a digital signature created by the private key; "law" includes any Act of Parliament or of a State Legislature, Ordinances promulgated by the President under article 240, Bills enacted as President's Act under sub-clause (a) of clause (1) of article 375 of the Constitution and includes rules, regulations, bye-laws and order issued or made thereunder; "licence" means a licence granted to a Certifying Authority under section 24; (za) "originator" means a licence granted to a Certifying Authority under section 24; (zb) "prescribed" means prescribed by rules made under the Act; (zc) "private key" means the key of a key pair used to create a digital signature; (zd) "public key" means the key of a key pair used to verify a digital signature and listed in the Digital Signature Certificate; (ze) "secure system" means computer hardware, software and procedure that

* * * *

(a) are reasonably secure from unauthorised access and misuses;

(b) provide a reasonable level of reliability and correct operation;

(c) are reasonably suited to performing the intended functions; and

(d) adhere to generally accepted security procedures; (zf) "security procedure" means the security procedure prescribed under section 16 by the Central Government; (zg) "subscriber" means a person in whose name the Digital Signature Certificate is issued; (zh) "verify", in relation to a digital signature, electronic record or public key, with its grammatical variations and cognate expressions, means to determine whether (a) the initial electronic record was affixed with the digital signature by the use of private key corresponding to the public key of the subscriber; (b) the initial electronic record is retained intact or has been altered since such electronic record was so affixed with the digital signature.

(2) Any reference in this Act to any enactment or any provision thereof shall, in relation to an area in which such enactment or such provision is not in force, be construed as a reference to the corresponding law or the relevant provision of the corresponding law, if any, in force in that area.

CHAPTER II

DIGITAL SIGNATURE

3. Authentication of electronic records.—(1) Subject to the provisions of this section, any subscriber may authenticate an electronic record by affixing his digital signature.

(2) The authentication of the electronic record shall be effected by the use of asymmetric crypto system and hash function which envelop and transform the initial electronic record into another electronic record.

Explanation: For the purposes of this sub-section, "hash function" means an algorithm mapping or translation of one sequence of bits into another, generally smaller, set known as "hash result" such that an electronic record yields the same hash result every time the algorithm is executed with the same electronic record as its input making it computationally infeasible—

(a) to derive or reconstruct the original electronic record from the hash result produced by the algorithm;

(b) that two electronic records can produce the same hash result using algorithm.

(3) Any person by the use of a public key of the subscriber can verify the electronic record.

(4) The private key and the public key are unique to the subscriber and constitute a functioning key pair.

CHAPTER III

ELECTRONIC GOVERNANCE

4. Legal recognition of electronic records.— Where any law provides that information or any other matter shall be in writing or in the typewritten or printed form, then, notwithstanding anything contained in such law, such requirement shall be deemed to have been satisfied if such information or matter is—

(a) rendered or made available in an electronic form; and

(b) accessible so as to be usable for a subsequent reference.

5. Legal recognition of digital signatures.—Where any lay provides that information or any other matter shall be authenticated by affixing the signature or any document shall be signed or bear the signature of any person, then, notwithstanding anything contained in such law, such requirement shall be deemed to have been satisfied if such information or matter is authenticated by means of digital signature affixed in such manner as may be prescribed by the Central Government.

Explanation: For the purposes of this section, "signed", with its grammatical variations and cognate expressions, shall, with reference to a person, means affixing of his hand written signature or any mark on any document and the expression "signature" shall be construed accordingly.

6. Use of electronic records and digital signatures in Government and its agencies.—(1) Where any law provides for—

(a) the filing of any form, application or any other document with any office authority, body for agency owned or controlled by the appropriate Government in a particular manner;

(b) the issue or grant of any licence, permit, sanction or approval by whatever name called in a particular manner;

(c) the receipt or payment of money in a particular manner, then, notwithstanding anything contained in any other law for the time being in force, such requirement shall be deemed to have been satisfied if such filing, issue, grant, receipt or payment, as the case be, is effected by means of such electronic form as may be prescribed by the appropriate Government.

(2) The appropriate Government may, for the purposes of sub-section (1), by rules, prescribe—

(a) the manner and format in which such electronic records shall be filed, created or issued;

(b) the manner or method of payment of any fee or charges for filing, creation or issue any electronic record clause (a).

7. Retention of electronic records.—(1) Where any law provides that documents, records or information shall be retained for any specific period, then, that requirement shall be deemed to have been satisfied if such documents, records or information are retained in the electronic form, if:

(a) the manner and format therein remains accessible so as to be usable for a subsequent reference;

(b) the electronic record is retained in the format in which it was originally generated, sent or received or in a format which can be demonstrated to represent accurately the information originally generated, sent or received;

(c) the details which will facilitate the identification of the origin, destination, date and time of dispatch or receipt of such electronic record:

Provided that this clause does not apply to any information which is automatically generated solely for the purpose of enabling a record to be dispatched or received.

(2) Nothing in this section shall apply to any law that expressly provides for the retention of documents, records or information in the form of electronic records.

8. Publication of rule, regulation, etc. in Electronic Gazette.—Where any law provides that any rule, regulation, order, bye-law, notification or any other matter shall be published in the Official Gazette, then, such requirement shall be deemed to have been satisfied if such rule, regulation, order, bye-law, notification or any other matter is published in the Official Gazette or Electronic Gazette:

Provided that where any rule, regulation, order, bye-law, notification or any other matter is published in the Official Gazette or Electronic Gazette, the date of publication shall be deemed to be the date of the Gazette which was first published in any form.

9. Sections 6, 7 and 8 not to confer right to insist document should be accepted in electronic form.—Nothing contained in sections 6, 7 and 8 shall confer a right upon any person to insist that any Ministry or Department of the Central Government or the State Government or any authority or body established by or under any law or controlled or funded by the Central or State Government should accept, issue, create, retain and preserve any document in the form of electronic records or effect any monetary transaction in the electronic form.

CHAPTER IV

ATTRIBUTION, ACKNOWLEDGEMENT AND DESPATCH OF ELECTRONIC RECORDS

11. Attribution of electronic records.—An electronic record shall be attributed to the originator,

(a) if it was sent by the originator himself;

(b) by a person who had the authority to act on behalf of the originator in respect of that electronic record; or

(c) by an information system programmed by or on behalf of the originator to operate automatically.

12. Acknowledgement of receipt.—(1) Where the originator has not agreed with the addressee that the acknowledgement of receipt of electronic record be given in a particular form or by a particular method, an acknowledgement may be given by—

(a) any communication by the addressee, automated or otherwise; or

(b) any conduct of the addressee, sufficient to indicate to the originator that the electronic record has been received.

Where the originator has stipulated that the electronic record shall be binding only on receipt of an acknowledgement of such electronic record by him, then, unless acknowledgement has been so received, the electronic record shall be deemed to have been never sent by the originator.

Where the originator has not stipulated that the electronic record shall be binding only on receipt of such acknowledgement, and the acknowledgement has not been received by the originator within the time specified or agreed or, if no time has been specified or agreed to within a reasonable time, then, the originator may give notice to the addressee stating that no acknowledgement has been received by him and specifying a reasonable time by which the acknowledgement must be received by him and if no acknowledgement is received within the aforesaid time limit he may after giving notice to the addressee, treat the electronic record as though it has never been sent.

13. Time and place of desptach and receipt of electronic record—(1) Save as otherwise agreed to between the originator and the addressee, the despatch of an electronic record occurs when it enters a computer resources outside the control of the originator.

(2) Save as otherwise agreed between the originator and the addressee, the time of receipt of an electronic record shall be determined as follows, namely:—

(a) if the addressee has designated a computer resource for the purpose of receiving electronic record,

(i) receipt occurs at the time when the electronic record enters the designated computer resource; or

(ii) if the electronic record is spent to a computer resource of the addressee that is not the designated computer resource, receipt occurs at the time when the electronic record is retrieved by the addressee;

(b) if the addressee has not designated a computer resource along with specified timings, if any, receipt occurs when the electronic record enters the computer resource of the addressee.

(3) Save as otherwise agreed to between the originator and the addressee, an electronic record is deemed to be received at the place where the addressee has his place of business.

(4) The provisions of sub-section (2) shall apply notwithstanding that the place where the computer resource is located may be different from the place where the electronic record is deemed to have been received under sub-section (3).

(5) For the purpose of this section,

(a) if the originator or the addressee has more than one place of business, the principal place of business, shall be the place of business;

(b) if the originator or the addressee does not have a place of business, his usual place of residence shall be deemed to be the place of business;

(c) "usual place of residence", in relation to a body corporate, means the place where it is registered.

CHAPTER V

SECURE ELECTRONIC RECORDS AND SECURE DIGITAL SIGNATURES

14. Secure electronic record.— Where any security procedure has been applied to an electronic record at a specific point of time, then such record shall be deemed to be a secure electronic record from such point of time to the time of verification.

15. Secure digital signature.—If, by application of a security procedure agreed to by the parties concerned, it can be verified that a digital signature, at the time it was affixed, was—

(a) unique to the subscriber affixing it;

(b) capable of identifying such subscriber;

(c) created in a manner or using a means under the exclusive control of the subscriber and is linked to the electronic record to which related in such a manner that if the electronic record was altered the digital signature would be invalidated, then such digital signature shall be deemed to be a secure digital signature.

29. Access to computers and data.—(1) Without prejudice to the provisions of sub-section (1) of section 68, the Controller or any person authorised by him shall, if he has reasonable cause to suspect that any contravention of the provisions of this Act, rules or regulations made thereunder has been committed, have access to any computer system, any apparatus, data or any other material connected with such system, for the purpose of searching or causing a search to be made for obtaining any information or data contained in or data contained in or available to such computer system.

(2) For the purposes of sub-section (1), the Controller or any person authorised by him may, by order, direct any person incharge of, or otherwise concerned with the operation of, the computer system, data apparatus or material, to provide him with such reasonable technical and other assistance as he may consider necessary.

30. Certifying Authority to follow certain procedures.— Every Certifying Authority shall,

(a) make use of hardware, software, and procedures that are secure from intrusion and misuse;

(b) provide a reasonable level of reliability in its services which are reasonably suited to the performance of intended functions;

(c) adhere to security procedures to ensure that the secrecy and privacy of the digital signatures are assured; and

(d) observe such other standards as may be specified by regulations.

34. Disclosure.—(1) Every Certifying Authority shall disclose in the manner specified by regulations—

(a) Its Digital Signature Certificate which contains the public key corresponding to the private key used by that Certifying Authority to digitally sign another Digital Signature Certificate;

(b) and certification practice statement relevant thereto;

(c) notice of the revocation or suspension of its Certifying Authority certificate if any; and

(d) any other fact that materially and adversely affects either the reliability of a Digital Signature Certificate, which that Authority has issued, or the Authority's ability to perform its services.

(2) Where in the opinion of the Certifying Authority any event has occurred or any situation has arisen which may materially and adversely affect the integrity of its computer system or the conditions subject to which a Digital Signature Certificate was granted, then, the Certifying Authority shall,

(a) use reasonable efforts to notify any person who is likely to be affected by that occurrence: or

(b) act in accordance with the procedure specified in its certification practice statement to deal with such event or situation.

67. Publishing of information which is obscene in electronic form.— Whoever publishes or transmits or causes to be published in the electronic form, any material which is lascivious or appeal to the prurient interest or if its effect is such as to tend to deprave and corrupt persons who are likely, having regard to all relevant circumstances, to read, see or hear the matter contained or embodied in it, shall be punished on first conviction with imprisonment of either description for a term which may extend to five years and with fine which may extend to one lakh rupees and in the event of a second or subsequent conviction with imprisonment of either description for a term which may extend to ten years and also with fine which may extend to two lakh rupees.

70. Protected system.— (1) The appropriate Government may, by notification in the Official Gazette, declare that any computer, computer system or computer network to be a protected system.

(2) The appropriate Government may, by order in writing, authorise the persons who are authorised to access protected systems notified under sub-section.

(3) Any person who secures access or attempts to secure access to a protected system in contravention of the provisions of this section shall be punished with imprisonment of either description for a term which may extend to ten years and shall also be liable to fine.

72. Penalty for breach of confidentiality and privacy.—Save as otherwise provided in this Act or any other law for the time being in force, if any person who, in pursuance of any of the powers conferred under this Act, rules or regulations made thereunder, has secured access to any electronic record, book, register, correspondence, information, document or other material without the consent of the person concerned discloses such electronic record, book, register, correspondence, information, document or other material to any other person shall be punished with imprisonment for a term which may extend to two years, or with fine which may extend to one lakh rupees, or with both.

THE MEDICAL TERMINATION OF PREGNANCY REGULATIONS, 2003

(Relevant Provisions)

G.S.R. 486 (E).—In exercise of powers conferred by section 7 of the Medical Termination of Pregnancy Act, 1971 (34 of 1971), the Central Government hereby makes the following regulations, namely:

1. Short title, extent and commencement.—(1) These regulations may be called the Medical Termination of Pregnancy Regulations, 2003.

(2) They extend to all the Union territories.

(3) They shall come into force on the date of their publication in the Official Gazette.

2. Definitions.—In these regulations, unless the context otherwise requires,

(a) "Act" means the Medical Termination of Pregnancy Act, 1971 (34 of 1971);

(b) "Admission Register" means the register maintained under regulation 5;

(c) Chief Medical Officer of the District means the Chief Medical Officer of the District by whatever name called;

(d) "Form" means a form appended to these regulations;

(e) "hospital" means a hospital established or maintained by the Central Government or the Government of Union territory;

(f) "section" means a section of the Act.

3. Form of certifying opinion or opinions.—(1) Where one registered medical practitioner forms or not less than two registered medical practitioners form such opinion as is referred to in sub-section (2) of section 3 or 5, he or she shall certify such opinion in Form I.

(2) Every registered medical practitioner who terminates any pregnancy shall, within three hours from the termination of the pregnancy certify such termination in Form I.

4. Custody of forms.—(1) The consent given by a pregnant woman for the termination of her pregnancy, together with the certified opinion recorded under section 3 or section 5, as the case may be and the intimation of termination of pregnancy shall be placed in an envelope which shall be sealed by the registered medical practitioner or practitioners by whom such termination of pregnancy was performed and until that envelope is sent to the head of the hospital or owner of the approved place or the Chief Medical Officer of the State, it shall be kept in the safe custody of he concerned registered medical practitioner or practitioners, as the case may be.

(2) On every envelope referred to in sub-regulation (1), pertaining to the termination of pregnancy under section 3, there shall be noted the serial number assigned to the pregnant woman in the Admission Register and the name of the registered medical practitioner or practitioners by whom the pregnancy was terminated and such envelope shall be marked "SECRET".

(3) Every envelope referred to in sub-regulation (2) shall be sent immediately after the termination of the pregnancy to the head of the hospital or owner of the approved place where the pregnancy was terminated.

(4) On receipt of the envelope referred to in sub-regulation (3), the head of the hospital or owner of the approved place shall arrange to keep the same in safe custody.

(5) Every head of the hospital or owner of the approved place shall send to the Chief Medical Officer of the State, in Form II a monthly statement of cases where medical termination of pregnancy has been done.

(6) On every envelope referred to in sub-regulation (1), pertaining to the termination of pregnancy under section 5, there shall be noted the name and address of the registered medical practitioner by whom the pregnancy was terminated and the date on which the pregnancy was terminated and such envelope shall be marked "SECRET".

Explanation. The columns pertaining to the hospital or approved place and the serial number assigned to the pregnant woman in the Admission Register shall be left blank in Form I in the case of termination performed under section 5.

(7) Where the pregnancy is not terminated in an approved place or hospital, every envelope referred to in sub-regulation (6) shall be sent by registered post to the Chief Medical Officer of the State on the same day on which the pregnancy was terminated or on the working day next following the day on which the pregnancy was terminated:

Provided that where the pregnancy is terminated in an approved place or hospital, the procedure provided in sub-regulations (1) to (6) shall be followed.

5. Maintenance of Admission Register.—(1) Every head of the hospital or owner of the approved place shall maintain a register in Form III for recording there in the details of the admissions of women for the termination of their pregnancies and keep such register for a period of five years from the end of the calendar year it relates to.

(2) The entries in the Admission Register shall be made serially and a fresh serial shall be started at the commencement of each calendar year and the serial number of the particular year shall be distinguished from the serial number of other years by mentioning the year against the serial number, for example, serial number 5 of 1972 and serial number 5 of 1973 shall be mentioned as 5/1972 and 5/1973.

(3) Admission Register shall be a secret document and the information contained therein as to the name and other particulars of the pregnant woman shall not be disclosed to any person.

6. Admission Register not to be open to inspection.—The Admission Register shall be kept in the safe custody of the head of the hospital or owner of the approved place, or by any person authorized by such head or owner and save as otherwise provided in sub-regulation (5) of regulation 4 shall not be open for inspection by any person except under the authority of law:

Provided that the registered medical practitioner on the application of an employed woman whose pregnancy has been terminated, grant a certificate for the purpose of enabling her to obtain leave from her employer;

Provided further that any such employer shall not disclose this information to any other person.

7. Entries in registers maintained in hospital or approved place.—No entry shall be made in any case-sheet, operation theatre register, follow-up card or any other document or register other than the Admission Register maintained at any hospital or approved place indicating therein the name of the pregnant woman and reference to the pregnant woman shall be made therein by the serial number assigned to the woman in the Admission Register.

THE PROTECTION OF PLANT VARIETIES AND FARMERS' RIGHTS ACT, 2001

(Relevant Provisions)

84. Document open to public inspection.—Any person may, on an application to the Authority or the Registrar, as the case may be, and on payment of such fees as may be prescribed, obtain a certified copy of any entry in the Register or any other document in any proceedings under this Act pending before such Authority or Registrar or may inspect such entry or document.

86. Government to be bound.—The provisions of this Act shall be binding on the Government.

THE PROTECTION OF PLANT VARIETIES AND FARMERS' RIGHTS RULES, 2003

(Relevant Provisions)

9. Size, etc. of documents.—All documents and copies of documents, except affidavits and drawings, sent to or left at the office of the Authority or otherwise furnished to the Registrar shall be written, typewritten, lithographed, or printed (either in the Hindi or in the English language unless otherwise directed or allowed by the Authority or the Registrar-General) in large and legible characters with deep indelible ink with lines widely spaced upon one side only of strong white paper of a size of approximately 33.00 centimetres by 20.50 centimetres (13 inches by 8 inches) or 29.7 centimetres by 21 centimetres (11 3/4 inches by 8 1/4 inches) with a margin of at least four centimetres (one and a half inches) on the left-hand part thereof.

THE REPRESENTATION OF THE PEOPLE ACT, 1951
(Relevant Provisions)

[1][**33A. Right to information.**—(1) A candidate shall, apart from any information which he is required to furnish, under this Act or the rules made thereunder, in his nomination paper delivered under sub-section (1) of section 33, also furnish the information as to whether—

(i) he is accused of any offence punishable with imprisonment for two years or more in a pending case in which a charge has been framed by the court of competent jurisdiction;

(ii) he has been convicted of an offence [other than any offence referred to in sub-section (1) or sub-section (2), or covered in sub-section (3), of section 8] and sentenced to imprisonment for one year or more.

(2) The candidate of his proposer, as the case may be, shall, at the time of delivering to the returning officer the nomination paper under sub-section (1) of section 33, also deliver to him an affidavit sworn by the candidate in a prescribed form very fine the information specified in sub-section (1).

(3) The returning officer shall, as soon as may be after the furnishing of information to him under sub-section (1), display the aforesaid information by affixing a copy of the affidavit, delivered under sub-section (2), at a conspicuous place at his

1. Ins. by Act 72 of 2002, s. 2 (w.e.f. 24-8-2002).

office for the information of the electors relating to a constituency for which the nomination paper is delivered.

[1]**33B. Candidate to furnish information only under the Act and the rules.**—Notwithstanding anything contained in any judgment, decree or order of any court or any direction, order or any other instruction issued by the Election Commission, no candidate shall be liable to disclose or furnish any such information, in respect of his election which is not required to be disclosed or furnished under this Act or the rules made thereunder.]

[2]**38. Publication of list of contesting candidates.**—(1) Immediately after the expiry of the period within which candidatures may be withdrawn under sub-section (1) of section 37, the returning officer shall prepare and publish in such form and manner as may be prescribed a list of contesting candidates, that is to say, candidates who were included in the list of validly nominated candidates and who have not withdrawn their candidature within the said period.

[3][(2) For the purpose of listing the names under sub-section (1), the candidates shall be classified as follows, namely:

(i) candidates of recognised political parties;

(ii) candidates of registered political parties other than those mentioned in clause (i); and

(iii) other candidates.

(3) The categories mentioned in sub-section (2) shall be arranged in the order specified therein and the names of candidates in each category shall be arranged in alphabetical order and the addresses of the contesting candidates as given in the nomination papers together with such other particulars as may be prescribed.]

1. Subs. by s. 3, ibid. (w.e.f. 2-5-2002).
2. Subs. by Act 27 of 1956, s. 21, for s. 38.
3. Subs. by Act 21 of 1996, s. 8, for sub-section (2) (w.e.f. 1-8-1996).

CHAPTER VII

PUBLICATION OF ELECTION RESULTS AND NOMINATIONS

[1][**71. Publication of results of elections to the Council of States and of names of persons nominated by the President.**— After the elections held in any year in pursuance of the notifications issued under section 12, there shall be notified by the appropriate authority in the Official Gazette the names of members elected by the elected members of the Legislative Assemblies of the States and by the members of the electoral colleges for the various Union territories at the said elections together with the names of any persons nominated by the President of the Council of States under sub-clause (a) of clause (1) of Article 80 or under any other provisions.

73. Publication of results of general elections to the House of the People and the State Legislative Assemblies and of names of penous neminated thereto.—Where a general election is held for the purpose of constituting a new House of the People or a new State Legislative Assembly, there shall be notified by the Election Commission in the Official Gazette, as soon as may be after the results of the elections in all the constituencies other than those in which the poll could not be taken for any reason on the date originally fixed under clause (d) of section 30 or for which the time for completion of the election has been extended under the provisions of section 153 have been declared by the returning officer under the provisions of section 53 or, as the case may be, section 66, the names of the members elected for those constituencies [4]* * * and upon the issue of such notification that House or Assembly shall be deemed to be duly constituted:

Provided that the issue of such notification shall not be deemed—

(a) to preclude,

(i) the taking of the poll and the completion of the election in any Parliamentary or Assembly constituency or constituencies in which the poll

1. Subs. by Act 27 of 1956, s. 38, for certain words.

could not be taken for any reason on the date originally fixed under clause (d) of section 30; or

(ii) the completion of the election in any Parliamentary or Assembly constituency or constituencies for which time has been extended under the provisions of section 153.

(b) to affect the duration of the House of the People or the State Legislative Assembly, if any, functioning immediately before the issue of the said notification.

74. Publication of results of elections to the State Legislative Councils and of names of persons nominated to such Councils.—After the elections held [1][in pursuance of the notifications issued under section 15A or] in any year in pursuance of the notifications issued under section 16, there shall be notified by the appropriate authority in the Official Gazette the names of the members elected for the various Council constituencies and by the members of the Legislative Assembly of the State at the said elections together with the names of any persons nominated by the Governor[2] under subclause (e) of clause (3) of article 171.

[3]*CHAPTER VIIA*

DECLARATION OF ASSETS AND LIABILITIES

75A. Declaration of assets and liabilities.—(1) Every elected candidate for a House of Parliament shall, within ninety days from the date on which he makes and subscribes an oath or affirmation, according to the form set out for the purpose in the third Schedule to the Constitution, for taking his seat in either House of Parliament, furnish the information, relating to—

(i) the movable and immovable property of which he, his spouse and his dependant children are jointly or severally owners or beneficiaries;

1. Ins. by Act 37 of 1957, s. 13.
2. The words "or Rajpramukh, as the case may be" omitted by the Adaptation of Laws (No. 2) Order, 1956.
3. Ins. by Act 72 of 2002, s. 4 (w.e.f. 24-8-2002).

(ii) his liabilities to any public financial institution; and

(iii) his liabilities to the Central Government or the State Government, to the Chairman of the Council of States or the Speaker of the House of the People, as the case may be.

(2) The information under sub-section (1) shall be furnished in such form and in such manner as may be prescribed in the rules made under sub-section (3).

(3) The Chairman of the Council of States or the Speaker of the House of the People, as the case may be, may make rules for the purposes of sub-section (2).

(4) The rules made by the Chairman of the Council of States or the Speaker of the House of the People, under sub-section (3) shall be laid, as soon as may be after they are made, before the Council of States or the House of the People, as the case may be, for a total period of thirty days which may be comprised in one session or in two or more successive sessions and shall take effect upon the expiry of the said period of thirty days unless they are sooner approved with or without modifications or disapproved by the Council of States or the House of the People and where they are so approved, they shall take effect on such approval in the form in which they were laid or in such modified form, as the case may be, and where they are so disapproved, they shall be of no effect.

(5) The Chairman of the Council of States or the Speaker of the House of the People, as the case may be, may direct that any wilful contravention of the rules made under sub-section (3) by an elected candidate for a House of Parliament referred to in sub-section (1) may be dealt with in the same manner as a breach of privilege of the Council of States or the House of the People, as the case may be.

Explanation. For the purposes of this section,

(i) "immovable property" means the land and includes any building or other structure attached to the land or permanently fastened to anything which is attached to the land;

(ii) "movable property" means any other property which is not the immovable property and includes corporeal and incorporeal property of every description;

(iii) "public financial institution" means a public financial institution within the meaning of section 4A of the Companies Act, 1956 (1 of 1956), and includes bank;

(iv) "bank" referred to in clause (iii) means—

(a) State Bank of India constituted under section 3 of the State Bank of India Act, 1955 (23 of 1955);

(b) subsidiary bank having the meaning assigned to it in clause (k) of section 2 of the State Bank of India (Subsidiary Banks) Act, 1959 (38 of 1959);

(c) Regional Rural Bank established under section 3 of the Regional Rural Banks Act, 1976 (21 of 1976);

(d) corresponding new bank having the meaning assigned to it in clause (*da*) of section 5 of the Banking Regulation Act, 1949 (10 of 1949); and

(e) Co-operative Bank having the meaning assigned to it in clause (*cci*) of section 5 of the Banking Regulation Act, 1949 (10 of 1949) as modified by sub-clause (i) of clause (*c*) of section 56 of that Act; and

(v) "dependant children" means sons and daughters who have no separate means of earning and are wholly dependant on the elected candidate referred to in sub-section (1) for their livelihood.

PART VA

FREE SUPPLY OF CERTAIN MATERIAL TO CANDIDATES OF RECOGNISED POLITICAL PARTIES

78A. Free supply of copies of electoral rolls.—(1) The Government shall, at any election to be held for the purposes of constituting the House of the People or the Legislative Assembly of a State, supply, free of cost, to the candidates of recognised political parties such number of copies of the electoral roll, as finally published under the Representation of the People Act, 1950 (43 of 1950) and such other material as may be prescribed.

(2) The material referred to in sub-section (1) shall be supplied,

(i) subject to such conditions as may be imposed by the Central Government in consultation with the Election Commission with respect to the reduction of the maximum expenditure which may be incurred by the candidate under section 77; and

(ii) through such officers as may be specified by the Election Commission who shall act in accordance with such general or special directions as may be given by the Election Commission.

78B. Supply of certain items to candidates, etc.—(1) The Election Commission shall, at any time between the date of publication of the notification calling the election for the purposes of constituting the House of the People or the Legislative Assembly of a State and the date on which the poll is to be taken, supply or cause to be supplied, such items as the Central Government may, by order, determine in consultation with the Election Commission, to the electors in the constituencies concerned or to the candidates set up by the recognised political parties.

(2) Where the Election Commission supplies the items to the candidates under sub-section (1), the Central Government may, in consultation with the Election Commission, impose conditions with respect to the reduction of the maximum expenditure which may be incurred by the candidate under section 77.

Explanation. For the purposes of section 39A, this chapter and clause (hh) of sub-section (2) of section 169, the expression "recognised political party", has the meaning assigned to it in the Election Symbols (Reservation and Allotment) Order, 1968.

THE SEMICONDUCTOR INTEGRATED CIRCUITS LAYOUT-DESIGN ACT, 2000
(Relevant Provisions)

87. Documents open to public inspection.—(1) Save as otherwise provided in sub-section (4) of section 25,

(a) the register and any document upon which any entry in the register is based;

(b) every notice of opposition to the registration of a layout-design application for rectification before the Registrar, counter-statement thereto, and any affidavit or document filed by the parties in any proceedings before the Registrar; and

(c) the indexes mentioned in section 86 and such other documents as the Central Government may, by notification in the Official Gazette, specify; shall, subject to such conditions as may be prescribed, be open to public inspection at the Semiconductor Integrated Circuits Layout-Design Registry.

(2) Any person may, on an application to the Registrar and on payment of such fees as may be prescribed, obtain a certified copy of any entry in the register or any document referred to in sub-section (1).

THE TRADE MARKS ACT, 1999
(Relevant Provisions)

148. Documents open to public inspection.—(1) Save as otherwise provided in sub-section (4) of section 49,

(a) the register and any document upon which any entry in the register is based;

(b) every notice of opposition to the registration of a trade mark application for rectification before the Registrar, counter-statement thereto, and any affidavit or document filed by the parties in any proceedings before the Registrar;

(c) all regulations deposited under section 63 or section 74, and all applications under section 66 or section 77 for varying such regulations;

(d) the indexes mentioned in section 147; and

(e) such other documents as the Central Government may, by notification in the Official Gazette, specify,

shall, subject to such conditions as may be prescribed, be open to public inspection at the Trade Marks Registry:

Provided that when such register is maintained wholly or partly on computer, the inspection of such register under this section shall be made by inspecting the computer print-out of the relevant entry in the register so maintained on computer.

(2) Any person may, on an application to the Registrar and on payment of such fees as may be prescribed, obtain a certified copy of any entry in the register or any document referred to in sub-section (1).

PART V

REPORTS AND GUIDELINES

(Relevant Provisions)

REPORT OF NATIONAL COMMISSION TO REVIEW THE WORKING OF THE CONSTITUTION, 2002*
(Relevant Provisions)

CHAPTER 3

C. FUNDAMENTAL RIGHTS

3.4. Background and Approach

3.4.1. Constitutional guarantees for the human rights of our people were one of the persistent demands of our leaders throughout the freedom struggle. By the year 1949, when the Constituent Assembly had completed the drafting of the Fundamental Rights Chapter, it had before it the 'Universal Declaration of Human Rights, 1948'.

3.4.2. The International Covenant on Civil and Political Rights, 1966 (ICCPR) broadly referred to the inherent right to life and liberty and the right against arbitrary deprivation of those rights and its various aspects (Articles 6 to 14); privacy, family, etc. (Article 17); freedom of conscience and religion (Article 18); freedom of expression and information (Article 19); right of peaceful assembly (Article 21); freedom of association (Article 22); rights of minorities (Article 27), etc. The International Covenant on Economic, Social and Cultural Rights, 1966 (ICESCR) broadly referred to the "right to work" and its various aspects (Articles 6 and 7); right to form trade unions for

* *Vide* the Report of NCRWC under the Chairmanship of Justice M.N. Venkatachaliah, dated March 31, 2002.

promotion of economic or social interests and the right to strike (Article 8); right to social security and social insurance (Article 9); family, marriage, children and mothers' rights (Article 10); adequate standard of living, right to food, clothing and housing, freedom from hunger (Article 11); physical and mental health (Article 12); education (Article 13); compulsory primary education (Article 14) and culture (Article 15). The treaty obligations under the covenant enjoined the State Parties to ensure these rights without discrimination and "to take steps" to promote them "to the maximum of its available resources", with a view to achieving "progressively" the full realisation of these rights. The Directive Principles of State Policy in Part IV of the Constitution are indeed the precursor to economic, social and cultural rights specified in the ICESCR.

3.4.3. During the last three decades, a vast number of human rights have found place in new constitutions and bills of rights of more than eighty countries and of supra-national entities. Countries which enacted these new constitutions have had the benefit of all the developments in the human rights jurisprudence which have taken place since 1950. Also, our Supreme Court has by judicial interpretation expanded the scope of the fundamental rights, particularly in relation to article 21, and this has included more civil and political rights which were not explicit in Part III.

3.4.4. A new development is that of the principle of 'basic structure' of the Constitution enunciated by the Supreme Court in 1973 in *Kesavananda Bharati* vs *State of Kerala.* As to what are these basic features, the debate still continues. The Supreme Court has also held that the scope of certain fundamental rights could be adjudged by reading into them or reading them not only in the light of the Directive Principles of State Policy but also international covenants or conventions which were in harmony with the Fundamental Rights.

3.4.5. The Commission feels that after fifty years, time is ripe to review and enlarge suitably the contents of some of the Fundamental Rights, particularly those Fundamental Rights which have been judicially deduced.

3.8. Freedom of Press and Freedom of Information

3.8.1. Article 19(1)(a) refers to "freedom of speech and expression". It is proposed that the article must expressly include the freedom of the press and other media, the freedom to hold opinion and to seek, receive and impart information and ideas. It is also proposed to amend article 19(2) by adding a further restriction on disclosure of information received in confidence except if required in public interest.

The Commission recommends that article 19(1)(a) and (2) be amended to read as follows:

"Art. 19(1): All citizens shall have the right—

(a) to freedom of speech and expression which shall include the freedom of the press and other media, the freedom to hold opinions and to seek, receive and impart information and ideas;"

19(2): "Nothing in sub-clause (a) of clause (1) shall affect the operation of any existing law, or prevent the State from making any law, in so far as such law imposes reasonable restrictions on the exercise of the right conferred by the said sub-clause in the interests of the sovereignty and integrity of India, the security of the State, friendly relations with foreign States, public order, decency or morality, or in relation to contempt of court, defamation or incitement to an offence, or preventing the disclosure of information received in confidence except when required in public interest."

3.8.2. A mere legislation by the Parliament by amending the Contempt of Courts Act, 1971 alone may not suffice because the power of the Supreme Court and the High Courts to punish for contempt is recognized in the Constitution. Therefore, the Commission recommends that an appropriate proviso to article 19(2) of the Constitution may be added as under:

"Provided that, in matters of contempt, it shall be open to the Court to permit a defence of justification by truth on satisfaction as to the *bona fides* of the plea and it being in public interest."

3.12. The Supreme Court has included.—"Right to Privacy" in the Right to "Life" under article 21.

It is, therefore, proposed that a new article, namely, article 21-B, should be inserted on the following lines:

"21-B. (1) Every person has a right to respect for his private and family life, his home and his correspondence.

(2) Nothing in clause (1) shall prevent the State from making any law imposing reasonable restrictions on the exercise of the right conferred by clause (1), in the interests of security of the State, public safety or for the prevention of disorder or crime, or for the protection of health or morals, or for the protection of the rights and freedoms of others."

3.26. Justiciability and Enforceability

3.26.1. The judiciary is not suited, according to several writers to enforce some of the ICESCR rights. Where the resources of the nation are involved and a question of priority arises, the remedy cannot be judicial. However, the concept here is not "justiciability" at the instance of individuals in courts of law, but the concept is one of "enforceability" which means that the State must "recognize", and "take steps", by adopting "legislative" or other measures for the "full realisation" and "to the maximum of the State's available resources, both individually and through international assistance and co-operation". These are the words actually used by the ICESCR and have been the subject matter of voluminous literature. These rights are described as "entitlements" of the people and give rise to "obligations" on the part of the State parties. The enforcement must first be of the "minimum core obligations" as stated in para 10 of the General Comment No. 3 of 1990 of the U.N. Committee on Economic, Social and Cultural Rights.

3.26.2. It is felt that an appropriate mechanism must be devised to oblige the State to take action step by step and progressively for the realisation of these rights to the maximum within the resources of the State.

3.26.3. The Commission recommends that the heading of Part IV of the Constitution should be amended to read as "Directive Principles of State Policy and Action".

6.10. Right to Information

6.10. 1. Major assumption behind a new style of governance is the citizen's access to information. Much of the common man's distress and helplessness could be traced to his lack of access to information and lack of knowledge of decision-making processes. He remains ignorant and unaware of the processes which vitally affect his interest. Government procedures and regulations shrouded in a veil of secrecy do not allow the clients to know how their cases are being handled. They shy away from questioning officers handling their cases because of the latter's snobbish attitude and bow-wow style. Right to information should be guaranteed and needs to be given real substance. In this regard, government must assume a major responsibility and mobilize skills to ensure flow of information to citizens. The traditional insistence on secrecy should be discarded. In fact, we should have an oath of transparency in place of an oath of secrecy. Administration should become transparent and participatory. Right to information can usher in many benefits, such as speedy disposal of cases, minimizing manipulative and dilatory tactics of the babudom, and, last but most importantly, putting a considerable check on graft and corruption.

6.11. Freedom of Information Bill, 2000

6.11. The object of the Freedom of Information Bill, 2000 now pending before Parliament is to promote transparency in government activity. The public has a right to know what decisions are being taken and why. Dissemination of information about policies and actions in the public realm leads to a more accountable government. This deserves full support. The Commission recommends that the Union Government should take steps to move the Parliament for early enactment of the Freedom of Information Legislation. It will be a major step forward in strengthening the values of a free and democratic society.

CHAPTER 11

SUMMARY OF RECOMMENDATIONS SYNOPSIS

[Of the various recommendations, 58 recommendations involve amendment to the Constitution, 86 involve legislative measures and the rest involve executive action.]

CHAPTER 3

FUNDAMENTAL RIGHTS, DIRECTIVE PRINCIPLES AND FUNDAMENTAL DUTIES

FUNDAMENTAL RIGHTS

(1) In article 12 of the Constitution, the following Explanation should be added:

Explanation: 'In this article, the expression "other authorities" shall include any person in relation to such of its functions which are of a public nature.' [para 3.5]

* * * *

(3) Article 19(1)(a) and (2) should be amended to read as follows:

"Art. 19(1): All citizens shall have the right—

(a) to freedom of speech and expression which shall include the freedom of the press and other media, the freedom to hold opinions and to seek, receive and impart information and ideas."

19(2): "Nothing in sub-clause (a) of clause (1) shall affect the operation of any existing law, or prevent the State from making any law, in so far as such law imposes reasonable restrictions on the exercise of the right conferred by the said sub-clause in the interests of the sovereignty and integrity of India, the security of the State, friendly relations with foreign States, public order, decency or morality, or in relation to contempt of court, defamation or incitement to an offence, or preventing the disclosure of information received in confidence except when required in public interest." [Para 3.8.1]

(8) A new article, namely, article 21-B, should be inserted on the following lines:

"21-B. (1) Every person has a right to respect for his private and family life, his home and his correspondence.

179TH REPORT OF LAW COMMISSION OF INDIA ON THE PUBLIC INTEREST DISCLOSURE AND PROTECTION OF INFORMER, 2001*
(Relevant Provision)

CHAPTER 4

FREEDOM OF SPEECH, RIGHT TO KNOW AND RIGHT TO PRIVACY

Before discussing the proposals for a Bill enabling public servants to provide information about corruption or mal-administration in their department, it is necessary to refer to the Constitutional provisions relating to Freedom of Speech, Right to Know and the Right to Privacy.

Freedom of speech and expression is guaranteed by sub-clause (a) of Article 19(1) of the Constitution of India. This right is, however, subject to Article 19(2) which permits law to be made for the purpose of imposing reasonable restrictions in the interests of the sovereignty and integrity of India, the security of State, friendly relations with foreign States, public order, decency or morality or in relation to contempt of court, defamation or incitement to an offence.

In this context, we may point out that Art. 19(a) of the Universal Declaration of Human Rights and Art. 19(2) of the Covenant on Civil and Political Rights and Art. 10 of the

---

* *Vide* Chapter 41 of the 179th Report of the Law Commission of India Under the Chairmanship of Justice B.P. Jeevan Reddy, Submitted on 14 December, 2001.

European Convention on Human Rights and Fundamental Freedoms expressly refer to the:

"freedom to seek, receive and impart information and ideas of all kinds, regardless of frontiers, either orally, in writing or in print, in the form of art, or through any other media of his choice" and this right is, however, subject to restrictions that may be imposed by law, (a) for respecting the rights or reputations of others or (b) for the protection of national security or of public order or of public health and morals.

The First Amendment to the American Constitution also refers to the Right of Free Speech. The American Supreme Court has held in one of the most celebrated judgments in New York *Times* vs *Sullivan*, (1964) 376 US 254 that the "central meaning" of the First Amendment was the:

"profound national commitment to the principle that debate on public issues should be uninhibited, robust and wide open and that it may well include vehement, caustic and sometimes unpleasantly sharp attacks on government and public servants".

The above case involved the right of the public official to seek damages for libel and the court held:

"The constitutional guarantees require...a federal rule that prohibits a public official from recovering damages for a defamatory falsehood relating to his official conduct unless he proves that the statement was made with 'actual malice'—that is, with knowledge that it was false or with reckless regard of whether it was false or not."

The word "Public official" would include an elected representative, an appointed official and all governmental employees, even those located near the bottom of any organization provided they are government officials "who have or appear to have substantial responsibility or control over the conduct of governmental affairs". *Rosenblatt* vs *Baer*, (1966), 383 US 75. In principle, not every person in government is a "public official". His position must be one which could invite the public scrutiny and discussion occasioned by the particular charges in controversy. Again, in relation to what is "official conduct" of the public servant, the law has been laid down expansively. In *Garrison* vs *Louisiana* (1964) 379 US 64, the Supreme Court held that allegations of "laziness, inefficiency and obstruction directed against local criminal court judges were relevant to official conduct of such judges". Allegations could be "anything which might touch on an official's fitness for office" and they would be relevant.

Our Supreme Court had occasion to deal with the exposure of the conduct of government through the media or otherwise. In one of the earliest cases *in S. Rangarajan* vs *P. Jagjivan Ram*, 1989 (2) SCC 574, the Supreme Court held that criticism of government policies was not prohibited though there should be a proper balance between freedom of expression and social interests. But courts cannot simply balance the two interests as if they are of equal weight. The court's commitment to freedom of expression demands that it cannot be suppressed unless the situations created by allowing the freedom are pressing and the community interest will be endangered. The anticipated damage should not be remote, or conjectural or farfetched. It should have proximate and have a direct nexus with the expression.

In *Life Insurance Corporation* vs *Manubhai D. Shah*, (1992) 3 SCC 637, the Supreme Court held that there is nothing wrong in requesting the publication of the respondent's rejoinder in the Life Insurance Corporation's (LIC's) inhouse journal though the rejoinder referred to the discriminatory practices of the Corporation which were adversely affecting the interests of a large number of policy holders. This was because; the statute required the Corporation to function in the best interests of the community. The Court observed that the 'community is, therefore, entitled to know whether or not this requirement of the statute is being satisfied in the functioning of the LIC. The LIC was bound to publish the rejoinder of the organization be it, in its inhouse journal, so that the readers who read the magazine obtained a complete picture of the corporation and not a one sided one. The LIC's refusal to publish the rejoinder was therefore violative of the right of the community to know the internal functioning of the Corporation'.

The legal foundation for exposure of corruption, misconduct or maladministration by public servant was laid down by the

Supreme Court in *R. Rajagopal* vs *State of Tamil Nadu*, (1994) 6 SCC 632. The case involved the publication of serious misconduct of public servants by a convict who was serial-killer. The case squarely deals with the right to know and the limits of privacy of public servants. The Supreme Court referred to the judgments of the American Court in *New York Times* vs Sullivan, already referred to and another judgment of the House of Lords in England reported in *Derbyshire* vs *Times Newspaper Ltd*, 1993(2) WLR 449. The Supreme Court held that while decency and defamation were two of the grounds referred to in Clause (2) of Art. 19, still any publication against any person will not be objectionable if such publication was based on "public record". In addition, in the case of "public official", the right to privacy or for that matter, the remedy of action for damages is simply not available with respect to their acts and conduct relevant to the discharge of their official duties. This is so even where the publication is based upon facts and statements which are not true, unless the public official establishes that the publication was made with reckless disregard for truth. In such a case, it would, however, be enough for the person who published the news to prove that he reacted after a reasonable verification of the facts. It is not necessary for him to prove that what he has published is true. Of course, where the publication is proved to be false and actuated by malice or personal animosity, damages can be awarded. No doubt, in matters not relevant to his official duties, the public official enjoys the same protection in respect of his privacy as any other citizen (The judiciary and Parliament and legislatures are not subject to these principles and enjoy greater immunity). The above principle does not, however, mean that the press is not bound by the Official Secrets Act, 1923 or any similar enactment.

The above declaration of law by the Supreme Court is of fundamental importance on the subject of exposure of corrupt officials. If the law permits furnishing of information regarding corruption, past/present or impending and gives protection to the informants from reprisals, unless the disclosure is proved to be malicious, such a law can play a very useful role.

Recently, the Supreme Court has traced the origins of the community's "right to know" from his right to freedom of speech and expression. The Court observed in *Dinesh Trivedi* vs *Union of India*, 1997 (4) SCC 306 that in modern constitutional democracies, it is axiomatic that citizens have a right to know about the affairs of the government which, having been elected by them, seeks to formulate sound policies of governance aimed at their welfare. To ensure that the continued participation of the people in the democratic process, they must be kept informed of the vital decisions taken by the government and the basis thereof. The Court was dealing with the Vohra Committee Report and stated that though it was not advisable to make public the basis on which certain conclusions were arrived at in that Report, the conclusion reached in that Report should be examined by a new body or institution or a special committee to be appointed by the President of India on the advice of the Prime Minister and after consideration with the Speaker of the Lok Sabha.

It is therefore clear that the Supreme Court has accepted that the right to know is part of the fundamental right of freedom of speech and expression guaranteed under Art. 19(1)(a). Of course, it will be subject to the reasonable restrictions, as may be imposed by law under article 19(2).

It is now recognized that while a public servant may be subject to a duty of confidentiality, this duty does not extend to remaining silent regarding corruption of other public servants. Society is entitled to know and public interest is better served more if corruption or mal-administration is exposed. The Whistleblower laws are based upon this principle.

In the light of the above judgment of the American and English Courts and our Supreme Court, on the question as to the scope of "free speech", the Commission is of the view that a statute enabling complaints to be made by public servants, or persons or NGOs against other public servants and the grant of protection to such complainants is perfectly valid and will not offend the right to privacy emanating from sub-clause (a) of clause (1) of Art. 19. The right to privacy has to be adequately balanced against the right to know. Both these rights emanate from same sub-clause in Art. 19.

THE PUBLIC INTEREST DISCLOSURE (PROTECTION OF INFORMERS) BILL, 2002*

A Bill to encourage disclosure of information relating to the conduct of any public servant involving the commission of any offence under the Prevention of Corruption Act, 1988 or any other law for the time being in force, abuse of official position or mal-administration, to protect the persons making such disclosures and for matters connected therewith or incidental thereto.

Be it enacted in Parliament in the Fifty-third Year of Republic of India as follows:

1. Short title and extent.—(1) This Act may be called as the Public Interest Disclosure (Protection of Informers) Act, 2002.

(2) It extends to the whole of India and applies also to public servants outside India.

2. Definitions.—In this Act unless the context otherwise requires—

(a) "action" means action taken by way of decision, recommendation or finding or any other proceeding and includes failure to act and all other expressions connoting action or act shall be construed accordingly;

(b) "Competent Authority" in relation to,

(i) a Minister, means any Authority notified by the President in this behalf;

---

* *Vide* Chapter 8 paras 111 to 121 of the 179th Report of the Law Commission of India under the Chairmanship of Justice B.P. Jeevan Reddy, Submitted on 14 December, 2001.

(ii) any other public servant, means the Central Vigilance Commission constituted under the Central Vigilance Commission Ordinance, 1999 which ceased to operate, and continued under the Government of India in the Ministry of Personnel, Public Grievances and Pensions (Department of Personnel and Training) Resolution No.371/20/99-AVD-III dated the 4 April 1999.

(c) "disclosure" means a disclosure of information that the person making the disclosure reasonably believes, that it tends to show disclosable conduct;

(d) "disclosable conduct" means such conduct as a public servant may engage in or has engaged or is engaging, or proposes to engage in, which amounts to,

(i) abuse or misuse of power or discretion vested in him; or

(ii) an attempt to commit or the commission of an offence under the Prevention of Corruption Act, 1988, the Indian Penal Code, 1860 or any other law for the time being in force; or

(iii) mal-administration;

(e) "mal-administration" includes any action taken or purporting to have been taken or being taken or proposed to be taken in the exercise of administrative or statutory power or discretion,

(i) where such action is unreasonable, unjust, oppressive or discriminatory;

(ii) where there has been negligence or undue delay in taking such action;

(iii) where there has been reckless, excessive or unauthorized use of power in taking such action;

(iv) where such action amounts to breach of trust;

(v) where such action involves the conduct of a public servant which would result in wastage of public funds or causes loss or prejudice to the State or is prejudicial to public interest in any manner; or

(vi) where such action is outside the authority of law or amounts to violation of systems and procedures.

(f) "Minister" means a member of the Council of the Ministers for the Union and includes the Minister of State and Deputy Minister but does not include the Prime Minister;

(g) "prescribed" means prescribed by rules made under this Act;

(h) "public servant" denotes a person falling under any of the descriptions hereinafter following, namely:

(i) every Minister;

(ii) every officer who is appointed to a public service or post in connection with the affairs of the Union;

(iii) every person in the service or pay of,

(1) a ny local authority in any Union territory, (which is notified by the Central Government in this behalf in the Official Gazette),

(2) any corporation (not being a local authority) established by or under a Central Act and owned or controlled by the Central Government,

(3) any Government company within the meaning of section 617 of the Companies Act, 1956, in which not less than fifty-one per cent. of the paid up share capital is held by the Central Government, or any company which is a subsidiary of a company in which not less than fifty-one per cent of the paid up share capital is held by the Central Government,

(4) any cooperative society receiving any financial aid from the Central Government; or

(5) any society registered under the Societies Registration Act, 1860, which is subject to the control of the Central Government and which is notified by that Government in this behalf in the Official Gazette;

(i) "victimisation" with all its grammatical variations, in relation to a public servant other than a Minister, shall include,

(A) suspension pending inquiry, transfer, dilution or withdrawal of duties, powers and responsibilities, recording adverse entries in the service records, issue of memos, verbal abuse, all classes of major or minor punishment specified in the disciplinary rules, orders or regulations applicable to such public servant and such other type of harassment;

(B) any of the acts referred to in sub-clause (A) whether committed by the person against whom a disclosure is made or by any other person or public authority at his instance.

3. Requirements of a public interest disclosure.—(1) Any disclosure of information revealing a disclosable conduct shall be a public interest disclosure for the purposes of this Act.

(2) Notwithstanding anything contained in the Official Secrets Act, 1923, any public servant other than those referred to clauses (a) to (d) of article 33 of the Constitution or any other person including any non-governmental organization, may make a public interest disclosure to the Competent Authority.

(3) Every disclosure shall be made in good faith and the person making it shall solemnly affirm that he reasonably believes that the information disclosed and any allegation contained therein is substantially true.

(4) Every disclosure shall be in writing and shall contain as full particulars as possible and shall be accompanied by supporting documents or other material.

(5) The Competent Authority may, if it deems fit call for further information or particulars from the person making the disclosure.

(6) The Competent Authority shall not entertain a disclosure under sub-section (1) unless the identity of the person making it is disclosed in the disclosure.

4. Procedure on receipt of Public Interest Disclosure.—(1) On receipt of a public interest disclosure under section 3, if the Competent Authority considers, after conducting a preliminary inquiry that such disclosure—

(a) is frivolous or vexatious;

(b) is misconceived or lacking in substance;

(c) is trivial; or

(d) has already been dealt with adequately; it shall dismiss the complaint and inform the person making the disclosure accordingly.

(2) If an issue raised in a disclosure has been determined by a court or tribunal authorised to determine the issue, after consideration of the matters raised in the disclosure, the Competent Authority shall decline to act on the disclosure to the extent that the disclosure seeks to reopen the issue.

(3) If the Competent Authority is of the opinion that the disclosure should be inquired into then it shall proceed in accordance with the provisions of section 5, to inquire into the facts and allegations contained in the disclosure.

5. Procedure of inquiry.—(1) Where the Competent Authority proposes to conduct an inquiry under sub-section (3) of section 4, it

(a) shall forward a copy of the disclosure along with relevant documents and material, if any, to the public servant concerned and to his superior in the official hierarchy;

(b) shall afford to the public servant concerned an opportunity to offer his comments upon the disclosure and the accompanying documents and material, if any; and

(c) may make such orders as to the safe custody of documents and material relevant to the inquiry, as it deems fit.

(2) The inquiry by the Competent Authority shall not be open to public and the name of the public servant making the

disclosure and the public servant named in the disclosure shall not be disclosed to the public.

(3) The name of the person making the disclosure shall be disclosed to the public servant:

Provided that if the person making the disclosure requests that his identity should not be disclosed to the public servant named in the disclosure, and if the Competent Authority is satisfied that such a request may be acceded to in public interest or the safety of such person, it shall make necessary directions in that behalf after recording its reasons.

(4) The Competent Authority shall be bound by the principles of natural justice and subject to the other provisions of this Act, the Competent Authority shall have the power to regulate its own procedure including the fixing of places and times of its inquiry.

(5) If, after conducting an inquiry, the Competent Authority is of the opinion that—

(a) the facts and allegations contained in the disclosure are frivolous or vexatious or are not made in good faith; or

(b) there are no sufficient grounds for proceeding with the inquiry, it shall close the inquiry and inform the concerned persons, the reasons for its opinion.

(6) If after conducting such inquiry, the Competent Authority is of the opinion that disclosable conduct is established against a public servant,

(a) it shall, if such public servant is other than a Minister, record the appropriate findings and send its findings along with the relevant records, to the Authority competent to take disciplinary action against the public servant;

(b) it shall, if such public servant is a Minister, record the appropriate findings and send its findings along with the relevant records, to the Prime Minister.

(7) The authorities referred to in clauses (a) or (b) of sub-section (6), as the case may be, shall upon receipt of the findings

under that sub-section, take appropriate action immediately against the person named in its findings.

(8) If the inquiry held by the Competent Authority discloses conduct, which constitutes an offence punishable under any law, the Competent Authority shall direct the appropriate authority or agency to initiate criminal proceedings against such public servant including a Minister in accordance with law:

Provided that where such a direction is made, any requirement of sanction or prior approval for such prosecution under any law for the time being in force, shall not be necessary to be complied with.

(9) The conduct of an inquiry under this Act in respect of any action shall not affect such action, or any power or duty of any public servant to take further action with respect to any matter subject to the inquiry, in accordance with any law for the time being in force.

6. Matters not subject to inquiry by Competent Authority.— (1) The Competent Authority shall not entertain or inquire into any disclosure,

(a) in respect of which a formal and public inquiry has been ordered under the Public Servants Inquiries Act, 1850, or

(b) in respect of a matter which has been referred for inquiry under the Commissions of Inquiry Act, 1952.

(2) The Competent Authority shall not investigate,

(a) any disclosure which is made after the expiry of twelve months from the date on which the action complained against becomes known to the complainant;

(b) any disclosure involving an allegation, if the complaint is made after the expiry of five years from the date on which the action complained against is alleged to have taken place:

Provided that the Competent Authority may entertain a disclosure referred to in clause (a), if the person making it satisfies him that he had sufficient cause for not making the disclosure within the period specified in this clause.

(3) Subject to the provisions of sub-section (2) the provisions of this Act shall apply to all disclosable conduct committed before the commencement of this Act.

(4) Nothing in this Act shall be construed as empowering the Competent Authority to question, in any inquiry under this Act, any administrative or statutory action taken in the exercise of a discretion except where it is satisfied that the discretion is so exercised because of the disclosable conduct.

7. Powers of the Competent Authority.—(1) Without prejudice to the powers conferred on the Competent Authority under any other law for the time being in force, the Competent Authority or any person or agency authorized by it in writing, for the purpose of any inquiry (including preliminary inquiry, if any, before such inquiry) under this Act, may require any public servant or any other person who in its opinion will be able to furnish information or produce documents relevant to the inquiry, to furnish any such information or produce any such document.

(2) For the purpose of any such inquiry (including the preliminary inquiry), the Competent Authority or any person or agency authorized by it in writing shall have all the powers of a civil court while trying a suit under the Code of Civil Procedure, 1908, in respect of the following matters, namely:

(a) summoning and enforcing the attendance of any person and examining him on oath;

(b) requiring the discovery and production of any document;

(c) receiving evidence on affidavits;

(d) requisitioning any public record or copy thereof from any court or office;

(e) issuing commissions for the examination of witnesses or documents;

(f) such other matters as may be prescribed.

(3) All proceedings before the Competent Authority or any person or agency authorized by it in writing shall be deemed to

be judicial proceedings within the meaning of section 193 of the Indian Penal Code.

(4) Subject to the provisions of sub-section (5), no obligation to maintain secrecy or other restriction upon the disclosure of information obtained by or furnished to Government or any public servant, whether imposed by the Official Secrets Act 1923 or any other enactment or by any rule of law, shall be claimed by any public servant in the proceedings before the Competent Authority or any person or agency authorized by it in writing and the Government or any public servant shall not be entitled in relation to any such inquiry, to any such privilege in respect of the production of documents or the giving of evidence as is allowed by any enactment or by any rule of law in legal proceedings.

(5) No person shall be required or be authorized by virtue of this Act to furnish any such information or answer any such question or produce so much of any document—

(a) as might prejudice the security or defence or international relations of India (including India's relations with the Government of any other country or with any international organization), or the ongoing investigation of crime; or

(b) as might involve the disclosure of proceedings of the Cabinet of the Union Government or any Committee of that Cabinet and for the purpose of this sub-section a certificate issued by a Secretary to the Government of India certifying that any information, answer or portion of a document is of the nature specified in clause (a) or clause (b), shall be binding and conclusive.

(6) Subject to the provisions of sub-section (4), no person shall be compelled for the purposes of inquiry under this Act to give any evidence or produce any document which he could not be compelled to give or produce in proceedings before a Court.

8. Report on disclosures.—(1) Every Competent Authority shall prepare annually a consolidated annual report of the performance of its activities in such form as may be prescribed and forward it to the President.

(2) On receipt of the annual report under sub-section (1), the President shall cause a copy thereof together with an explanatory memorandum to be laid before each House of Parliament.

9. Time limit for completion of inquiry.—(1) The Competent Authority shall hold every such inquiry as expeditiously as possible and in any case complete the inquiry within a period of six months from the date of the receipt of the complaint:

Provided that if the Competent Authority is of opinion that the inquiry cannot be completed before the said period, it may, for reasons to be recorded in writing, extend the said period and in no case the said period shall be extended beyond a period of two years from the date of receipt of the complaint.

(2) Nothing contained in sub-section (1) shall operate as a bar against initiation or continuance of any action or proceedings under any other law for the time being in force against the public servant named in the complaint.

10. Safeguards against victimisation.—(1) The Central Government shall ensure that no person who has made a disclosure under this Act is victimized by initiation of any proceedings or otherwise merely on the ground that such person had made a disclosure under this Act.

(2) If any person other than the Minister, is aggrieved by any action on the ground that he is being victimized due to the fact that he had filed a complaint under section 3, he may file an application before the Competent Authority seeking redress in the matter.

(3) On receipt of an application of under sub-section (2), the Competent Authority may, after making such inquiry as it deems fit, is of opinion that allegation of victimization—

(a) is true and is relatable to the complaint or its subject matter, it may give appropriate directions as it may consider necessary, to the concerned public servant or public authority as the case may be;

(b) is not true or is not maintainable for the reason that the alleged victimisation is not relatable to the complaint or its subject matter, it may dismiss the application.

(4) Notwithstanding anything contained in any other law for the time being in force, the power to give directions under sub-section (3), in relation to a public servant, shall include the power to direct the restoration of the public servant making the disclosure, to the *status quo* ante.

(5) The Competent Authority issuing directions under sub-section (3), shall take such action as is necessary and reasonable to prevent the victimization continuing or occurring in the future.

(6) Every direction given by the Competent Authority shall be binding upon the public servant or the public authority against whom the allegation of victimization has been proved.

11. Transfer of public servant for avoiding victimisation.— (1) The public servant making a disclosure may, during or at the conclusion of the inquiry, apply to the Competent Authority for transfer from the Office or Department in which he is currently posted to another Office or Department.

(2) The Competent Authority on receipt of an application under sub-section (1) shall, if it is satisfied that the applicant has been victimized or is likely to be victimized because of the disclosure, direct the appropriate authority, even if the inquiry has not resulted in any finding against the public servant, to transfer the applicant to another Office or Department, if such transfer is feasible having regard to the qualification and experience of the applicant and the availability of an equivalent post.

12. Protection of witnesses and other persons.—The Competent Authority may pass such orders granting adequate protection to the witnesses and other persons assisting the inquiry as may be necessary in the circumstances of the case.

13. Power to pass interim orders.—During the pendency of the inquiry and at any time after the first disclosure of the disclosable conduct, the Competent Authority may pass such interim orders as it may deem fit, to prevent victimization of the public servant making the disclosure or to prevent the disclosable conduct continuing or occurring in the future.

14. Burden of proof in certain cases.—Where the Competent Authority conducts inquiry into an application under sub-section (3) of section 10, the burden of proving that such action or proceeding which is the subject of victimization would have been taken even if no disclosure had been made by the applicant, shall be upon such public servant or public authority against whom allegation of vitimisation has been made.

15. Protection of action taken in good faith.—No suit, prosecution or other legal proceedings shall lie against the Competent Authority or against any officer, employee, agency or person acting on its behalf, in respect of anything which is in good faith done or intended to be done under this Act.

16. Punishment for false or frivolous disclosures.—Any person who makes any disclosure which was false to his knowledge or reckless or malicious, shall be punishable with imprisonment for a term which may extend up to three years and also to fine which may extend up to fifty thousand rupees.

17. Power to make rules.—(1) The President may, by notification in the Official Gazette, make rules for the purpose of carrying out the provisions of this Act.

(2) Every rule made under this Act shall be laid, as soon as may be after it is made, before each House of Parliament, while it is in session, for a total period of thirty days which may be comprised in one session or in two or more successive sessions, and if, before the expiry of the session immediately following the session or the successive sessions aforesaid, both Houses agree in making any modification in the rule, or both Houses agree that the rule should not be made, the rule shall thereafter have effect only in such modified form or be of no effect, as the case may be; so, however, that any such modification or annulment shall be without prejudice to the validity of anything previously done under that rule.

ELECTION COMMISSION'S GUIDELINES FOR PUBLICATION AND DISSEMINATION OF RESULTS OF OPINION POLLS/EXIT POLLS, 1998*

The Election Commission has observed that during the run up to any general elections to the House of the People or State Legislative Assemblies, Opinion Polls are often conducted by different organisations. The results of such opinion polls are published in newspapers, magazines and other periodicals, and sometimes telecast/broadcast on the electronic media. The dissemination of such results of Opinion Polls receives wide publicity and coverage in the print and electronic media and such dissemination, particularly on the eve of polls, has the potential to influence the electors when they are in the mental process of making up of their minds to vote or not to vote for a certain political party or a candidate. The methodology followed by different organisations conducting such opinion polls varies from organisation to organisation, or the agencies, conducting such polls. Similarly, the sample size of the electorate covered by such polls and geographic spread of the survey also differs substantially in each case.

2. Apart from the Opinion Polls, Exit Polls are also conducted by some organisations on the days of polls. Considering the magnitude of the electorate in the country, particularly at the time of countrywide general elections to the House of the People, and the complexity of operations involved in the conduct of such general elections, the poll is taken in a phased manner,

---

* Guidelines of Election Commission of India for 1998 General Elections of Lok Sabha and State Legislative Assemblies.

spread over a period of two to three weeks. Publication of result of any Exit Poll, in the intervening period when the poll in any of the States or Union Territories or constituencies is yet to be taken, is likely to affect the unbiased exercise of franchise by the elector, one way or the other.

3. Representations have been made to the Commission by various political parties and others concerned that the conduct of such Opinion Polls and Exit Polls, and publication of their results, when the election process is on, should be stopped, so that no political party or candidate suffers adversely or gain an undue advantage, because of the above.

4. The Commission has discussed the matter with all recognised National and State political parties at the meetings held in New Delhi on 22 and 23 December 1997. Almost all the political parties, with the exception of one or two, emphatically stated that Opinion Polls, the way the same are conducted, are unscientific. According to them, there is considerable bias in the size and the nature of the sample drawn to make such an opinion poll and they tend to influence the voters in an unbecoming manner. They further stated that many of the polls are motivated and are not impartial, because of the known leanings or prejudices of some of the organisations conducting such polls, towards or against certain political parties and/or their leaders. While some parties were in favour of opinion polls not being allowed, right from the date of announcement of elections by the Commission, a large number of parties were in favour of such restrictions being applied from the date of notification for the elections.

5. Almost all the parties were also opposed to allowing the exercise of Exit Polls and emphatically stated that the results of such Exit Polls, even if permitted, should, in no way, come out before the polling in all the constituencies in all States and Union Territories were over in all respects.

6. The Commission has carefully examined the matter. It has also examined the position as obtaining in some of the other advanced democracies in various parts of the world. It has been observed that in many of these democracies, like, Canada, France, Italy, Poland, Turkey, Argentina, Brazil, Colombia, etc.

restrictions, in one way or the other, are placed on the conduct of Opinion Polls and Exit Polls.

7. The Canadian Elections Act, (vide Section 322.1) peremptorily prohibits the publication of any results of any Opinion Poll two days before the voting begins. The said Section provides as under:

"No person shall broadcast, publish or disseminate the results of an opinion survey respecting how electors will vote at an election or respecting an election issue that would permit the identification of a political party or candidate from midnight the Friday before polling day (which is always a Monday) until the close of all polling stations."

8. The Italian Decree Law of 18.11.1995, n. 488, titled "Urgent Provisions for equal access to the Media during electoral and referendary campaign" provides, vide Art. 8, as follows:

"Starting from the 20th day before the elections till the closing date of voting, it is forbidden to publish or circulate the results of exit polls, even if such surveys were carried out before the above mentioned period."

9. In this context, the provisions of Section 126 of our Representation of the People Act, 1951, as amended by the Representation of the People (Amendment) Act, 1996, w.e.f. 1.8.1996, also deserve to be taken special note of. That Section provides as under:

"126. Prohibition of public meetings during the period of forty-eight hours ending with hour fixed for conclusion of poll.

(1) No person shall—

(a) convene, hold, attend, join or address any public meeting or procession in connection with an election; or

(b) display to the public any election matter by means of cinematography, television or other similar apparatus; or

(c) propagate any election matter to the public by holding, or by arranging the holding of, any musical concert or any theatrical performance or any other entertainment or amusement with a view to attracting the members of the public thereto, in any polling area during the period of forty-eight hours ending with the hour fixed for the conclusion of the poll for any election in that polling area.

2. Any person who contravenes the provisions of sub-section (1) shall be punishable with imprisonment for a term which may extend to two years or with fine, or with both.

3. In this section, the expression "election matter" means any matter intended or calculated to influence or affect the result of an election."

10. The law, as contained in the above quoted section 126, is clear manifestation of recognition of ground reality by Parliament, in its collective wisdom and as a measure of electoral reform carried out by it as recently as August 1996 after the last general election to the House of the People in 1996, that the voter needs a period of at least 48 hours before the completion of the poll, during which he should not be disturbed in the process of weighing the merits and demerits of political parties and contesting candidates in the electoral fray and he can absorb, what he has heard or witnessed during the campaign period, in a tranquil and balanced frame of mind.

11. Viewed in the light of the above statutory restrictions, allowing results of Opinion Polls and Exit Polls to be published, on the eve of polls or during the polling process, would be a deleterious intrusion into the mind of the voter, which is prohibited by law during the aforesaid period of 48 hours. The Commission is statutorily bound to take all such steps as will give effect to the Parliamentary intent and implement the law, in letter and spirit, as laid down by Parliament.

12. The Commission is conscious of the fact that, in any democratic society, the electors, who choose their representatives to give them a government, do have a right to have information, and be informed and educated, about the policies, programmes, manifestos, etc. of political parties and candidates, who are vying for their votes, and who, if voted to power, will form the

government. The Commission is equally conscious of the 'freedom of press' in any democratic country, and the rights of the print and electronic media to gather information, on any issue or event of public importance, and disseminate it to the general public for their information and decision making. But the Commission also has to balance between such rights of the print and electronic media and the rights of the electorate in the matter of exercise of their franchise in a free and fair manner, uninfluenced by any extraneous factors. In striking such balance, it would not be unreasonable and unfair to place certain reasonable restrictions on the dissemination of information, particularly unverified information, by the print and electronic media, on the eve of polls.

13. In this context, the guidelines framed by the Press Council of India, established under an Act of Parliament with the object of preserving the freedom of Press and of maintaining and improving its standards, in regard to the dissemination of results of Opinion Polls and Exit Polls, also deserve special attention. The attention of the Commission has been invited to these guidelines by none other than Hon'ble Justice P.B. Sawant, Chairman of Press Council of India and President of World Association of Press Councils. These guidelines of Press Council of India provide, *inter alia*, as follows:

Guidelines on 'Pre-poll' and 'Exit-polls' Survey

The Press Council of India having considered the question of desirability or otherwise of publication of findings of pre-poll surveys and the purpose served by them, is of the view that the newspapers should not allow their forum to be used for distortions and manipulations of the elections and should not allow themselves to be exploited by the interested parties.

The Press Council, therefore, advises that in view of the crucial position occupied by the electoral process in a representative democracy like ours, the newspapers should be on guard against their precious forum being used for distortions and manipulations of the elections. This has become necessary to emphasise today since the print media is sought to be increasingly exploited by the interested individuals and groups to misguide and mislead the unwary voters by subtle and not so subtle propaganda on casteist, religious and ethnic basis as well as by the use of sophisticated means like the alleged pre-poll surveys. While the communal and seditious propaganda is not difficult to detect in many cases, the interested use of the pre-poll survey, sometimes deliberately planted, is not so easy to uncover. The Press Council, therefore, suggests that whenever the newspapers publish pre-poll surveys, they should take care to preface them conspicuously by indicating the institutions which have carried such surveys, the individuals and organisations which have commissioned the surveys, the size and nature of sample selected, the method of selection of the sample for the findings and the possible margin of error in the findings.

Further in the event of staggered poll dates; the media is seen to carry exit-poll surveys of the polls already held. This is likely to influence the voters where the polling is yet to commence. With a view to ensuring that the electoral process is kept pure and the voters' minds are not influenced by any external factors, it is necessary that the media does not publish the exit-poll surveys till the last poll is held.

The Press Council, therefore, requests the Press to abide by the following guideline in respect of the exit-polls:

Guideline: "No newspaper shall publish exit-poll surveys, however, genuine they may be, till the last of the polls is over."

14. Having regard to all the above mentioned facts and circumstances, and the constitutional and legal provisions relevant to the issue under consideration, the Election Commission has, in pursuance of its sacred and solemn duty of conducting free and fair elections to Parliament and State Legislatures, entrusted to it by Article 324 of the Constitution, decided to lay down the following Guidelines for observance by print and electronic media, including government controlled electronic media in connection with the conduct of Opinion Polls and Exit Polls by them, during the forthcoming general elections to the House of the People and the Legislative Assemblies of Gujarat, Himachal Pradesh, Meghalaya, Nagaland and Tripura.

Guidelines of the Election Commission of India

(i) The organisations or agencies conducting Opinion Polls shall be free to conduct such polls, and publish results thereof, in or by any print or electronic media, at any time, except the period mentioned in clause (ii), during the run up to the polls for the aforesaid general elections to the House of the People and State Legislative Assemblies mentioned above.

(ii) No result of any opinion poll conducted at any time shall be published, publicised or disseminated, in any manner whatsoever, in or by any print or electronic media, after 1700 hours on 14 February 1998 (16 February 1998 being the first day of poll for the aforesaid general elections) and till half an hour after the closing of poll in all States and Union Territories, three Parliamentary Constituencies in the State of Jammu and Kashmir i.e. 1730 hours on 28 February, 1998.

(iii) The above organisations and agencies shall also be free to conduct exit polls. But the result of any such exit poll conducted at any time shall also not be published, publicised or disseminated, in any manner whatsoever, in or by any print or electronic media, at any time from 0700 hours on 16 February 1998 (being the first day of poll for the aforesaid general elections) and till half an hour after the closing of poll in all States and Union Territories, except three Parliamentary Constituencies, i.e. 1730 hours on 28 February 1998.

(iv) Any organisations or agencies conducting any Opinion Poll or Exit Poll, while publishing, publicising or disseminating the result of any such poll, must indicate the sample size of the electorate covered by such polls and geographic spread of survey so conducted. They must invariably give the details of methodology followed, likely percentage of errors, the professional background and experience of the organisation or organisations and the key professionals involved in the conduct and analysis of the poll.

Explanation: In this Order,

(a) "Electronic media" includes Radio and Television—both Government owned and Private and covers Satellite, Terrestrial and Cable Channels.

(b) "Dissemination" includes publication in any newspaper, magazine or periodical, or display on electronic media, or circulation by means of any pamphlet, poster, placard, handbill or any other document.

15. The above guidelines shall also apply mutatis mutandis at all future elections to Parliament and State Legislatures.

GUIDELINES ON THE RIGHT TO KNOW PROMOTING OPEN GOVERNMENT COMMONWEALTH PRINCIPLES *

I. Introduction

The Commonwealth Law Ministers at their meeting in Barbados in 1980 emphasised that "public participation in the democratic and governmental process was at its most meaningful when citizens had adequate access to official information".

Since that time a number of Commonwealth countries have enacted freedom of information legislation establishing a public right of access to government information. Their experience has demonstrated that these laws enhance the effectiveness of government. Other Commonwealth countries are preparing legislation drawing on this practical experience.

During the 1990s the Commonwealth, guided by its Fundamental Political Values enshrined in the 1991 Harare Commonwealth Declaration, has sought to promote democracy, the rule of law, just and honest government and fundamental human rights. In consolidation the achievements of the past decade the Commonwealth seeks to focus its efforts on strengthening the processes of open and accountable government together with the promotion of sustainable development.

The 1990s has been a decade of democratisation with a number of countries, many within the Commonwealth, making the transition from one party and authoritarian regimes to elected representative governments.

---

* Commonwealth Expert Group meeting on Right to know and Promotion of Democracy and Development, Marlborough House, London, dated 1st March, 1999.

The new millennium promises to be an era for transparency and accountability on the part of government and all sectors of society concerned with public life. These trends will be further stimulated by the growth of information technology and increased globalisation and inter-dependency of national economies.

II. Benefits of Freedom of Information

Freedom of information has many benefits. It facilitates public participation in public affairs by providing access to relevant information to the people who are then empowered to make informed choices and better exercise their democratic rights. It enhances the accountability of government, improves decision-making, provides better information to elected representatives, enhances government credibility with its citizens, and provides a powerful aid in the fight against corruption. It is also a key livelihood and development issue, especially in situations of poverty and powerlessness.

Following a review of the successful experience of Commonwealth freedom of information laws, the Expert Group of the Right to Know submits for the consideration and endorsement of Commonwealth Law Ministers, at their forthcoming meeting in Trinidad from 3-7 May 1999, the following *Principles and Guidelines on the Right to Know*. The Group further recommends that the Law Ministers submit the Principles and Guidelines to the Commonwealth Heads of Government at their summit in South Africa from 12-15 November 1999 for their consideration and adoption.

III. Principles

- Freedom of information should be guaranteed as a legal and enforceable right permitting every individual to obtain records and information held by the executive, the legislative and the judicial arms of the state, as well as any government owned corporation and any other body carrying out public functions.
- The legislation should contain a presumption in favour of maximum disclosure.
- The right of access may be subject to only such exemptions, which are narrowly drawn, permitting

government to withhold information only when disclosure would harm essential interests such as national defence and security, law enforcement, individual privacy or commercial confidentiality, provided that withholding the information is not against public interest.

- Decisions under the legislation should be subject to independent review capable of ensuring compliance.

IV. Guidlines

- Governments should enact freedom of information legislation containing appropriate administrative measures for its implementation.
- Governments should permit any individual to obtain information promptly and at low or no cost.
- Legislation should provide for an independent review of decisions capable of providing an effective remedy in any case of delay or denial.
- Governments should maintain and preserve records.
- Government should promote a culture of openness, publicly disseminating information related to the exercise of their functions and the information held by them.

V. The Role of the Commonwealth

The Commonwealth through its various institutions should take steps to promote these principles and report periodically on their progress in this regard. The Secretariat should report to the Commonwealth Law Ministers about the progress achieved at their meeting in 2002.

In particular, the Commonwealth Secretariat should facilitate and assist governments in promoting these principles through technical and other assistance including measures to promote the sharing of experience between member states and the involvement of civil society in this process.

Commonwealth associations and organisations are encouraged to consider ways in which they can contribute to this process.

PART VI

STATE LAWS ON THE RIGHT TO INFORMATION

THE ANDAMAN & NICOBAR ISLANDS RIGHT TO INFORMATION RULES, 2005*

In exercise of powers conferred under section 28 of the Right to Information Act, 2005 (Central Act No. 22 of 2005) read with section 2(e)(v) thereof, the Lt Governor, Andaman & Nicobar Islands hereby makes the following rules, namely:

1. Short title and commencement.—(1) These rules may be called the Andaman and Nicobar Islands Right to Information (Regulation of Fee and Cost) (amendment) Rules, 2007.

(2) They shall come into force from the date of their publication in the Official Gazette.

2. Definitions.—(1) In these rules, unless the context otherwise requires—

(a) 'Rules' means the Right to Information Rules, 2005;

(b) 'Authorised person' means a person nominated by the competent authority to accept fee prescribed under these rules;

(c) 'Section' means a section of the Act.

(2) Words and expressions used but not defined in these rules shall have the meaning as assigned to them in the Act.

3. A request for obtaining information under sub-section (1) of section 6 shall be accompanied by an application fee of rupees 25 by way of cash against proper receipt or by demand draft or bankers cheque payable to the Accounts Officer of the Public Authority.

---

* *Vide* 314/2005/F. No. 1-252/2005/TSM/RTI R-2005, dated 24th November, 2005.

4. For providing the information under sub-section (1) of the section 7, the fee shall be charged by way of cash against proper receipt or by a demand draft or bankers cheque payable to the Accounts Officer of the public authority at the following rates:

(a) Rupees two for each page (in A4 or A3 size paper) created or copied;

(b) Actual charges or cost prize of a copy in large size paper;

(c) Actual cost or price for samples or models; and

(d) For inspection of records no fee for the first hour and a fee of rupees five for each fifteen minutes (or fraction thereof) thereafter.

5. For providing the information under sub-section (5) of the section 7, the fee shall be charged by way of each against proper receipt or by demand draft or bankers cheque payable to the Accounts Officer of the public authority at the following rates:

(a) For information provided in diskette or floppy rupees fifty per diskette or floppy; and

(b) For information provided in printed form, at the price fixed for such publication or rupees two per page of the photocopy for extracts from the publication.

No fee will be charged from the applicants under BPL category. However, the applicant seeking the information has to enclose a xerox copy of the BPL certificate in support of his claim failing which application will be summarily rejected without giving any reason.

Form A

FORM OF APPLICATION FOR SEEKING INFORMATION

I.D. No..........

(For Official Use)

To

The Competent Authority,

....

....

1. Name of the Applicant :
2. Address :
3. Particulars of Information :

Concerned department :

Particulars of information required :

(i) Details of information required :

(ii) Period for which information required :

(iii) Other details :

4. I state that the information sought does not fall within the restrictions contained in section 8 of the Act and to the best of my knowledge it pertains to your office.

5. A fee of Rs. ....has been deposited in the office of the Competent Authority *vide* No. ....dated...........

Place:

Date:

Signature of Applicant...............

E-mail address, if any................

Tel. No. (Office)........................

(Residence).................................

Note: (i) Reasonable assistance can be provided by the Competent Authority in filling up the Form A.

(ii) Please ensure that the Form A is complete in all respect and there is no ambiguity in providing the details of information required.

ACKNOWLEDGEMENT OF APPLICATION IN FROM A

I.D. No...............

1. Received an application in Form A from Shri/Ms..........resident of.......under section 28 of the A&N Islands Right to Information Rules, 2005.

2. The information is proposed to be given normally within 15 days and in any case within 30 days from the date of receipt of application and in case it is found that the information asked for cannot be supplied, the rejection letter shall be issued stating reason thereof.

3. The applicant is advised to contact the undersigned on........between 11 a.m. and 1 p.m.

4. In case the applicant fails to turn up on the scheduled date(s), the Competent Authority shall not be responsible for delay if any.

5. The applicant shall have to deposit the balance fee, if any, with the authorised person before collection of information.

6. The applicant may also consult Web-site of the department from time to time to ascertain the status of his application.

....

Signature and Stamp of the

Dated: Competent Authority

E-mail address...............

Web-site...............

Tel. No................

Form B

OUTSIDE THE JURISDICTION OF COMPETENT AUTHORITY

From...............

....

To,

....

....

Sir/Madam,

Please refer to your application with I.D. No. ....dated....... addressed to the undersigned regarding supply of information on................

The requested information does not fall within the jurisdiction of this Competent Authority and, therefore, your application is being returned herewith.

This is in supersession of the acknowledgement given to you on....

You are requested to apply to the concerned Competent Authority.

Yours faithfully

Competent Authority..................

E-mail address...........................

Web-site......................................

Tel. No......................................

Form C

FORM OF SUPPLY OF INFORMATION TO THE APPLICANT

From...............

....

To,

....

....

Sir/Madam,

Please refer to your application with I.D. No. ....dated....... addressed to the undersigned regarding supply of information on.........

1. The information asked for is enclosed for reference,

Or

*The following partly information is being enclosed:

(i)

(ii)

and/or

*The remaining information about the other aspects cannot be supplied due to following reasons:—

(i)

(ii)

(iii)

and/or

* Strike out if not applicable.

*The following requested information does not fall within the jurisdiction of this Competent Authority:

(i)

(ii)

2. As per section 19(1) specified in sub-section (1) or clause (a) of sub-section (3) of section 7 of the Right to Information Act, 2005, you may file an appeal to the immediate superior to the Public Information Officer as first appeal and second appeal to Central Information Commission, Government of A&N Administration, within 30 days of the issue of this order.

Yours faithfully

Competent Authority....................

E-mail address...........................

Web-site.......................................

Tel. No...

THE ANDHRA PRADESH RIGHT TO INFORMATION BILL, 2001

To provide for Right to Information to every citizen in order to promote openness, transparency and accountability in administration and ensure effective participation of the people in all matters related to governance.

Whereas Right to Information is accepted by the Supreme Court as an inherent part of Right to Freedom of Speech and Expression under Article 19(1)(a) and the Right to Life and Personal Liberty under Article 21 of the Constitution;

Whereas Right to Information is a facet of the Fundamental Right to Free Speech and Expression, the provisions made here under are for the enforcement of the said Right;

Whereas securing information has been hitherto largely dependent on administrative circulars, and no clear law exists for obtaining information, it has become necessary to set out procedures for acquiring such information, and as such the procedures in order to comply with Article 21 of the Constitution shall be fair and reasonable;

Be it enacted by the Andhra Pradesh State Legislature in the 52nd year of the Republic of India as follows:

1. Short title, object and commencement.—(1) This Act may be called the Andhra Pradesh Right to Information Act, 2001.

(2) This Act is in furtherance and for the enforcement of Right to Information, a facet of Freedom of Speech and Expression. The interpretation of the provisions of this Act shall be in furtherance and for effective access to the said Right.

(3) It shall come into force on such date as the State Government may, by notification, appoint, which shall not be later than 60 days from the date of obtaining the assent of the Governor.

2. Definitions.—In this Act, unless the context otherwise requires:

(a) "Competent Authority" means the:

- Speaker in the case of the Legislative Assembly,
- Chief Justice of the High Court in the case of the High Court and all the subordinate courts,
- Governor in the case of other authorities created by or under the Constitution,
- Chairperson of the Zilla Parishad in the case of all subjects and departments under the Jurisdiction of the Panchayats in the district,
- Chairperson of the Municipality, Municipal Corporation or Nagar Palika in the case of the respective urban local governments,
- The District Magistrate in the case of all state government departments or organizations or bodies in the district, and
- Lok Ayukta in the case of all other public authorities.

(b) "information" means any material or information relating to the affairs, administration, decisions or conduct of public authority and includes any document or record relating to the affairs of the public authority;

(c) "prescribed" means prescribed by rules under this Act by the State Government;

(d) "project" means any public work or scheme or programme launched by the government or public authority;

(e) "public authority" means all offices of the State of Andhra Pradesh including the Andhra Pradesh Public Service Commission, the State Election Commission or any other constitutional body established by the State of Andhra Pradesh; all local authorities; all authorities constituted by or under any Act of the State Legislature for the time being in force, such as a company, corporation, trust, society, any statutory or other authority, or any organisation or body funded, owned and controlled by the State Government;

(f) "public information officer" means the Public Information Officer appointed under Sub-section (1) of Section 6;

(g) "publish" means communication of information through all generally accepted forms including media briefings, advertisements where necessary and feasible, displaying in a prominent place accessible to the general public, making copies available to the public at a reasonable cost, making copies available in electronic format including posting on an official website, and publication in an official journal or periodical made widely available to the public on demand;

(h) "record" includes any document, manuscript or file; any microfilm, microfiche and facsimile copy of a document; any reproduction of image or images embodied in such microfilm (whether enlarged or not); and any other material produced by a computer or by any other device;

(i) "right to information" means the right of access to information from any public authority by means of inspection, taking of extracts and notes; obtaining certified copies of any records of such public authority; diskettes, floppies, photocopies or in any other electronic mode or through print-outs where such information is stored in a computer or in any other device;

(j) "trade secret" means information contained in a formula, pattern, compilation, programme, device, product, method, technique or process which is not generally known and which may have economic value.

3. Right to information.—Subject to the provisions of this Act, all citizens shall have freedom of information and Right to Information from a public authority.

4. Obligations of public authorities.—Every public authority shall—

(1) Maintain and keep updated all records duly catalogued and indexed.

(2) Publish periodically, and in any case at least once in a calendar year:

(a) particulars of its organization, structure, functions and responsibilities;

(b) the powers and duties of officers and employees and the procedure followed by them in the decision making process;

(c) norms for discharge of its functions including prescribed periods for processing and completion of physical and financial targets and the actual achievements with reference to such norms;

(d) classes of records under its control including the rules, regulations, instructions and list of manuals, etc. used by its employees for carrying out the activities;

(e) norms for classification of information and mode of storage and retrieval;

(f) the details of facilities available to citizens for access to information;

(g) the name, designation and other relevant particulars of the Public Information Officer, to whom requests for information may be addressed.

(3) Before initiating or causing to sanction any project, publish or communicate to the public generally and to the persons affected or likely to be affected by the project in particular, the relevant facts available to it or to which it has reasonable access.

(4) Publish and display in a tamper-proof notice board in a prominent place accessible to the general public all its decisions which have a bearing on public interest immediately after a decision is taken and in any case not later than two working days.

(5) Give reasons for decisions, whether administrative or adjudicative, to those affected and disclose the relevant facts and analysis when major policies or decisions are announced.

(6) Publish such other information as may be prescribed or necessary:

Provided it shall be mandatory for each custodial establishment such as a police lock-up, jail, mental asylum, remand house, women's home, beggars home, etc. to appoint a Visitors' Committee comprising independent citizens which shall have full access to the establishment, their records and inmates at all hours of the day and night.

5. Report to competent authority.—(1) Before or on 30 June of every calendar year, the public authority shall submit to the Competent Authority a report covering the preceding financial year and the report shall include:

(a) the number of determinations made by the public authority not to comply with requests for records made to such public authority under Section 8(1) and the reasons for each such determination;

(b) the number of appeals made by persons under Section 12, the result of such appeals, and the reason for the action upon each appeal that results in a denial of information;

(c) the names and titles or positions of each person responsible for the denial of records requested under Section 8, and the number of instances of participation for each;

(d) the results of each proceeding conducted pursuant to Section 13 including a report of the disciplinary action taken against the officer or employee who was primarily responsible for improperly withholding records or an explanation of why disciplinary action was not taken;

(e) a copy of every rule, regulation or guideline issued by such public authority for the purpose of implementation of this Act;

(f) a copy of the fee schedule and the total amount of fees collected by the public authority for making records available under Section 7; and

(g) such other information as indicates efforts to administer fully Section 7.

(2) Each public authority shall make each such report available to the public including by computer telecommunications, or by other electronic means.

(3) The Competent Authority shall make all such reports available at a single electronic access point.

(4) The Competent Authority shall notify the Speaker of the Legislative Assembly and the Leader of the Opposition no later than 31st August of the year in which each such report is issued, that such reports are available by electronic and other means.

(5) The Competent Authority shall develop reporting and performance guidelines in connection with reports required by this section within three months from the date on which this Act comes into effect.

(6) Before or on August 31 of every year, the Competent Authority shall submit to the Speaker an annual report, which shall include for the prior fiscal year a listing of the number of cases of rejection of requests for information arising under Section 8, the exemption involved in each case, the disposition of such case, and the fee schedule fixed under Section 7.

6. Designation of Public Information Officers.—(1) Every public authority shall for the purposes of this Act, designate one or more officers as Public Information Officers.

(2) Every Public Information Officer shall deal with requests for information and shall render reasonable assistance to any person seeking such information.

(3) Any officer whose assistance has been sought by the Public Information Officer, shall render all such assistance.

7. Procedure for supply of information.—(1) A person desiring information from a public authority shall make an application in writing, orally or through electronic means, to the Public Information Officer. For the said purpose the applicant may be allowed to inspect the concerned document(s): Provided that where such request cannot be made in writing, the Public Information Officer shall render all reasonable assistance to the person making the request to reduce it in writing.

(2) The information asked for under Sub-section (1) shall be supplied in writing, either in the official language of the State in that area or the language in which the said information is recorded.

(3) Every public authority may have a right to charge a reasonable fee for the supply of any document subject to the condition that such fee shall not exceed the cost of making and supplying the document. The fee charged shall not be such that it may amount to denial of the right. The fee charged shall not be a source of revenue for the government, and shall not be subject to periodical enhancement. The fee may be waived when the disclosure of information is sought in larger public interest.

(4) The information asked for under Sub-section (1) shall be furnished to the applicant by the public authority:

(a) within twenty-four hours where such information relates to forfeiture of the life or liberty of any individual;

(b) within seven days if the information is readily available and is of routine nature; and

(c) as expeditiously as possible, and in any case within fifteen working days from the date of receipt of the application for all other categories of information.

8. Processing of requests for information.—(1) On the receipt of an application requesting for information, the public authority shall consider it and pass orders thereon either granting or refusing it, as soon as practicable and in any case within the time limits prescribed in Sub-section (4) of Section 7 from the date of receipt of the application;

Provided that where the public authority does not have the information, he shall within the period specified under Section 7(4) from the date of receipt of application transfer the application to the officer or person with whom such information is available and inform the applicant accordingly, and thereafter such officer or person to whom such application is transferred shall furnish information within the period specified under Section 7(4) from the date of receipt of the application by him.

(2) Where a request is rejected under Sub-section (1), such a rejection shall be with the prior approval of the higher officer to be designated by the respective public authority. In such a case, the Public Information Officer shall communicate to the person making the request as expeditiously as possible and in no case not later than 7 days:

(a) the reasons for such rejection;

(b) the period within which the appeal against such rejection may be preferred;

(c) the particulars of the appellate authority.

(3) Information shall ordinarily be provided in the form in which it is sought unless it would disproportionately divert the resources of a public authority or would be detrimental to the safety or preservation of the record in question.

(4) In certain special circumstances as specified in this sub-paragraph, the time limits prescribed by this Act may be extended by written notice to the person making such request, setting forth the reasons for such extension and the date on which the information sought is expected to be dispatched. No such notice shall specify a date that would result in an extension of more than ten working days.

Explanation: 'certain special circumstances' means, only to the extent reasonably necessary to the proper processing of the particular request including:

(a) the need to search for and collect the requested records from field facilities or other establishments that are separate from the office processing the request;

(b) the need to search for, collect, and appropriately examine a voluminous amount of separate and distinct records which are demanded in a single request; or

(c) the need for consultation, which shall be conducted with all practicable speed, with another public authority having a substantial interest in the matter or among two or more components of the public authority having substantial subject-matter interest therein.

9. Exemption from disclosure of information.— Notwithstanding anything herein before but subject to the provisions of Section 10 the following information shall be exempted from disclosure, namely:

(a) information, the disclosure of which would prejudicially affect the sovereignty and integrity of India, security of the State, strategic, scientific or economic interest of India or conduct of international relations;

(b) information, the disclosure of which would prejudicially affect public safety and order, detection and investigation of an offence or which may lead to incitement to commit an offence;

(c) record of deliberations of the Council of Ministers for a specified period; but does not include the documents relied upon by the Council of Ministers or its decisions except in respect of matters covered by items (a) and (b): Provided that the decisions arrived at in the Cabinet meetings, and the reasons therefor shall be made public immediately;

(d) minutes or records of advice, opinions or recommendations made by an officer of a public authority during the decision making process prior to the executive decision or policy formulation;

Provided all such records and information shall be made available to the public after an executive decision is taken or policy formulated;

(e) information the disclosure of which would constitute a breach of privilege of the Parliament or the State Legislature;

Provided that the Public Information Officer shall before withholding information under this clause refer the matter to the AP Legislative Assembly Secretariat for determination of the issue and act according to the advice tendered by the Secretariat;

(f) trade and commercial secrets protected by law, or information the disclosure of which would prejudicially affect the legitimate economic and commercial interests or the competitive position of a public authority, or would cause unfair gain or loss to any person or institution;

(g) patentable information or information relating to specific results of sponsored ongoing research work in scientific establishments of government during the course of such research, until the results are published in a scientific journal or made public in an appropriate forum:

Provided that nothing in the foregoing provisions of this section shall preclude the right of any person to obtain such information as would affect life or liberty of any person in whom he or she is interested:

Provided that information which cannot be denied to the Parliament or State Legislature or to a local government shall not be denied to any citizen:

Provided that all declassified information shall be made available to the public on request:

Provided that norms for declassification shall be reviewed periodically as determined by the appropriate public authority, and made public.

10. Grounds for refusal of access in certain cases.—There shall be free access to all information excepting what is contained in Section (9). Subject to this provision, a Public Information Officer may reject a request for information where such request:

(a) is too general in nature or is of such a nature that, having regard to the volume of information required to be retrieved or processed would involve disproportionate diversion of the resources of a public authority or would adversely interfere with the functioning of such authority;

Provided that where such request is rejected on the ground that the request is too general, it would be the duty of the Public Information Officer to render help as far as possible to the person making the request to reframe his request in such a manner as may facilitate the supply of information:

Provided that if the Public Authority finds it difficult to furnish copies of the required information, the applicant shall be allowed to inspect the record and make notes in the manner and within such time as may be prescribed:

Provided that difficulties encountered by the authorities under this Act shall not be a ground for denial of access to information.—

(b) relates to personal information, the disclosure of which has no relationship to any public activity, or which would cause unwarranted invasion of the privacy of an individual, except where larger public interest is served by disclosure:

Provided that the information relating to returns of assets and liabilities filed by any public servant or public representative shall be made available to the public.

11. Severability.—If a request for information is rejected on the ground that it is in relation to information which is exempted from disclosure, then notwithstanding anything contained in this Act, access shall be given to that part of the record which does not contain any information that is exempted from disclosure under this Act and which can reasonably be severed from any part that contains exempted information.

12. Appeals.—(1) Where a request for information is registered under Section 8(1), the public authority shall communicate the details of such a rejection to the prescribed appellate authority immediately. The appellate authority shall treat such information as suo motu appeal and shall pass appropriate orders within the periods prescribed under Section 7(4).

(2) Any person who has not received any communication within the period prescribed under Section 7(4), or who is aggrieved by a decision of the public authority may within thirty days next after such period appeal to such authority as may be prescribed. Any such appeal shall be disposed of within the period prescribed in Section 7(4):

Provided that such authority may entertain the appeal after the expiry of the said period of thirty days if it is satisfied that the appellant was prevented by sufficient cause from filing the appeal in time:

Provided that no appeal shall lie against an order of withholding of information under clause (e) of Section 9.

(3) On rejection of a first appeal for access to information under the provisions of this Act, the applicant shall have the right for a second appeal to the Competent Authority within 30 days, who shall then dispose of the appeal within the period prescribed in Section 7(4).

13. Penalties.—(1) Any individual responsible for providing any information under this Act shall be personally liable for failure to furnish the information within the period specified therein.

(2) Where the information asked for under this Act is not furnished within the time specified, the person responsible for supplying the information shall be punishable with a fine of Rs. 100 (Rupees one hundred only) per every day of delay beyond the day by which the information was supposed to be supplied in compliance with the provisions of this Act:

Provided that departmental disciplinary action shall be initiated in all such cases, and appropriate punishment shall be awarded.

(3) In case of wilful concealment of information or deliberate furnishing of false information, the person or persons responsible shall be punished with a fine and imprisonment for six months:

Provided that in all such cases mandatory disciplinary action shall be taken by the appropriate authority simultaneously irrespective of the outcome of criminal prosecution.

(4) And to remove all doubts, such offences as outlined in sub-section (3) will entail punishment of reduction of rank or removal and dismissal from service, if found guilty after disciplinary proceedings by the respective public authority's administrative mechanism:

Provided that the public authority shall report to the Competent Authority within 30 days all information relating to the cases covered in this section, including the disciplinary action taken, penalty imposed, and such other details as may be prescribed or pertinent.

14. Protection of action taken in good faith.—No suit, prosecution or other legal proceeding shall lie against any person for anything which is done or intended to be done in good faith under this Act or any rule made thereunder.

15. Protection for public interest disclosures.—A public servant who is in possession of information on serious wrongdoing by any individual or agency in government which might pose a serious and imminent threat to the safety or health of an individual or the public, or severely compromise public interest or cause serious loss to the public exchequer, shall not be penalized in any way for disclosing to the public such information backed by reasonable evidence.

16. Bar on Jurisdiction of Courts.—No court shall entertain any suit, application or other proceeding in respect of any order made under this Act and no such order shall be called in question otherwise than by way of an appeal under this Act:

Provided that when an offence is committed under this Act, the case will be tried by the appropriate criminal court.

17. Act to have an overriding effect.—The provisions of this Act shall have effect notwithstanding anything inconsistent contained in any other law made by the State Legislature in respect of any matter falling under the State List or the Concurrent List, in the Seventh Schedule of the Constitution, except the provisions of any existing law made by Parliament in respect of any matter falling under the Concurrent List.

18. Power to make rules.—(1) The State Government by notification in the Official Gazette, shall make rules to carry out the provisions of this Act, within sixty days from the date of enactment of this Act.

(2) In particular and without prejudice to the generality of the foregoing power, such rules may provide for all matters relevant to the application of this Act.

(3) Every rule made under this Act by the State Government shall be laid before the State Legislature, within 30 days of such rule being made.

19. Power to remove difficulties.—(1) If any difficulty arises in giving effect to the provisions of this Act, the State Government may, by order published in the Official Gazette, make such provisions not inconsistent with the provisions of this Act as appears to it to be necessary or expedient for removal of the difficulty, provided no such order shall be made after two years after commencement of the Act.

(2) Every order made under this Section shall, as soon as maybe after it is made, be laid before the Legislature.

THE ARUNACHAL PRADESH RIGHT TO INFORMATION RULES, 2005*

In exercise of the powers conferred by sub-section (1) of section 28 of the Right to Information Act, 2005 (Central Act No. 22 of 2005), the Governor of Arunachal Pradesh hereby makes the following rules, namely:—

1. Short title and commencement.—(1) These rules may be called the Arunachal Pradesh Right to Information Rules, 2005.

(2) They shall come into force from the date of their publication in the official Gazette.

2. Definitions.—(1) In these rules, unless the context otherwise requires,—

(a) 'Act' means the Right to Information Act, 2005 (Central Act No. 22 of 2005);

(b) 'Competent Authority' means the Competent Authority to accept fee prescribed under these rules;

(c) 'Form' means the 'Form' appended to these rules;

(d) 'Section' means a section of the Act.

(2) Words and expressions used but not defined in these rules shall have the meaning as assigned to them in the Act.

3. Application for seeking information.—Any person seeking information under the Act shall make an application in Form 'A' to the competent authority and deposit application fees as per rule 8 with the authorised person. The competent authority shall duly acknowledge the application as provided in Form 'A':

---

* *Vide* No. OM-43/2005, Government of Arunachal Pradesh, Department of Personnel, Administrative Reforms & Training, Administrative Reforms Branch, dated 15th September, 2005.

Provided that a person who makes a request through electronic form shall ensure that the requisite fee is deposited in Treasury Challan under the Head of Account '0070—other administrative service within seven days of his request sent through electronic form, failing which his application shall be treated as withdrawn by the applicant.

4. Disposal of application by the competent authority.— (1) If the requested information does not fall within the jurisdiction of the competent authority, it shall order return of the application to the applicant in Form 'B' as soon as practicable, normally within fifteen days and in any case within thirty days of the receipt of the application, advising the applicant, wherever possible, about the competent authority to whom the application should be made. The application fee deposited in such cases shall not be refunded.

(2) If the requested information falls within the competent authority's jurisdiction and also in one or more of the categories of restrictions listed in section 8 of the Act, the competent authority, on being satisfied, will issue the rejection order in Form 'C' as practicable, normally within fifteen days and in any case, within thirty days from the date of the receipt of the application.

(3) If the requested information falls within the competent authority's jurisdiction but not in one or more of the categories listed in section 8 of the Act, the competent authority, on being so satisfied, shall supply the information to the applicant in Form 'D', falling within his jurisdiction. In case, the information sought is partly outside the jurisdiction of the competent authority or partly falls in the categories listed in section 8 of the Act, the competent authority shall supply only such information as is permissible under the Act and is within its own jurisdiction and reject the remaining part giving reasons thereof.

(4) The information shall be supplied as soon as practicable, normally within fifteen days and in any case within thirty days from the date of the receipt of the application on deposit of the balance amount, if any, in Treasury Challan and original copy of the Challan is submitted to the authorised person, before collection of information. A proper acknowledgment shall be obtained from the applicant in token of receipt of information.

5. Appeal.—(1) Any person—

(a) who fails to get a response in Form 'B', or Form 'C' from the competent authority within thirty days of submission of Form 'A'; or

(b) who is aggrieved by the response received within the prescribed period, may appeal in Form 'E' to the State Information Commission and deposit fee for appeal as per rule 8 in Treasury Challan and original copy of the Challan is submitted with the authorised person.

(2) On receipt of the appeal, the State Information Commission shall acknowledge the receipt of appeal and after giving the applicant an opportunity of being heard, shall endeavor to dispose it of within thirty days from the date on which it is presented and send a copy of the decision to the competent authority concerned.

(3) (a) Where the appeal is filed on the ground specified in clause (a) of sub-rule (1) of this rule, no appeal shall be admissible after sixty days of the submission of the application in Form 'A'.

(b) Where the appeal is filed on the ground specified in Rule in clause (b) of sub-rule (1) of this rule, no appeal shall be admissible after thirty days of the issue of the response appealed against.

(4) In case the appeal is allowed, the information shall be supplied to the applicant by the competent authority within such period as ordered by the appellate authority. This period shall not exceed thirty days from the date of the receipt of the order.

6. Penalties.—(1) Whoever being bound to supply information under sub-section (1) of section 20 of the Act fails to furnish the information asked for under the Act within the time specified or fails to communicate the rejection order under section 9 of the Act, shall be liable to pay a penalty of fifty rupees per day for the delayed period beyond thirty days subject to a maximum of five hundred rupees per application filed under rule 3.

(2) Where the information supplied is found to be false in any material particular and which the person bound to supply it

knows or has reasonable cause to believe it to be false or does not believe it to be true, the person supplying the information shall liable to pay a penalty of one thousand rupees per amplication, filed under rule 3.

7. ***Suo moto*** **publication of information by public authorities.**—(1) The public authority shall *suo moto* publish information as per sub-section (3) of section 26 of the Act by publishing booklets, folders and pamphlets at the following intervals:

S. No.	Particulars of information to be published	Interval
1.	Particular of its organisation, functions . and duties	. Once in five years
2.	Powers and duties of its officers and employees and the procedure followed by them in the decision making process.	Once in two years
3.	Norms set by the public authority for the discharge of its functions.	Once in two years
4.	Laws, bye-laws, rules, regulations, instruction, manuals and other categories of records under its control used by its employees for discharging its functions.	Once in five years
5.	Details of facilities available to citizens for obtaining information.	Annually
6.	Name, designation and other particulars of the competent authority.	Annually

(2) Such information shall also be made available to the public through information counters, medium of internet and display on notice board at conspicuous places in the office of the competent authority and the State Public Information Commission.

8. Charging of fees.—(1) The competent authority shall charge the fee at the following rates, namely:—

(A) *Application Fees*

(i) Information relating to tender documents/bids/ Five hundred rupees quotation/Business contracts;	Five hundred rupees per application.

(ii) Information other than (i) above — Fifty rupees per application.

(A) *Other Fees*

S. No.	Description of information	Price/Fees in Rupees
1.	Where the information is available in the form of a priced publication.	Price so fixed
2.	For other than priced publication.	Five rupees per page

(2) The appellate authority shall charge a fee of fifty rupees per appeal through Treasury Challan.

(3) The Fees charfed shall be deposited through Treasury Challan in the Head of Account "0070-Other administrative charge" by the applicant.

9. State infromation commission.—(1) The State Infromation Commission shall be constituted by the State Government by a separate notification.

10. Maintence of records.—(1) The competent authority shall maintain records of all applications received for supply of information and fee charged and deposited in the Government account.

(2) The State Infromation Commission shall maintain records of all appeals filed before it and fee charged and deposited in the Government account.

THE ASSAM RIGHT TO INFORMATION ACT, 2001

An act to provide for right to information to the citizens and in relation to the matters connected therewith or incidental thereto.

PREAMBLE

Whereas it is expedient to provide for right to information to the citizens so as to promote openness, transparency and accoutability in administration;

It is hereby enacted in the 52nd year of the Republic of India as follows:

1. Short title, extent and commencement.—(1) This Act may be called the Assam Right to information Act, 2001.

(2) It shall come into force on such date, as the State Government may, by notification in the Official Gazette, appoint.

2. Definitions.—In this Act, unless the context otherwise requires—

(a) *Controlling Officer* means the immediate superior officer above the Incharge of the Office, who supervises and controls the works of the Incharge of the Office or such officer as may, from time to time, be specified as such by the State Government for the purposes of this Act;

(b) *Incharge of the Office* means an officer or a functionary of the State Government or a Public Authority who is in the charge and actual control of the office of the State Government or the Public Authority, as the case may be, or such officer or functionary as may from time to time be specified as such by an order by the State Government or the Public Authority, as the case may be for the purposes of this Act;

(c) *Information* means and includes information relating to any matter in respect of the affairs of the administration or decisions of the State Government or a Public Authority but does not include any such information the publication of which has been prohibited by any law for the time being in force or by any notification issued by the State Government from time to time under this Act;

(d) *Prescribed* means prescribed by the rules made under this Act;

(e) *Public Authority* means and includes the officer of,

(i) all local bodies and other authorities constituted by the State Government under any law for the time being in force; or Central Act No. 1 of 1956;

(ii) a Government Company or corporation incorporated under the Companies Act 1956 in which not less than fifty-one per cent of the paid up share capital is held by the State Government, or other State Government undertakings, organizations or institutions financed either wholly or partly and owned, or controlled by the State Government or any other company, corporation, undertaking or institution in which the State Government stands guarantor in respect of any loan or financial advance availed of by such company corporation, institution, organization or undertaking, as the case may be; or

(iii) a cooperative society or any other society, a trust or any other organization or institution established under any law for the time being in force by the State Government and directly controlled or funded by it; or

(iv) any body, authority, institution, organization, agency or instrumentally including the District

Rural Development Agencies, funded either wholly or partly by the State Government; and

(v) any other body, authority institution or organization receiving substantial financial assistance from the State Government as may be notified by the State Government from time to time for the purposes of this Act;

Provided that the *Public Authority* as defined above shall not include:

(i) the offices of the Central Government,

(ii) any establishment of the armed forces or central para-military forces,

(iii) any body or corporation owned or controlled by the Central Government,

(iv) the High Court of Assam and other courts of Law including the Tribunals and other organization which have the status of a Court whose proceedings are deemed to be the judicial proceedings,

(v) the Secretariat of the Government of Assam,

(vi) the Secretariat of the Assam Legislative Assembly, and

(vii) any office, body or authority as may be notified by the State Government.

(f) *Right to information* means and includes the right of access to information relating to them affairs of the State Government or any Public Authority by means of,

(i) obtaining certified copy of any record, or

(ii) inspection of accessible records and taking notes and extracts, or

(iii) inspection of public works, or

(iv) taking of samples of materials from public works, or

(v) obtaining diskettes, floppies or any other electronic mode or through printouts where such information is stored in a computer or in any other device, or

(vi) in such other manner as may be prescribed, but does not include any such information the publication of which has been prohibited by any law for the time being in force or by any notification issued by the State Government from time to time under this Act;

(g) *Record* means and includes any document, manuscript, file; diskette, floppy or other computerized record maintained by the State Government or any Public Authority, as the case may be, in transacting the day to day affairs of their business;

(h) *State Government* means the Government of Assam;

(i) *Trade secret* means information contained in a formula, pattern, compilation, programme, device, product, method, technique or process which is not generally known and which may have economic value.

3. Maintenance of records.—Every office of the State Government or Public Authority shall maintain the records in such manner and form as may be prescribed in this behalf by the State Government or the Public Authority, as the case may be, from time to time.

4. Right to information (Central Act No. XIX of 1923).—(1) Subject to the provisions of this Act, and the Official Secrets Act, 1923 every citizen shall have the right to obtain information from the Incharge of the Office and such Incharge shall be liable to provide the information in accordance with the provisions of this Act. (2) Notwithstanding anything contained in sub-section (i), no. person shall be given:

(a) (i) information, the disclosure of which may prejudicially affect the sovereignty and integrity of India, security of the State, strategic, scientific or economic interest of India or conduct of international relations,

(ii) information, the disclosure of which would prejudicially affect the conduct of Centre-State relations, including information exchanged in confidence between the Central and State Government or any of their authorities or agencies.

(b) information the disclosure of which may prejudicially affect public safety and order or which may lead to an incitement to commit an offence or prejudicially affect fair trial or adjudication of a pending case,

(c) information relating to Cabinet papers including records of the deliberations of the Council of Ministers, Secretaries and other officers,

(d) information, the disclosure of which may harm, frankness and candour of internal discussions including inter-departmental notes, correspondence and papers containing advice or opinion as also of projections and assumptions relating to internal policy analysis,

(e) information, the disclosure of which may prejudice the assessment or collection of any tax, cess, duty or fee or assist in avoidance or evasion of tax, cess, duty or fee,

(f) information, the disclosure of which may constitute a breach of privilege of the Parliament or the State Legislative or may amount to violation of an order of a competent court,

(g) information regarding trade or commercial secrets protected by law or information, the disclosure of which may prejudicially affect the legitimate economic and commercial interest or the competitive position of the State Government or a public authority; or may cause unfair gain or loss to any person,

(h) information, the publication of which has been prohibited by the State Government by way of notification issued in exercise of any provision of this Act,

(i) information regarding any matter the disclosure of which may,

(i) help or facilitate escape from legal custody or affect prison security;

(ii) impede the process of investigation or apprehension or prosecution of offenders;

(iii) prejudicially affect the enforcement of any law including detection, prevention, investigation or suppression of crime or contravention of any law or the apprehending of offender and the operations of any intelligence organization including any operation against extremism, terrorism and insurgency;

(iv) endangered the life or physical safety of any person or identify the source of information or assistance given in confidence for law enforcement or security purposes;

(v) prejudicially affect the fair trial or adjudication of a pending case or the proceeding of any Tribunal or public inquiry;

(vi) reveal the existence or identity of confidential record or source of information; or may prejudice future supply of information relating to violation or contravention of any law;

(vii) prejudicially affect the ability of the State Government to management the economy or the legitimate economic or commercial interest of the State Government or a Public Authority; or may cause unfair gain or loss to any individual or organization;

(viii) cause unwarranted invasion to the privacy of an individual and which has no relationship to any public activity;

(j) information held in consequence of having been supplied in confidence by a person who,

(i) gave the information under a guarantee that its confidentiality would be protected; or

(ii) was not under any legal obligation whether actual or implied to supply and has not consented to its disclosure; Central Act No. 1 of 1872.

(k) the record and information referred to in sections 123 and 124 of the Indian Evidence Act, 1872 and claimed privileged.

(l) information on the following grounds also,

(i) that the request is too general or is of such a nature that having regard to the volume of the information required to be retrieved or processed for fulfilling it, it would involve or processed for fulfilling it, it would involve disproportionate diversion of the resources of the State Government or the Public Authority, as the case may be, or would adversely interfere with the functioning of such Authority:

Provided that where access is being refused on the ground that the request is too general it would be the duty of the Incharge of the office concerned to render help as far as possible to the person seeking information to re-frame his request in such a manner as may facilitate supply of information,

(ii) that the request relates to information that is required by law or convention to be published at a particular time, or

(iii) that the request relates to information that is contained in published material for sale.

5. Procedure for supply of information.—(1) Any person desirous of obtaining information shall make an application to the Incharge of the Office in the prescribed manner, along with such fee, in such form and with such particulars, as may be prescribed.

(2) On receipt of an application under sub-section (1), the Incharge of the office shall consider it and if the information is such which can be provided and does not fall within the category specified under sub-section (2) of section 4, the Incharge of the Office shall provide the information within thirty days of the receipt of the application.

(3) Where the information sought by the applicant falls under any of the restricted categories specified under sub-section (2) of section 4, the Incharge of the office shall refuse to provide the information and shall communicate his reasoned decision to the applicant within thirty days from the date of receipt of the application.

(4) The information sought may be provided in the form it is available in the office by copying or photocopying the same which shall be certified, and signed and sealed on each page thereof by the Incharge of the office.

(5) When it appears to the Incharge of the office that the information sought for by the applicant is not available in the office, he shall forward the application to the office where he reasonably believes the information to have originated or be available and communicate the same to the applicant.

6. Appeals.—(1) Subject to such rules as may be prescribed any person,

(i) aggrieved by an order of the Incharge of the office may within thirty days from the date of receipt of such order, or

(ii) who has not received any communication within a period of thirty working days from the date of the application under section 5, may within thirty days next after such period, prefer an appeal before the Controlling Officer.

(2) Every appeal shall be accompanied by such fee to be deposited or paid in such manner as may be prescribed.

(3) The Controlling Officer may, after giving the person affected a reasonable opportunity of being heard, pass such order as it deems fit:

Provided that every appeal so preferred shall be decided and disposed of by all means within thirty days from the date of presentation there of Assam Act VII of 1977.

(4) Any person aggrieved by the order of the Controlling Officer under sub-section (1) may prefer a Second Appeal before the Assam Administrative Tribunal constituted under section 3 of the Assam Administrative Tribunal Act, 1977 within a period of thirty days from the date of receipt of such order.

(5) The Assam Administrative Tribunal may, after giving the person affected a reasonable opportunity of being heard, pass such order as it deems fit:

Provided that every Second Appeal so preferred shall be decided and disposed of by all means within sixty days from the date of presentation of the appeal.

7. Power to remove difficulties.—If any difficulty arises in giving effect to the provisions of this Act, the State Government may, by an order make such provision not inconsistent with the provision of this Act and appear to them to be necessary or expedient for removing the difficulty.

8. Protection of action taken in good faith.—No suit, prosecution or other legal proceeding shall lie against the State Government or any Public Authority or any officer or functionary thereof any person for anything which is done in pursuance of this Act or the rules made thereunder.

9. Penalties.—Where any Incharge of the office, without any reasonable cause fails to supply the information sought for within the period specified under section 4 or furnishes information which is false with regard to any material and which he knows or has reasonable cause to believe to be false shall be liable to disciplinary action by Disciplinary Authority under the relevant service rules governing the service of the officer concerned.

10. Bar of jurisdiction of court.—No court shall entertain any suit, application or other proceeding in respect of any order made under this Act and no such order made under this Act and no such order shall be called in question otherwise than by way of an appeal under this Act.

11. Power to make rules.—(1) The State Government may make rules for carrying out the purposes of this Act.

THE ASSAM RIGHT TO INFORMATION FEE NOTIFICATION, 2005*

The Governor of Assam is pleased to prescribe following fees to be charged under various Sections of the Right to Information Act, 2005 (No. 22 of 2005) enacted by the Parliament:

Section 6(1)

(i) Rs 10 per application Section 7(1)

(i) Rs 2 for each page (In A4 or A3 size paper)

(ii) Actual charge or cost price of a copy in larger size paper

(iii) Actual cost or price for samples or models

(iv) For inspection of records no fee for the first hour and a fee of Rs 5 for each 15 minutes thereafter

Section 7(5)

(i) Rs 50 per diskette or floppy

(ii) Price fixed for printed publication at printed price or Rs. 2 per page of photocopy for extracts from the publication

Provided that:

(a) No fee prescribed under Sections 6(1), 7(1) and 7(5) shall be charged from the persons who are of below poverty line as may be determined by the State Government as stipulated under Section 7(5) of the Right to Information Act, 2005.

---

* *Vide* File No. AR 78/2005/91, Government of Assam, dated 7th October, 2005.

(b) No fee prescribed under Section 7(1) and 7(5) shall be charged where the "State Public Information Officer" fails to provide information within the time limits prescribed under Section 7(1) as stipulated under Section 7(6) the Right to Information Act, 2005.

(c) The above fees shall be collected in form of Demand Draft or Banker's Cheque or cash against proper receipt to be issued by an officer authorized in this behalf by the State Public Information Officer or the Assistant State Public Information Officer, as the case may be and shall be deposited through Treasury Challan under the Head of Account "0070-other Administrative Services".

This will come into force with immediate effect.

THE DELHI RIGHT TO INFORMATION ACT, 2001

(Delhi Act No. 7 of 2001)

An act to make provision for securing right to information in the National Capital Territory of Delhi and for matters relating thereto.

Be it enacted by the Legislative Assembly of the National Capital Territory of Delhi in the Fifty-second Year of the Republic of India as follows:

1. Short title and commencement.—(1) This Act may be called the Delhi Right to Information Act, 2001.

(2) It shall come into force on such date as the Government may, by notification in the official Gazette, appoint.

2. Definitions.—In this Act, unless there is anything repugnant in the subject or contexts,

(a) "competent authority" means any authority or officer notified by the Government from time to time in official gazette for the purpose of this Act;

(b) "electronic form" with reference to information means any information generated, sent, received or stored in media, magnetic, optical, computer memory, microfilm, computer generated microfiche or similar device;

(c) "Government" means the "Lt Governor referred in article 239 AA of the Constitution";

(d) "information" means any material or information relating to the affairs of the National Capital Territory of Delhi except matters with respect to entries 1, 2 and 18 of the State List and entries 64, 65 and 66 of that list in so far as they relate to the said entries 1, 2 and 18 embodied in the Seventh Schedule of the Constitution;

(e) "Lt Governor" means the Lt Governor of the National Capital Territory of Delhi appointed by the President under article 239 of the Constitution;

(f) "prescribed" means as prescribed in rules;

(g) "public authority" means any authority or body established or constituted—

(i) by or under the Constitution;

(ii) by any law made by the Government and includes any other body owned, controlled or substantially financed by funds provided directly or indirectly by the Government.

(h) "Public Grievances Commission" means the Public Grievances Commission setup by the Government vide their Resolution No. 4/14/94-AR dated 25 September 1997 as amended from time to time;

(i) "right to information" means the right of access to information and includes the inspection of works, documents, records, taking notes and extracts and obtaining certified copies of documents or records, or taking samples of material.

3. Right to information.— Subject to the provisions of this Act, every citizen shall have right to obtain information from a competent authority.

4. Obligations on public authorities.—Every public authority shall—

(a) maintain all its records, in such a manner and form as is consistent with its operational requirements duly catalogued and indexed;

(b) publish at such intervals as may be prescribed by the Government;

(i) the particulars of its organisation, functions and duties;

(ii) the powers and duties of its officers and employees and the procedure followed by them in the decision making process;

(iii) the norms set by the public authority for the discharge of its functions;

(iv) laws, bye-laws, rules, regulation, instructions, manuals and other categories of records under its control used by its employees for discharging its functions;

(v) the details of facilities available to citizens for obtaining information; and

(vi) the name, designation and other particulars of the competent authority;

(c) publish all relevant facts concerning important decisions and policies that affect the public while announcing such decisions and policies;

(d) give reasons for its decisions, whether administrative or quasi-judicial to those affected by such decisions;

(e) before initiating any project, publish or communicate to the public generally or to the persons affected or likely to be affected by the project in particular, the facts available to it or to which it has reasonable access which, in its opinion, should be known to them in the best interests of maintenance of democratic principles.

5. **Procedure for supply of information.**—(1) A person desiring information shall make a request in writing or through electronic form, to the competent authority giving the particulars of the matter relating to which he seeks information:

Provided that where a person cannot, for valid reasons, make a request in writing, the competent authority may either accept an oral request which may, subsequently, be reduced in writing or render reasonable assistance to such person in making a written request.

(2) Upon receipt of an application requesting for an information, the competent authority shall consider it and furnish the information required by the applicant or pass orders thereon refusing the request as soon as practicable but normally within 15 days and in any case within thirty days from the date of receipt of application.

(3) The information shall be supplied in writing, either in English or in the official language.

(4) Where a request is rejected under sub-section (2), the competent authority shall communicate to the person making the request, (i) the reasons for such rejection; (ii) the period within which the appeal against such rejection may be preferred; (iii) the particulars of the appellate authority.

6. Restrictions on right to information.—The competent authority may, for reasons to be recorded in writing, withhold:

(a) the information the disclosure or contents of which will prejudicially affect the sovereignty and integrity of India or security of the National Capital Territory of Delhi or international relations or which leads to incitement to an offence;

(b) the information relating to an individual or other information, the disclosure of which would constitute a clear and unwarranted invasion of personal privacy and has no relationship to any activity of the Government or which will not sub-serve any public interest;

(c) papers containing advice, opinion, recommendations or minutes submitted to the Lt Governor for discharge of his constitutional functions and any information, disclosure of which would prejudicially affect the conduct of the Centre-State/Union territory relations, including information exchanged in confidence between the Centre and the Government or any of their authorities or agencies;

(d) trade and commercial secrets or any other information protected by law;

(e) information whose release would constitute a breach of privilege of Parliament or Legislative Assembly of the National Capital Territory of Delhi:

Provided that the competent authority shall, before withholding information under this clause, refer the matter to the Legislative Assembly Secretariat for determination of the issue and act according to the advice tendered by that Secretariat:

Provided further that no appeal shall lie under section 7 against an order withholding supply of information under this clause;

(f) information whose disclosure would endanger the life or physical safety of any person or identify the source of information or assistance given in confidence for law enforcement or security purposes or in public interest:

Provided that the information, which cannot be denied to the Legislative Assembly of the National Capital Territory of Delhi, shall not be denied to any person.

(g) minutes or records of advice including legal advice, opinions or recommendations made by an officer of a public authority during the decision making process prior to the executive decision or policy formulation.

(h) Cabinet papers including records of the deliberations of the Council of Ministers, Secretaries and other officers.

7. **Appeal.**—(1) Any person aggrieved by an order of the competent authority, or any person who has not received any order from the competent authority within thirty working days, may appeal to the Public Grievances Commission;

(2) The decision of the Public Grievances Commission shall be final.

(3) No order adversely affecting any person shall be passed, except after giving that person a reasonable opportunity of being heard.

(4) Every appeal shall be disposed as expeditiously as possible and endeavour shall be made to dispose of the appeal within thirty days from the date on which it is presented.

8. **Obligation on competent authority.**—Every competent authority shall be under a duty to maintain all its records, as per its operational requirements, duly catalogued and indexed, and grant access to information, subject to the provisions of this Act, to any citizen requesting for such access.

9. Penalties.—(1) Any person responsible for providing any information under this Act shall be personally liable for furnishing the information within the period specified.

(2) Where a person responsible to supply information fails to furnish the information asked for under this Act within the time specified or furnishes any information which is false in any material particulars, and which he knows or has reasonable cause to believe to be false or does not believe it to be true, he shall be liable, after such inquiry as may be required under the service rules pertaining to disciplinary action applicable to him, for imposition of such penalty as may be determined by the disciplinary authority under such rules or as prescribed in the Rules.

10. State Council for Right to Information.—(1) The Government shall, by notification in the official Gazette, establish with effect from such date as specified in the notification, a Council to be known as State Council for Right to Information.

(2) The State Council shall consist of the following members, namely:

(a) the Chief Minister, Government of National Capital Territory of Delhi shall be its Chairman;

(b) the Minister Incharge of the Department of Administrative Reforms in the Government shall be its member; provided if the Chief Minister is the Minister Incharge of Administrative Reforms Department, then the Finance Minister shall be the Member;

(c) such number of other officials not exceeding ten of which three members shall be elected representatives of the Legislative Assembly of the NCT of Delhi and of which one shall be woman to be nominated by the Speaker of Assembly of NCT of Delhi and non-official members not exceeding ten representing such interests as may be prescribed by the Government.

(3) The time and place of the meeting of the Council shall be as the Chairman may decide and it shall observe such procedures as may be laid down by the Council to transact its business.

(4) The object of the State Council shall be to promote the right to information in the National Capital Territory of Delhi and it shall deal with all matters related to right to information, such as:

(a) review of the operation of this Act and the rules made thereunder;

(b) review of the administrative arrangements and procedures to secure for citizens the fullest possible access to information;

(c) research and documentation as regards management of information with a view to improving the extent and accuracy of information being made available under this Act; and

(d) to advise the Government on all matters related to the right to information, including training, development and orientation of employees to bring in a culture of openness and transparency.

11. Act to have overriding effect.—The provisions of this Act shall have effect notwithstanding anything inconsistent therewith contained in any other enactment of the Legislative Assembly of Delhi, for the time being in force.

12. Protection of action taken in good faith.—No suit, prosecution or other legal proceedings shall lie against any person for anything done in good faith or intended to be done in pursuance of this Act.

13. Charging of fees.—The competent authority shall charge such fees for supply of information as may be prescribed by rules, but which shall not exceed the cost of processing and making available of the information.

14. Laying of annual report of State Council.—The Chairperson shall cause to be laid on the Table of the House Annual Report of the State Council.

15. Power to make rules.—(1) The Government may, by notification in the official Gazette, make rules to carry out the purposes of this Act. (2) In particular, and without prejudice to the generality of the foregoing power, such rules may provide for all or any of the following matters, namely:

(a) the interval at which particulars and other material and information shall be published by the public authorities; (b) the composition of the State Council with reference to the interest to be represented therein; (c) prescription of fee to be charged for supply of information; (d) any matter which is to be, or may be prescribed under this Act.

(3) Every rule made under this Act shall be laid, as soon as may be after it is made, before the House of the Legislative Assembly of the National Capital Territory of Delhi while it is in session, for a total period of thirty days which may be comprised in one session or in two or more successive sessions, and if, before the expiry of the session immediately following the session or the successive sessions aforesaid, the House agrees in making any modification in the rule or the House agrees that the rule should not be made, the rule shall thereafter have effect only in such modified form or be of no effect, as the case may be; so, however, that any such modification or annulment shall be without prejudice to the validity of anything previously done under that rule.

16. Removal of difficulties.—(1) If any difficulty arises in giving effect to the provisions of this Act, the Government may, by general or special order published in the official Gazette, make such provision not inconsistent with the provisions of this Act as appear to it to be necessary or expedient for the purposes of removing difficulty:

Provided that no such order shall be made after the expiration of two years from the commencement of this Act.

(2) Every order made under this section shall, as soon as may be after it is made, be laid before the Legislative Assembly of the National Capital Territory of Delhi.

THE DELHI RIGHT TO INFORMATION RULES, 2001*

In exercise of the powers conferred by sub-section (1) of section 15 of the Delhi Right to Information Act, 2001 (Delhi Act No. 7 of 2001), the Government of Delhi hereby makes the following rules, namely:

1. Short title and commencement.—(1) These rules may be called the Delhi Right to Information Rules, 2001.

(2) They shall come into force from the date of their publication in the official Gazette.

2. Definitions.—(1) In these rules, unless the context otherwise requires,

(a) "Act" means the Delhi Right to Information Act, 2001 (Delhi Act No. 7 of 2001);

(b) "Authorized person" means a person nominated by the competent authority to accept fee prescribed under these rules;

(c) "Form" means the "Form" appended to these rules;

(d) "section" means a section of the Act.

(2) Words and expressions used but not defined in these rules shall have the meaning as assigned to them in the Act.

3. Application for seeking information.—Any person seeking information under the Act shall make an application in Form 'A' to the competent authority and deposit application fees in cash or in the form of affixing non-judicial stamp on the

* *Vide* Notification No. F. 17/3/2001/AR/11653-11952, dated 19th October, 2001, published in the Delhi Gazette, Extra., Pt. IV, dated 19th October, 2001.

application or postal order or Bank draft in the name of "Govt of NCT of Delhi" as per Rule 8 with the authorized person. The competent Authority shall duly acknowledge the application as provided in Form 'A':

Provided that a person who makes a request through electronic form shall ensure that the requisite fee is deposited in cash or in form of postal order or Bank draft in the name of "Govt of NCT of Delhi" as per Rule 8 with the authorized person within seven days of his request sent through electronic form, failing which his application shall be treated as withdrawn by the applicant.

4. Disposal of application by the competent authority.— (1) If the requested information does not fall within the jurisdiction of the competent authority, it shall order return of the application to the applicant in Form 'B' as soon as practicable, normally within fifteen days and in any case within thirty days of the receipt of the application, advising the applicant, wherever possible, about the competent authority to whom the application should be made. The application fee deposited in such cases shall not be refunded.

(2) If the requested information falls within the competent authority's jurisdiction and also in one or more of the categories of restrictions listed in Section 6 of the Act, the competent authority, on being satisfied, will issue the rejection order in Form 'C' as soon as practicable, normally within fifteen days and in any case, within thirty days from the date of the receipt of the application.

(3) If the requested information falls within the competent authority's jurisdiction but not in one or more of the categories listed in section 6 of the Act, the competent authority, on being so satisfied, shall supply the information to the applicant in Form 'D', falling within his jurisdiction. In case, the information sought is partly outside the jurisdiction of the competent authority or partly falls in the categories listed in section 6 of the Act, the competent authority shall supply only such information as is permissible under the Act and is within its own jurisdiction and reject the remaining part giving reasons thereof.

(4) The information shall be supplied as soon as practicable, normally within fifteen days and in any case within thirty days from the date of the receipt of the application on deposit of the balance amount, if any, to the authorized person, before collection of information. A proper acknowledgement shall be obtained from the applicant in token of receipt of information.

(5) For inspection of document the applicant shall deposit fee with the authorized person in addition to the application fee as prescribed in Rule 8. Only those documents shall be allowed for inspection, copies of which can be given under the Act.

5. Appeal.—(1) Any person:

(a) who fails to get a response in Form 'B', or Form 'C' from the competent authority within thirty days of submission of Form 'A', or

(b) is aggrieved by the response received within the prescribed period, may appeal in Form 'E' to the Public Grievances Commission and deposit fee for appeal as per Rule 8 with the authorized person.

(2) On receipt of the appeal, the Public Grievances Commission shall acknowledge the receipt of appeal and after giving the applicant an opportunity of being heard, shall endeavour to dispose it of within thirty days from the date on which it is presented and send a copy of the decision to the competent authority concerned.

(3) (a) Where the appeal is filed on the ground specified in clause (a) of sub-rule (1) of this rule, no appeal shall be admissible after sixty days of the submission of the application in Form 'A'.

(b) Where the appeal is filed on the ground specified in clause (b) of sub-rule (1) of this rule, no appeal shall be admissible after thirty days of the issue of the response appealed against.

(4) In case the appeal is allowed, the information shall be supplied to the applicant by the competent authority within such period as ordered by the appellate authority. This period shall not exceed thirty days from the date of the receipt of the order.

6. Penalties.—(1) Whoever being bound to supply information under sub-section (1) of section 5 of the Act fails to furnish the information asked for under the Act within the time specified or fails to communicate the rejection order under sub-section (2) of section 5 of the Act, shall be liable to pay a penalty of fifty rupees per day for the delayed period beyond thirty days subject to a maximum of five hundred rupees per application, filed under Rule 3.

(2) Where the information supplied is found to be false in any material particular and which the person bound to supply it knows or has reasonable cause to believe it to be false or does not believe it to be true, the person supplying the information shall be liable to pay a penalty of one thousand rupees per application, filed under Rule 3.

7. *Suo motu* publication of Information by public authorities.—(1) The public authority shall suo motu publish information as per clause (b) of section 4 of the Act by publishing booklets, folders and pamphlets at the following intervals.

S. No.	Particulars of information to be published	Interval
1.	Particulars of its organization, functions and duties	Once in five years
2.	Powers and duties of its officers and employees and the procedure followed by them in the decision making process.	Once in two years
3.	Norms set by the public authority for the discharge of its functions	Once in two years
4.	Laws, bye-laws, rules, regulations, instructions, manuals and other categories of records under its control used by its employees for discharging its functions	Once in five years
5.	Details of facilities available to citizens for obtaining information	Annually
6.	Name, designation and other particulars of the competent authority	Annually

(2) Such information shall also be made available to the public through information counters, medium of internet and display on notice board at conspicuous places in the office of the competent authority and the Public Grievances Commission.

8. Charging of fee.—(1) The competent authority shall charge the fee at the following rates, namely:

(a) Application fees

(i)	information relating to tender documents/bids/quotation/business contracts;	five hundred rupees per application
(ii)	information other than (a) above	fifty rupees per application

(b) Other fees

S. No	Description of Information	Price/Fees in Rupees
1.	Where the information is available in the form of a priced publication	Price so fixed
2.	For other than priced publication	Five rupees per page
3.	Inspection of documents	Fifteen rupees per 15 minutes (or fraction thereof)

(2) The appellate authority shall charge a fee of fifty rupees per appeal.

9. State Council for Right to Information.—(1) The State Council for Right to Information shall consist of the following members:

1.	Chief Minister	Chairman
2.	Minister Incharge of the Administrative Reforms Department/Finance Minister (if Chief Minister is the Minister Incharge of the Department of Administrative Reforms)	Member
3.	Three Members of the Legislative Assembly of NCT of Delhi	Members
4.	Chief Secretary, Government of NCT of Delhi	Member
5.	Five officers from amongst Principal Secretaries/ Secretaries/Head of Departments, Government of NCT of Delhi	Members
6.	Two representatives of the Media (Print/Electronic)	Members
7.	Four representatives of non-government institutions	Members
8.	Two representatives of resident welfare associations	Members
9.	Two representatives of industry/trade /commerce	Members
10.	Secretary Incharge of the Department of Administrative Reforms.	Member Secretary

(2) The three members of the Legislative Assembly of the National Capital Territory of Delhi, of whom one shall be woman, shall be nominated as members of the State Council for Right to Information by the Speaker of the Legislative Assembly.

(3) The seven officials and ten non-official members of the State Council, as listed above at serial numbers 4, 5 and 10 and from serial numbers 6 to 9 respectively, shall be nominated by the Government.

10. Maintenance of Records.— (1) The competent authority shall maintain records of all applications received for supply of information and fee charged.

(2) The Public Grievances Commission shall maintain records of all appeals filed before it and fee charged.

Form A

[*See* Rule 3]

FORM OF APPLICATION FOR SEEKING INFORMATION

I.D. No. ....

(For official use)

To

The Competent authority

....

....

1. Name of the Applicant
2. Address
3. Particulars of information—
   (a) Concerned department
   (b) Particulars of information required
      (i) Details of information required
      (ii) Period for which information asked for
      (iii) Other details

4. I state that the information sought does not fall within the restrictions contained in section 6 of the Act and to the best of my knowledge it pertains to your office.

5. A fee of Rs......... has been deposited in the office of the Competent Authority vide No. .... dated ....

Place ....

Date ....

Signature of Applicant
E-mail address, if any ....
Tel. No. (Office)................
(Residence)......................

Note: (i) Reasonable assistance can be provided by the Competent Authority in filling up the Form A.

(ii) Please ensure that the Form A is complete in all respects and there is no ambiguity in providing the details of information required.

Acknowledgement of Application in Form - A

I.D. No.......... Dated............

1. Received an application in Form A from Shri/Ms. .... resident of .... under Section 5(1) of the Delhi Right to Information Act, 2001.

2. The information is proposed to be given normally within 15 days and in any case within 30 days from the date of receipt of application and in case it is found that the information asked for can not be supplied, the rejection letter shall be issued stating reason thereof.

3. The applicant is advised to contact the undersigned on........... between 11 a.m. to 1 p.m.

4. In case the applicant fails to turn up on the scheduled date(s), the Competent Authority shall not be responsible for delay, if any.

5. The applicant shall have to deposit the balance fee, if any, with the authorized person before collection of information.

6. The applicant may also consult website of the department from time to time to ascertain the status of his application.

Signature and Stamp of the Competent Authority
E-mail address..................
Website:.........................
Tel. No..........................
Dated............................

Form B

[*See* Rule 4 (1)]

OUTSIDE THE JURISDICTION OF COMPETENT AUTHORITY

From ....

No. F........................... Date _______

To,

....

....

....

Sir/Madam,

Please refer to your application, I.D. No.......... dated .... addressed to the undersigned regarding supply of information on.....................

2. The requested information does not fall within the jurisdiction of this Competent Authority and, therefore, your application is being returned herewith.

*3. This is in supersession of the acknowledgement given to you on ....

4. You are requested to apply to the concerned Competent authority:

Yours faithfully,

Competent Authority

E-mail address............

Website.....................

Tel. No......................

---

* Strike out wherever not applicable.

Form C

[*See* Rule 4(2)]

REJECTION ORDER

From ....

No. F............................. Date ....

To,

......................................,

......................................,

....

Sir/Madam,

Please refer to your application, I.D. No.......... dated .... addressed to the undersigned regarding supply of information on......................

2. The information asked for cannot be supplied due to following reasons:

(i)

(ii)

3. As per Section 7 of Delhi Right to Information Act, 2001, you may file an appeal to the Public Grievances Commission, Government of Delhi, within 30 days of the issue of this order.

Yours faithfully,

Competent Authority

E-mail address............

Website.....................

Tel. No......................

Form D

[*See* Rule 4(3)]

FORM OF SUPPLY OF INFORMATION TO THE APPLICANT

From ....

No. F.................................. Date............

To

....,

....,

....

Sir/Madam,

Please refer to your application, I.D. No.......... dated .... addressed to the undersigned regarding supply of information on.....................

2. The information asked for is enclosed for reference.

Or

The following partly information is being enclosed.*

(i)

(ii)

The remaining information about the other aspects cannot be supplied due to following reasons:—

(i)

(ii)

(iii)

3. The requested information does not fall within the jurisdiction of this Competent Authority.*

4. As per Section 7 of Delhi Right to Information Act, 2001, you may file an appeal to the Public Grievances Commission, Government of Delhi, within 30 days of the issue of this order.*

Yours faithfully,

Competent Authority

E-mail address..................

Web-site...........................

Tel. No...........................

* Strike out if not applicable.

Form E

[*See* Rule 5(1)]

APPEAL UNDER SECTION 7(1) OF THE DELHI RIGHT TO INFORMATION ACT, 2001

I.D. No.................

(For official use)

To

The Secretary

Public Grievances Commission

M Block , Vikas Bhawan

New Delhi 110002

1. Name of the appellant
2. Address
3. Particulars of the Competent Authority
   (a) Name
   (b) Address
4. Date of submission of application in Form A
5. Date on which 30 days from submission of Form A is over:
6. Reasons for appeal
   (a) No response received in Form B, or C within 30 days of submission of Form A [Rule 5(1)(a)];
   (b) Aggrieved by the response received within prescribed period (Rule 5(1)(b)) (A copy of the reply receipt be attached);
   (c) Grounds for appeal.
7. Last date for filing the appeal. (please see Rule 5 (3):
8. Particulars of Information—
   (i) Information requested:
   (ii) Subject:
   (iii) Period:

9. A fee of Rs. 50 for appeal has been deposited in P.G.C. vide receipt No.......... dated ....

Place.................

Date ....

Signature of Appellant

E-mail address, if any

Tel. No. (Office)..................

(Residence).......................

Acknowledgement

I.D. No................ Dated:............

Received an Appeal application from Shri .... resident of .... under Section 7(1) of the Delhi Right to Information Act, 2001.

Signature of the Receipt Clerk

Public Grievances Commission

Tel.No............................

E-mail address ....

Website ....

By order and in the name of the Lt Governor of the National Capital Territory of Delhi.

THE DELHI RIGHT TO INFORMATION NOTIFICATION, 2005*

To,

All Principal Secrtaries/Secretaries/Heads of departments under GNCTD/Autonomous Bodies/Undertakings and Local Bodies

Sub: RTI Act, 2005—"The Right to Information (Regulation of Fee and Cost) Rules, 2005"

Sir/Madam,

Please find enclosed herewith a copy of Notification dated 16th September, 2005 issued by the Government of India, Ministry of Personnel, Public Grievances and Pensions (DOPT) i.e. "The Right to Information (Regulation of Fee and Cost) Rules, 2005".

It is requested that the above notification may please be brought to the notice of all the State Public Information Officers/ State Assistant Public Information Officers and Appellate Authorities for strict compliance in connection with implementation of Right to Information Act, 2005.

Encl: As above:**

Yours faithfully,
(Prakash Kumar)
Secretary (AR)

---

* *Vide* F. No. 13/9/05/AR/12098-12247, dated 28th September, 2005.

** This is in contemplation of the amount of fee variations between Delhi RTI Rules, 2001 and (Central) RTI (Fee and Cost) Rules, 2005. The (Central) RTI (Fee and Cost) Rules, 2005 is given at p. 46 of this book and Delhi RTI Rules, 2001 is given at p. 323 of this book.

THE GOA RIGHT TO INFORMATION ACT, 1997

[Goa Act 28 of 1997]

An act to make provision for securing Right to Information in the State of Goa and for matters relating thereto.

Whereas it is necessary that every Governmental action should be transparent to the public;

And whereas to achieve this object, every citizen should be able to get information from the Government;

Be it enacted by the Legislative Assembly of Goa in the Forty-eighth Year of the Republic of India as follows:

1. Short title and commencement.— (1) The Act may be called the Goa Right to Information Act, 1997.

2. Definitions.—(a) "Competent Authority" (see appendix) means any authority or officer notified by the Government for the purpose of the Act.

(b) "Government" means Government of Goa.

(c) "Information" means any material or information relating to affairs of the State or any local or other authorities constituted under any enactment passed by the Legislative Assembly of Goa for the time being in force or a Statutory Authority or a Company, Corporation, Trust, Firm, Society or a Co-operative Society, or any Organisation funded or controlled by the Government or executing any public work or service on behalf of or as authorised by the Government;

(d) "Right to Information" means the Right to access to information and includes the inspection of works, documents, records, taking notes and extracts and obtaining certified copies of documents or records, or taking samples of material.

3. Right to information.— Subject to the provisions of this Act, every citizen shall have right to obtain information from a Competent Authority.

4. Procedure for supply of information.—(1) A person desiring information shall make an application to the Competent Authority giving the particulars of the matter relating to which he seeks information:

Provided that where a person cannot, for valid reasons, make a request in writing, the Competent Authority may either accept an oral request which may subsequently be reduced in writing or render reasonable assistance to such person in making a written request.

(2) Upon receipt of an application requesting for an information, the Competent Authority shall consider it and furnish the information required by the applicant or pass orders thereon refusing the request as soon as practicable and in any case, within thirty working days from the date of receipt of application:

Provided that where such information relates to the life or liberty of an individual, the Competent Authority shall either furnish information or pass order refusing the request within 48 hours on receipt of the application.

(3) The information shall be supplied in writing either in English or in the Official Language.

5. Restrictions on right to information.—The Competent Authority may, for reasons recorded in writing, withhold—

(a) Information, the disclosure or contents of which will prejudicially affect the sovereignty and integrity of India or security of the State or International relations or Public Order or administration of justice or investigation of an offence or which leads to incitement to an offence;

(b) Information relating to an individual or other information, the disclosure of which has no relationship to any activity of the Government or which will not subserve any public interest and would constitute a clear and unwarranted invasion of personal privacy;

[(bb) papers containing advice, opinion, recommendations or minutes submitted to the Governor for discharge of his constitutional functions and any information, disclosure of which, would prejudicially affect the conduct of the Centre-State relations, including information exchanged in confidence between the Centre and the Government or any of their authorities or agencies.] [Inserted by Amendment Act, 1997 (Goa Act No. 1 of 1998)]

(c) Trade and commercial secrets or any other information protected by Law;

(d) Information whose release would constitute a breach of Parliament or Legislative Assembly Privilege:

[Provided that the Competent Authority shall, before withholding information under this clause, refer the matter to the Legislature Secretariat for determination of the issue and act according to the advice tendered by that Secretariat:

Provided further that no appeal shall lie under section 6 against an order withholding supply of information under this clause; [Inserted by Amendment Act, 1997 (Goa Act No. 1 of 1998)]

(e) Information whose disclosure would endanger the life or physical safety of any person or identify the source of information or assistance given in confidence for law enforcement or security purposes or in public interest:

Provided that information which cannot be denied to the State Legislature shall not be denied to any person.

6. Appeal.—(1) Any person aggrieved by an Order of the Competent Authority, or any person who has not received any Order from the Competent Authority within thirty working days may appeal to the Administrative Tribunal constituted under the Goa Administrative Tribunal Act, 1965 (6 of 1965).

(2) The decision of the Administrative Tribunal shall be final.

(3) No order adversely affecting any person shall be passed except after giving that person a reasonable opportunity of being heard.

(4) Every appeal shall be disposed as expeditiously as possible and the endeavour shall be made to dispose of the appeal within 30 days from the date on which it is presented.

7. Obligation on Competent Authority.—Every Competent Authority shall be under a duty to maintain all its records, as per its operational requirements, duly catalogued and indexed and grant access to information, subject to the provisions of this Act to any citizen requesting for such access.

8. Penalties.—(1) Any person responsible for providing any information under this Act shall be personally liable for furnishing the information within the period specified.

(2) Where a person responsible to supply information fails to furnish the information asked for under this Act within the time specified [or furnishes any information which is false in any material particulars and which he knows or has reasonable cause to believe to be false or does not believe it to be true] [Inserted by Amendment Act, 1997 (Goa Act No. 1 of 1998)] he shall be liable, after such inquiry as may be necessary under the service rules applicable to him, for imposition of such penalties as may be determined by the disciplinary authority under such rules. In addition the disciplinary authority may order him to pay a fine of Rs 100 for every day of delay after the day by which the information is required to be supplied.

[9,10] [Omitted by Amendment Act, 1997 (Goa Act No. 1 of 1998)]

11. State Council for Right to Information.—(1) The Government shall, by Notification in the Official Gazette, establish with effect from such day as specified in the Notification, a Council to be known as State Council for Right to Information.

(2) The State Council may consist of the following members

(a) the Minister-in-Charge of the Department of Administrative Reforms in the Government who shall be its Chairman; and

(b) (i) such other official Members not exceeding four;

(ii) two MLAs to be nominated by the Speaker;

(iii) non-official Members not exceeding four representing journalists, Editors of Newspapers, News agencies, Non-Government Organisations;

[(iv) non-official members not exceeding two other than those falling under item;

(iv) above. [Inserted by Amendment Act, 1997 (Goa Act No. 1 of 1998)]

(c) the time and place of the meeting of the Council shall be as the Chairman may decide and it shall observe such procedure as may be laid down by the council to transact its business.

(3) The object of the State Council shall be to promote right to information in the State and it shall deal with all matters related to right to information such as—

(a) review the operation of the Act and rules made thereunder;

(b) review of the administrative arrangements and procedures to secure for citizens the fullest possible access to information;

(c) research and documentation as regards management of information with a view to improving the extent and accuracy of information being made available under the Act; and

(d) to advise the Government on all matters related to right to information, including training, development and orientation of employees to bring in a culture of openness and transparency.

12. Act to have overriding effect.—The provisions of this Act shall have effect notwithstanding anything inconsistent therewith contained in any other enactment of the Legislative Assembly of Goa, for the time being in force.

13. Protection of action taken in good faith.—No suit, prosecution or other legal proceedings shall lie against any person for anything done in good faith or intended to be done in pursuance of this Act.

14. Charging of fees.—The Competent Authority shall charge fees for supply of information which shall not exceed the cost of processing and making available of information.

THE GUJARAT RIGHT TO INFORMATION RULES, 2005*

In exercise of the powers conferred by section 27 of the Right to Information Act, 2005 (22 of 2005), the Government of Gujarat hereby makes the following rules, namely:

1. Short title and commencement.—(1) These rules may be called the Gujarat Right to Information Rules, 2005.

(2) They shall come into force on 12 October 2005.

2. Definitions.—(1) In these rules, unless the context otherwise requires,

(a) "Act" means the Right to Information Act, 2005;

(b) "Commission" means the State Information Commission constituted under section 15 of the Act;

(c) "Form" means form appended to these rules;

(d) "fees" means fees prescribed under rule 5.

(2) The words and expressions used but not defined in these rules shall have the meaning assigned to them in the Act.

3. Application for obtaining information.— (1) A person who desires to obtain information shall make an application in Form A accompanying with the fees prescribed in Rule 5, or through the e-media to the Public Information Officer and the receipt of the application shall be given to the applicant in Form B. The fees may be paid in cash wherever facility for cash receipt is available, or by demand draft or by pay order or in the form of non-judicial stamp.

---

* *Vide* No. GS-30-2005-VHS-1005-2664-RTI Cell, dated 5th October, 2005.

(2) (i) The applicant shall be required to pay the application fee as provided under clause (a) of sub-rule (1) of Rule 5:

Provided that a person applying through the e-media shall have to pay the fees within seven days from the date of application, failing which the application shall be treated as withdrawn.

(ii) The Public Information Officer shall inform the applicant in Form C regarding other fees and charges to be paid as provided under clause (b) of sub-rule (1) of Rule 5:

Provided that no fees and charges shall be payable by a person belonging to the Below Poverty Line families provided that such person encloses with the application, a certified copy of the Below Poverty Line Card or a certificate issued in that behalf by the concerned authority.

(3) The fees and charges payable under clause (b) of sub-rule (1) of Rule 5 may be paid in cash wherever facility for cash receipt is available, or by demand draft or by pay order.

4. Disposal of the application.—(1) The Public Information Officer shall be required to provide the information sought for, to the applicant within thirty days of the receipt of the request in Form D or inform the applicant about rejection of application in Form F taking into consideration the provisions of Sections 8 and 9 of the Act:

Provided that the applicant shall be given reasons for not giving the information which are exempted from disclosure under section 8; or under section 9 of the Act.

(2) In case where the information sought for does not fall within the jurisdiction of the Public Information Officer to whom the application is made, he shall transfer such application in Form E to concerned Public Authority/Public Information Officer within five days of the receipt of the application and inform the applicant immediately about such transfer:

Provided that where the information sought for concerns the life or liberty of a person, the Public Information Officer shall be required to provide such information within forty-eight hours of the receipt of such request or application.

5. Rates of fees.—(1) The rates of fees and other charges for obtaining required information and documents shall be as under:

(a) Application fees: Rs 20 per application

(b) Other fees and charges

No.	Details of Information required	Price in Rs
1	Any information available in the form of publication	Actual price of publication.
2	Other information/documents	
	A. Information provided in	
	(i) A4, A3 size paper	Rs 2 per page
	(ii) Larger size paper	
	B. For sample model or photographs.	Amount of actual cost
	Note: Procedure stipulated by the Department for the sample or the model shall have to be followed	
	C. For inspection of records	No fees for the first half an hour and thereafter Rs 20 for each half an hour Note: The existing rates of fees for inspection of records shall continue wherever such system or procedure exists and the aforesaid fees shall not be applicable
	D. For information to be furnished in a floppy or a disc, wherever possible	Rs 50 per floppy or disc.

6. Appeal.—(1) Any person aggrieved by a decision of the Public Information Officer in Form D or in Form F, or does not receive any decision, as the case may be, he may prefer an appeal in Form G within thirty days from the date of receipt or non-receipt of such decision, to appellate authority appointed by the Government in this behalf.

(2) The applicant aggrieved by an order of the appellate authority under sub-rule (1) may prefer the second appeal to the State Information Commission within ninety days from the date of the receipt of the order of the appellate authority giving following details:

(i) Name and address of the applicant;

(ii) Name and office address of the Public Information Officer;

(iii) Number, date and details of the order against which the second appeal is filed;

(iv) Brief facts leading to second appeal;

(v) Grounds for appeal;

(vi) Verification by the appellant;

(vii) Any information which commission may deem necessary for deciding the appeal.

(3) Every appeal made to the Commission shall be accompanied by the following documents—

(i) Certified copy of the order against which second appeal is preferred.

(ii) Copies of documents referred and relied upon by the appellant along with a list thereof.

(4) While deciding appeal the Commission may,

(i) take oral or written evidence on oath or on affidavit;

(ii) evaluate the record;

(iii) inquire through the authorized officer further details or truthfulness;

(iv) summon the Public Information Officer or the appellate authority who has heard the first appeal;

(v) hear the third party; and

(vi) obtain necessary evidence from the Public Information Officer or the appellate authority who has heard the first appeal.

(5) The Commission shall serve the notice in any one of the following mode,

(i) service by the party itself;

(ii) by hand delivery;

(iii) by registered post with acknowledgement due; or

(iv) through the Head of the Department or its subordinate office.

(6) The Commission shall after hearing the parties to the appeal, pronounce in open proceedings its decision and issue a written order which shall be authenticated by the registrar or such officer as may be authorized by the Commission in this behalf.

7. Maintenance of records.—(1) The Public Information Officer shall maintain the record in respect of the applications received for information and the fees collected for giving the information. (2) The State Information Commission shall maintain the record regarding all appeals received and disposed of.

8. Miscellaneous.— For the purpose of removing any doubt it is hereby clarified that the 'forms', as prescribed under these rules, need not be in authorized pre-printed stationery, but any format neatly typed, handwritten or in electronic form which covers essential details prescribed in the form shall be valid.

Form A

[*See* Rule 3(1)]

APPLICATION FORM FOR OBTAINING INFORMATION

I.D. No.

(For office use)

To

The Public Information Officer,

(Department/Office)

1. Name of the applicant
2. Full address
3. Particulars of Information required (in brief)
4. I, hereby, state that the information sought is not covered under the categories which is exempted from disclosure of information under section 8 or under section 9 of the Right to Information Act, 2005 and to the best of my knowledge, it is pertaining to your Department/Office.

5. *(1) I have paid the fees Rs............in words rupees..................on dated .... vide receipt No........... in the Department/Office of ....

*(2) I enclose herewith demand draft/pay order No......... dated........... drawn in favour of .... Officer, issued by .... Bank towards the fees payable.

*(3) Non-judicial stamp of Rs.................is affixed on this application.

*(4) I belong to B.P.L. family. Xerox copy of my card/ certificate is enclosed herewith.

Place: .... Signature of applicant

Date: .... e-mail address, if any

Telephone No.(Office)

(Residence)

N.B.— Person belonging to B.P.L. family need not pay any type of fees

Form B

[*See* Rule 3(1)]

RECEIPT OF AN APPLICATION

From:

The Public Information officer,

(Department/Office)

I.D. No. .... Date:..............

1. Received the application dated .... in Form A, prescribed under sub-rule (1) of rule 3 of the Right to Information Rules, 2005 from Shri/Smt/Kum...................., resident of ....

2. The information shall be provided within 30 days. In any case, if it is found that it is not possible to give the required information, a letter showing reasons thereof for rejecting the request shall be issued.

* Strike out whichever is not applicable.

3. The applicant may contact the undersigned during 11.00 a.m. to 1.00 p.m. on dated .... (here mention the date not later than thirty days from the date of the receipt of an application).

4. In case of failure to remain present on the stipulated date by the applicant, the Public Information Officer shall not be held responsible for delay in providing information.

5. The applicant shall be required to deposit the outstanding amount of fees or charges, if any, prior to collection of the information or the documents.

Your faithfully,
Public Information Officer
Name of the Department/Office:
Telephone No.:
E-mail:
Website:

Form C

[*See* Rule 3(2)]

INTIMATION TO APPLICANT TO DEPOSIT FEE AND CHARGES FOR REQUIRED INFORMATION AND/OR DOCUMENTS

To

Shri/Smt/Kum.....................

Address...........................

Sir,

With reference to your request/application dated.............. (I.D. No....... dated..............), I am to state that you are required to deposit Rs.................... (in words Rupees....................only) for required information and documents sought for. It is requested to obtain the copies of the required information/documents after depositing the amount in this Department/Office.

(1)	Total No. of pages .... x Rs 2 per page A3, A4 size	Rs
(2)	Total No. of large size pages (except A3, A4 size)	Rs (Amount of actual cost)
(3)	Floppy/disc charges.......... x Rs 50 per piece	Rs

(4) Charges for inspection of record.......... Rs
(5) Charges for sample/model.................... Rs

Total Rs............

....

Yours faithfully,

( )
Public Information Officer:
Name of the Department/Office
Telephone No.:
E-mail:
Website:

Form D

[*See* Rule 4(1)]

SUPPLY OF INFOR2MATION TO THE APPLICANT

From:

The Public Information Officer
(Department/Office)
No................ Date ....

To,

Shri/Smt./Kum..................
Address..........................

Sir,

This is with reference to your application dated:............(I.D. No............date...............) requesting for supply of information.

*2. Details of required information is enclosed herewith.

*3. Out of the required information sought for the partial information is supplied as under:

(1)

(2)

(3)

(4)

*4. With reference to your request for supplying information, the following information/documents cannot be supplied for the following

* Strike out whichever is not applicable.

reasons:

1.

2.

3.

4.

5. If you are aggrieved by the above decision, you may prefer an appeal to *................within thirty days from the date of receipt of the decision.

6. The information whichever is given to you is as a member of Below Poverty Line families and shall not be used for any other purpose.

Yours faithfully,

( )

Public Information Officer

Name of the Department/Office

Telephone No.

e-mail:

Website:

Form E

[*See* Rule 4(2)]

TRANSFER OF APPLICATION PERTAINING TO OTHER AUTHORITY

From: No..............

Dated...........

Public Information Officer

..............Department/Office

Address..............................

To

Shri/Smt

Public Information Officer

..............Department/Office

---

* Here pls. specify Name/Address of the Appellate Authority.

Address...............................

Sir,

Please find enclosed herewith an application from Shri...........dated........... (I.D. No............), for the reasons stated below:

Required information does not fall within the jurisdiction of this Department/Office. As it falls within the jurisdiction of your Department/Office, the same is transferred herewith to you for further necessary action.

It is certified that the applicant has paid Rs............ (Rupees............only) on account of fees/charges for obtaining required information, which has been credited in the Government treasury/account.

Copy to:

Shri/Smt/Kum......................

(Applicant)

1. As your application pertaining to required information doesn't fall within the jurisdiction of this Department/Office, it has been transferred to the Public Information Officer having jurisdiction.

You are requested to contact the Public Information Officer mentioned above.

Form F

[*See* Rule 4(1)]

ORDER OF REJECTION OF INFORMATION

From:

Public Information Officer

...............Department/Office

Address...............................

No...............Dated.............

To

Shri/Smt/Kum........................

Address.............................

Sir,

With reference to your application dated.............. I.D. No............ requesting for supplying information, I am to state that ....:

1. The information requested cannot be provided for the following reasons:
   The information requested falls within the exempted categories under sub-rule..........of Section 8 or under Section 9 of the Act.
2. If you are aggrieved by the above decision, you may prefer an appeal to*............. within thirty days from the date of receipt of the decision.

Yours faithfully,
( )
Public Information Officer:
Name of the Department/Office:
Telephone No.:
e-mail:
Website:

Form G

[*See* Rule 6(1)]

FORM OF FIRST APPEAL

I.D. No...............
Date...................
(For office use)

To

The Appellate Authority
(Department/Office)...........

Sir,

As I have not received any decision/As I am aggrieved by the decision of the Public Information Officer________________, I, hereby file this appeal. The particulars of my application are as follows:

1. Name of the Appellant
2. Address of Appellant
3. (A) Name of the Public Information Officer:

* Here pl. specify Name/Address of the Appellate Authority.

Address of Public Information Officer:

(B) Department/Office and address:

(C) Particulars of the decision against which the appeal is preferred including the No. & date of such decision.

4. Date of application submitted in Form A:

5. Details of Information:

(1) Information asked for

(2) Period for which information is sought

6. Date as on completion of 30 days after submitting application in Form A

7. Reasons for Appeal—

(A) No decision is received within 30 days of submission of application in Form A

(B) Aggrieved by the decision of Public Information Officer Dated:

8. Ground for appeal. Brief facts of the case

9. Last date for filing the appeal

10. Prayer/reliefs sought for

I hereby state that the information and particulars given above are true to the best of my knowledge and belief.

Place...........

Date...........

Name of appellant

Signature of appellant:

e-mail address, if any:

Telephone No.(Office):

(Residence):

Acknowledgement

From:

Public Information Officer

...............Department/Office

Address..............

I.D. No................ Date:...............

1. Received an appeal application of Shri ....a resident of .... in Form G prescribed under sub-rule (1) of Rule 6 of the Gujarat Right to Information Rules, 2005.

Signature of the receipt clerk,
Office of the Appellate Authority:
Telephone No.:
e-mail:
Website:

By order and in the name of the Governor of Gujarat.

THE HARYANA RIGHT TO INFORMATION RULES, 2005*

In exercise of the powers conferred by sub-section (I) read with sub-section (2) of section 27 of the Right to Information Act, 2005 (Central Act 22 of 2005), the Governor of Haryana hereby makes the following rules providing for information under the said Act, namely:

1. Short title and commencement.—(1) These rules may be called the Haryana Right to Information Rules, 2005.

(2) They shall come into force on the date of their publication in the official Gazette.

2. Definitions.—(1) In these rules, unless the context otherwise requires,

(a) "Act" means the Right to Information Act, 2005 (Central Act 22 of 2005;

(b) "Commission" means the Haryana Information Commission;

(c) "Form" means a form, appended to these rules;

(d) "Section" means the section of the Act.

(2) The words and expressions used in these rules, but not defined, shall have the same meaning as assigned to them in the Act.

3. Application for obtaining information.—(1) A person, who desires to obtain any information admissible under the Act, shall make an application in Form A to the State Public

---

* *Vide* No. 5/4/2005-IAR, Government of Haryana, dated 28th Oct., 2005.

Information Officer/State Assistant Public Information Officer along with a fee as specified in Rule 5 of these rules.

(2) On the receipt of an application, made under sub-rule (1), the State Public Information Officer/State Assistant Public Information Officer shall give a receipt in token thereof to the applicant.

4. Deposit of fee.—(1) The fee shall be deposited with the State Public Information Officer/State Assistant Public Information Officer either in cash against proper receipt or by treasury challan.

(2) The amount of fee shall be credited to the receipt head/ account number of the concerned public authority.

(3) On receipt of an application, submitted under sub-rule (1) of Rule 3, the State Public Information Officer/State Assistant Public Information Officer shall scrutinize the application and shall assess how much fee is required to be paid by the applicant for obtaining the information.

(4) The fee assessed under sub-rule (3), shall be informed to the applicant by the State Public Information Officer/State Assistant Public Information Officer in Form B within a period of seven days from the receipt of application.

(5) In case the applicant fails to deposit the requisite fee within a period of fifteen days after the issuance of the intimation given to him under sub-rule (4), it shall be construed that the applicant is no longer interested in obtaining the information, sought for, and his application shall be deemed to have been filed.

5. Quantum of fee.—(1) An application for obtaining any information under sub-section (1) of section 6 shall be accompanied with a fee of Rs 50

(2) For providing an information under sub-section (1) of Section 7, the fee shall be charged from the applicant at the following rates, namely:

(a) Rs 10 for each page in A-4 or A-3 size paper, created or copied; and

(b) if information is to be provided on a large size of paper than that of specified in clause (a), the actual cost price of such a paper shall be charged.

(3) For providing an information under sub-section (5) of Section 7, the fee shall be charged from the applicant at the following rates, namely:

(a) Rs 50 for providing information in a floppy;

(b) Rs 100 for providing information in diskette; and

(c) if information sought is of such a nature, which is contained in a printed document of which a price has been fixed, then that information shall be provided after charging the price, fixed for that printed document. However, if only an extract or page of such a printed document is asked for, then a fee of Rs 10 per page shall be charged.

(4) No fee for inspection of record shall be charged, if such an inspection is made for one hour only. However, if inspection is made for a period of more than one hour, then a fee of rupees ten shall be charged for every fifteen minutes in excess of first hour. Every fraction of the period above fifteen minutes, shall be construed as a complete period of fifteen minutes and it shall be charged as full period of fifteen minutes.

6. Procedure to be followed in deciding appeal.—Before deciding an appeal, the Commission shall,

(a) serve notice to the concerned persons;

(b) entertain any evidence in support of appeal, which may be oral or in writing from the concerned persons;

(c) examine on oath or by having affidavits from the persons concerned;

(d) persue or inspect the documents or any records or copies thereof;

(e) inquire through the authorized officer the facts of an appeal or may require facts in detail, if it so deems appropriate, hear the State Public Information

Officer or any other senior officer who had decided the first appeal, as the case may be; and

(f) receive evidence on affidavits from the State Public Information Officer or any senior officer who had decided the first appeal or from any other person from whom the evidence may be deemed necessary.

7. Mode of serving notice.—The Commission may serve notice to the persons concerned in any of the following modes, namely

(a) by hand delivery (dasti) through process server; or

(b) by registered post with acknowledgement due; or

(c) by publication in the newspaper.

8. Order by the Commission.—(1) The Commission shall make order in writing and pronounce the same in the presence of the concerned parties.

(2) The party concerned may, obtain the copy of the order from the Commission.

Form A

[*See* Rule 3(1)]

To

The State Public Information Officer/

State Assistant Public Information Officer

(Name of the office with address)

1. Full name of the applicant
2. Address
3. Particulars of information required:

   (i) Subject matter of information*

   (ii) The period to which the information relates**

   (iii) Description of the information required***

---

* Broad category of the subject to be indicated (such as Grant/ Government land/Service matters/Licenses, etc.).

** Relevant period for which information is required to be indicated.

*** Specific details of the information are required to be indicated.

(iv) Whether information is required by post or in person (the actual postal charges shall be included in addition to the fees)

(v) In case by post (Ordinary, Registered or Speed)

Place.............. Signature of the Applicant

Date..............

Acknowledgement

Received your application dated ...., vide Diary No............... dated ....

(Signature)

State Public Information Officer/

State Assistant Public Information Officer

Name of the Department/Office

Form B

[*See* Rule 4(4)]

From

State Public Information Officer/

State Assistant Public Information Officer

(Name of Department/Office)

To,

Name and address of the applicant

Sir,

Please refer to your application dated ....addressed to the undersigned requesting information regarding.............. The additional fee for supplying this information to you is Rs..............

2. You are hereby informed to pay the fee at this office either in cash or in a Government treasury through challan and send a copy of the challan to this office within a period of fifteen days and collect the information on..............

3. The amount of fee shall be deposited in the receipt head/account No. (to be intimated to the applicant by the concerned department.)

State Public Information Officer/

State Assistant Public Information Officer

THE JAMMU AND KASHMIR RIGHT TO INFORMATION ACT, 2004
[J&K ACT NO. 1 OF 2004]

An Act to make provision for securing right to information and

Be it enacted by the Jammu and Kashmir State Legislature in the Fifty-fourth Year of the Republic of India as follows:

1. Short title, extent and commencement.—(1) This Act may be called the Jammu and Kashmir Right to Information Act, 2004. (2) It shall extend to the whole of the State of Jammu and Kashmir. (3) It shall come into force on such date as the Government may, by notification in the Government Gazette, appoint.

2. Definitions.— In this Act, unless the context otherwise requires,

(a) "Controlling Officer" means the immediate superior officer above the incharge of office, who supervises and controls the work of incharge of office or such officer as may from time to time, be specified as such by the Government for the purposes of this Act;

(b) "Department" means any department or office of the Government;

(c) "Government" means the Government of Jammu and Kashmir;

(d) "Incharge of the Office" means an Officer/ functionary of a department of the Government or a public body, who is in actual control of any office of the Government or public body, as the case may be, or such officer/functionary as may, from time to time, be specified as such by the Government for the purposes of this Act;

(e) "Information" means any document or information relating to the affairs of the State or a public body;

(f) "Public body" shall include,

(i) offices of all local bodies and other authorities constituted under any law for the time being in force; or

(ii) any other statutory authority constituted by the Government under any law for the time being in force; or

(iii) a Government Company/Corporation incorporated under the Companies Act, 1956 (Central Act No. 1 of 1956) in which not less than fifty one per cent of the paid up share capital, is held by the Government or a trust established by the Government under any law for the time being in force and controlled by it; or

(iv) a Society or a Co-operative Society or any other organization established under any law for the time being in force, by the Government and directly controlled or funded by it; or

(v) any other body, which may be receiving substantial financial assistance from the Government, as may be specified by notification, in the Government Gazette for the purposes of this Act;

(g) "Right to information" means right to obtain information relating to the affairs of the State or Public bodies by means of,

(i) obtaining certified copies of documents or records; or

(ii) inspection of accessible records and taking notes and extracts; or

(iii) inspection of public works; or

(iv) taking of samples of material from public works; and

(v) diskettes, floppies or in any other electronic mode or through print outs where such information is stored in a computer or in any other device.

3. Obligation of Departments and Public Bodies.—Every Department and public body shall,

(a) maintain all its records, in such manner and form as is consistent with its operational requirements duly catalogued and indexed;

(b) publish at such intervals as may be prescribed by the Government,—

(i) the particulars of its organization, functions and duties;

(ii) the powers and duties of its officers and employees and the procedure followed by them in the decision making process;

(iii) the norms set by the public authority for the discharge of its functions;

(iv) rules, regulations, instructions, manuals and other categories of records under its control used by its employees for discharging its functions;

(v) the details of facilities available to citizens for obtaining information; and

(vi) the name, designation and other particulars of the in charge of the office and of the Controlling Officer.

(c) publish all relevant facts concerning important decisions and policies that affect the public while announcing such decisions and policies;

(d) give reasons for its decisions, whether administrative or quasi-judicial to those affected by such decisions;

(e) before initiating any project, publish or communicate to the public generally or to the persons affected or likely to be affected by the project in particular, the facts available to it or to which it has reasonable access which in its opinion should be known to them in the best interests of maintenance of democratic principles.

4. Right to information.—Subject to the provisions of this Act, every citizen shall have right to obtain information from the incharge of office and such incharge shall be liable to provide information under and in accordance with the provisions of this Act.

5. Procedure for supply of information.—Any person seeking information shall make an application to the incharge of the office giving particulars of the matter relating to which information is sought,

(a) if the incharge of the office is in possession of the information requested and the information does not fall in any one or more categories mentioned in section 6, the incharge of the office shall supply the information to the applicant as far as may be practical within a period of thirty working days from the receipt of the application;

(b) if the incharge of the office is in possession of the information requested but, the information sought falls in any one or more categories mentioned in section 6, the incharge of the office shall reject the request and communicate the reasons for the rejection to the applicant as early as possible;

(c) if the incharge of the office is dealing with the subject matter but the information cannot be compiled without considerable financial expenditure or without considerable extra work, the incharge of the office may after recording the reasons in writing, send a regret reply to the applicant. The incharge of the office shall, however, supply any related information readily available.

(d) the incharge of the office may seek the assistance of any other officer as he may consider necessary for the proper discharge of his duties;

(e) any officer whose assistance has been sought under clause (d) shall render all assistance to the incharge of the office seeking his assistance.

6. Restriction of right to information.—(1) Notwithstanding anything hereinbefore contained, the following information shall be exempted from disclosure, namely:

(a) information, the disclosure of which would prejudicially affect the sovereignty and integrity of India, security of the State, or conduct of international relations;

(b) information, the disclosure of which would prejudicially affect public safely and order, detection and investigation of an offence, or which may lead to an incitement to commit an offence;

(c) information, the disclosure of which would prejudicially affect the conduct of Centre-State relations, including information exchanged in confidence between the Central and State Government or any of their authorities/agencies;

(d) Cabinet papers including record of deliberations of the Council of Ministers;

(e) minutes of records of advice including legal advice, opinions of recommendations made by any officer of a public authority during the decision making process prior to the executive decision or policy formulation;

(f) information, the disclosure of which may result in the breach of privileges of Parliament or the Legislature of the State, or contravention of a lawful order of a court;

(g) Information held in consequence of having been supplied in confidence by a person who—

(i) gave the information under a guarantee that its confidentiality would be protected; or

(ii) was not under any legal obligation, whether actual or implied, to supply, and has not consented to its disclosure.

(2) The incharge of the office may, for reasons to be recorded in writing, withhold—

(a) information, the disclosure of which,

(i) would prejudicially affect the enforcement of any law including detection, prevention, investigation or suppression of crime or contravention of any law or the apprehending of offenders and the operations of any intelligence organizations;

(ii) would endanger the life or physical safety of any person, or identify the source of information or assistance given in confidence for law enforcement or security purposes;

(iii) would prejudicially affect fair trial or adjudication of a pending case or the proceedings of any tribunal, public inquiry;

(iv) would reveal the existence or identity of a confidential record or would prejudice future supply of information relating to violation or contravention of any law;

(v) may help or facilitate escape of any person from legal custody or affect his present security;

(b) information the disclosure of which would prejudicially affect the Government's ability to manage the economy or the legitimate economic and commercial interests of a public authority; or would cause unfair gain or loss to any individual or organization; these would include trade and commercial secrets protected by law;

(c) personal information, the disclosure of which has no relationship to any public activity or which would cause unwarranted invasion of the privacy of an individual;

(d) the record and information referred to in sections 123 and 124 of the Evidence Act, Samvat 1977 and claimed privileged;

(e) information on the following grounds also—

(i) that the request is too general or is of such nature that, having regard to the volume of information required to be retrieved or processes for fulfilling it, it would involve disproportionate diversion of the resources of a public authority or would adversely interfere with the functioning of such authority:

Provided that, where access is being refused on the ground that the request is too general, it would be duty of the incharge of office concerned to render help, as far as possible, to the persons seeking information to reframe his request in such a manner as may facilitate supply of information;

(ii) that the request relates to information that is required by law or convention to be published at a particular time;

(iii) that the request relates to information that is contained in published material for sale.

7. Third party information.—Where an incharge of office intends to disclose information on a request made by a party which relates to or has been supplied by a third party and has been treated as confidential by that party, the incharge of office shall by notice to that third party invite representation against such proposed disclosure.

8. Act not to apply to certain organizations.—Nothing contained in this Act shall apply to intelligence and security organizations by whatever name called, discharging their functions as such under the Government.

9. Appeals.—(1) Any person aggrieved by the order of the incharge of the office or any person who has not received Required information within the time stipulated under section 5, may appeal to the controlling officer, within thirty days of the decision rejecting his request for information or the expiry of period stipulated under section 5 for furnishing such information:

Provided that the controlling officer may entertain appeal after the expiry of the said period of thirty days, if it is satisfied that the appellant was prevented by sufficient cause from filing the appeal.

(2) A second appeal against the decision under sub-section (1) shall lie within 30 days of such decision to the Government:

Provided that the Government may entertain appeal after the expiry of the said period of thirty days if it is satisfied that the appellant was prevented by sufficient cause from filing the appeal.

(3) The appeals preferred under sub-sections (1) and (2) shall be heard and decided expeditiously and by all means be disposed of within thirty days of presentation of appeal:

Provided that no order adversely affecting the person making the appeal shall be passed unless an opportunity of being heard is afforded to him.

(4) The appeal shall be accompanied with the proof of fee deposited or tendered in the manner provided in accordance with section 10.

10. Fee.—(1) The request for seeking information under this Act shall be accompanied by a proof of payment of such fee as may be prescribed for furnishing of information.

(2) If requisite fee as prescribed under sub-section (1) is not paid for the required information, the information sought under section 5 may not be made available.

(3) The appeal shall be accompanied with such fee, and be deposited and tendered in such manner, as may be prescribed.

11. Obligation of the incharge of office.—(1) Every incharge of the office shall have a duty to maintain all records in accordance with the procedure laid down under relevant law or Departmental manuals.

(2) While maintaining the records proper indexing, listing, numbering and paging of records shall be done and the same may be kept ready for access to information, subject to the provisions of this Act, to any citizen requesting for such access.

(3) Any person responsible for providing any information under this Act shall be personally liable for furnishing information within the period specified under this Act.

12. Penalties.—Where any person responsible for making available information under this Act, fails without any reasonable cause to furnish information sought by any citizen under the provisions of this Act within the time specified or furnishes any information which is false with regard to any material particulars and which he knows and has reasonable cause to believe it to be false or does not believe it to be true, he shall be liable, after such inquiry as may be required under rules pertaining to disciplinary action applicable to him, for imposition of such penalty as may be determined by the disciplinary authority under such rules.

13. Protection of action taken in good faith.—No suit, prosecution or legal proceedings shall lie against any person for anything done or intended to be done in good faith in pursuance to the provisions of this Act or rules made thereunder.

14. Bar to the legal proceedings.—No court shall entertain any suit, application or other proceedings in respect of any order made under this Act and no such order shall be called in question otherwise, than by way of appeal under this Act.

15. Power to make rules.—The Government may make rules for carrying out the purposes of this Act.

(2) All rules under this Act shall be laid, as soon as may be after they are made, before the two Houses of the State Legislature. If the State Legislature makes any modification in such rules, or resolves that any such rule should not be made, such rules thereafter have effect only in such modified form or be of no effect as the case may be:

Provided that any such modification or annulment shall be without prejudice to the validity of anything previously done thereunder.

THE JAMMU AND KASHMIR RIGHT TO INFORMATION RULES, 2005*

In exercise of the powers conferred by sub-section (1) of Section 15 of the Jammu and Kashmir Right to Information Act, 2004 (Act No. 1 of 2004), the Government of Jammu and Kashmir hereby makes the following rules, namely:

1. Short title and commencement.—(i) These rules may be called the Jammu and Kashmir Right to Information Rules, 2005.

(ii) These rules shall come into force from the date of their publication in the Official Gazette.

2. Definitions.—In these rules, unless the context otherwise requires,

(a) "Act" means the Jammu and Kashmir Right to Information Act, 2004.

(b) "Authorized person" means a person nominated by the incharge of the Office to accept fee prescribed under these rules.

(c) "Controlling Officer" means the Officer as specified in schedule I specified as such in schedule annexed to these rules.

(d) "Form" means the form appended to these rules.

(e) "Incharge of the Office" means an Officer/ functionary specified as such in schedule annexed to these rules.

(f) "Section" means a section of the Act.

---

* *Vide* S.R.O. 181, Government of Jammu & Kashmir, dated 30th June, 2005.

(iii) Words and expressions used but not defined in these rules shall have the same meaning as has been assigned in the Act.

3. Application for seeking information.—(i) Any person seeking information under the Act shall make an application in Form 'A' to the incharge of the office and deposit application fee as per Rule 8 with the Authorized person. The incharge of the Office shall duly acknowledge the application as provided in Form 'A'. Provided that the person who makes a request shall ensure that the requisite fee is deposited in cash with the Authorized person within 7 days of his request, failing which his application shall be treated as withdrawn.

4. Disposal of application seeking information.—(i) If the information sought for falls in any of the restrictions mentioned in section 6 of the Act and/or pertains to the organizations mentioned in section 8 of the said Act, the incharge of the office shall order return of the application to the applicant in Form 'B' as soon as practicable, within 15 days of receipt of the application assigning the reason(s) for such return. The application fee deposing in such cases shall not be refunded.

(ii) If the information sought for does not fall within any of the restrictions mentioned in section 6 and do not pertain to the organizations mentioned in section 8 of the Act, the incharge of the Office, on being satisfied, shall supply the information to the applicant in Form 'C'. In case the information sought is partially falling under the preview of section 6 and/or 8 of the Act and partly falls outside the restrictions, the incharge of the office shall supply only such information as is permissible under the Act and reject the remaining part giving reasons thereof.

(iii) The information shall be supplied as soon as practicable within a period of thirty (30) working days from the receipt of the application on deposit of fee. A proper acknowledgement shall be obtained from the applicant in token of receipt of the information.

5. Inspection of documents.—(i) In case the applicant desires the inspection of documents, the applicant shall deposit fee with the incharge of the Office in addition to the application fee as prescribed in rule 8. Only those documents shall be allowed for inspection, copies of which can be given under the Act.

(ii) Inspection of public works: In case the applicant desires the inspection of public works, the applicant shall deposit fee with the Authorized person in addition to the application fee as prescribed in rule 8. Inspection of only such public works shall be allowed which are provided by this Act and not prohibited by any other law.

(iii) Taking of samples or material from public works: In case the applicant desires taking samples or material from public work, the incharge of the Office shall decide the quantum of fee on case to case basis so as to cover the cost of the material and the labour in providing such sample. The applicant shall deposit the fee so calculated with the Authorized person in addition to application fee as prescribed in rule 8. Only such sample and material shall be made available which is permissible under the provision of this Act.

6. Appeal.—(1) Any person—

(a) who fails to get a response in Form 'C' from the incharge of the Office within 30 working days of submission of Form 'A' or

(b) is aggrieved by the response received within the prescribed period, may appeal in Form 'D' to the controlling officer within 30 days of the decision of incharge of the office.

(2) On receipt of the appeal, the controlling officer shall acknowledge the receipt of appeal and after giving the applicant the opportunity of being heard, shall endeavour to dispose it off within 30 days from the date on which it is presented and send a copy of the decision to the incharge of the office concerned.

(3) The second appeal against the decision of the controlling officer shall lie within 30 days of such decision with the Government in Form 'E'.

(4) In case the appeal is allowed, the information shall be supplied to the applicant by the incharge of the Office within such period as ordered by the appellate authority. This period

shall not exceed thirty working days from the date of receipt of the order.

7. Publication of information.—(i) Every department and public body shall publish the information as per the sub-section (b) of Section 3 of the Act, in the form of booklets, folders and pamphlets within three months from the date these rules are notified in the official Gazette and then at the following intervals:

No.	Particulars of Information to be published	Interval
1.	Particulars of its organizations, functions and duties	Once in five years
2.	Powers and duties of its Officers and employees and the procedure followed by them in the decision-making process	Once in two years
3.	Norms set by the public authority for the discharge of its functions	Once in two years
4.	Laws, bye-laws, rules, regulations, instructions, manuals and other categories of records under its control used by its employees for discharging its functions	Once in five years
5.	Details of facilities available to citizens for obtaining information	Annually
6.	Name, designation and other particulars of the incharge of the Office and Controlling Officer	Annually

(ii) Such information shall also be made available to the public information counters, medium of Internet and display on notice board at conspicuous places in the office of the Incharge of the Office and in the office of the Controlling Officer.

8. Charging of fee.—(i) The incharge of the Office shall charge the fee at the following rates:

1 Application fee Five rupees per application

No.	Description of Information	Fees in Rupees
1.	Where the information is available in the form of a priced publication	Price fixed for the publication
2.	For other than priced publication	As fixed or determined for the same
3.	Inspection of documents	Rupees 5 (Five)

4.	Inspection of public works	Rupees 500
5.	Taking of samples of material from public works	Rupees 500

(ii) The appellate authority shall charge a fee of Ten rupees per appeal: Provided that the said prescribed fee shall be deposited in the Government Treasury under:

Major Head: 0070-Other Administrative Services

60- Other Services

800-Other Receipts

Receipts on account of Right to Information Act.

9. Interpretation.—In case there seems any ambiguity in these rules the interpretation of the Government in the General Administration Department in consultation with Law Department shall be the final.

10. Maintenance of records.—(i) The incharge of the Office shall maintain records of all applications received for supple of information and fee charged.

(ii) The controlling officer shall maintain records of all appeals filed before him and the fee charged.

THE KARNATAKA RIGHT TO INFORMATION ACT, 2000

(Karnataka Act No. 28 of 2000)

An Act to provide for right of access to information to the citizens of the State and in relation to the matters connected there with or incidental thereto.

Whereas right to Government held information is accepted by the Supreme Court as a part of right to speech and expression guaranteed to citizens in the Constitution.

And whereas providing right of access to information to the citizens of the State promotes openness, transparency and accountability in administration and ensures effective participation of people in the administration and thus makes democracy meaningful.

And whereas it is expedient to provide for right of access to information to the citizens of the State and in relation to the matters connected therewith or incidental thereto and for the purpose hereinafter appearing;

Be it enacted by the Karnataka State Legislature in the fifty-first year of the Republic of India as follows:

1. Short title and commencement.— This Act may be called the Karnataka Right to Information Act, 2000.

It shall come into force from such date, as the State Government may, by notification, appoint and different dates may be appointed for different provisions of this Act.

2. Definitions.—In this Act, unless the context otherwise requires

(a) "Competent authority" means head of the office or any officer or person as may be notified by the State Government for the purpose of this Act:

Provided that where the Competent Authority transfers application to any officer or person under the proviso to sub-section (2) of section 5, such officer or person shall be deemed to be the "Competent Authority".

(b) "Information" means information relating to any matter in respect of the affairs of the administration or decisions of a public authority.

(c) "Public authority" means:

(i) all offices of the State Government including the Karnataka Public Service Commission;

(ii) all local authorities, all authorities constituted by or under any Act of the State Legislature for the time being in force, a company, corporation, trust, society, any statutory or other authority, co-operative society or any organisation or body funded, owned or controlled by the State Government but does not include:

(a) Offices of the Central Government;

(b) Any establishment of the armed forces or Central Para Military forces;

(c) Any body or corporation owned or controlled by the Central Government.

(d) "Right to Information" means right of access to information from any public authority:

(i) by obtaining certified copies of any records;

(ii) by obtaining diskettes, floppies or any other electronic mode or through print-zouts where such information is stored in a computer or in any other device;

(iii) in such other manner as may be prescribed;

(e) "Record" includes:

(i) any document, manuscript and file;

(ii) any microfilm, microfiche and facsimile copy of document;

(iii) any reproduction of image or images embodied in such microfile (whether enlarged or not) and

(iv) any other material produced by a computer or by any other device.

(f) "Trade secret" means information contained in a formula, pattern, compilation, programme, device, product, method, technique or process which is not generally known and which may have economic value.

3. Obligation of Public Authorities.—Every public authority shall—

(a) maintain all records in such manner and form as is consistent with its operational requirements duly catalogued and indexed.

(b) publish at such intervals as may be prescribed:

(i) The particulars of its organisation, functions and duties;

(ii) The powers and duties of officers and employees and the procedure followed by them in the decision making process;

(iii) The norms setup by the public authority for the discharge of its functions;

(iv) The details of facilities available to citizens for obtaining information.

(c) publish all relevant facts concerning such of the important decisions and policies that affect the public as may be prescribed while announcing such decisions and policies.

(d) before sanctioning or initiating or causing to sanction or initiate any project, scheme or activity as may be specified by the State Government, publish or communicate to the public generally or to the persons affected or likely to be affected by the project, scheme or activity in particular in such manner as may be prescribed, the facts available to it or to which it has reasonable access which in its opinion should be known to them in the best interests of maintenance of democratic principles.

(e) publish such other information as may be prescribed.

4. Right to information.—(1) Subject to the provisions of this Act every citizen shall have the right to information.

(2) Notwithstanding anything contained in sub-section (1), no person shall be given:

(a) information, the disclosure of which would prejudicially affect the sovereignty and integrity of India, security of the State, strategic scientific or economic interest of India or conduct of international relations.

(b) information, the disclosure of which would prejudicially affect public safety and order or which may lead to an incitement to commit an offence or prejudicially affect fair trial or adjudication of a pending case.

(c) information relating to Cabinet papers including records of the deliberations of the Council of Ministers, Secretaries and other Officers:

Provided that information regarding the decisions of the Cabinet along with the reasons leading to the decision shall be made available and every Government Order issued on the basis of the Cabinet decision shall be accompanied by a statement explaining the reasons for and the circumstances under which the decision is taken.

(d) information the disclosure of which would harm, frankness and candour of internal discussions including inter-departmental or intra-departmental notes, correspondence and papers containing advice or opinion as also of projections and assumptions relating to internal policy analysis:

Provided that information regarding minutes or records, advice including legal advice, opinion or recommendation made or given in respect of the executive decisions or policy formulations shall be made available after an executive decision taken or policy formulation is done.

(e) information the disclosure of which would prejudice the assessment or collection of any tax, cess, duty or fee or assist in avoidance or evasion of the tax, cess, duty or fee.

(f) information the disclosure of which would constitute a breach of privilege of the Parliament or the State Legislature:

Provided that the Competent Authority shall before withholding information under this clause refer the matter to the Karnataka Legislative Assembly Secretariat or the Karnataka Legislative Council Secretariat, as the case may be for determination of the issues and act according to the advice tendered by the Secretariat:

Provided further that in computing the period of fifteen working days under sub-section (2) of section 5 for the purpose of this clause, the time required for determination of issues under the first proviso shall be excluded.

(g) information regarding trade or commercial secrets protected by law or information, the disclosure of which would prejudicially affect the legitimate economic and commercial interest or the competitive position of a public authority; or would cause unfair gain or loss to any person.

(h) information regarding any matter which is likely to:

(i) help or facilitate escape from legal custody or affect prison security; or

(ii) impede the process of investigation or apprehension or prosecution of offenders.

5. Procedure for supply of information.—(1) A person desirous to obtain information shall make an application to the competent authority in the prescribed manner, along with such fee, in such form and with such particulars, as may be prescribed:

Provided that the fee payable shall not exceed the actual cost of supplying information.

(2) On the receipt of an application requesting for information, the competent authority shall consider it and except for justifiable reasons, pass orders thereon either granting or refusing it, as soon as practicable and in any case within fifteen working days from the date of receipt of the application:

Provided that where the competent authority does not have the information, he shall within fifteen days from the date of receipt of application transfer the application to the officer or person with whom such information is available and inform the applicant accordingly and thereafter such officer or person to whom such application is transferred shall furnish information within fifteen working days from the date of receipt of the application from the competent authority.

(3) Where a request is rejected under sub-section (2), the competent authority shall communicate in writing to the person making the request:

- The reasons for such rejection.
- The period within which the appeal against such rejection may be preferred.
- The particulars of the appellate authority.

6. Grounds for refusal to supply information in certain cases.—Without prejudice to the provisions of section 4, the competent authority may also reject a request for supply of information where such request:

(a) is too general in nature and the information sought is of such nature that, it is not required to be ordinarily collected by the public authority:

Provided that where such request is rejected on the aforesaid ground, it shall be the duty of the competent authority to render help as far as possible to the person seeking information to reframe the request in such a manner as may facilitate the supply of information.

(b) relates to information that is required by law, rules, regulations or orders to be published at a particular time; or

(c) relates to information that is contained is published material available to public;

(d) relates to personal information the disclosure of which has no relationship to any public activity or which would cause unwarranted invasion of the privacy of an individual except where larger public interest is served by disclosure:

Provided that the information relating to returns of assets and liabilities filed by any Government servant shall be made available to the public.

7. Appeals.—(1)Subject to such rules as may be prescribed, any person (i) aggrieved by an order of the competent authority may, within thirty days from the date of receipt of such order or (ii) who has not received any communication within a period of fifteen working days from the date of making application under Section 5, may within thirty days next after such period; appeal to such authority as may be prescribed:

Provided that no appeal shall lie against an order of withholding of information under clause (f) of sub-section (2) of section 4.

(2) The appellate authority may, after giving the person affected a reasonable opportunity of being heard, pass such order as it deems fit.

(3) Any person aggrieved by the order of the appellate authority under sub-section (2) may prefer an appeal to the Karnataka Appellate Tribunal.

(4) Appeals referred to in sub-section (1) and (3) shall be disposed of within thirty days from the date of receipt of such appeals.

8. Power to remove difficulties.—If any difficulty arises in giving effect to the provisions of this Act, the State Government may, by an order make such provisions not inconsistent with the provisions of this Act and appear to them to be necessary or expedient for removing the difficulty, provided that no such order shall be made after the expiry of two years from the date of commencement of this Act.

9. Penalties.—Where any competent authority, without any reasonable cause fails to supply information sought for within the period specified under section 5 or furnishes information which is false with regard to any material particulars and which it knows or has reasonable cause to believe it to be false.

(1) The authority immediately superior to the competent authority may impose a penalty not exceeding two thousand rupees on such competent authority as it thinks appropriate after giving him a reasonable opportunity of being heard and such a penalty shall be recoverable from his salary or if no salary is drawn as arrears of land revenue; and he shall also be liable to disciplinary action under the service rules applicable to him.

10. Bar of Jurisdiction of Courts.—No Court shall entertain any suit, application or other proceeding in respect of any order made under this Act and no such order shall be called in question otherwise than by way of an appeal under this Act.

11. Act to have overriding effect.—The provisions of this Act shall have effect notwithstanding anything inconsistent therewith contained in any other law made by the State Legislature in respect of any matter falling under State list or concurrent list except the provisions of any existing law or a law made by Parliament in respect of any matter falling under concurrent list.

12. Power to make rules.—(1) The State Government may, after previous publication by notification make rules to carry out the provisions of this Act.

(2) In particular, and without prejudice to the generality of the foregoing power such rules may provide for all or any of the following matters, namely:

(a) the fee payable under section 5;

(b) any other matter which is required to be, or may be, prescribed.

(3) Every rule made under this Act shall be laid as soon as may be after it is made, before each House of the State Legislature while it is in session for a total period of thirty days which may be comprised in one session or in two or more successive sessions and if before the expiry of the session in which it is so laid or the session immediately following, both the Houses agree in making modification in the rule or both the Houses agree that rule should not be made the rule thereafter, shall have effect only in such modified form or be of no effect, as the case may be, so however, that any such modification or annulment shall be without prejudice to the validity of anything previously done under that rule.

13. Repeal and savings.—(1) The Karnataka Right to Information Ordinance, 2000 (Karnataka Ordinance No. 9 of 2000) is hereby repealed.

(2) Notwithstanding such repeal anything done or any action taken under the said Ordinance shall be deemed to have been done or taken under this Act.

The above translation of the Karnataka Right to Information Ordinance, 2000 be published in the Official Gazette under clause (3) of Article 348 of the Constitution of India.

THE KARNATAKA RIGHT TO INFORMATION RULES, 2005*

In exercise of the powers conferred by the sub-section (1) and (2) of Section 27 of the Right to Information Act, 2005 (Central Act No. 22 of 2005) the Government of Karnataka hereby makes the following rules, namely:

1. Title and commencement.—(1) These rules may be called the Karnataka Right to Information Rules, 2005.

(2) They shall come into force from the date of their publication in the official Gazette.

2. Definitions.—In these rules, unless the context otherwise requires,

(i) "Act" means the Right to Information Act, 2005 (Act 22 of 2005);

(ii) "Section" means Section of the Act.

3. Publication of certain other informations, etc. under section 4.—(1) The information under Section 4(4) shall be easily accessible to the public. It shall be indicated on the notice board by the Public Information Officer where these particulars are available. Further the public authorities can adopt any of the methods provided under the Act for disseminating the information.

(2) The information so disseminated shall also contain the details of phone numbers, fax number, etc. of the State Public Information Officers and the Assistant State Public Information Officers of the office in question.

---

* *Vide* No. DPAR: 74/RTI/2005 (*Part* 2), dated 11th October, 2005.

4. Fee.—(1) Any person desirous of obtaining information under sub-section (1) of section 6 of the Act shall make an application in Form A or in any other format as far as possible containing the particulars specified under the format to the State Public Information Officer or State Assistant Public Information Officer as the case may be along with an initial fee of Rs 10 with his application. Every officer receiving request under the Act shall give an acknowledgement.

(2) (a) For providing information under sub-section (1) of section 7, the fees for supplying the information shall be charged at Rs 2 for each page in respect of matters in A4 size paper.

(b) For providing information under sub-section (1) of section 7, in the case of Maps, Plans, Reports, a partial record or any technical data or sample or models, a reasonable fee shall be fixed by the State Public Information Officer in each case depending upon the cost of labour and material required to be employed.

(c) As regards inspection of records and documents, no fee for the first hour. For every subsequent half an hour or fraction thereof, Rs 20 shall be charged from persons making application with initial payment as prescribed under rule 4(1) above. For inspection of works a reasonable fee shall be fixed by the State Public Information Officer in each case depending upon the cost of labour and material required to be employed apart from initial fee as prescribed under rule 4(1).

(3) For providing information under sub-section (5) of section 7, the fees for supplying information in diskette or floppy or C.D. or in any other electronic mode shall be Rs 50

(4) The fee shall be collected in the form of Indian Postal Order or Demand Draft or Bankers Cheque or pay order drawn in favour of the State Public Information Officer or in cash or by remitting it to the Treasury as per Karnataka Financial Code (KFC).

(5) A person claiming exemption under proviso to sub-section (5) of section 7 shall produce a valid certificate issued by the competent authority that he/she belongs to the Below Poverty Line category.

5. Salary and allowances and conditions of service of officers and employee of the State Information Commission.—(1) The salary and allowances payable to the officers and employees of State Information Commission shall be on a par with other State Government employees of equivalent rank.

(2) The rules governing conditions of service and disciplinary matter of the State Government employees shall mutatismutandis apply to the employees of State Information Commission subject to modifications specified in schedule to these rules.

(3) The method of recruitment shall be in accordance with the provisions under K.C.S. (General Recruitment) Rules, 1977 by deputation of government servants of equivalent rank from any of the State Civil Services or public sector undertakings or by outsourcing:

Provided that the outsourcing shall be restricted to posts of cleaning, housekeeping, home orderlies and security guards.

6. Appeal under sub-section (1) of section 19.—(1) The Public Authority shall by Notification specify the designation of the officer to whom the appeals under sub-section (1) of section 19, shall lie.

(2) Every such appeal shall be accompanied by a copy of the order, if any, appealed against, and it shall specify:

(i) The name and address of the applicant and the particulars regarding the State Public Information Officer appealed against;

(ii) The date of receipt of order, if any, from the State Public Information Officer appealed against;

(iii) The grounds of appeal; and

(iv) The relief which the applicant claims.

(3) The Appellate Authority under sub-section (1) of section 19 shall fix a day for hearing of the appeal. On the date fixed for hearing the appeal or on further date to which, the appeal may be adjourned, the Appellate Authority shall after hearing the parties pass such orders on the appeal as it deems fit.

7. Procedure in Appeals under sub-section (3) of Section 19.—The provisions of Rule 6 shall *mutatis mutandis* apply to an appeal preferred under Section 19(3).

SCHEDULE

Class of Posts	Authority empowered to appoint	Authority empowered to impose penalties and penalties which he may impose		Appellate Authority
		Authority	Penalties	
1	2	3	4	5
Senior Stenos/ Stenos/Senior Assistants/ Assistants/Junior Assistants/Drivers and any other Group C posts	Secretary of the State Information Commission	Secretary of the State Information Commission Principal Secretary/Secretary to Government concerned/Disciplinary Authority Concerned in the Parent Dept/Chief Executive of the respective Public Sectors Undertakings	(ii) to (iva) of Rule 8 of KCS (CCA) Rules 1957 (v) to (viii) of Rule 8 of KCS (CCA) Rules 1957 (ii) to (iva) of KCS(CCA) Rules 1957	State Chief Information Commissioner. Chief Secretary to Government/Appellate Authority concerned in the Parent Dept/Board of Directors of Public Sectors Undertakings Government
Private Secretary/Section Officers/Under Secretary	Secretary of the State Information Commission	State Chief Information Commissioner Government/Disciplinary Authority Concerned in the Parent Dept/Chief Executive of the respective Public Sectors Undertakings	(v) to (viii) of Rule 8 of KCS(CCA) Rules 1957 (i) to (iva) of KCS(CCA) Rules 1957	Governor/ Appellate Authority concerned in the Parent Dept/Board of Directors of Public Sectors Undertakings. Secretary Information Commission
Peons/Other Group D employees	Under Secretary to the Information Commission	Under Secretary to the Information Commission Appointing Authority of the concerned parent department	(v) to (viii) of Rule 8 of KCS(CCA) Rules 1957	Concerned Appellate Authority in parent Department

FORM A (SECTIONS 6(1) AND 7(1) OF THE RTI ACT, 2005)

1. Full name of the applicant
2. Address
3. Details of the document/inspection/samples required
4. Year to which the above pertains
5. Designation and address of the Public Information Officer from whom the Information is required

Place..............

Date..............

Signature of the applicant

THE KARNATAKA TRANSPARENCY IN PUBLIC PROCUREMENTS ACT, 1999

(Karnataka Act No. 29 of 2000)

An Act to provide for ensuring transparency in public procurement of goods and services by streamlining the procedure in inviting, processing and acceptance of tenders by Procurement Entities, and for matters related thereto.

Whereas it is expedient in public interest to render the process of procurement of goods and services by Procurement Entities transparent by streamlining the procedure in inviting, processing and acceptance of tenders.

Be it enacted by the Karnataka State Legislature in the fiftieth year of the Republic of India as follows:

CHAPTER I

1. Short title and commencement.—(1) This act may be called the Karnataka Transparency in Public Procurements Act, 1999. (2) It shall be deemed to have come into force with effect from the fourth day of October 2000.

2. Definitions.—In this act, unless the context otherwise requires,

(a) "Construction works" means putting up, demolishing, repairs or renovation of buildings, roads and bridges or other structures including fabrication of steel structures and other civil works;

(b) "Goods" means machinery, motor vehicles, equipment, furniture, articles of stationery, textiles raw materials, drugs, scientific instruments, chemicals, foodgrain, oils and oilseeds or other commodity required for consumption, use or distribution by a procurement entity in discharge of its public duties;

(c) "Government" means the State Government;

(d) "Procurement Entity" means any Government Department, a State Government Undertaking, Local Authority or Board, Body or Corporation established by or under any law and owned or controlled by the Government, and any other body or authority owned or controlled by the Government and as may be specified by it.

(e) "Public Procurement" or "Procurement" means purchase of goods, obtaining of services or undertaking of construction works by the procurement entities;

(f) "Services" means the action of serving, attending upon, helping or benefiting a Procurement Entity in the course of discharging its public duties and includes construction works;

(g) "Specified goods or Services" means the goods or services as the case may be specified in a tender and identified in the contract resulting from acceptance of a tender on account of a procurement entity;

(h) "Tender" means the formal offer made for supply of goods or services in response to an invitation for tender published in a Tender Bulletin;

(i) "Tender Accepting Authority" means an Officer or a Committee appointed to accept tenders and a "Tender Inviting Authority" means an Officer or a Committee appointed to invite tenders, under Section 9;

(j) "Tender Bulletin" means a bulletin published for the State as a whole or for any district or districts within the State containing the details of invitation, processing and acceptance of Tenders;

(k) "Tender Bulletin Officer" means a State Tender Bulletin Officer or a Tender Bulletin Officer referred to in Section 7;

(l) "Tender Document" means the set of papers detailing the schedule of works, calendar of events, requirement of goods and services, technical specifications, procurement criteria and such other particulars, as may be prescribed for evaluation and comparison of tenders.

3. Provisions not to apply to certain projects.—The provisions of this Act in so far as they are inconsistent with the procedure specified in respect of the Projects funded by International Financial Agencies or Projects covered under International Agreements, shall not apply to procurement of goods or services for such project.

4. Exceptions to applicability.—The provisions of Chapter II shall not apply to procurement of goods and services:

(a) during the period of natural calamity or emergency declared by the Government;

(b) where the goods or services are available from a single source or where a particular supplier or contractor has exclusive rights in respect of the goods or services or construction work and no reasonable alternatives or substitutes exist. Provided that for the purpose of this clause there shall be a committee of three experts containing of one technical representative of the procuring entity one technical representative of the Government organization dealing with similar procurement and one representative from a reputed Academic or Research Institution or Non-Commercial Institution having expertise in such line to examine and declare that the goods or services are available from a single source;

(c) where the procuring entity having procured goods, services or technology from a supplier or contractor determines that additional supplies must be procured from the same supplier or contractor for reasons of standardization and compatibility with the existing goods, service or technology;

(d) where the goods or services are procured from certain Departments of Government, public sector undertakings, statutory boards and such other institutions specified by the Government and such goods are manufactured or services are provided by them, for a period not exceeding two years from the date of commencement of this Act;

(e) where the procurement is by the Government Departments, State Government Undertakings, or any Board, Body or Corporation established by or under any law and owned or controlled by the Government or Zilla Panchayats constituted under the Karnataka Panchayat Raj Act, 1993 or City Municipal Corporations established under the Municipal Corporation Act, 1976 or City Municipal Councils established under the Karnataka Municipalities Act, 1964 or the Hyderabad Karnataka Areas Development Board constituted under the Hyderabad Karnataka Area Development Board Act, 1993 or Malnad Area Development Board constituted under the Malnad Area Development Board Act, 1991 or the Bayaluseeme Development Board constituted under the Bayaluseeme Development Board Act, 1994,

(i) in case of construction works of all types the value of which does not exceed rupees five lakhs;

(ii) in case of goods or services other than construction works the value of which does not exceed rupees one lakh;

(ee) where the procurement of goods or services is by the Grama Panchayats and Taluk Panchayats constituted under the Karnataka Panchayat Raj Act, 1993, Town Municipal Councils or Town Panchayats constituted under the Karnataka Municipalities Act, 1964 or Urban Development Authorities constituted under the Karnataka Urban Development Authorities Act, 1987;

(i) for the purpose of implementing mini water supply scheme or construction of school rooms and the value of such procurement does not exceed rupees two lakhs; and

(ii) for other purposes and the value of such procurements does not exceed rupees one lakh.

(f) where the goods or services are procured under rate contracts from the Director General of Supplies and Disposals or from the Stores Purchase Department of the State; and

(g) in respect of specific procurements as may be notified by the Government from time to time.

(h) in respect of spot purchase of cotton by Spinning Mills, purchase of oil seeds by the Karnataka Agro-industries Corporation or the Karnataka Cooperative Oilseeds Grower's Federation, purchase of sugarcane by Sugar Mills, direct purchase of paddy by the Agricultural Produce Market Committees and the Karnataka Food and Civil Supplies Corporation, purchase of cloth by the Karnataka Handloom Development Corporation, purchase of silk by the Karnataka Silk Industries Corporation, purchase of milk by the Karnataka Milk Producers Co-operative Federation, purchase of palm oil by the Karnataka Food and Civil Supplies Corporation and the Karnataka Co-operative Oil seeds Grower's Federation, purchase of cloth by the Government Departments and public sector undertaking from the Karnataka Handloom Development Corporation and purchase by such other organizations or purchase of any other material as may be notified by the Government from time to time.

CHAPTER II

REGULATION OF PROCUREMENT

5. Procurement other than by tender prohibited.—On and from the date of commencement of this Act no Procurement

Entity shall procure goods or services except by inviting tenders for supply.

6. Procurement entities to follow procedure.— No tender shall be invited, processed or accepted by Procurement Entity after the commencement of this Act except in accordance with the procedure laid down in this Act or the rules made thereunder.

7. Tender Bulletin Officers.—(1) The Government may by notification appoint an officer not below the rank of a Deputy Secretary to Government of the concerned department to be the State Tender Bulletin Officer for the State in respect of that Department where the procurement of that department covers more than one district. (2) Deputy Commissioner of the District shall be the District Bulletin Officer.

8. Publication of Tender Bulletin.—(1)The State Tender Bulletin Officer, or as the case may be, the District Tender Bulletin Officer shall on receipt of intimation relating to notice of invitation of tenders from tender inviting authority or information relating to details of acceptance of tender under section 13 or rejection of tender under section 14 from the tender Accepting Authority, publish within the prescribed time, the State Tender Bulletin or as the case may be District Tender Bulletin. (2) The Tender Bulletin shall be made available for sale in the office of the Tender Bulletin Officer and in such other places as the Tender Bulletin Officer deems fit to make available.

9. Tender Inviting Authority and Tender Accepting Authority.—(1) The procurement Entity may, by order, appoint,

(i) one or more of officers or a committee of officers to be the Tender Inviting Authority for any specified area, specified procurement or specified class of goods or services, and

(ii) one or more of officers or a Committee of Officers to be the Tender Accepting Authority for any specified area or Specified Procurement, specified class of goods and services:

Provided that where a multi-member Committee is already appointed for any Procurement Entity for discharging the function of accepting tenders, such Committee shall be deemed to be a Tender Accepting Authority appointed under this Act.

10. Tender Scrutiny Committee.—The Tender Accepting Authority may constitute a Tender Scrutiny Committee consisting of such persons as it deems fit to scrutinise tenders above five crores in the case of the Public Works, Irrigation and Minor Irrigation Departments of the Government and above rupees one crore in other cases.

11. Opening of tenders.—(1) The Procurement entity may authorise either the tender Inviting Authority or the Tender Accepting Authority or any other Officer to open the Tenders and draw up a list of Tenderers responding to the notice inviting tender, in each case.

(2) The Authority, or as the case may be the officer referred to in sub-section (1) shall open the tender, draw up a list of tenderers in the prescribed manner and unless it is also the Tender Accepting Authority, forward the tenders along with the list of tenderers, to the Tender Accepting Authority.

12. Duties of Tender Inviting Authority.—(1) It shall be the duty of every Tender Inviting Authority,

(a) to take out notice inviting tenders at the behest of the Procurement Entity in the prescribed manner;

(b) to communicate the notice inviting tenders by marking a copy thereof to the Tender Bulletin Officer concerned immediately after issue of the notice;

(c) to cause publication of notice inviting tenders in the prescribed manner; and

(d) to supply the Schedule of Rates and Tender Documents to every intending tenderer who has applied to get such documents.

(2) The Tender Inviting Authority shall take out notices, communications and publications required to be taken out under this section in such form, in such manner, by such mode and at such time and intervals as may be prescribed and different manner and mode of publication may be prescribed for different procurements depending on the value of the procurement.

(3) The Tender Inviting Authority shall collect all the details received in response to the notice inviting tender, within the time stipulated and unless it is itself authorized to open the tender shall compile and forward all the tenders received to the Authority or Officer authorized to open the tenders.

13. Acceptance of tender.—The Tender Accepting Authority shall, after following such procedure as may be prescribed pass order accepting the tender and shall communicate the information relating to acceptance of tender together with a comparative analysis and reasons for accepting of tender to the procurement Entity and the Tender Bulletin Officer:

Provided that where the Tender Accepting Authority consists of single officer who is due to retire within the next six months, from the date fixed for the acceptance for tender, he shall not act to accept the tender without obtaining prior approval of the Procurement Entity:

Provided further that subject to such general or special order as may be issued by the Government from time to time, the Tender Accepting Authority may before passing order accepting a tender negotiate with lowest tenderer.

Notes

The State must not act arbitrarily in the matter of acceptance or rejection of tender or for that matter in the discharge of any of its intention can be well established in India by a series of Judicial decisions particularly of the Court being those of Kasturi vs J&K and Ramana vs International Airport Authority, AIR 1978 SC 1992, AIR 1979 SC 1628.

Rates fixed by the Govt cannot be revised subsequently and unilaterally unless, there are specific rules in this regard. G.S. Fernandez vs State of Karnataka, AIR 1990 SC 958.

A tender notice is only an invitation extended to contractors for making offers. It does not amount to an offer or proposal and the question of rates made by the contractor does not amount to an acceptance of offer. N.P. Singh vs Forest Officer, AIR 1962 Mani.

A tender is an offer. It is something which invites and is communicated to notify acceptance. Following are the requisites of a valid tender. (1) It must be unconditional. (2) Must be made at the proper place. (3) Conform to the terms of obligation. (4) Should be made at the proper time. (5) Should be made in the proper form. (6) The person by whom the tender is made must be able to and willing to perform his obligations. (7) There must be reasonable opportunity for inspection. (8) Must be made to the proper person. Tata Cellular vs. Union of India, AIR 1996 SC (11).

14. General rejection of tenders.—(1) The Tender Accepting Authority may at any time before passing an order of acceptance under Section 13, reject all the tenders on the ground of changes in the scope of procurement, failure of anticipated financial resource, accidents, calamities, or any other ground as may be prescribed which would render the procurement unnecessary or impossible and report the same to the Procurement Entity.

(2) The Procurement Entity shall thereafter communicate the fact of the rejection under this section to all the tenderers and also cause the same to be published in the Tender Bulletin.

15. Power to give directions.—It shall be competent for the Government to give appropriate directions to the Procurement Entity or the Authorities under this Act in order to secure and maintain transparency at any stage of the process of procurement, and it shall be duty of the Procurement Entity or such authority to comply with the directions.

16. Appeal.—(1) Any tenderer aggrieved by an order passed by the Tender Accepting Authority other than the Government under Section 13 may appeal to the prescribed authority within thirty days from the date of receipt of the order:

Provided that the prescribed authority may, in its discretion allow further time not exceeding thirty days for preferring any such appeal, if it is satisfied that the appellant had sufficient cause for not preferring the appeal in time.

(2) The prescribed authority may after giving opportunity of being heard to both the parties pass such order thereon as it deems fit and such order shall be final.

(3) The prescribed authority shall as far as possible dispose of the appeal within thirty days from the date of filing thereof.

17. Power to obtain information.—Notwithstanding anything contained in this Act or in any other law for the time being in force, the Government may with a view to ensuring transparency call for and obtain, from any Authority under this Act, any information relating to any matter in the process of procurement.

18. Power to call for records.—The Government may at any time, with a view to ensuring transparency in the procurement process call upon any authority under this Act,

(i) to produce records relating to invitation, processing and acceptance of tenders;

(ii) to furnish the tender document, estimates/statements/accounts or statistics relating to such tenders; and

(iii) to furnish report on any specific point incidental to the procurement.

CHAPTER III

MISCELLANEOUS

19. Officers deemed to be public servants.—Every officer acting under or in pursuance of the provisions of this Act or under a rule, order or notification made hereunder, shall be deemed to be a public servant within this meaning of Section 21 of the Indian Penal Code 1860 (Central Act XLV of 1860).

20. Immunity for action taken in good faith.—No suit or other legal proceeding shall lie against the Government or any officer or authority empowered to exercise powers or perform the functions under the Act in respect of anything which is in good faith done or intended to be done under this Act.

21. Bar of jurisdiction of courts.—Save as otherwise provided in this Act no order passed or proceedings taken by any officer or authority under this Act shall be called in question in any court, and no injunction shall be granted by any court in respect of any action taken or to be taken by such officer or authority in exercise of powers conferred on him or it, by or under this Act.

22. Act to override other laws.—The provisions of this Act shall have effect notwithstanding anything inconsistent there with contained in any other law for the time being in force or any custom or usage, agreement, decree or order of a Court or a Tribunal or other Authority.

23. Penalty.—Whoever contravenes the provisions of this Act or the rules made thereunder shall be punishable with imprisonment for a term which may extend to three years and with fine which may extend to five thousand rupees.

24. Power to remove difficulties.—If any difficulty arises in giving effect to the provisions of this Act, the Government may, by order published in the Gazette make such provisions not inconsistent with the provisions of the Act as appear to them to be necessary or expedient for removing the difficulty:

Provided that no such order shall be made after expiry of a period of two years from the date of commencement of the Act.

25. Power to make rules.—(1) The Government, may by notification, make such rules as are necessary for carrying out the purposes of this Act.

(2) Every rule made or notification or order issued under this Act shall as soon as possible, after it is made or issued, be placed before each House of the State Legislature while it is in session for a total period of thirty days, which may be comprised in one session or in two or more successive sessions and if before the expiry of the session in which it is laid or the sessions immediately following both Houses agree in making any modifications in the rule, notification or order or both Houses agree that the rule, notification or order shall not be made, the rule or notification or order shall thereafter have effect only in such modified form or be of no effect, as the case may be, so, however that any such modification or annulment shall be without prejudice to the validity of anything previously done under that rule or notification or order.

26. Savings.—All rules, regulations, orders, notifications, departmental codes, manuals, bye-laws, official memoranda, circular or any other order made or issued before the commencement of this Act and in force on the date of such commencement providing for or relating to any of the above matters for the furtherance of which this Act is enacted shall continue to be in force and effective as if they are made under the corresponding provisions of this Act, to the extent they are not inconsistent with the provisions of this Act and unless and until superseded by anything done or any action taken or any rule, notification or order, is made under this Act.

Repeal and savings.—(1) The Karnataka Transparency in Public Procurements Ordinance, 2000 (Karnataka Ordinance No. 8 of 2000) is hereby repealed. (2) Notwithstanding such repeal anything done or any action taken under the principal Act as amended by the said ordinance shall be deemed to have been done or taken under this Act.

THE KARNATAKA TRANSPARENCY IN PUBLIC PROCUREMENTS RULES, 2000

In exercise of the powers conferred by sub-section (1) of Section 23 of the Karnataka Transparency in Public Procurement Ordinance 2000, the Government of Karnataka hereby makes the following Rules namely:

CHAPTER I

PRELIMINARY

1. Short title and commencement.—(a) These rules may be called the Karnataka Transparency in Public Procurements Rules, 2000,

(b) They shall come into force on the date of publication in the Gazette.

2. Definitions.— In these Rules, unless the context otherwise requires—

(a) "Earnest money deposit" means the amount required to be deposited by a tenderer along with his tender indicating his willingness to implement the contract;

(b) "Pre-qualification" means the process by which the tenderer are first screened for their capability and resources to implement the contract before they are permitted to offer their tenders;

(c) "Two-cover system" means a procedure under which the tenderers are required simultaneously to submit two separate sealed covers, one containing the Earnest Money Deposit and the details of their capability to undertake the tender which will be opened first and the second cover containing the price quotation which will be opened only if the tenderer is found to be qualified to execute the tender.

CHAPTER II

GENERAL

3. Categories of procurement.—(1) For the purpose of application of these rules, procurement is categorized as:

(i) Construction; and

(ii) Supply of goods and services.

CHAPTER III

PUBLICITY

4. Publication of tender bulletin.—(1) The District Tender Bulletin shall be published by the District Bulletin Officer at least once in every week.

(2) The State Tender Bulletin shall be published by the State Tender Bulletin Officer at least once in every week.

(3) The Tender Bulletin Officer shall cause to be published call notices inviting tenders and intimations of acceptance of tenders received up to forty-eight hours prior to the actual publication of the bulletin.

(4) In case notice inviting tender or information relating to acceptance of the tender needs to be published urgently, then the Secretary to Government of the concerned administrative department in the case of the State Tender Bulletin or the Deputy Commissioner in the case of the District Tender Bulletin may for the reasons to be recorded in writing, direct the respective tender bulletin officers to publish an extraordinary issue of the tender bulletin.

5. Distribution of tender bulletins.—(1) The Tender Bulletin Officer shall make the tender bulletin available in the concerned office of the Government department, local authority statutory board, public sector undertaking, university or cooperative institution.

(2) The Tender Bulletin Officer shall make available adequate copies of the tender Bulletin at the office of the Tender Inviting Authority whose notice inviting tenders and intimation of tender acceptance finds place in the bulletin.

(3) Any person or institution can be enrolled as a regular subscriber to the Tender Bulletin on payment of a fixed fee annually, half-yearly or quarterly as the case may be.

6. Tender Bulletin to contain information only.—(1) The Tender Bulletin shall contain only information of the notice inviting tenders.

(2) Intimation of acceptance of tender shall not in itself create a legal right.

(3) A notice inviting tender will not be invalidated merely on the grounds that the notice has not been published in the newspapers.

7. Information to be published in the State Tender Bulletin.—The notice inviting tenders and decisions on tenders shall be published in the State Tender Bulletin in cases where—

(a) The Tender Inviting Authority is a secretary to Government, or head of a government department, or the Chief Executive of a Public Sector Undertaking, Statutory board, apex co-operative Institution, university or state level society formed by the Government.

(b) The value of the procurement is rupees one crore and above.

8. Information to be published in the district tender bulletin.—Subject to the provisions of Rule 10, notices inviting tenders and decisions on tenders shall be published in the district Tender Bulletin of the district where the headquarters of the Tender Inviting Authority is located.

Provided that where a value of procurement is rupees one crore and above, it shall also be published in the State Bulletin.

9. Details to be mentioned in notice inviting tenders.—The Notice Inviting Tenders shall contain the following details, namely,

(a) The name and address of the procuring entity and the designation and address of the Tender Inviting authority;

(b) Name of the scheme, project or programme for which the procurement is to be effected;

(c) The date up to which and places from where the tender documents can be obtained;

(d) The amount of earnest money deposit payable;

(e) The last date and time for receipt of tenders;

(f) The date, time and place for opening of tenders received; and

(g) Any other information which the Tender Inviting Authority considers relevant.

10. Publication of notice inviting tenders in newspapers.—(1) The Tender Inviting Authority shall have the notice inviting tenders published in the Indian Trade Journal in all cases where the value of procurement exceeds rupees ten crore.

(2) The number, editions and language of the newspapers in which the notices inviting tenders shall be published will be based on the value of procurement as per departmental rules.

(3) In cases where publication of Tender Notices is to be done only in newspapers with circulation within the district, the Information and Publicity Officer of the District shall be the competent authority; to release the advertisement shall be the Director of Information and Publicity, Bangalore.

(4) The Notice Inviting Tender shall be given due publicity in newspapers and also affixing on notice boards in the District Offices. The Director of Information and Publicity shall publish the Notice Inviting Tenders as per instructions of the tendering department.

CHAPTER IV

NOTICE INVITING TENDERS AND TENDER DOCUMENTS

11. Technical specifications contained in the tender documents.—(1) The technical specifications contained in the tender documents shall include a detailed description of what is proposed to be procured.

(2) Unbiased technical specifications shall be prepared by observing the following safeguards, namely:

(a) use of brand names and catalogue numbers shall be avoided and where it becomes unavoidable, along with the brand name the expression "or equivalent" shall be added;

(b) wherever possible the appropriate Indian Standard with the number shall be incorporated;

(c) in the case of construction tenders, detailed estimates shall be prepared by the competent technical authorities based on the schedule or rates and standard data as revised from time to time.

12. Commercial conditions.—(1) The tender documents shall require all tenders to pay an earnest money deposit at the rates as per the departmental rules by means of a demand draft, bankers cheque, specified small savings instruments or where the procuring entity deems fit, irrevocable bank guarantee in a specified form of the department. The tender documents shall clearly state that any tender submitted without the earnest money deposit be summarily rejected:

Provided that any category of tenders specifically exempted by the Government from the payment of earnest money deposit will not be required to make such a deposit.

(2) The tender documents shall specify the period for which the tenderer should hold the prices offered in the tender valid:

Provided that the initial period of validity shall not be less than ninety days.

(3) The tender documents shall require that as a guarantee of the tenderer performance of the contract, a security deposit be taken from the successful tenderer as per departmental rules.

(4) The tender documents and the contract shall include a clause for payment of liquidated damages and penalty payable by the tenderer in the event of non-fulfilment of any of the terms or whole of the contract.

(5) The tender documents shall indicate the quantity proposed to be procured in the tender, and the Tender Accepting Authority shall be ordinarily permitted to vary the quantity finally ordered only to the extent of twenty-five percent either way of the requirement indicated in the tender documents.

13. Supply of tender documents.—(1) The Tender Inviting Authority shall make available the tender documents from the date indicated in the notice inviting tender.

(2) The Tender Inviting Authority shall ensure that the tender documents are made available to any person who is willing to remit the cost of the documents:

Provided that in the cases where the procuring entity has a system of registration of contractors, the tender documents will be supplied only to registered contractors in the appropriate class.

(3) The Tender Inviting Authority shall be registered post or courier the tender documents to any prospective tenderer who makes a request for the documents on payment of cost along with postal charges at the risk and responsibility of the prospective tenderer.

14. Clarification to tender documents.—At any time after the issue of the tender documents and before the opening of the tender, the Tender Inviting Authority may make any changes, modifications or amendments to the tender documents and shall send intimation of such change to all those who have purchased the original tender documents.

CHAPTER V

RECEIPT OF TENDERS AND TENDER OPENING

15. Place and time for receipt of tenders.—(1) The Tender Inviting Authority shall ensure that adequate arrangements are made for the proper receipt and safe custody of the tender at the place indicated for the receipt of the tenders.

(2) The Tender Inviting Authority shall permit the submission of tenders by post or courier:

Provided that the Tender Inviting Authority shall not be responsible for any delay in transit in such cases.

(3) The Tender Inviting Authority may extend the last date and time for receiving tender after giving adequate notice to all intending tenderer in cases where:

(a) The publication of the tender notice has been delayed;

(b) The communication of changes, in the tender documents to the prospective tenderer under Rule 14 took time;

(c) Any other reasonable grounds exist, for such extension which shall be recorded in writing by the Tender Inviting Authority.

16. Marking of covers in which the tender is submitted.— The tenderer shall be responsible for properly superscribing and sealing the cover in which the tender is submitted and the Tender Inviting Authority shall not be responsible for accidental opening of the cover that are not properly super scribed and sealed as required in the tender documents before the time appointed for tender opening.

17. Minimum time for submission of tenders.—(1) The Tender Inviting Authority shall ensure that adequate time is provided for the submission of tenders and minimum time is allowed between date of publication of the notice inviting tenders in the relevant tender bulletin and the last date for the submission of tenders. This minimum period shall be as follows:

(a) For tender up to Rs two crore in value, thirty days, and

(b) For tenders in excess of Rs two crore in value, sixty days.

(2) Any deduction in the time stipulated under sub-rule (1) has to be specifically authorized by an authority superior to the tender inviting authority for reasons to be recorded in writing.

18. Opening of tenders.—(1) All the tenders received by the Tender Accepting Authority shall be opened at the time specified in the Notice Inviting Tenders and in cases where an extension of time for the submission of tenders has been given subsequent to the original Notice Inviting Tenders in accordance with sub-rule (3) of Rule 15 at the time so specified subsequently.

(2) The tenders will be opened in the presence of the tenderer or one of the representatives of the tenderer who chose to be present.

19. Procedure to be followed at tender opening.—The following procedure shall be followed at the tender opening:

(a) All the envelopes received containing tenders shall be counted;

(b) All the tenders received in time shall be opened;

(c) A record of the correction noticed at the time of the bid opening shall be maintained;

(d) The name of the tenderer and the quoted prices, should be read out;

(e) The fact whether earnest money deposit has been made and other documents required have been produced may be indicated, but this shall be merely an examination of the documents and not an evaluation;

(f) minutes of the tender opening shall be recorded. The signatures of the tenderer present shall be obtained unless any of the tenderer or his representative refuses to sign the minutes.

20. Tenders scrutiny committee.—(1) Tender Accepting Authority may constitute a Tender Scrutiny Committee consisting of such officers as it deems fit to scrutinize the tender document, supervise opening of tender carry out the preliminary examination and detailed evaluation of the tenders received and prepare the evaluation report for the consideration of the Tender Accepting Authority.

(2) The Tender Accepting Authority shall constitute Tender Scrutiny Committee, where the value of the tender exceeds

Rs five crore in respect of public works, irrigation department and minor irrigation department and one crore in respect of all the other departments.

CHAPTER VI

TENDER EVALUATION

21. Tender evaluation to be in accordance with evaluation criteria.—The Tender Accepting Authority shall cause the evaluation of tenders to be carried out strictly in accordance with evaluation criteria indicated in tender documents.

22. Time taken for evaluation and extension of the tender validity.—(1) The evaluation of tenders and award of contract shall be completed, as far as possible, within the period for which the tenders are held valid.

(2) The Tender Accepting Authority shall seek extension of the validity of tenders from the tenderer for the completion of evaluation, if it is not completed within the validity period of tender.

(3) In case the evaluation of tenders and award of contract is not completed within extended period, all the tenders shall be deemed to have become invalid and fresh tenders may be called for.

23. Process of tender evaluation to be confidential until the award of the contract is notified.—(1) The Tender Inviting Authority shall ensure the confidentiality of the process of tender evaluation until orders on the tender are passed.

(2) Tenderer shall not make attempt to establish unsolicited and unauthorized contact with the Tender Accepting Authority, Tender Inviting Authority or Tender Scrutiny Committee after the opening of the tender and prior to the notification of the Award and if any attempt by the tenderer to bring bear extraneous pressures on the Tender Accepting Authority shall be sufficient reason to disqualify the tenderer.

(3) Notwithstanding anything contained in sub-rule (2), the Tender Inviting Authority or Tender Accepting Authority or the Tender Scrutiny Committee may seek *bona fide* clarification from tenderer relating to the tender submitted by them during the evaluation of tenders.

24. Initial examination to determine substantial responsiveness.—(1) The Tender Inviting Authority shall cause an initial examination of the tender submitted to be carried out in order to determine their substantial responsiveness.

(2) During the initial examination the following factors shall be considered, namely:

(a) Whether the tenderer meets the eligibility criteria laid down in the tender document;

(b) Whether the crucial document have been duly signed;

(c) Whether the requisite earnest money deposit has been furnished;

(d) Whether the tender is substantially responsive to the technical specification set out in the bidding documents including the testing of samples where required.

(3) Tenders which on initial examination are found not to be substantially responsive under any of the clauses under sub-rule (2) may be rejected by the Tender Accepting Authority.

25. Determination of the lowest evaluated price.—(1) Out of the tenders found to be substantially responsive after the initial examination the tenderer who has bid the lowest evaluated price in accordance with the evaluation criteria or tenderer scoring the highest on the evaluation criteria specified as the case may be, shall be determined.

(2) In determining the lowest evaluated price, the following factors shall be considered, namely:

(a) The quoted price shall be corrected for arithmetical errors;

(b) In case of discrepancy between the price quoted in words and in figures, lower of the two shall be considered;

(c) Adjustment to the price quoted shall be made for deviations in the commercial conditions such as the delivery schedule and minor variations in the payment terms which are quantifiable but deemed to be non-material in the context of the particular tender;

(d) The evaluation shall include all central duties such as customs duty and central excise duty inclusive of local levies as part of the price;

(e) In case of purchase of equipment, the operation and maintenance and spare parts cost for appropriate periods as may be specified in bid documents may be quantified, where practicable and considered:

Provided that for a period of five years from first day of April 2001, Small Scale Industries in the State shall be given fifteen per cent price preference in accordance with the New Industrial Policy 2001-2006 issued by the Government in Order No. CI 167 SPI 2001, dated 30 June 2001 while determining the lowest evaluated price.

Explanation: For the purpose of this provision Small Scale Industry means an Industrial undertaking in which the investment in fixed assets in plant and machinery whether held on ownership terms or on lease or by hire purchase does not exceed Rs one hundred lakhs.

26. Preparation of evaluation report and award of tenders.—(1) Tender Scrutiny Committee or the officer inviting the tender shall prepare detailed evaluation report which shall be considered by the Tender Accepting Authority before taking a final decision on the tender.

(2) As soon as the tenderer qualified to perform the contract is identified in accordance with [section 13], the Tender Accepting Authority shall pass orders accepting the tender and communicate the order of acceptance to the successful tenderer. The Tender Accepting Authority shall also send to the Tender Bulletin Officer a statement of evaluation of the tenders with a comparative statement of tender received and decision thereon for publication in the Tender Bulletin.

(3) Within such reasonable time as may be indicated in the tender document, the tenderer whose tender has been accepted will be required to execute the contract agreement in the specified format.

(4) In case the successful tenderer fails to execute necessary agreement under sub-rule (3) within the period specified, then Earnest Money Deposit shall be forfeited and his tender held as non-responsive.

27. Pre-qualification procedure.—(1) The Tender Inviting Authority shall for reasons to be recorded in writing provide for pre-qualification of tenderer on the basis of:

(a) Experience and past performance in the execution of similar contracts;

(b) Capabilities of the tenderer with respect to personnel, equipment and construction or manufacturing facilities;

(c) Financial status and capacity.

(2) Only the tenders of pre-qualified tenderer shall be considered for evaluation:

Provided that notwithstanding anything contrary contained in these Rules, The Tender Inviting may adopt the list of pre-qualified tenderer empanelled by the directorate of Information Technology, Government of Karnataka in respect of computer, Peripheral and related services and call for price bids from all such pre-qualified tenderer and the price bids received from the pre-qualified shall be considered for evaluation by the Tender Accepting Authority, so far as may in accordance with these rules.

28. Two cover tenders.—(1) In the case of construction or supply and installation of equipment, tenders exceeding rupees fifty lakhs in value where the pre-qualification procedure or Turn Key Tender System are not being followed the Tender Inviting Authority shall follow the two-cover tender system.

(2) The first cover shall contain the following information about the tender namely;

(a) Experience and past performance in the execution of similar contracts;

(b) Capabilities with respect to personnel, equipment and construction or manufacturing facilities;

(c) Financial status and the capacity;

(d) Any other information considered relevant.

(3) The second cover shall contain the prices quoted by the tenderer.

(4) The Tender Inviting Authority shall cause the first cover to be opened first and evaluate the tenderer capacity on the basis of criteria specified in a tender document and on this basis, prepare a list of qualified tenderer.

(5) Thereafter, the second cover containing the price quotation of only those tenderer qualified under sub-rule (4) shall be opened by the Tender Inviting Authority.

(6) The Tender Inviting Authority shall follow the procedure outline in Rules 25 and 26.

CHAPTER VII

APPEALS

29. Appeals.—An appeal under [section 16] shall lie:

(a) To the head of the department concerned if the order is passed by the Tender Accepting Authority subordinate to the Head of Department;

(b) To the Government if the order is passed by a Tender Accepting Authority which is Head of Department, or a Local Authority or State Government Undertaking or a Board, Body Corporation or any other Authority owned or controlled by the Government.

THE KARNATAKA LEGISLATIVE ASSEMBLY SECRETARIAT RIGHT TO INFORMATION RULES, 2006*

In exercise of the powers conferred by section 28 of the Right to Information Act, 2005 (Central Act No. 12 of 2005), the Speaker, Karnataka Legislative Assembly hereby makes the following rules, namely—

1. **Short title and commencement.**—(1) These rules may be called the Karnataka Legislative. Assembly Secretariat Right to Information Rules, 2006.

(2) They shall come into force on the date of their publication in the Official Gazette.

2. **Definitions.**—In these rules, unless the context otherwise requires—

(a) "Act" means the Right to Information Act, 2005;

(b) "Section" means section of the Act; and

(c) All other words and expressions used herein but not defined in the Act shall have the meanings assigned to them in the Act.

3. Any person who desires to obtain information under sub-section (1) of section 6 shall make an application in writing in Form 'A' or in any other format as far as possible containing the particulars specified in Form 'A' to the State Public Information Officer or the State Assistant Public Information Officer as the case may be along with a fee of rupees ten by way

* *Vide* No. KLAS/ADM-1/LGA/138/RIA/2006, Bangalore, dated 15th May, 2006 Karnataka Gazette, Extra., No. 519, dated 16-5-2006.

of cash against proper receipt or by demand draft or banker's cheque payable to the Under Secretary (Accounts), Karnataka Legislative Assembly Secretariat.

4. For providing information under sub-section (1) of section 7, the fee shall be charged by way of cash against proper receipt or by demand draft or banker's cheque payable to the Under Secretary (Accounts), Karnataka Legislative Assembly Secretariat at the following rates—

(a) rupees two for each page (in A-4 or A-3 size paper) created or copied;

(b) actual charge or cost price of a copy in larger size paper;

(c) actual cost or price of samples or models; and

(d) for inspection of records, no fee for the first hour; and a fee of rupees twenty for each subsequent hour (or fraction thereof).

5. For providing information under sub-section (5) of section 7, the fee shall be charged by way of cash against proper receipt or by demand draft or banker's cheque payable to the Under Secretary (Accounts), Karnataka Legislative Assembly Secretariat at the following rates—

(a) for information provided in diskette or floppy rupees fifty per diskette or floppy; and

(b) for information provided in printed form at the price fixed for such publication or rupees two per page of photocopy for extracts from the publication.

Form A

[*See* Rule 3(1)]

APPLICATION FORM FOR OBTAINING INFORMATION

The State Public Information Officer/

The State Assistant Public Information Officer,

Karnataka Legislative Assembly Secretariat,

P.B. No. 5074, Vidhana Soudha, Bangalore-560 001

1. Name of the applicant:
2. Full address:
3. Brief particulars of information required:
4. I hereby state that the information sought for is not covered under the categories which are exempted from disclosure of information under section 8 or under section 9 of the Right to Information Act, 2005 and to the best of my knowledge it pertains to your Secretariat.
5. (1) I hereby state that the prescribed application fee of Rs............... (Rupees......) has been paid *vide* receipt No............dated.......... in the Accounts Branch of your Secretariat.

   (2) I state that I have paid the fee for the information desired in your Accounts..........Branch *vide* receipt No........... dated............/I am enclosing herewith a demand draft/pay order No. ....dated........ drawn in favour of the Under Secretary (Accounts), Karnataka Legislative Assembly Secretariat towards the fee payable.

   (3) I belong to the BPL family. A Xerox copy of my BPL card/certificate is enclosed herewith.

Signature of the applicant:

Place: e-mail address, if any:

Date: Telephone No. office:

Residence:

NB: A person belonging to B.P.L. family need not pay any type of fees.

THE KARNATAKA PUBLIC SERVICE COMMISSION RIGHT TO INFORMATION RULES, 2006*

NOTIFICATION

In exercise of the powers conferred by sub-sections (1) and (2) of section 28 of the Right to Information Act, 2005 (Central Act 22 of 2005), the Governor of Karnataka being the Competent Authority in respect of the Karnataka Public Service Commission, hereby makes the following rules, namely—

1. **Title and commencement.**—(1) These rules may be called the Karnataka Public Service Commission Right to Information Rules, 2006.

(2) They shall come into force from the date of their publication in the Official Gazette.

2. **Definitions.**—In these rules, unless the context, otherwise requires—

(a) "Act" means the Right to Information Act, 2005 (Central Act 22 of 2005);

(b) "Commission" means the Karnataka Public Service Commission;

(c) "Governor" means the Governor of Karnataka;

(d) "Section" means a section of the Act.

3. **Request for information under section 6.**—(1) A request to obtain information under sub-section (1) of section 6 shall be in the Form annexed to these rules or in any other format as far

---

* *Vide* No. DPAR 8 SSC 2006, Bangalore, dated 9th May, 2006 Karnataka Gazette, Extra., No. 510, dated 10-5-2006.

as possible containing the particulars specified under the format addressed to the State Public Information Officer or the Assistant State Public Information Officer as the case may be and shall be accompanied by—

(i) an application fee of rupees ten; and

(ii) the approximate fees at the rates specified in Rule 4 for the information sought for, by way of cash against a proper receipt from the Section Officer (Accounts Branch) of the Commission.

(2) The State Public Information Officer shall give an acknowledgment for every application received.

4. Fees payable for providing information.—The fees payable for providing information under sub-sections (1) and (5) of section 7 shall be as follows—

(a) rupees two for each page in A4 size paper;

(b) actual charge or cost of providing a copy in larger size paper;

(c) actual cost of reasonable price fixed by the State Public Information Officer, in each case, for samples, maps, reports or models or technical data material held in any electronic form or in printed form;

(d) reasonable price fixed by the State Public Information Officer but not less than rupees fifty for information provided in diskette or floppy or CD or any other electronic mode;

(e) for inspection of records or documents no fee is payable for the first one hour and a fee of rupees twenty per hour (or fraction thereof) thereafter.

ANNEXURE

Form

(*See* Rule 3)

FORM OF REQUEST FOR INFORMATION UNDER SECTION 6

1. Name and address of the applicant:
2. Details of the information required:

3. Year or period to which it rentes:
4. Amount paid Rs. Number and date of receipt:

Place:

Date: Signature of applicant

THE KERALA RIGHT TO INFORMATION BILL, 2002

A Bill to provide for right of access to information to the citizens and in relation to the matters connected therewith or incidental thereto.

PREAMBLE

Whereas, right to Government held information is accepted by the Supreme Court as a part of right to speech and expression guaranteed to citizens in the Constitution;

And whereas, providing right of access to information to the citizens of the State promotes openness, transparency and accountability in administration and ensures effective participation of people in the administration and thus makes democracy meaningful;

And whereas, it is necessary that every Governmental action should be transparent to the public;

And whereas to achieve this object, every citizen should be able to get information from the Government;

Be it enacted in the Fifty-third Year of the Republic of India as follows:

1. Short title and commencement.—(1) This Act may be called the Kerala Right to Information Act, 2002. (2) It shall come into force from such date, as the Government may by notification, appoint and different dates may be appointed for different provisions of this Act.

2. Definition.—In this Act, unless the context otherwise requires,

(a) "competent authority" means any authority, officer or person as may be notified by the Government for the purposes of this Act;

(b) "information" means information relating of any matter in respect of the affairs of the administration or decisions of a public authority;

(c) "Local Self Government Institutions" means a Panchayat constitute under the Kerala Panchayat Raj Act, 1994 (13 of 1994) or a Municipality constituted under the Kerala Municipality Act, 1994, (20 of 1994);

(d) "public authority" means,

(i) all offices of the State Government;

(ii) all authorities constituted by or under any Act of the State Legislature for the time being in force, a company, Corporation, trust, society, any statutory or other authority, cooperative society or any organisation or body funded, owned or controlled by the State Government, but does not include,

(i) offices of the Central Government;

(ii) any establishment of the Armed Forces or Central Para Military Forces;

(iii) any body or corporation owned or controlled by the Central Government;

(iv) the High Court of Kerala and other courts of law including Tribunals, and other organisations which have the status of courts and whose proceedings are deemed to be judicial proceedings;

(v) the Secretariat of the Governor of Kerala;

(vi) all Local Self Government Institutions.

(e) "right to information" means right of access to information from any public authority,

(i) by obtaining certified copies of any records;

(ii) by obtaining diskettes, floppies or any other electronic mode or through printouts where such information is stored in a computer or in any other device;

(iii) in such other manner as may be prescribed.

(f) "record" includes,

(i) any document, manuscript and file;

(ii) any microfilm, microfiche and facsimile copy of a document;

(iii) any reproduction of image or images embodied in such microfile (whether enlarged or not); and

(iv) any other material produced by a computer or by any other device.

(g) "trade secret" means information contained in a formula, pattern, compilation, programme, device, product, method, technique or process which is not generally known and which may have economic value.

3. Obligation of public authorities.—Every public authority shall,

(a) maintain all records in such manner and form as is consistent with its operational requirements duly catalogued and indexed;

(b) publish at such intervals as may be prescribed,

(i) the particulars of its organisation, functions and duties;

(ii) the powers and duties of officers and employees and the procedure followed by them in the decision making process;

(iii) the norms setup by the public authority for the discharge of its functions;

(iv) the details of facilities available to citizens for obtaining information;

(c) publish all relevant facts concerning such of the important decisions and policies that affect the public, as may be prescribed, while announcing such decisions and policies;

(d) before sanctioning or initiating or causing to sanction or initiate any project scheme or activity, as may be specified by the State Government, publish or communicate to the public generally or to the persons affected or likely to be affected by the project, scheme or activity in particular in such manner, as may be prescribed, the facts available to it or to which it has reasonable access which in its opinion should be known to them in the best interests of maintenance of democratic principles;

(e) publish such other information as may be prescribed.

4. **Right to information.**—(1) Subject to the provisions of this Act every citizen shall have the right to information.

(2) Notwithstanding anything contained in sub-section (1), no person shall be given,

(a) information, the disclosure of which would prejudicially affect the sovereignty and integrity of India, security of the State, strategic scientific or economic interest of India, or conduct of international relations;

(b) information, the disclosure of which would prejudicially affect public safety and order or which may lead to an incitement to commit an offence or prejudicially affect fair trial or adjudication of a pending case;

(c) information relating to cabinet papers including records of the deliberations of the Council of ministers, Secretaries and other officers;

(d) information, the disclosure of which would harm, frankness and candour of internal discussions including inter-departmental or intra-departmental notes, correspondence and papers containing advice or opinion of projections and assumptions relating to internal policy analysis;

(e) information, the disclosure of which would prejudice the assessment or collection of any tax, cess, duty or fee or assist in avoidance or evasion of the tax, cess duty or fee;

(f) information, the disclosure of which would constitute a breach of privilege of the Parliament or the State Legislature;

(g) information regarding trade or commercial secrets protected by law or information, the disclosure of which would prejudicially affect the legitimate economic and commercial interest or the competitive position of a public authority or would cause unfair gain or loss to any person;

(h) information regarding any matter which is likely to,

(i) help or facilitate escape from legal custody or affect prison security; or

(ii) impede the process of investigation or apprehension or prosecution of offenders.

5. Procedure for supply of information.—(1) A person desirous to obtain information shall make an application to the competent authority in the prescribed manner, along with such fee, in such form and with such particulars, as may be prescribed:

Provided that the fee payable shall not exceed the actual cost of supplying information.

(2) On receipt of an application requesting for information, the competent authority shall consider it and except for justifiable reasons, pass orders thereon either granting or refusing it, as soon as practicable and in any case within thirty working days from the date of receipt of the application:

Provided that where the competent authority does not have the information he shall within fifteen days from date of receipt of application transfer the application to its next higher authority with whom such information is available and inform the applicant accordingly and thereafter such next higher authority to whom such application is transferred shall furnish information within thirty working days from the date of receipt of the application from the competent authority.

(3) Where a request is rejected under sub-section (2), the competent authority shall communicate, in writing, to the person making the request,

(i) the reasons for such rejection;

(ii) the period within which the appeal against such rejection may be preferred;

(iii) the particulars of the appellate authority.

6. Grounds for refusal to supply information in certain cases.—Without prejudice to the provisions of Section 4, the competent authority may also reject a request for supply of information where such request,

(a) is too general in nature and the information sought is of such nature that, it is not required to be ordinarily collected by the public authority:

Provided that where such request is rejected on the aforesaid ground, it shall be the duty of the competent authority to render help as far as possible to the person seeking information to reframe the request in such manner as may facilitate the supply of information;

(b) relates to information that is required by law, rules, regulations or orders to be published at a particular time; or

(c) relates to information that is contained in published material available to public;

(d) relates to personal information the disclosure of which has no relationship to any public activity or which would cause unwarranted invasion of the privacy of an individual except where larger public interest is served by disclosure:

Provided that the information relating to returns of assets and liabilities filed by any Government servant shall be made available to the public under such circumstances as may be prescribed.

7. Appeals.—(1) Subject to such rules as may be prescribed, any person,

(i) aggrieved by an order of the competent authority may, within thirty days from the date of receipt of such order; or

(ii) who has not received any communication within a period of thirty working days from the date of making application under Section 5, may within next thirty days after such period; appeal to such authority as may be prescribed:

Provided that no appeal shall lie against an order of withholding of information under clause (f) of sub-section (2) of Section 4.

(2) The appellate authority may, after giving the person affected a reasonable opportunity of being heard, pass such order as it deems fit.

(3) The decision of the appellate authority shall be final.

(4) Appeals referred to in sub-sections (1) shall be disposed of within thirty days from the date of receipt of such appeals.

8. Power to remove difficulties.—If any difficulty arises in giving effect to the provisions of this Act, the Government may, by an order, make such provisions not inconsistent with the provisions of this Act and appear to them to be necessary or expedient for removing the difficulty:

Provided that no such order shall be made after the expiry of two years from the date of commencement of this Act.

9. Protection of action taken in good faith.—No suit, prosecution or other legal proceedings, shall lie against the Government or any public authority or any person for anything which is done in good faith or intended to be done, under or in pursuance of this Act or rules made thereunder.

10. Penalties.—Where any competent authority, without any reasonable cause, fails to supply information sought for within the period specified under Section 5 or furnishes information which is false with regard to any material particulars and which he knows or has reasonable cause to believe it to be false,

(i) the authority superior to the competent authority may impose a penalty not exceeding two thousand rupees on such competent authority as it thinks appropriate after giving him a reasonable opportunity of being heard and such a penalty shall be recoverable from his salary or if no salary is drawn, as arrears of public revenue due on land; and

(ii) he shall also be liable to disciplinary action under the service rules applicable to him.

11. State Council for Right to Information.—(1) The Government shall, by notification in the Gazette, establish with effect from such date as may be specified in the notification, a council to be known as State Council for Right to Information.

(2) The State Council shall consist of the following members namely:

(a) the Minister-in-charge of the Department of Administrative Reforms in the Government who shall be its chairman; and

(b) (i) such other official members not exceeding four; (ii) non-official members not exceeding four representing journalists, non- government organisations;

(3) the time and place of the meeting of the State Council shall be decided by the Chairman and shall observe such procedure, as may be laid down by the council to transact its business.

(4) The function of the State Council shall be to promote right to information in the state and to deal with all matters relating to right to information, such as,

(a) review the operation of the Act and the rules made there under;

(b) review of the administrative arrangements and procedures to secure for citizens the fullest possible access to information;

(c) research and documentation as regards management of information with a view to improving the extent and accuracy of information being made available under the Act; and

(d) to advise the Government on all matters relating to right to information, including training, development and orientation of employees to bring in a culture of openness and transparency.

12. Overriding effect of Act.—The provisions of this Act or any rule or order made thereunder shall have effect notwithstanding anything inconsistent therewith contained in any law other than this Act or may instrument having effect by virtue of any law other than this Act.

13. Power to make rules.—(1) The Government may, after previous publication, by notification, make rules to carrying out all or any of the purposes of this Act.

(2) In particular, and without prejudice to the generality of the foregoing power, such rules may provide for all or any of the following matters, namely:

(a) the fee payable under section 5;

(b) any other matter which is to be, or may be, prescribed.

(3) Every rule made under this Act shall be laid as soon as may be after it is made, before the Legislative Assembly while it is in session for a total period of fourteen days which may be comprised in one session or in two successive sessions and if before the expiry of the session in which it is so laid or the session immediately following, the Legislative Assembly makes any modification in the rule or decides that the rule should not be made, the rule shall, thereafter have effect only in such modified form or be of no effect, as the case may be; so whoever, that any such modification or annulment shall be without prejudice to the validity of anything previously done under that rule.

Statement of objects and reasons.—Right of access to information to the citizens of the State promotes openness, transparency and accountability in the administration and ensures effective participation of people in the administration and makes democracy meaningful. Therefore, it is proposed to direct all public authorities *inter alia* to publish periodically the details of facilities available to citizens and announce the details of schemes, projects, etc. before its implementation and also supply of information as and when a request to that effect is made by a citizen.

2. The Bill seeks to achieve the above objects.—Financial Memorandum:

The Bill, if enacted, and brought into operation, would not involve any additional expenditure from the consolidated fund of the State.

Memorandum regarding delegation legislation.—1. Sub-clause (2) of clause 1 of the Bill seeks to empower the Government to notify the data of commencement of the Act.

2. Sub-clause (a) of clause 2 of the Bill seeks to empower the Government to appoint any authority or officer or person to be competent authority for the purposes of the Act.

3. Sub-clause (e) of clause 2 of the Bill seeks to empower the Government to prescribe the manner of obtaining certified copies, floppies, etc.

4. Sub-clause (d) and (c) of clause 3 of the Bill seeks to empower the Government to specify the scheme or activity and such other information that may be published.

5. Sub-clause (1) of clause 5 of the Bill seeks to empower the Government to prescribe the manner of making application, fee, form and other particular.

6. Clause 8 of the Bill seeks to empower the Government by order make provisions for removing any difficulty when arises in giving effect to the provisions of the Act.

7. The matter in respect of which rules may be made or orders may be issued are matters of procedure or details and are of routine and administrative nature. Further, every rule made under this Act is subject to scrutiny by the legislative assembly. The delegation of legislative power is there of a normal character.

THE MADHYA PRADESH RIGHT TO INFORMATION BILL, 2003

(Madhya Pradesh Act No. 3 of 2003)

Received the assent of the Governor on the 24 January, 2003, assent first published in the Madhya Pradesh Gazette (Extra ordinary) dated the 31 January 2003.

An act to provide for freedom to every citizen of the State to secure access to information under the control of public authorities consistent with public interest and as a right to promote openness and transparency in administration and for matters connected therewith or incidental thereto.

Be it enacted by the Madhya Pradesh Legislature in the Fifty-third year of the Republic of India as follows:

1. Short title and commencement.—(1) This act may be called the Madhya Pradesh Jankari Ki Swatantrata Adhiniyam 2002. (2) It extends to the whole of the State of Madhya Pradesh.

2. Definitions.—In this Act unless the context otherwise requires:

(a) 'Personal information' means recorded information about an individual.

(b) "public body" means

(i) all offices of the State Government;

(ii) all local authorities and statutory authorities constituted under any Act of the State Legislature for the time being in force and all companies. Corporations and cooperative societies in which not less than fifty-one per cent of the paid up share capital is held by the State Government.

(i) offices of the Central Governor situated in Madhya Pradesh.

(ii) any establishment of the Armed forces or Central para Military forces in the state of Madhya Pradesh.

(iii) corporations owned by the Central Government.

(iv) religious organisations.

(v) the Madhya Pradesh Vidhan Sabha.

(vi) the High Court of Madhya Pradesh and other Courts of Law including Tribunals, and other Organisations which have the Status of Courts and whose proceedings are deemed to be judicial proceedings.

(vii) the Secretariat of the Governor of Madhya Pradesh.

(viii) the office of the Lokayukt.

(c) "head of a public body" means a person who is the Chief Executive and in charge of the affairs of a public body.

(d) "Designated Officer" means an officer appointed by the head of a public body to carry out the provisions of this Act.

(e) "record" means

(i) any document, manuscript and file;

(ii) any microfilm, microteche and facsimile copy of a document

(iii) any reproduction of image or images embodied in such microfilm (whether enlarged or not); and

(iv) any other material produced by a computer or by any such device.

3. Obligations of public bodies.—Every public body shall

(a) Maintain all records in such manner and form as is consistent with its operational requirements...;

(c) Publish the details of facilities available to citizens for obtaining information.

4. Freedom of inspection and obtaining certified copies.—(1) Subject to the provisions of this Act every citizen shall have the freedom to inspect and obtain copies of any record created within three preceding calendar years which is in possession of a public body.

(2) Notwithstanding anything contained in sub-section (1), no person shall be given:

(a) Information, the disclosure of which would prejudicially affect the sovereignty and integrity of India, security of the State, strategic scientific or economic interest of India or conduct of international relations;

(b) Information, the disclosure of which would prejudicially affect public safety and order or which may lead to an incitement to commit an offence or prejudicially affect fair trial or adjudication of a case;

(c) Information relating to Cabinet papers and every Government order issued on the basis of the Cabinet decision including records of the deliberations of the Council of Ministers, Secretaries and other Officers;

(d) Information the disclosure of which would harm, frankness and candour of internal discussions including inter-departmental or intra-departmental notes, correspondence and papers containing advice or opinion as also of projections and assumptions relating to internal policy analysis;

(e) Information the disclosure of which would prejudice the assessment or collection of any tax, cess, duty or fee or assist in avoidance or evasion of the tax, cess, duty or fee;

(f) Information the disclosure of which would constitute a breach of privilege of the Parliament or the State Legislature;

(g) Information regarding trade or commercial secrets protected by law or such information, the disclosure of which would prejudicially affect the legitimate economic and commercial interest or the competitive position of a public body or would cause unfair gain or loss to any person;

(h) Information regarding any matter which is likely to—

(i) help or facilitate escape from legal custody or affect prison security; or

(ii) which relates to the process of investigation or apprehension or prosecution of offenders; and

(iii) information the disclosure of which is prohibited under any enactment regulation or international agreement.

Explanation: The period of three years shall be reckoned from 1 January of the calendar year in which any person applies to inspect or obtain copies of any record.

5. Procedure and fees.—(1) A person desiring to inspect or obtain a copy of record under this Act may make an application in writing to the designated officer.

(2) The designated officer shall, as soon as possible, but not later than thirty days, of receipt of such an application subject to the provisions of sub-section (2) of Section 4 and Section 6 of this Act, permit inspection of the record or supply copies, as the case may be unless the application fails to pay the requisite fee or refuse such permission if information can not be supplied under the provisions of this Act.

(3) Where a request is rejected under sub-section (2) the designated officer shall communicate to the person making request:

(i) the reasons for such rejection;

(ii) the period within which an appeal against such rejection may be preferred;

(iii) the particulars of the appellate authority.

(4) Every public body shall charge fees for the information supplied or inspection of document allowed at such rates as may be notified by the State Government.

6. Grounds for refusal to supply information in certain cases.—Without prejudice to the provisions of Section 4, the designated officer may also reject a request for supply of information where such request—

(a) is too general in nature and the information sought is of such nature that, it is not required to be ordinarily collected by the public body;

(b) relates to information that is required by law, rules, regulations or orders to be published at a particular time;

(c) relates to information that is contained in published material available to public;

(d) relates to personal information the disclosure of which has no relationship to any public activity or which would cause unwarranted invasion of the privacy of an individual;

(e) relates to matters classified as 'Secret' or 'Confidential'.

(f) is vague or meaningless; or too large in volume to prepare copies.

7. Appeal.—(1) Any person aggrieved by an order of the designated officer refusing to provide information may prefer an appeal within thirty days of the impugned order to the State Government or to such appellate authority as may be notified by the State Government subject to such rules as may be prescribed.

Explanation: An application made under sub-section (1) of Section 5 shall be deemed to have been refused if no communication is received within a period of forty days from the date of such application.

(2) An appeal shall be decided within thirty days from the date of filing it.

(3) The decision in appeal shall be final and binding on all concerned.

8. Penalties.—(1) Where the head of a public body or designated officer fails to supply the desired information within a period of thirty days from the date of receipt of the copy of the order of the appellate authority, the appellate authority may impose a penalty not exceeding two thousand rupees on the concerned head of the public body or designated officer as it thinks appropriate after giving him a reasonable opportunity of being heard and such a penalty shall be recoverable in such manner as may be prescribed. (2) The head of the public body or designated officer or whom a penalty under sub-section (1) has been imposed may within thirty days from the date of communication of such order to him, prefer an appeal to the State Government.

9. Responsibilities of head of public body.—(1) The head of every public body shall be responsible for monitoring the implementation of the provisions of this Act. (2) Every head of public body shall for the purposes of this Act, appoint one or more officials as designated officer.

10. Power to make rules.—(1) The State Government may make rules to carry out the provisions of this Act. (2) All rules made under this Act shall, as soon as possible after they are made, be laid on the table of the Legislative Assembly.

11. Protection of action taken in good faith.—No suit prosecution or other legal proceedings shall lie against the State Government or any public body or any person for anything which is done or intended to be done in good faith in pursuance of this Act or the rules made there under.

12. Bar of jurisdiction of courts.—No court shall entertain any suit, application or other proceeding in respect of any order made under this Act and no such order shall be called in question otherwise than by way of an appeal if any provided under this Act.

13. Removal of difficulties.—If any difficulty arises in giving effect to the provisions of this Act the State Government may by order, make such provisions not inconsistent with the provisions of this Act, as appears to it to be necessary or expedient for removing the difficulty.

14. Act to have overriding effect.—The provisions of this Act shall have effect notwithstanding anything inconsistent herewith contained in any other law made by the State Legislature in respect of any matter falling under State list or Concurrent list except the provisions of any existing law or a law made by Parliament in respect of any matter falling under Concurrent list.

THE MADHYA PRADESH RIGHT TO INFORMATION (FEES AND APPEAL) RULES, 2005

In exercise of the powers conferred by section 27 of the Right to Information Act. 2005 (Central Act No. 22 of 2005) the State Government, hereby makes the following rules, namely:

CHAPTER I

PRELIMINARY

1. Short title and commencement.—(1) These rules may be called the Madhya Pradesh Right to Information (Fees and Appeal) Rules, 2005. (2) They shall come into force with effect from the date of publication in the Madhya Pradesh Gazette.

2. Definitions.—In these rules, unless the context otherwise requires,

(a) "Act" means the Right to Information Act, 2005 (No. 22 of 2005).

(b) "Below Poverty Line" means such citizen of State of Madhya Pradesh who is declared as below poverty line by the Government of Madhya Pradesh.

(c) "Cost" means the cost which is chargeable for providing information as defined in clause (f) of Section 2 of the Act.

(d) "Fees" means the fees payable under the provisions of the Act.

(e) "Forms" means the forms attach to these rules.

(f) "Sections" means the sections of the Act.

(g) The words used in these rules but not defined shall have the same meaning as they are defined in Section 2 of the Act.

CHAPTER II

FEES

3. (1) Any person, who is not below the poverty line, desires any material under sub-section (4) of Section 4 of the Act shall submit the application himself to the State Public Information Officer/ Assistant Public Information Officer with non-judicial stamp of Rs 10 or with the receipt of Rs 10 (Rupees ten) after making payment in cash. If the application is being sent by post, the applicant shall enclose the non-judicial stamp of Rs 10 Rupees ten).

(2) After receiving the application by the State Public Information Officer or the State Assistant Public Information Officer as the case may be, the printing cost or medium cost price of the material of the information as determined by above officer shall be deposited by the applicant to the above said officers in cash or in the form of non-judicial stamp. If the amount is deposited in cash by the applicant, the State Public Information Officer or the officer as directed by him shall give a receipt of such amount. The amount so deposited shall be deposited into the treasury by a challan.

4. Any person, who is not below the poverty line, desires to seek an information under sub-section (1) of Section 6 and sub-section (1) of Section 7 of the Act shall produce the application before the public Authority or State Public Information Officer or State Assistant Public Information Officer, as the case may be, with the non-judicial stamp of Rs 10 (Rupees ten) or with the receipt of Rs 10 (Rupees ten) by paying in cash.

5. (1) For the purposes of sub-section (5) of Section 7 where access to information is to be provided in the printed or in any electronic format, the applicant, who is not below the poverty line, shall deposit the actual cost of the Information as determined by the public Authority or State Public Information Officer or State Assistant Public Information Officer in cash or in the form of non-judicial stamp within three days from the date of direction to such officers as directed by the public Authority or State Public Information Officer.

(2) If the applicant wants to examine any document or record, the State Public Information Officer or State Assistant Public Information Officer shall depute any sub-ordinate officer for such purpose and the applicant, who is not below the poverty line, shall pay Rs 50 (Rupees fifty) for first hour or fraction thereof and Rs 25 (Rupees twenty-five) for every additional fifteen minutes or fraction thereof in cash or in the form of non-judicial stamp.

(3) If the applicant wants the certified samples of any material, the cost determined by the State Public Information Officer or State Assistant Public Information Officer of such material, shall be deposited by the applicant to such officer who is directed by the State Public Information Officer, in cash or in the form of non-judicial stamp.

(4) Where the information is stored in the computer, the actual cost of the diskettes or floppies or tape or video cassette as determined by the State Public Information Officer or the State Assistant Public Officer shall be deposited by the applicant in cash or in the form of non-judicial stamp.

CHAPTER III

PAY AND OTHER SERVICE CONDITIONS

6. The officer and servants deputed under sub-section (6) of the Section 16 shall be paid the same pay and allowances as they were receiving before deputation and for these service conditions the same rules shall be applicable as were applicable before such deputation.

CHAPTER IV

APPEAL

7. First appeal.—(1) Any person who does not receives a decision within the time specified in sub-section (1) or clause (a) of sub-section (3) of Section 7, or is aggrieved by a decision of the State Public Information Officer, may within thirty days from the expiry of such period or from the receipt of such a decision prefer an appeal, with a memorandum of appeal and the fee of Rs 50 (Rupees fifty) either in cash or in the form of non-judicial stamp, to such officer who is senior in rank to the State Public Information Officer in each Public Authority.

Provided that such officer may admit the appeal after the expiry of the period of thirty days if he is satisfied that the appellant was prevented by sufficient cause from filing the appeal in time.

(2) In the memorandum of appeal the name and address of the appellant, the basis of the subject matter of the information, with the name and the post of the competent officer, the orders of the competent authority and payment of fee shall be clearly specified.

(3) An appeal under sub-rule (1) shall be disposed of within thirty days of the receipt of the appeal or within such extended period not exceeding a total of forty-five days from the date filing thereof, as the case may be, for reasons to be recorded in writing.

(4) The Copy of order passed in appeal shall be given free of cost.

8. Second appeal.—(1) A second appeal against the decision under sub-rule (3) of Rule 7 shall lie within ninety days from the date on which the decision should have been made or was actually received, with the State Information Commission:

Provided that the State Information Commission may admit the appeal after the expiry of the period of ninety days if it is satisfied that the appellant was prevented by sufficient cause from filing the appeal in time.

(2). With the memorandum of appeal filed before the State Information Commission the fee of Rs 100 (Rupees one hundred) in cash or in the form of non-judicial stamp shall be deposited.

(3). The State Information Commission shall after giving reasonable opportunity of being heard to public Authority or State Public Information Officer or appellant, as the case may be, disposed of the appeal within thirty days from the date of the receipt of the appeal for reasons to be recorded in writing.

(4). The decision of the State Information Commission shall be final and binding.

(5). A copy of the decision of the State Information Commission shall be given free of cost. If the appellant wants to receive the copy of the order by post then after receiving the fee of postal charges, shall be sent within three days.

(9). The fee chargeable under Rules 7 and 8 shall not be charged from the persons who are of below poverty line.

THE MAHARASHTRA RIGHT TO INFORMATION ACT, 2002*

An Act to make provisions for effectively securing and enforcing the right to information in the State of Maharashtra and for matters connected therewith or incidental thereto.

Whereas the right to information has been recognized by the Supreme Court as a part of the fundamental right guaranteed to the citizens under Article 19(1) of the Constitution of India ;

And whereas the right to information is the bed-rock of democracy and can pave the way for transparency, openness and accountability in governance of the affairs of the State and ensure effective participation of the people in a democratic society;

And whereas it was expedient to make provision for effectively securing and enforcing the right to information in the State of Maharashtra and for matters connected therewith or incidental thereto;

And whereas both Houses of the State Legislature were not in session;

And whereas, Shri Chunilal Karsandas Thakker, discharging the functions of the Governor of Maharashtra, was satisfied that circumstances exist which render it necessary for him to take immediate action to make a law for the purposes hereinafter appearing; and therefore, promulgated the Maharashtra Right to Information Ordinance, 2002, on 23 September 2002;

And whereas it is expedient to replace the said ordinance by an Act of the State Legislature; it is hereby enacted in the fifty-third year of the Republic of India as follows:

---

* Repeated by Maharashtra Right to Information (Repeal) Act, 2005, w.e.f. 11 October, 2005.

1. Short title, extent and commencement.—(1) This Act may be called the Maharashtra Right to Information Act, 2002.

(2) It shall extend to the whole of the State of Maharashtra.

(3) It shall come into force on 23 September 2002.

2. Definitions.—In this Act, unless the context otherwise requires—

(1) "appellate authority" means the concerned Competent Authority mentioned in clause (3) and shall also include such officer or officers authorised by the concerned Competent Authority to act as the Appellate Authority, by general or special order, for the purposes of this Act.

(2) "Committee" means the Committee constituted by the Government for the purposes of Section 7(a), under the Chairmanship of the Additional Chief Secretary (Home) to the Government and other two members as may be specified by the Government by an order issued in this behalf;

(3) "Competent Authority" means:

(i) the Head of every Administrative Department of the State Government;

(ii) the Administrative Heads of the public and other authorities in the State;

(iii) the Registrar of Cooperative Societies for the Cooperative Societies registered under the Maharashtra Cooperative Societies, 1960;

(iv) the Registrar of Societies for the Societies registered under the Societies Registration Act, 1860;

(v) the Charity Commissioner for Charity Commissioner's Office and the Public Trusts registered under the Bombay Public Trusts Act, 1950;

(vi) the Commissioner of Labour for the trade unions registered with him;

(vii) the Secretary of the Maharashtra Public Service Commission for the administrative wing of the Maharashtra Public Service Commission;

(viii) the Registrar of the Lokayukta and Upa-Lokayuktas for the administrative wing of the Office of Lokayukta and Upa-Lokayuktas.

(4) "Government" means the Government of Maharashtra;

(5) "Information" means information relating to any matter in respect of the affairs of the Government and of any public authority and includes a copy of any record in the form of a document, diskettes, floppy or any other electronic mode.

(6) "public authority" means any authority or body established or constituted by any Central or State law and includes any other body owned and controlled by the State or which receives any aid directly or indirectly by the Government and shall include the bodies whose composition and administration are predominantly controlled by the Government or the functions of such body are of public nature or interest or on which office bearers are appointed by the Government.

Explanation: For the purposes of this clause the expression "aid" shall include Government aid in the form of Government land at concessional rates or any other monetary concessions like exemption from tax, etc. by Government as specified by Government, from time to time.

(7) "Public Information Officer" means an Officer designated by any Competent Authority under sub-section (1) of Section 5 and shall include such Officer or Employee whose assistance has been taken by the Public Information Officer for the performance of his duties under this Act.

(8) "prescribed" means prescribed by rules made under this Act.

(9) "record" means and includes,

(i) any document, manuscript or file;

(ii) any microfilm, microfiche and facsimile copy of the document;

(iii) any reproduction of image or images embodied in such microfilm (whether enlarged or not); and

(iv) any other material produced by a computer or by any other device.

(10) "State" means the State of Maharashtra.

3. Right to Information.— Subject to the provisions of this Act, every citizen shall have the right to get information.

4. Obligation on Public Authorities.—Every Competent Authority shall,

(a) maintain all its records, in such manner and form, as is consistent with its operational requirements duly catalogued and indexed;

(b) publish in the manner prescribed, from time to time,

(i) the particulars of its organization, functions and duties;

(ii) the powers and duties of its officers and employees and the procedure to be followed by them in decision making process;

(iii) the norms set by the public authority for the discharge of its functions;

(iv) the rules, regulations, instructions, manuals, government resolutions, orders and guidelines and the list of record in the office, which can be made available to the citizens;

(v) the details of facilities available to citizens for obtaining information;

(vi) the name, designation and other particulars of the Public Information Officer; and

(vii) such additional information as may be prescribed by the Competent Authority concerned from time to time.

(c) publish all relevant facts concerning important decisions whether administrative or quasi-judicial and policies that affect the public while announcing such decisions and policies.

(d) before initiating any project, publish or communicate to the public generally and to the persons affected by the project in particular, the facts available to it or to which it has reasonable access and which in its opinion should be known to the affected persons.

5. Appointment of Public Information Officers.—(1) Every Competent Authority shall for the purposes of this Act, designate one or more officers as Public Information Officers in all administrative units and offices under such Authority.

(2) Every Public Information Officer shall deal with a request for information and shall render reasonable assistance to any person seeking such information.

(3) The Public Information Officer may seek the assistance of any other Officer or Employee as he considers necessary for the proper discharge of his duties.

(4) Any Officer or Employee whose assistance has been sought under sub-section (3), shall render all assistance to the Public Information Officer seeking his assistance.

6. Procedure of getting information.—(1) A person desirous of obtaining information shall make an application to the Public Information Officer in the prescribed manner along with such fees, in such form and with such particulars, as may be prescribed.

(2) On receipt of an application requesting for information under sub-section (1), the Public Information Officer shall, as expeditiously as possible and in any case, not later than fifteen working days from the date of receipt of the application, either provide the information as requested or reject the request for any of the reasons specified under the provisions of this Act:

Provided that, in a suitable case for the reasons to be recorded and communicated to the applicant, the time limit may be extended by another fifteen working days:

Provided further that, where it is decided to provide the information on payment of any additional fees than the fees prescribed representing the cost of providing the necessary information, the Public Information Officer shall send an intimation to the applicant giving the details of the additional fees determined by him, requesting him to deposit the additional fees, and the period intervening the dispatch of the said intimation and payment of such additional fees, if any, shall be excluded for the purpose of calculating the period of fifteen working days or the additional period of fifteen days as the case may be, referred to in this sub-section:

Provided also that, the fees prescribed or the additional fees payable, as the case may be, shall not exceed the actual cost of supplying the information.

(3) Where a request is rejected under sub-section (2), the Public Information Officer shall communicate in writing to the person making the request.

(i) the reasons for such rejection;

(ii) the period within which an appeal, against such rejection may be preferred; and

(iii) the officer or authority before whom the appeal shall be preferred by the applicant.

(4) The information shall be provided in the language and in the form in which it is maintained by the public authority.

(5) **Whenever and wherever the information.**—Applied for, involves the life and liberty of a person, such information shall, subject to the provisions of section 7, be supplied to the applicant within twenty-four hours of the receipt of the application.

7. Exemption from disclosure of information Notwithstanding anything contained in this Act, no person shall be given the,

(a) information, disclosure of which would prejudicially affect the sovereignty and integrity of India, the security or interests of the State, relation with foreign State or lead to incitement of an offence:

Provided that, whenever any information sought is to be withheld on the aforementioned grounds, the request for such information shall forthwith be put up by the Public Information Officer through the Competent Authority to the Committee for consideration and decision;

Provided further that, the Public Information Officer shall, after obtaining the 'approval from such Committee for rejection of the request, while communicating such rejection to the applicant mention that such rejection is with the approval of the Committee;

(b) information which has been expressly forbidden to be published by any court of law or tribunal or the disclosure of which may constitute contempt of court;

(c) information, the disclosure of which would cause a breach of privilege of Parliament or the State Legislature;

(d) information including commercial confidence, trade secrets or intellectual property, the disclosure of which would harm the competitive position of a third party, unless the Competent Authority is satisfied that larger public interest warrants the disclosure of such information;

(e) information available to a person in his fiduciary relationship, unless the Competent Authority is satisfied that the larger public interest warrants the disclosure of such information;

(f) information pertaining to service record of a person;

(g) information received in confidence from foreign government or International Organization;

(h) information, the disclosure of which would endanger the life or physical safety of any person or identify the source of information or assistance given in confidence for law enforcement or security purposes;

(i) information the disclosure of which is prohibited under the provisions of the Official Secrets Act, 1923;

(j) information which would impede the process of investigation or apprehension or prosecuton of offenders; and

(k) information which relates to personal information the disclosure of which has no relationship to any public activity or interest, or which would cause unwarranted invasion of the privacy of the individual unless the Competent Authority is satisfied that the larger public interest justifies the disclosure of such information.

8. Grounds for refusal to supply of information in certain cases.—Without prejudice to the provisions of Section 7, the Public Information Officer may also reject the request for supply of information, where—

(a) the information is already published in the Official Gazette or otherwise, and is available to public or is of such a nature that the volume of information required to be retrieved or processed, would involve disproportionate diversion of the resources of a public authority:

Provided that, where such request is rejected on the aforesaid ground, it shall be the duty of the Public Information Officer to render help, as far as possible, to the person seeking information to reframe the request in such a manner as may facilitate the supply of information;

(b) it relates to information that is required by law, rules, regulations or order to be published at a particular time.

9. Other information.—(1) Without prejudice to the provisions of Section 7,

(a) the information pertaining to decision making in a case, shall be made available to any applicant after the decision has been taken or deemed to have been taken in such case and the matter is complete or over;

(b) any information relating to any occurrence, event or matter which has taken place, occurred or happened fifteen years before the date on which any request is made under sub-section (1) of Section 6, shall be provided to any person making such request.

(2) Any information which cannot be withheld from the Parliament and the State Legislature shall necessarily be made available to the applicant under the provisions of this Act.

10. Severability.—No request for an information shall be totally rejected on the ground that it is in relation to an information or record which is exempted from the disclosure, if, it is possible to give that information from the part of the record which does not contain any information that is exempted from disclosure under this Act and which can reasonably be severed from any part of the record that contains the exempted information.

11. Appeals.—(1) (i) Any person aggrieved by an order of the Public Information Officer may, within thirty days from the date of receipt of such order; or

(ii) any person who has not received any communication within the period of fifteen working days as specified in sub-section (2) of section 6 or the extended period as specified in the second proviso to the said sub-section (2), from the date of making such application; may, appeal to the appellate authority, within a period of thirty days of the lapse of such period in such form and with such fees, as may be prescribed:

Provided that, when the order of the Public Information Officer is passed under clause (a) of section 7 with the approval of the Committee referred to in the proviso to the said clause (a), the appeal against such order shall lie only to the Lokayukta or Upa-Lokayuktas.

(2) The appellate authority may, after giving the person or persons affected a reasonable opportunity of being heard, pass such order as it deems fit.

(3) Any person aggrieved by the order of the appellate authority under sub-section (2), may within thirty days from the receipt of such order, prefer second appeal to the Lokayukta or Upa-Lokayuktas, as the case may be, of the State.

(4) The appeals referred to in sub-sections (1) and (3) shall, as far as possible be disposed of within thirty days of the receipt of such appeals or within such extended period not exceeding a further period of thirty days, after recording the reasons for such extension of period.

(5) The decision of the Lokayukta or Upa-Lokayuktas, as the case may be, in appeals shall be final.

12. Penalty.—(1) Where any Public Information Officer has without any reasonable cause, failed to supply the information sought, within the period specified under sub-section (2) of section 6, the appellate authority may, in appeal impose a penalty of rupees two hundred fifty, for each day's delay in furnishing the information, after giving such Public Information Officer a reasonable opportunity of being heard.

(2) Where it is found in appeal that any Public Information Officer has knowingly given,

(a) incorrect or misleading information, or (b) wrong or incomplete information; the appellate authority may impose a penalty not exceeding rupees two thousand, on such Public Information Officer as it thinks appropriate after giving such officer a reasonable opportunity of being heard.

(3) An appeal shall lie against the order of the appellate authority, with the Lokayukta or Upa-Lokayuktas and the provisions of sub-sections (3), (4) and (5) or section 11 shall *mutatis mutandis* apply to such appeal.

(4) The penalty under sub-sections (1) and (2) as imposed by the appellate authority, shall be recoverable from the salary of the Public Information Officer concerned, or if no salary is drawn, as an arrears of land revenue.

(5) The Public Information Officer on whom the penalty under sub-sections (1) and (2) is imposed shall also be liable to appropriate disciplinary action under the service rules applicable to him.

13. Constitution of Councils.—(1) The Government shall set up a Council for monitoring the working of this Act, at the State level under the Chairmanship of the Chief Secretary, or any Additional Chief Secretary and for every Revenue Division, under the Chairmanship of the concerned Divisional Commissioner. Such Council shall generally comprise such members who are the persons of repute and standing in society including representatives of media and non-government organisations, and academicians, as may be prescribed.

(2) The Councils may take review of the working of the Ordinance, not less than once in six months and make suitable recommendations to the government.

14. Constitution of commission of Records.—(1) The Government shall set up a Commission of Records comprising the representatives of the Government, persons of repute and standing in society including academicians, as may be prescribed. It shall be the duty of the Records Commission to advise the Government on release of the old record for being made available for public information.

(2) The decision of the Commission of Records shall be binding on the Government and it shall be implemented within three months unless the Government, for reasons to be recorded decides to overrule the decision of the Commission.

(3) In each such case of overruling of the decision of the Records Commission, the Government shall lay a statement on the table of the State Legislature at the earliest.

15. Protection of action taken in good faith.—No suit, prosecution or other legal proceeding shall lie against any Government servant or officer for anything done or purported to have been done in good faith in pursuance of the provisions of this Act or the rules made thereunder.

16. Bar of jurisdiction of courts.—No court shall entertain any suit, application or other proceeding in respect of any order made under this Act and no such order shall be called in question otherwise than by way of an appeal under this Act.

17. Act to have overriding effect.—The provisions of this Act shall have effect notwithstanding anything inconsistent therewith contained in any other law made by the State Legislature or any rules, regulations or order made thereunder.

18. Powers to make rules.—(1) The State Government may by notification in the *Official Gazette*, make rules to carry out the purposes of this Act.

(2) Except when the rules are made for the first time, all rules made under this Act shall be subject to the condition of previous publication.

(3) Every rule made under this Act shall be laid, as soon as may be, after it is made, before each House of the State Legislature, while in session for a total period of thirty days, which may be comprised in one session or in two or more successive sessions, and if, before the expiry of the session in which it is so laid or the session immediately following, both Houses agree in making any modification in rule or both Houses

agree that the rule should not be made, and notify their decision to the effect in the *Official Gazette*, the rule shall, from the date of publication of such decision in the *Official Gazette,* have effect only in such modified form or be of no effect. as the case may be, so however, that any such modification or annulment shall be without prejudice to the validity of anything previously done or omitted to be done under that rule.

19. Powers to remove difficulties.—(1) If any difficulty arises in giving effect to the provisions of this act, the Government may, as occasion arises, by an order published in the *Official Gazette,* do anything, not inconsistent with the provisions of this Act, which appears to be necessary or expedient for removing the difficulty.

(2) Every order made under this section shall be laid, as soon as may be, after it is made, before each House of the State Legislature.

20. Repeal of Maharashtra XXXVIII of 2000.—The Maharashtra Right to Information Act, 2000 is hereby repealed.

21. Repeal of Mah. Ord. X of 2002 and saving.—(1) The Maharashtra Right to Information Ordinance, 2002, is hereby repealed.

(2) Notwithstanding such repeal, anything done or any action taken (including any notification or order issued) under the said Ordinance, shall be deemed to have been done, taken or issued, as the case may be, under this Act.

THE MAHARASHTRA RIGHT TO INFORMATION RULES, 2005*

In exercise of the powers conferred by sub-section (2) of section 27 of the Right to Information Act, 2005 (22 of 2005), the Government of Maharashtra hereby makes the following rules, namely:—

1. Short title and commencement.—(1) These rules may be called the Maharashtra Right to Information Rules, 2005.

(2) They shall come into force on the 12th October, 2005.

2. Definitions.—In the rules, unless the context otherwise requires,—

(a) 'Act' means the Right to Information Act, 2005 (22 of 2005);

(b) 'section' means section of the Act;

(c) Words and expressions used in these rules but not defined shall have the same meanings respectively, assigned to them, in the Act.

3. Procedure for seeking information.—A request for obtaining information under sub-section (1) of section 6 shall be made to the concerned State Public Information Officer on plain paper in the format given in Annexure "A" and shall be accompanied by an application fee of rupees ten by way of cash against proper receipt or by demand draft or banker's cheque payable to the public authority or by affixing a court fee stamp of rupees ten.

---

* *Vide* No. RTI. 2005/C.R. 315/05/5, Government of Maharashtra, Ministry of General Administration, dated 11th October, 2005 (w.e.f. 12-10-2005).

4. Fee for information.—(1) For providing the information under sub-section (1) of section 7, the fee shall be charged by way of cash against proper receipt or by demand draft or banker's cheque payable or by way of money order to the public authority, at the following rates, namely:—

(A)	(a) when the concerned Department has already fixed the price of some documents, maps, etc.	The price so fixed *plus* postal charges.
	(b) when the information is readily available, either by way of photocopying, or by other way (copy)	(i) rupees two for each page (in A-4 or A-3 size paper) created or copied *plus* postal charges; or (ii) actual charge or cost price of a copy in large siza paper *plus* postal charges.

(B) for inspection of records, no fee for the first hour; and a fee of rupees five for each fifteen minutes (or fraction thereof) thereafter:

Provided that no postal charges shall be charged if the applicant collects the information personally.

(2) For providing the information under sub-section (5) of section 7, the fee shall be charged by way of cash against proper receipt or by demand draft or banker's cheque or by way of money order payable to the public authority at the following rates:—

(a) for information provided in diskette or floppy, rupees fifty per diskette or floppy *plus* postal charges; and

(b) for information provided in printed form at the price fixed for such publication or rupees two per page of photocopy for extracts from the publication *plus* postal charges:

Provided that no postal charges shall be charged if the applicant collects the information personally.

5. Appeal.—(1) Any person who, does not receive a decision within the time specified in sub-section (1) or clause (a) of sub-section (3) of section 1, or is aggrieved by an order of the State Public Information Officer may, within thirty days from the date of receipt of the order of the State Public Information Officer, prefer an appeal to the concerned appellate authority on plain paper in the format given in Annexure "B", which shall be accompanied by an appeal fee of rupees twenty by way of cash against proper receipt or by demand, draft or banker's cheque payable to the public authority or by affixing a court fee stamp of rupees twenty, with a copy of such order appealed against.

(2) Any person aggrieved by an order of the appellate authority under sub- section (1) of section 19 may, within ninety days from the date of receipt of the order of the appellate authority, prefer a second appeal to the State Information Commission on plain paper in the format given in Annexure "C", which shall be accompanied by an appeal fee of rupees twenty by way of cash against proper receipt or by demand draft or banker's cheque payable to the State Information Commission or by affixing a court fee stamp of rupees twenty, with a copy of such order appealed against.

ANNEXURE "A"

(*See* Rule 3)

Affix here Court Fee Stamp of Rs. 10

FORMAT OF APPLICATION FOR OBTAINING INFORMATION UNDER THE RIGHT TO INFORMATION ACT, 2005

To,

The State Public Information Officer,

(Name of the office with address)

(1) Full name of the applicant:

(2) Address:

(3) Particulars of information required

(i) Subject matter of information.*:

(ii) The period to which the information relates.**:

---

* Broad category of the subject to be indicated (such as grant of Government land/Service matters/Licenses, etc.)

** Relevant period for which information is required to be indicated.

*** Specific details of the information is required to be indicated.

(iii) Description of the information required.***:

(iv) Whether information is required by post or in person.:

(The actual postal charges shall be included in additional fees)

(v) In case by post:

(Ordinary, Registered or Speed)

(4) Whether the applicant is below poverty line:

(if yes, attach the photocopy of the proof thereof).

Place:

Date: Signature of the Applicant.

ANNEXURE "B"

[See Rule 5(1)]

Affix here Court Fee Stamp of Rs. 20

APPEAL UNDER SECTION 19(1) OF THE RIGHT TO INFORMATION ACT, 2005

From:............

(Appellant's name and address)

To:...........

(Name/designation/address of the appellate authority)

(1) Full name of the Appellant:

(2) Address:

(3) Particulars of the State Public Information Officer:

(4) Date of receipt of the order appealed against (if order passed):

(5) Last date for filing the appeal:

(6) The grounds for appeal:

(7) Particulars of information—

(i) Nature and subject matter of the information required.

(ii) Name of the Office or Department to which the information relates.

Place:

Date: Signature of Appellant

ANNEXURE "C"

[*See* Rule 5(2)]

SECOND APPEAL UNDER SECTION 19(3) OF THE RIGHT TO INFORMATION ACT, 2005

From: ....

(Appellant's name and address)

To: ....

(1) Full name of the Appellant:

(2) Address:

(3) Particulars of State Public Information Officer:

(4) Particulars of the First Appellate Authority:

(5) Date of receipt of the order appealed against:

(6) Last date for filing the appeal:

(7) The grounds for appeal:

(8) Particulars of information—

(i) Nature and subject-matter of the information required.

(ii) Name of the Office or Department to which the information relates.

Place:

Date: Signature of Appellant

THE MEGHALAYA RIGHT TO INFORMATION NOTIFICATION, 2005*

From:

Shri P.J. Bazeley
Chief Secretary to the Government of Meghalaya

To:

1. Additional Chief Secretary to the Government of Meghalaya
2. Principal Secretaries/Commissioner & Secretaries/ Secretaries of Administrative Departments
3. All Commissioner of Division
4. All Heads of Departments
5. All Deputy Commissioners

Sub: Implementation of the Right to Information Act 2005

Dear Sir/Madam,

1. The Right to Information Act (RTI Act) received the assent of the President of India on 15 June 2005. Certain provisions (Sections 4, 5, 12, 13, 15, 16, 24, 27 and 28) related to the preparations necessary for the implementation of this Act came into immediate effect on 15 June 2005 itself. Other provisions of this RTI Act will come into force on the 120th day from 15 June 2005 that is on 12 October 2005.

2.1 In Sec. 2(h) of the RTI Act, 2005 the definition of "public authority" has been given.

* *Vide* No. IPR. 30/2005/Pt. II/14 Government of Meghalaya Information & Public Relations Department, dated 19th August, 2005.

According to this definition the following bodies in the State of Meghalaya are "public authorities"

(i) All Administrative Departments of the Secretariat.

(ii) All Directorates of the Government, except for those Departments which do not have any Directorate.

Public authorities may be identified at the following levels as well depending upon the structure and nature of functions of each Directorate—

(a) Commissioner of Division level

(b) District level

(c) Sub-divisional level

(d) Block level

(iii) Autonomous District Councils.

(iv) All Public Corporations, Councils, Authorities, Institutes, Autonomous bodies and other similar bodies (whose offices may be located at different levels in the manner of Directorates).

(v) All local bodies such as Municipal Boards and Town Committees.

(vi) All such NGOs, which are substantially financed directly or indirectly by the State Government.

2.2 The following may also be noted:

(a) Below the State Level, each Department, in consultation with Directorate(s), under it will identify in the most optimal manner, the public authorities at lower tiers, i.e. at the District and Sub-Divisional levels.

(b) The Administrative Departments shall also list out Councils, Corporations, Authorities etc. which shall be identified as public authorities and transmit instructions contained in the Right to Information Act, 2005 to such bodies for compliance.

(c) The Urban Affairs Department shall take necessary steps to convey instructions in implementing the

Right to Information Act, 2005 to local bodies under its purview.

(d) The District Council Affairs Department will convey necessary instructions for implemetation of the Right to Information Act, 2005 to the Autonomous District Councils.

(e) The Administrative Departments shall also identify and list NGOs that are funded by public funds and such NGOs shall be informed that they may fall under the ambit of the provision of the Right to Information Act, 2005 and requested to take necessary action accordingly.

2.3 The above process of identification of the public authority may be completed within the target date and the list of "public authority" so identified may be communicated to Information & Public Relations Department.

3. Orders have been issued earlier requiring Officers and Employees of all public authorities to be appraised with a complete understanding of the RTI Act. Provision of necessary materials about this Act and organization of meetings and workshop in order to explain the scope of the Act must be ensured, by all concerned. Such action must be undertaken at all levels within public authorities located in all Departments.

4. All public authorities above mentioned in para 2 will be required to designate Officers as follows:

(i) Public Information Officer (PIO) Section 5

(ii) Assistant Public Information Officer Section 5

(iii) Departmental Appellate Authority first appeal Section 19.

The following guidelines may be observed while designating these Officers:

(i) It is the responsibility of the PIO to provide information within 30 days to a person making the request. Therefore, this officer has the greatest level of importance under the RTI Act. While designating a PIO it may be borne in mind that such Officers be designated who, to a large extent, will be able to provide the requested information at their level itself so that the need for obtaining the requested information from any other office is reduced as much as possible.

(ii) In every public authority as many PIOs may be designated, as may be required.

(iii) Every Department may appoint as many PIOs, as may be required, keeping in mind, its dimensions, activities, number of offices, nature of work and the information needs of common people. PIOs may be appointed at the level of the Administrative Departments, the Head of Department, the District etc. as per the requirement.

(iv) As far as possible PIOs should be officers who are not required to undertake frequent field visits as part of their main responsibilities.

(v) As far as possible PIOs may be Heads of their Offices, so that they are capable of providing information which is under the control of their office to the common people easily.

(vi) There is a provision in this Act for the designation of Assistant PIOs also. According to the provision of the Act, if an Assistant PIO receives an information request from an individual, he is required to dispatch the request to the concerned PIO within a maximum of 5 days. A subordinate officer or employee below every PIO is required to be designated Assistant PIO. Every department may, according to its requirement, designate Assistant PIOs at the level of the block and the sub-division. The objective (of appointing an Assistant PIO) being if the PIO is unable to contact the common people in far off places, then information may be made available to them through the Assistant PIO who is situated closest to them.

(vii) Every public authority is required to designate a Departmental Appellate Authority (DAA) who will be senior in rank to the PIO. In order to provide easy access to the common people, the DAA may as far as possible be appointed at the same place as that of the PIO.

(viii) PIOs, Assistant PIOs and Appellate Authorities may be designated in all NGOs which have been identified as public authorities.

(ix) The convenience of the common people must be borne in mind while deciding upon the numbers and levels of designation of PIOs and Assistant PIOs. It should also be ensured that agents and middle men are not allowed to flourish.

5. Under Section 4 of the RTI Act, every public authority is required to disclose information voluntarily on 16 points. The following points may be borne in mind in relation to 'proactive disclosure' of information—

(i) Every public authority will be required to prepare 16 information manuals.

(ii) These manuals will have to be prepared for the following levels (of operation) keeping in mind the dimensions, activities, nature of work and the information needs of the common people in each Department.

(a) Administrative Department Level

(b) HOD/Commissioner of Division Level

(c) District Level

(d) Sub-Divisional Level

(e) Block Level

Flexibility may be observed while preparing the contents of the manual. The contents of manuals prepared for different levels are themselves likely to be varied. Some contents may be similar to manuals at all levels. Some contents may be available in the manual prepared at the district level which may not be available in the manual prepared at the level of Administrative Department or the Head of Department.

While designing the contents of these manuals at different levels the probable information needs of the common people at those levels should be kept in mind.

(iii) The main objective of Sec. 4 is that all public authorities proactively publish to the maximum extent such information that will be of interest to the common people so that the need for requesting information under this Act becomes minimal. This basic principle may be borne in mind while preparing the manual.

(iv) As the main objective of proactive disclosure is to provide information to the common people voluntarily, every public authority may conduct an extensive study and analysis of the kinds of information that common people ordinarily seek by approaching their office.

(v) With a view to providing information to the common people easily, categories of information other than the 16 points mentioned in Sec. 4 of the Act may be incorporated in various departmental website so as to bring down to a minimum their need for seeking information through applications.

(vi) These manuals will require to be updated at regular intervals. A system regarding timelines for updating each category of information will be designed while formulating the rules under this Act.

(vii) The information contained in these manuals will be required to be made accessible to common people through the medium of books, notice boards, departmental libraries and the internet and be made available for inspection in offices. Every Department will decide as to which information should be made available in which medium at which level (of operation) after taking into consideration the available resources, the nature of information concerned and the convenience of the common people.

6. It is necessary to provide training to PIOs/Assistant PIOs and Departmental Appellate Authorities for implementing the RTI Act. For this purpose the Meghalaya Administrative Training Institute (MATI), Shillong will prepare a programme for providing the initial training for Masters Trainers. Through these Master Trainers 2-day training programmes for all PIO and Departmental Appellate Authorities will be organized in every district. These training programmes will be organized by the District Magistrates under the supervision of the MATI, Shillong as soon as possible.

   MATI may seek the assistance of external institutions like Commonwealth Human Rights Initiatives, New Delhi, while organizing these training programmes.

7. The following tasks also need to be undertaken in order to prepare for the implementation of the RTI Act—

   (i) Constitution of the Information Commission.

   (ii) Issue of notification exempting security and intelligence agencies from the purview of this Act.

   (iii) Framing of rules under this Act.

   (iv) Preparing a "Practical Guide Manual" about this Act in simple language for educating the common people and for the convenience of administrative offices.

   The above tasks will be completed by the Department of Information and Public Relations in coordination with the concerned Departments.

8. The Implementation Schedule for major activities is at Annexure I and the Time Schedule for preparation of manuals is at Annexure II.

9. Action may be taken in diligent and timely manner on all the points mentioned in this letter.

Kindly acknowledge receipt.

Yours faithfully,

(P. J. Bazeley)

Chief Secretary to the

Government of Meghalaya

THE ORISSA RIGHT TO INFORMATION ACT, 2002

An Act to make provision for securing Right to Information in the State of Orissa and for matters relating thereto.

Whereas it is necessary that every Governmental action should be transparent to the public;

And whereas to achieve this object, every member of the public should be able to get information from the Government;

Be it enacted by the Legislative Assembly of Orissa in the Fifty-Second Year of the Republic of India as follows:—

1. Short title and commencement.—The Act may be called the Orissa Right to Information Act 2002.

2. Definitions.—(a) "Public authority"—It includes all offices of the State Government, and local self-government bodies, statutory authorities or other authorities constituted under any enactment of the State Government, administrative offices of Courts, Tribunals and quasi-judicial bodies funded out of State exchequer, any Political Party, Company, Trust, Society or Organisation owned, funded or controlled by the State Government or any individual or organization executing any public work or service on behalf of or as authorised by them.

(b) "Government" means Government of Orissa.

(c) "Information" means any material or information relating to the affairs (decision, action or plan) of the public authorities, which may include on-the-spot verification of an office, interview with the concerned personnel, complete or partial copy of a file, complete or partial copy of a register or muster roll, samples and photo of construction materials, copy of and notes on the relevant correspondence and telephonic conversation, complete or partial copy of a video cassette, computer floppy, CD ROM or any other electronic medium in which information is stored.

(d) "Right to Information" means the Right of a person to access information available with public authorities.

(e) "Competent Authority" An Information Officer to be declared by every public authority for the purpose of this Act, who shall receive, dispose of, and remain accountable for all applications seeking information about the concerned office, and where such Information Officer could not be identified for valid reasons, the lowest-ranking Gezetted Officer working in that office of the Public Authority shall be deemed to be an Information Officer for the purpose of this Act.

3. Right to Information.—Subject to the provisions of this Act, every member of the public shall have right to obtain information from a Competent Authority by way of:

(i) Inspecting the records and files, taking hand written notes on them, or complete or partial photocopying of the same,

(ii) Obtaining complete or partial print-out, copy of a computer floppy, CD ROM, Cassette, or any electronic device storing the information,

(iii) Obtaining a Photo, a map or any special kind of document,

(iv) Visit to the concerned site and taking samples of construction or other related materials used, and interview with the concerned personnel related to the information sought, or

(v) In such other manner as may be felt necessary by the Applicant for Information.

4. Procedure for supply of information.—(i) A person desirous of obtaining information shall make an application to the Competent Authority in writing in the prescribed form along with payment of the prescribed fee, and shall obtain a receipt from the Competent Authority who shall specify the nature of the information sought and the date of disposing of the same:

Provided that where a person can not, for valid reasons, make a request in writing, the Competent Authority may either accept an oral request which may subsequently be reduced in writing in the presence of the applicant, or render reasonable assistance to such person in making a written application:

Provided further, that the fee to be charged shall in no case exceed the cost of photocopying of the requested information or the cost of the diskette, cassette or any other device, as the case may be.

(ii) Upon receipt of an application for information, the Competent Authority shall consider it and furnish the information required by the applicant or pass orders thereon refusing the request along with giving reasons of such refusal, as soon as practicable, and in any case, within fifteen working days from the date of receipt of the application:

Provided that where such information relates to the life or liberty of an individual, the Competent Authority shall either furnish information or pass order refusing the request along with reasons of refusal within 24 hours of the receipt of the application.

(iii) All information shall be supplied in writing in the Official Language of the State (Oriya), failing which it may be supplied either in English (Official Language of the nation) or in Hindi (National Language).

5. Limitations on the Disclosure of Information.—The Competent Authority may, for reasons recorded in writing, withhold—

(a) Information, the disclosure of the contents of which will prejudicially affect the sovereignty and integrity of India, International relations, ongoing investigation of an offence or ongoing adjudication of a case in the court of law.

(b) Information relating to an individual, the disclosure of which has no relationship to any public interest and would on the other hand constitute a clear and unwarranted invasion of personal privacy;

(c) Information whose release would constitute a breach of privilege of the Parliament or Legislative Assembly:

Provided that the Competent Authority shall, before withholding information under this Section, refer the matter to the concerned Secretariat of the Legislature for determination of the nature of the information and act according to the advice tendered by that Secretariat;

(d) Information whose disclosure would endanger the life or physical safety of any person or identify the source of information or assistance given in confidence for enforcement of a law or rule:

Provided that information which can not be denied to the State Legislature shall not be denied to any person.

6. Procedure of disposal of Request for Information by the Competent Authority.—Where the Competent Authority does not have the information, he shall, within 3 days from the date of the receipt of the Application, transfer it to the authority superior to him with whom such information is likely available and inform the Applicant accordingly. Such 'superior authority shall, thereupon, furnish the said information within 12 working days from the receipt of the request from the Competent Authority:

Provided that where the Application for information cannot be complied with for reasons falling under Sections 5 of this Act, the Competent Authority, or the superior authority as the case may be, shall, within 15 working days of reteiving the Application, reject the Application and communicate to the party concerned,

(i) the reasons for such rejection;

(ii) the period within which the appeal against such rejection may be preferred; and

(iii) the particulars of the appellate authority.

7. Appeal.—(i) Any person aggrieved by an order of the Competent Authority or his superior authority, or any person who has not received any order from the Competent Authority within fifteen working from the date of his Application, may appeal to the State Administrative Tribunal, Orissa constituted under the Government against the order so passed or non-passing of any order.

(ii) The decision of the State Administrative Tribunal shall be final.

(iii) No order adversely affecting any person shall be passed by the Appellate Authority except after giving that person a reasonable opportunity of being heard.

(iv) Every appeal shall be disposed of as expeditiously as possible and in no case exceeding 15 working days from the date of appeal.

8. Obligations on Competent Authority.—(i) Every Competent Authority shall be under a duty *suo moto* to maintain all their official records, duly catalogued and indexed so as to cater to the day-to-day information needs of the public, and grant access to information, subject to the provisions of this Act, to any person applying in the prescribed manner for such access.

(ii) Every Competent Authority shall be under a duty *suo moto* to proactively publish and announce the information in all possible mass media for forewarning in sufficient advance of the possible occurrence of a natural or man-made disaster, and the state of disaster preparedness at State, District, Block and Municipal/NAC level, and shall inform the public in similar manner on the damage caused by such disaster at different levels including the village level, and the day-to-day progress made in the Governmental and non-Governmental efforts for rescue, relief and rehabilitation of the people affected by the disaster.

(iii) Every Competent Authority, before sanctioning or initiating any project, scheme or programme *suo moto* shall publish or communicate to the public generally, and in particular to the persons affected, or likely to be affected by the said project, scheme or activity about all facts including the possible benefit or loss likely to emanate from the proposed project, scheme or programme of the Government.

(iv) Every Competent Authority *suo moto* shall publish information relating to the life, liberty and human rights, in particular of persons in custodial institutions, on day-to-day basis at such intervals and frequency as may be prescribed.

9. Penalties.—(i) Any Competent Authority responsible for providing any information under this Act shall be personally liable for furnishing or withholding the information within the period specified.

(ii) Where a Competent Authority responsible to supply information fails to furnish the information asked for under this Act within the time specified, or willfully furnishes any information which is false in material particulars, he shall be liable, after such inquiry as may be necessary to be conducted by the State Vigilance Commission, for imposition of such penalties as may be determined by the disciplinary authority under the relevant Public Service Conduct Rules applicable to him. In addition, the disciplinary authority may order him to pay a fine of Rs. 200 for every day's delay following the deadline within which the information was required to be supplied.

10. Compensation.—(i) Where a Competent Authority fails to respond to an Application for Information within the stipulated deadline, the Applicant concerned is eligible for receiving a compensation to the tune of Rs. 100 against every day's delay from the Department or Office of the Public Authority concerned.

(ii) Where a Competent Authority willfully refuses the disclosure of information or serves wrongful information in response to the application for information, the concerned Applicant is eligible for receiving from the concerned Competent authority or his higher authority as the case may be, an amount of compensation to be determined by the appellate authority on adjudication.

11. State Council for Right to Information.—(i) The Government shall, by Notification in the Official Gazette, establish with effect from such day as specified in the Notification, a Council to be known as State Council for Right to Information. The Council shall remain free from administrative control by any Department of the Government except the finance necessary for setting up and maintaining the said Council to be borne by the Government of Orissa in the Department of General Administration. The Council shall directly report once half-yearly to the Governor of Orissa and Orissa Legislative Assembly and remain accountable to them about its activities.

(ii) The State Council for Right to Information may consist of the following members—

(a) A Retired Judge of Orissa High Court shall be its Chairman;

(b) The Secretary to Government in the Department of General Administration shall be its ex-officio Secretary;

(c) Official Members not exceeding four three RDCs and Secretary to Government in the Information and Public Relations Department;

(d) Two MLAs to be nominated by the Speaker;

(e) Non-Official Members not exceeding four representing Press, Electronic Media, Industry and Non-Government Organisations.

(iii) The time, place and agenda of the meeting of the Council shall be fixed by the Chairman who shall conduct the business of such meetings as may be laid down by the Constitution of the Council which is required to be framed in its 1st Meeting following its formation.

(iv) The principal object of the State Council is to promote right to information in the State and shall deal with all matters related to right to information from this perspective.

(v) The Council shall advise the Government for abolishing or amending, as the case may be, the very pre-existing Acts or Rules the provisions of which are inconsistent with the Orissa Right to Information Act.

(vi) The Council shall frame the Rules for the State as a whole and amend them as and when necessary for proper enforcement of the Orissa Right to Information Act.

(vii) The Council shall ensure the compliance by the various Departments and agencies of the Government in the matter of framing their respective Rules for enforcement of the Act.

(viii) The Council shall review the over all administrative infrastructure and procedures operating for the purpose of the Act and advise the Government for effecting necessary reforms therein from the viewpoint of gradual expanding of the scope of public access to official information.

(ix) The Council on periodical review of the functioning of the Act may suggest to the Cabinet of Ministers and Orissa Legislative Assembly suitable amendment to the Act as and when necessary.

(x) The Council shall promote sustained research and studies on the application of latest information technology for expanding, verifying, indexing, classifying, cataloguing, and storing the information pool so as to secure to the citizens the fullest and quickest possible access to official information.

(xi) The Council shall advise the Government for undertaking suitable phase-wise programmes for training, skill development and orientation of the Competent Authorities and other employees of the Government in respect of management and dissemination of official information, which is essential for ushering in a culture of openness and transparency in public life.

12. An Act to have over-riding effect.—The provisions of this Act shall have effect notwithstanding anything inconsistent therewith, contained in any other enactment of the Legislative Assembly of Orissa, for the time being in force.

THE ORISSA RIGHT TO INFORMATION RULES, 2005*

In exercise of the power conferred by Section 27 of the Right to Information Act (No. 22 of 2005), the State Government do hereby make the following rules, namely:

1. Short title and commencement.—(1) These rules may be called the Orissa Right to Information Rules, 2005. (2) They shall come into force on the date of their publication in the Orissa Gazette.

2. Definitions.—(1) In these rules, unless there is anything repugnant in the subject or context—

(a) 'Act' means the Right to Information Act, 2005 (No. 22 of 2005);

(b) 'BPL Card' means a card issued to any citizen who is below the poverty line;

(c) "fee" means amount payable by the applicant for obtaining any information under the provisions of sub-section (1) of section 6 and sub-sections (1) and (5) of section 7 excluding the cost of providing information;

(d) 'form' means a form appended to these rules;

(e) 'identity' means an evidence to show the citizenship like an electoral photo identity card, a passport or any other document which can satisfy the authority about the citizenship of the person;

---

* *Vide* S.R.O. 477/2005, Information and Public Relations Deptt., Government of Orissa, dated 1st October, 2005.

(f) 'Nodal Officer' means the Commissioner-cum-Secretary to Government, Information & Public Relations Department;

(g) 'Public Information Officer' means the State Public Information Officer designated under sub-section (1) of section 5 of the Act and includes an Assistant Public Information officer designated as such under sub-section (2) thereof;

(h) 'Schedule' means a schedule appended to these rules; and

(i) 'State Government' means the Government of Orissa.

(2) Words and expressions used but not defined in these rules shall have the meaning as assigned to them in the Act.

3. Appointment & obligations of Public Information Officers.—(1) A public authority, if it is a department of State Government, shall designate as many officers as it deem proper, not below the rank of Under Secretary as Public Information Officers.

(2) In each sub-ordinate office of the Department of Government including the Heads of Department and offices in the district and Sub-divisional level the head of such offices shall designate as many officers as they deem proper as Public Information Officers and Assistant Public Information Officers.

(3) Every public authority other than those mentioned in sub-rules (1) and (2) of the said Rule 3 shall designate one or more Public Information Officers in all administrative units and offices under such authority:

Provided that every such public authority shall, while designating such officers as Public Information Officers so designated, ensure that an officer higher in rank to public Information Officer, is available to be specified as Appellate Authority.

(4) If, for any reason beyond the control of Public Information Officer furnishing of information is delayed, he shall

record reasons with justification thereof and shall communicate the Head of the office about such delay.

4. Procedure to obtain information.—(1) A citizen desirous of any information may apply for information in Form A to the Public Information Officer, with the required fee in shape of Treasury Challan or cash as specified in the Schedule under the appropriate head of Account:

Provided that application fee shall not be payable in case of a person whose name appears in the latest list of persons below poverty line for which he has to produce BPL Card.

Provided that a citizen seeking information through electronic means has to submit evidence regarding deposit of prescribed application fee.

(2) The Public Information Officer or any other officer authorized by him shall furnish the acknowledgement and after being satisfied with the identity of the applicant shall also intimate in form B as soon as possible the amount of cost for providing information required to be paid by the applicant in cash, as mentioned in the Schedule.

(3) The applicant may deposit the said amount within a period of fifteen days from the date of receipt of such information, failing which the application shall stand rejected.

5. Information regarding rejection.—(1) Where a request has been rejected under sub-section (1) of section 7, the Public Information Officer shall intimate the applicant, the reasons for such rejection in Form C.

(2) Wherever information applied for is available in electronic means, the Public Information Officer may advise in Form C to the applicant to obtain the information from the appropriate website to be specified by the Public Information Officer.

6. Meeting of the recommending committee.—For the purpose of appointment of the State Chief Information Commissioner and the State Information Commissioner under sub-section (3) of section 15, the Nodal Officer shall, in consultation with the State Government, convene the meeting of the Committee for their recommendation.

7. Memorandum of appeal.—(1) An appeal under sub-section (1) of section 19 shall be filed in Form D to the officer as designated by the Public Authority to hear such appeal.

(2) The Memorandum of appeal shall be accompanied with such fee as specified in the Schedule which shall be paid in the shape of court fee stamp.

(3) Any person aggrieved by the decision under sub-section (1) of section 19, may prefer a second appeal before the State Information Commission under sub-section (3) thereof in Form E which shall be accompanied with such fee in the shape of court fee stamp as specified in the Schedule.

(4) The appeal preferred under sub-rules (1) and (3), if not accompanied with the required fee, shall be rejected by the concerned Appellate Authority, but no fee is payable by the applicant holding a BPL Card.

(5) Every order of the Appellate Authority shall be communicated to the appellant concerned and to the Public Information Officer where such appeal is from the order of the Public Information Officer and to the first Appellate Authority in case it is a second appeal.

8. Guidelines by the State Government.—The State Government shall have the power to issue guidelines not inconsistent with the provisions of the Act and these rules for smooth implementation of the provisions of the Act and the rules.

9. Penalties.—In the event of imposition of penalty under section 20 on the Public Information Officer concerned, such penalty may be deposited by the said officer by Treasury Challan under the appropriate receipt Head of the State Budget within a period of thirty days, failing which the amount shall be recovered from the salary of the officer concerned.

10. Calculation of cost of damage.—If any damage is caused to the public property in the course of giving any information in the form of samples of materials, the damage caused to such property shall be included while calculating further fees representing the cost of providing the information.

11. Maintenance of register.—(1) The Public Information Officer shall maintain a register in Form F for recording the details of the applications received and the information supplied by him and keep the Head of Office informed after furnishing any information and it shall be the duty of the Head of office to ensure required assistance, if any, as would be sought for by the Public Information Officer to facilitate providing information.

(2) The Public Information Officer shall maintain a cash register in Form G for recording the details of money received by him relating to providing information and deposit the money in such head of account or in any Scheduled Bank in the name of such officer as the concerned Head of Office decides.

12. Deposit of expenditure.—The expenditure to be incurred for production of witness or documents before the State Information Commission shall be deposited before the Commission by the party at whose instance the witnesses or the documents are to be produced.

13. Realisation of penalties or damages.—Any penalty or damage or any other sum payable under the Act, if not paid within thirty days of the date of receipt of the order for realization of the same or cannot be recovered, it can be realized from such person as arrears of land revenue.

[No. 27163 – I & PR]

By Order of Governor

Sd/-

(Digambar Mohanty)

Commissioner-cum-Secretary to Government

Form A

[*See* Rule 4(I)]

APPLICATION FOR INFORMATION UNDER SECTION 6(1) OF THE ACT

To

The Public Information Officer

(Name of the office with address)

1. Full name of the applicant
2. Father/Spouse name
3. Permanent address
4. Particulars in respect of identity of the applicant
5. Particulars of information solicited
   - (a) Subject matter of information
   - (b) The period to which the information relates
   - (c) Specific details of information required
   - (d) Whether information is required by post or in person

     (The actual postal charges shall be included in providing information)
   - (e) In case by post (ordinary, registered or speed)
6. Address to which information will be sent & in which form
7. Has the information provided earlier
8. Is this information not made available by the public authority
9. Do you agree to pay the required fee
10. Have you deposited application fee

    (If yes details of such deposit)
11. Whether belongs to BPL category, have you furnished the proof of the same

Place:

Date: Full signature of the applicant

Address

OFFICE OF THE PUBLIC INFORMATION OFFICER

Received the application from ——————————

——————————————————————

—address——————————————————

—————————————————————— on——

——————————seeking information.

Place: Full name of Public Information Officer

Date: Designation

Seal

Form B

[*See* Rule 4(2)]

INFORMATION FOR PAYMENT

From

(Name & Designation of the Public Information Officer)

To

Name of the applicant

Address

Sir,

Please refer to your application dated ——————addressed to the undersigned requesting information on ——————————————————————————. I am to inform you that the following amount towards cost for providing information may be deposited in cash, to enable the undersigned to furnish information sought for.

Please make payment within a period of fifteen days from the date of receipt of this intimation failing which the application shall be rejected.

Fee——————————

Yours faithfully,

Place: Public Information Officer

Date: Seal

Form C

[*See* Rules 5(1) and (2)]

INTIMATION OF REJECTION

Sir,

The undersigned regrets to express his inability to furnish the information asked for on account of the following reasons—

(i) It comes under the exempted category covered under Sections 8 and 9 of the Act.

(ii) Your application was not complete in all respects.

(iii) Your identity is not satisfactory.

(iv) The information is contained in published material available to public.

(v) You did not pay the required cost for providing information within the prescribed time.

(vi) The information sought for is prohibited as per Section 24(4) of the Act.

(vii) The information would cause unwarranted invasion of the privacy of any person.

(viii) The information as sought for by you is available in our website——————————————— —————You may download the information.

(ix) For any other reason please see overleaf.

However, if you feel aggrieved for the above said refusal you may file an appeal before the ....within 30 days of the receipt of this letter.

Place:

Date: Name & Designation of Public Relations Officer

To,

Sri ______________________________

Form D

[*See* Rule 7(1)]

FORM OF MEMORANDUM OF APPEAL TO THE FIRST APPELLATE AUTHORITY UNDER SECTION 19(1) OF THE ACT

From______________________

(Applicant's name & address)

Before

The First Appellate Authority

1. Full name of the Appellant
2. Address
3. Particulars of Public Information Officer
4. Date of receipt of the order appealed against
5. Last date for filing the appeal
6. Particulars of information
   (a) Nature and subject matter of the information required
   (b) Name of the office or Department to which the: information relates
7. The grounds for appeal

(Details if any to be enclosed in separate sheet)

Verification

I, ________________________________(Name of the appellant), son of/daughter of/wife of ______________hereby declare that the particulars furnished in the appeal are to the best of my knowledge and belief, true and correct and that I have not suppressed any material fact.

Signature of the Appellant

Place:

Date:

To

____

Name and address of Appellate Authority

Form E

[*See* Rule 7(3)]

SECOND APPEAL UNDER SECTION 19(3) OF THE ACT

From

____

(Applicant's name & address)

To

The State Information Commission

1. Full name of the Appellant
2. Address
3. Particulars of the first Appellate Authority
4. Date of receipt of the order appealed against
5. Last date for filing the appeal
6. Particulars of information—
   (a) Nature of subject matter of the information required
   (b) Name of the office or Department to which the information relates
7. The grounds for appeal

(Details items to be enclosed in separate sheet)

Verification

I, ______________________(Name of the appellant, son of/ daughter of/wife of ___________________________hereby declare that the particulars furnished in the appeal are to the best of my knowledge and belief, true and correct and that I have not suppressed any material fact.

Signature of the Appellant

Place:

Date:

To

Orissa State Information Commission

Form F

[*See* Rule 11(1)]

FORMAT FOR THE INFORMATION REGISTER

Sl. No.	Date of application	Name of the person requiring the information	Address of the person	Nature of information	Whether all formalities have been complied by the person requiring the information	Name of the authority from which the infromation are to be collected	Date on which the iformation shall be supplied	Date on which the authority/ authorities concerned requested to supply the required information	No. & date of reminder issued authorities	Date on which the information are recieved by the P.I.O. from the authority/ the concerned	Date of supply of informtion to the person concerned requiring information	Reasons in brief for not supplying information	Remarks
1	2	3	4	5	6	7	8	9	10	11	12	13	14

Form G

[*See* Rule 11(2)]

CASH REGISTER

Name & Address of the Applicant

Date of application

Date of deposit of amount

Particulars of fee/with Challan/Bank draft/Cash

Refund, if any

Remarks

SCHEDULE

(*See* Rules 4 and 7)

FEES/AMOUNT TO BE CHARGED FOR PROVIDING INFORMATION

PART I

(A) *Application fee*	*Rate to be charged*	*Mode of deposit*
(i) Application fee seeking information	Rupees twenty per Application	Treasury Challan/ cash
(ii) Application fee for 1st Appeal	Rupees twenty	Court fee stamp
(iii) Application fee for 2nd Appeal	Rupees twenty-five	Court fee stamp
	PART II	
(B) *Amount to be charged for providing information*		
(i) A4 or A3 size paper created or copied	Rupees two per each	By Cash
(ii) Paper size larger than A4 or A3	Actual charge or cost price of a copy	
(iii) Inspection of records	No fee for the first hour & Rs. 5.00 for each 15 minutes (or fraction thereof) thereafter.	By Cash
(iv) CD with cover	Rs. 50 per CD	By Cash

(v) Floppy Diskette (1.44 MB)	Rs. 50 per Floppy	By Cash
(vi) Maps & Plans	Reasonable cost to be fixed by P.I.O. depending upon the cost of labour and material and equipment and other ancillary expenses	By Cash
(vii) Video Cassette/ Microfilm/Microfiche	Reasonable cost to be fixed by P.I.O. depending upon the cost of labour and material and equipment and other ancillary expenses	By Cash
(viii) Certified sample or models of material	Actual cost or price for sample or models	By Cash
(ix) Information in printed form	Price fixed for such publication	By Cash

N.B.— Proper and authentical money receipt to be issued for all cash payment. The office is to state the cash receipt No. on the application form 'A'.

THE PUNJAB RIGHT TO INFORMATION RULES, 2005*

In exercise of the powers conferred by sub-section (1) of section 27 of the Right to Information Act, 2005 (Central Act No. 22 of 2005), and all other powers enabling him in this behalf, the Governor of Punjab is pleased to make the following rules to provide for the matters specified in sub-section (2) of the said section, namely:

1. Short title and commencement.—(1) These rules may be called the Punjab Right to Information Rules, 2005. (2) They shall come into force on and with effect from the 12th day of October 2005.

2. Definitions.—(1) In these rules, unless the context otherwise requires—

(a) "Act" means the Right to Information Act, 2005 (Central Act No. 22 of 2005);

(b) "Commission" means the Punjab Information Commission, constituted under section 15 of the Act;

(c) "Form" means a Form, appended to these rules; and

(d) "Section" means a Section of the Act.

(2) The words and expressions used in these rules, but not defined, shall have the same meanings as assigned to them in the Act.

3. Application for obtaining information.— (1) A person, who desires to obtain any information admissible under the Act, shall.

* *Vide* No. G.S.R./C.A. 22/2005/S.27/2005, dated 12th October, 2005.

make an application in Form 'A' to the State Public Information Officer along with a fee, as specified in rule 5 of these rules.

(2) On the receipt of an application, made under sub-rule (1), the State Public Information Officer shall give a receipt in token thereof to the applicant.

4. Deposit of fee.—(1) The fee may be deposited either in cash or by draft or cheque or treasury challan.

(2) The amount of fee shall be credited to the account of the concerned public authority.

(3) On receipt of an application, submitted under sub-rule (1) of rule 3, the State Public Information Officer shall scrutinise the application and shall assess how much fee is required to be paid by the applicant for obtaining the information.

(4) The fee, assessed under sub-rule (3), shall be informed to the applicant by the State Public Information Officer in Form 'B' within a period of seven days from the receipt of application.

(5) In case the applicant fails to deposit the requisite fee within a period of fifteen days after the issuance of the intimation given to him under sub-rule (4), it shall be construed that the applicant is no longer interested in obtaining the information, sought for, and his application shall be deemed to have been filed.

5. Quantum of fee.—(1) An application for obtaining any information under sub-section (1) of section 6 shall be accompanied with a fee of rupees fifty.

(2) For providing an information under sub-section (1) of section 7, the fee shall be charged from the applicant at the following rates, namely:

(a) Rs. 10 for each page in A-4 or A-3 size paper, created or copied; and

(b) If information is to be provided on a large size of paper than that of specified in clause (a), the actual cost price of such a paper shall be charged.

(3) For providing an information under sub-section (5) of Section 7, the fee shall be charged from the applicant at the following rates, namely:

(a) Rs. 50 for providing information in floppy;

(b) Rs. 100 for providing information in diskette; and

(c) If information sought is of such a nature, which is contained in a printed document of which a price has been fixed, then that information will be provided after charging the price, fixed for that printed document. However, if only an extract or page of such a printed document is asked for, then a fee of Rs. 10 per page shall be charged from the applicant.

(4) No fee for inspection of record shall be charged, if such an inspection is made for one hour only. However, if inspection is made for a period of more than one hour, then a fee of rupees ten shall be charged for every fifteen minutes in excess of first hour. Every fraction of the period above fifteen minutes, shall be construed as a complete period of fifteen minutes and it shall be charged as full period of fifteen minutes.

6. Procedure to be followed in deciding appeal.—Before deciding an appeal, the Commission shall,

(a) serve notice to the concerned persons;

(b) entertain any evidence in support of appeal, which may be oral or in writing from the concerned persons;

(c) examine on oath or by having affidavits from the persons concerned;

(d) peruse or inspect the documents or any records or copies thereof;

(e) inquire through the authorised officer the facts of an appeal or may require facts in detail, if it so deems appropriate, hear the State Public Information Officer or any other senior officer, who had decided the first appeal, as the case may be; and

(f) receive evidence on affidavits from the State Public Information Officer or any senior officer, who had decided the first appeal or from any other person from whom the evidence may be deemed necessary.

7. Mode of serving notice.—The Commission may serve notice to the persons concerned in any of the following modes, namely:

(a) by hand delivery(dasti) through process server; or

(b) by registered post with acknowledgment due; or

(c) by publication in newspaper.

8. Order by the commissioner.—(1) The commissioner shall make order in writing and pronounce the same in the presence of the concerned parties.

(2) The party concerned may, obtain the copies of the order from the commission.

[Section 19(10)]

Form A

[*See* Rule 3(1)]

The Assistant Public Information Officer/

The Public Information Officer/AP10

(Name of the office with address)

(1) Full name of the applicant

(2) Address

(3) Particulars of information required

(i) Subject matter of information*

(ii) The period to which the information relates**

(iii) Description of the information required***

(iv) Whether information is required by post or in person

("the actual postal charges shall be included in additional fees)

---

* Broad category of the subject to be indicated (such as grant/Government land/Service matters/Licenses etc.).

** Relevant period for which information is required to be indicated.

*** Specific details of the information are required to be indicated.

(v) In case by post (Ordinary, Registered or Speed post.)

Signature of the applicant

Place:

Date:

Acknowledgement

Received your application dated———————————— vide

Diary No .... Dated

Signatures of Assistant Public Information Officer/
Public Information Officer

Name of the Department/Office ....

Form B

(*See* Rule 4 (4)

From

Designation of the

Public Information Officer

To

(Name of the applicant)

Address of the applicant

Sir,

Please refer to your application dated———————— addressed to the undersigned requesting information regarding——————————. The additional fee for supplying this information to you is Rs———————————.

2. You are requested to pay the fee at this Office or make payment in a Government Treasury through Challan and send a copy of the challan to this office and collect the information on————.

3. The amount of fee shall be deposited in the budget head No. (to be intimated to the applicant by the concerned department).

Public Information officer

B.R. BAJAJ

Principal Secretary to Government of Punjab

Department of Information Technology

Form 2

REJECTION ORDER UNDER THE RIGHT TO INFORMATION ACT, 2005

From..................... Date............

....

....

No. F.....................

To,

....

....

....

Sir/Madam,

Please refer to your application I.D. No. ....dated............. addressed to the undersigned regarding supply of information on.....................

2. The information asked for cannot be supplied due to following reasons:—

(i) ....

(ii) ....

3. As per section 19 of the Right to Information Act, 2005, you may file an appeal to the Appellate Authority of this Department/Undertaking/Public Authority, within 30 days of the issue of this order. (Please indicate the name and designation of the Appellate Authority).

Yours Faithfully,

Public Information Officer:

E-mail address:

Web-site:

Tel. No.:

THE RAJASTHAN RIGHT TO INFORMATION ACT, 2000*

(Rajasthan Act No. 13 of 2000)

An Act to provide for Right to Information to the citizens about the affairs of the State and public bodies.

Be it enacted by the Rajasthan State Legislature in the Fifty-first Year of the Republic of India as follows:

1. Short title, extent and commencement.—(1) This Act may be called the Rajasthan Right to Information Act, 2000.

(2) It shall extend to the whole of the State of Rajasthan.

(3) It shall come into force on such date as the State Government may, by notification in the Official Gazette, appoint.

2. Definitions.—In this Act, unless the context otherwise requires—

(i) "Controlling Officer" means the immediate superior officer above the incharge of office, who supervises and controls the work of incharge of office or such officer as may, from time to time, be specified as such by the State Government for the purposes of this Act;

(ii) "District Level Officer" means an officer or functionary of the State Government or a public body having jurisdiction over a District in the State or as may, from time to time, be specified as such by the State Government for the purposes of this Act;

---

* Repealed by the Rajasthan Right to Information (Repeal) Act, 2006 (10 to 2006) w.e.f. 20 April, 2006.

(iii) "Incharge of the Office" means an office/functionary of a Department of the State Government or a public body, who is in actual control of any office of the State Government or public body, as the case may be, or such officer/functionary as may, from time to time, be specified as such by the State Government for the purposes of this Act;

(iv) "Information" means any material or information relating to the affairs of the State or a public body;

(v) "Public Body" shall include,

(a) Offices of all local bodies and other authorities constituted under any enactment of the Rajasthan State Legislature for the time being in force; or

(b) any other statutory authority constituted by the State Government under any law for the time being in force; or

(c) a Government Company/Corporation incorporated under the Companies Act, 1956 (Central Act No. 1 of 1956) in which not less than fifty-one per cent of the paid up share capital is held by the State Government or a trust established by the State Government under any law for the time being in force and controlled by it; or

(d) a Society or a Co-operative Society or any other organisation established under any law for the time being force, by the State Government and directly controlled or funded by it; or

(e) any other body, which may be receiving substantial financial assistance from the State Government, as may be specified by notification in the official Gazette for the purposes of this Act.

(vi) "Right to information" means the right of access to information relating to the affairs of the State or public bodies by means of—

(a) obtaining certified copies of documents or records, or

(b) inspection of accessible records and taking notes and extracts, or

(c) inspection of public works, or

(d) taking of samples of material from public works; and

(vii) "Vigilance Committee" means a District Public Grievances-cum-vigilance Committee constituted by the State Government vide order No. F.33 (32)/AR/ Gr. 1/77 dated 17 December 1977 or as may be reconstituted or constituted by the State Government from time to time.

3. Right to information.—Subject to the provisions of this Act, every citizen shall have right to obtain information from the incharge of office and such incharge shall be liable to provide information under and in accordance with the provisions of this Act.

4. Procedure for supply of information.—(1) Any person seeking information shall make an application to the incharge of the office giving particulars of the matter relating to which information is sought.

(2) Upon receipt of an application under sub-section (1), the incharge of the office shall consider it and if the information is such which can be provided and does not fall within the categories specified under section 5, the incharge of office shall provide the information within thirty days of the receipt of application under sub-section (1).

(3) Where the information sought by the applicant falls under the restricted categories specified under section 5, the incharge of the office shall refuse to provide information and shall communicate his decision to the applicant within thirty days from the date of receipt of application under sub-section (1).

(4) The information sought may be made available in the form it is available by copying or photocopying the same.

(5) The information may be sought from and may be furnished by the incharge of the Office wherefrom the information has originated or where any record is normally maintained or deposited.

5. Restrictions on right to information.—The incharge of the office may, for reasons to be recorded in writing, withhold—

(i) information, the disclosure or contents of which will prejudicially affect the sovereignty and integrity of India, security of the State, conduct of international relations, including information received in confidence from foreign Governments, their agencies or international organisations;

(ii) information, the disclosure of which would prejudicially affect the conduct of Center-State relations, including information exchanged in confidence between the Central and State Government or any of their authorities/agencies;

(iii) information whose disclosure would harm the frankness and candour of internal discussions, including Cabinet papers, inter-departmental/intra-departmental notes, correspondence and papers containing advice, opinion etc. as also of projections and assumptions relating to internal policy analysis;

(iv) information, the disclosure of which—

(a) Would prejudicially affect the enforcement of any law including detection, prevention, investigation or suppression of crime or contravention of any law or the apprehending of offenders and the operations of any intelligence organisations;

(b) Would endanger the life or physical safety of any person, or identify the source of information or assistance given in confidence for law enforcement or security purposes;

(c) Would prejudicially affect fair trial or adjudication of a pending case or the proceedings of any tribunal, public inquiry;

(d) Would reveal the existence or identity of a confidential record or source of information; or would prejudice future supply of information relating to violation or contravention of any law;

(e) May help or facilitate escape of any person from legal custody or affect his present security;

(v) information the disclosure of which would prejudicially affect the governments ability to manage the economy or the legitimate economic and commercial interests of a public authority; or would cause unfair gain or loss to any individual or organisation;

(vi) personal information, the disclosure of which has no relationship to any public activity or which would cause unwarranted invasion of the privacy of an individual;

(vii) information held in consequence of having been supplied in confidence by a person who—

(a) gave the information under a guarantee that its confidentiality would be protected; or

(b) was not under any legal obligation, whether actual or implied, to supply, and has not consented to its disclosure;

(viii) information whose release would constitute a breach or privilege of Parliament/State Legislative Assembly, or would amount to violation of an order of a competent court;

(ix) the record and information referred to in sections 123 and 124 of the Indian Evidence Act, 1872 and claimed privileged;

(x) information on the following grounds also—

(a) that the request is too general or is of such a nature that, having regard to the volume of information required to be retrieved or processed for fulfilling it, it would involve disproportionate diversion of the resources of a public authority or would adversely interfere with the functioning of such authority:

Provided that, where access is being refused on the ground that the request is too general, it would be duty of the incharge of office concerned to render help, as far as possible, to the person seeking information to re-frame his request in such a manner as may facilitate supply of information;

(b) that the request relates to information that is required by law or convention to be published at a particular time; or

(c) that the request relates to information that is contained in published material for sale.

6. First appeal.—(1) Any person aggrieved by the order of: the incharge of the office or any person who has not received required information within the time stipulated under section 4, may appeal to the controlling officer:

Provided that no order adversely affecting the person making appeal shall be passed unless an opportunity of being heard is afforded to him.

(2) Every appeal shall be heard and decided expeditiously and by all means be disposed of within thirty days from the date of presentation of appeal.

(3) The appeal shall be accompanied with the proof of fee deposited or tendered in the manner provided in accordance with section 8.

7. Second appeal.—(1) Any person aggrieved by the order of—

(i) the controlling officer who is not above the rank of a District Level Officer, may appeal to the Vigilance Committee of the concerned District;

(ii) the controlling officer other than those specified in clause (i) may appeal to the Rajasthan Civil services Appellate Tribunal constituted under Section 3 of the Rajasthan Civil Services (Service Matters Appellate Tribunals) Act, 1976 (Act No. 34 of 1976):

Provided that no order adversely affecting the person making the appeal shall be passed unless an opportunity of being heard is afforded to him.

(2) Every appeal shall be heard and decided expeditiously and by all means disposed of within thirty days from the date of presentation of the appeal.

(3) The appeal shall be accompanied with the proof of fee deposited or tendered in the manner provided in accordance with section 8.

8. Fee.— Fee request for seeking information under this Act shall be accompanied by a proof of payment of such fee as may be prescribed for furnishing of information.

(2) If requisite fee as prescribed under sub-section (1) is not paid for the required information, the information as sought under section 4 may not be made available.

(3) The appeal shall be accompanied with such fee, and be deposited and tendered in such manner, as may be prescribed.

9. Obligation of the incharge of office.—(1) Every incharge of the office shall have a duty to maintain all records in accordance with the procedure laid down under relevant law or Departmental manuals.

(2) While maintaining the records proper indexing, listing, numbering and paging of records shall be done and the same may be kept ready for access to information, subject to the provisions of this Act, to any citizen requesting for such access.

(3) Any person responsible for providing any information under this Act shall be personally liable for furnishing information within the period specified under this Act.

10. Penalties.—Where any person responsible for making available information under this Act, fails without any reasonable cause to furnish information sought by any citizen under the provisions of this Act within the time specified or furnishes any information which is false with regard to any material particulars and which he knows and has reasonable cause to believe it to be false or does not believe it to be true, he shall be liable, after such inquiry as may be required under the service rules, pertaining to disciplinary action applicable to him, for imposition of such penalty as may be determined by the disciplinary authority under such rules.

11. Bar to the legal proceedings.—No legal proceedings shall be instituted for enforcing the right to information without first exhausting the remedies provided under this Act.

12. Protection of action taken in good faith.—No suit, prosecution or legal proceedings shall lie against any person for anything done or intended to be done in good faith in pursuance to the provisions of this Act or rules made thereunder.

12 A. *Suo moto* exhibition/exposure of information.—The State Government and public bodies may *suo moto* exhibit or expose such information, from time to time, as it may consider appropriate in public interest, in the manner as may be prescribed.

13. Power to make rules.—(1) The State Government may make rules for carrying out the purposes of this Act. (2) All rules made under this Act shall be laid, as soon as may be after they are made, before the House of the State Legislature while it is in session, for a period of not less than fourteen days, which may be comprised in one session or in two successive sessions and if, before the expiry of the session in which they are so laid or of the session immediately following, the House of the State Legislature makes any modification in any such rules, or resolves that any such rule should not be made, such rules shall thereafter have effect only in such modified form or be of no effect, as the case may be, so, however, that any such modification or annulment shall be without prejudice to the validity of anything previously done thereunder.

THE TAMIL NADU RIGHT TO INFORMATION ACT, 1997

(As introduced in the Assembly)

An Act to make provision for securing the right to information in the State of Tamil Nadu and for matters relating thereto.

Whereas it is necessary that every Governmental action should be transparent to the public;

And whereas to achieve this object, every citizen should be able to get information from the Government;

Be it enacted by the Legislative Assembly of the State of Tamil Nadu in the Forty-eighth Year of the Republic of India as follows:

1. Short title and commencement.—(1) This act may be called the Tamil Nadu Right to Information Act, 1997. (2) It shall come into force at once.

2. Definitions.—In this Act, unless the context otherwise requires—

(1) "Competent Authority" means any authority, officer not below the rank of Deputy Collector or an Officer of an equivalent grade and above empowered by the Government by notification, to be Competent Authority for the purpose of this Act;

(2) "Government" means the State Government;

(3) "Information" includes copy of any document relating to the affairs of the State or any local or other authorities constituted under any act for the time being in force or a statutory authority or a company, corporation or a cooperative society or any organisation owned or controlled by the Government.

3. Right of access to information.—(1) Every person *bona fide* requiring information may have access to such information in accordance with the procedure specified under this Act.

(2) Notwithstanding anything contained in sub-section (1), no person shall be given information relating to—

(a) information relating to defence security;

(b) information whose disclosure will prejudice the security, integrity and sovereignty of the Nation and the State;

(c) information whose disclosure would harm the conduct of international relations or affairs;

(d) information received in confidence from foreign Governments, foreign courts or international organisations;

(e) information whose disclosure would harm the frankness and candour of internal discussion, including;

(i) proceedings of Cabinet and Cabinet committees;

(ii) internal opinion, advice, recommendations, consultation and deliberation;

(iii) projections and assumptions relating to internal policy analysis; analysis of alternative policy options and information relating to rejected policy options;

(iv) confidential communications between departments, public bodies and regulatory bodies;

(f) information relating to confidential communications between Ministers and the Governor;

(g) information whose disclosure would prejudice the administration of justice, including fair trial and the enforcement or proper administration of the law;

(h) information whose disclosure would prejudice legal proceedings or the proceedings of any tribunal, public inquiry or other formal investigation (whether actual or likely) or whose disclosure has been or is likely to be addressed in the context of such proceedings;

(i) information covered by legal professional privilege;

(j) information whose disclosure would prejudice the prevention, investigation or detection of crime, the apprehension of offenders;

(k) information whose disclosure would harm public safety or public order;

(l) information whose disclosure would endanger the life or physical safety of any person, or identify the source of information or assistance given in confidence for law enforcement or security purposes;

(m) information whose disclosure would increase the likelihood of damage to the environment; or rare or endangered species and their habitats;

(n) information whose disclosure would harm the ability of the Government to manage the economy, prejudice the conduct of official market operations, or could lead to improper gain or advantage to any person;

(o) information whose disclosure would prejudice the assessment or collection of tax, duties, or assist tax avoidance or evasion;

(p) information including commercial confidences, trade secrets or intellectual property whose unwarranted disclosure would harm the competitive position of the third party;

(q) information whose disclosure could lead to improper gain or advantage or would prejudice,

  (i) the competitive position of a department or other public body or authority;

  (ii) negotiations or the effective conduct of personnel management or commercial or contractual activities;

(r) information held in consequence of having been supplied in confidence by a person who,

(i) gave the information under a statutory guarantee that its confidentiality would be protected; or

(ii) was not under any legal obligation, whether actual or implied, to supply it, and has not consented to its disclosure;

(s) information whose disclosure is prohibited under any enactment, regulation or international agreement;

(t) information whose release would constitute a breach of Parliament/Legislative Assembly/Council Privilege;

(u) the documents referred in sections 123 and 124 of the Indian Evidence Act, 1872;

(v) any matter which is likely to—

(i) help the commission of offence;

(ii) help or facilitate escape from legal custody or affect prison security; or

(iii) impede the process of investigation or apprehension or prosecution of offenders.

(3) (a) Any person who wants to have access to the information may make an application in the manner prescribed to the Competent Authority in such form with such particulars, as may be prescribed.

(b) Where an application is made under clause (a) and the information is not available with the Competent Authority but is available with another department or authority, the Competent Authority may transfer the application to the Competent Authority with whom such information is available and inform the applicant accordingly. The Competent Authority to whom such application is transferred shall furnish the information within thirty working days from the date of receipt of the application from the Competent Authority from whom it has been referred or received.

(c) Where an application is so transferred to a department or authority, the head of that department or authority shall be deemed to be Competent Authority.

(d) (i) Upon the receipt of an application requesting for an information, the Competent Authority shall consider it and pass orders thereon either granting or refusing the request, as soon as practicable and in any case, within thirty working days from the date of receipt of application.

(ii) In other cases, the Competent Authority shall take all reasonable steps to inform the applicant of its decision on the request as soon as practicable.

(4) (a) If in the opinion of the Competent Authority any information, if disclosed, is likely to cause breach of the peace or cause violence, or disharmony among the section of the people on the basis of religion, language, caste, creed, community or if it is prejudicial to public interest, the Competent Authority shall refuse to give information.

(b) Any application made under clause (a) shall be rejected, for reasons to be recorded in writing, if in the opinion of the Competent Authority,

(i) any such information sought falls in any one or more categories of items listed under section 3(2), or

(ii) the disclosure of the information sought would be prejudicial to the maintenance of public order, or maintenance of essential services and supplies.

4. Appeal.—(1) Any person aggrieved by an order of the Competent Authority or any person who has not received any order from the Competent Authority within thirty working days may appeal to the Government or to such other authority as may be notified by the Government, subject to such rules as may be prescribed.

(2) The decision of the Government or such other authority as may be prescribed shall be final.

(3) No order adversely affecting any person shall be passed except after giving that person a reasonable opportunity of being heard.

5. Protection or action taken in good faith.—No suit, prosecution or other legal proceeding shall lie against any authority or person for anything done in good faith or intended to be done in pursuance of this Act or the rules made thereunder.

6. Power to remove difficulties.—If any difficulty arises in giving effect to the provisions of this Act, the Government may, by an order published in the Tamil Nadu Government Gazette, make such provisions not inconsistent with the provisions of this Act and appear to them to be necessary or expedient for removing the difficulty:

Provided that no such order shall be made after the expiry of two years from the date of the commencement of this Act.

7. Power to make rules.—(1) The Government may make rules for carrying out the purposes of this Act.

(2) (a) All rules made under this Act shall be published in the Tamil Nadu Government Gazette and unless they are expressed to come into force on a particular day, shall come into force on the day on which they are so published.

(b) All notifications issued under this Act shall, unless they are expressed to come into force on a particular day, come into force on the day on which they are published.

(3) Every rule made or notification issued under this Act shall, as soon as possible, after it is made or issued, be placed on the table of the Legislative Assembly, and if, before the expiry of the session in which it is so placed or the next session, the Assembly makes any modification in any such rule or notification or the Assembly decides that the rule or notification should not be made or issued, the rule or notification shall, thereafter, have effect only in such modified form or be of no effect, as the case may be, so however, that any such modification or annulment shall be without prejudice to the validity of anything previously done under that rule or notification.

Statement of Objects and Reasons

In order to provide the public the right of access to information, about the administration and to enable them to get details about the schemes of the Government implemented by various departments, the works executed by various departments, the quantity of rice and other essential commodities supplied to each of the shops under public distribution system of their stocks and to pave the way for the people to question irregularities in the system, the Government have decided to bring a legislation.

The Bill seeks to give effect to the above decision.

Aladi Aruna

Minister of Law

Secretariat

Chennai

Date 17-04-97

Memorandum Regarding Delegated Legislation

Clauses 2(1), 3(3) 4, 6 and 7 of the Bill authorise the Government to prescribe the manner and method of giving effect to certain provisions of the proposed Act by making suitable Rules thereunder.

The powers delegated are normal and not of an exceptional character.